D1317621

DATE DUE

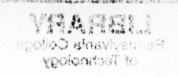

Professional
Ruby on Rails™

Noel Rappin

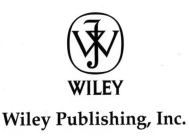

WILEY

Wiley Publishing, Inc.

Professional Ruby on Rails™

Published by
Wiley Publishing, Inc.
10475 Crosspoint Boulevard
Indianapolis, IN 46256
www.wiley.com

Copyright © 2008 by Wiley Publishing, Inc., Indianapolis, Indiana

ISBN: 978-0-470-22388-8

Manufactured in the United States of America

10 9 8 7 6 5 4 3 2 1

Library of Congress Cataloging-in-Publication Data is available from the publisher.

To Erin. Forever. And for everything.

About the Author

Noel Rappin is the Director of Rails Practice at Pathfinder Associates (www.pathfinderagile.com), and has nearly a decade of experience with web application programming. Noel has a Ph.D. from the Georgia Institute of Technology, where he studied how to teach object-oriented design concepts. He is the co-author of *Jython Essentials* and *wxPython in Action*. You can read more of Noel's writing at both the Pathfinder Agile Ajax blog (http://blogs.pathf.com/agileajax) and his own blog (http://10printhello.blogspot.com).

Credits

Acquisitions Editor
Jenny Watson

Development Editor
Maryann Steinhart

Technical Editor
Raymond Budd

Production Editor
Martine Dardignac

Copy Editor
Kathryn Duggan

Editorial Manager
Mary Beth Wakefield

Production Manager
Tim Tate

Vice President and Executive Group Publisher
Richard Swadley

Vice President and Executive Publisher
Joseph B. Wikert

Project Coordinator, Cover
Lynsey Stanford

Proofreader
Sossity Smith

Indexer
Johnna VanHoose Dinse

Acknowledgments

Many different people helped make this book possible. Thanks to my agent Neil Salkind for getting this project off the ground, and to Jenny Watson and Maryann Steinhart at Wiley for helping turn it from a proposal into a book. Thanks to the technical editor, Raymond Budd, for his attention to detail in verifying the source code for this book, and the copyeditor, Kathryn Duggan, for her attention to matters of style and clarity.

Without the Rails community as a whole, this book would have been a lot less interesting and more difficult. Thanks to David Heinemeier Hansson for creating Rails in the first place, and the entire core team for the ongoing implementation. Also thanks to people like Dave Thomas and Chad Fowler for their part in popularizing Rails. The Rails community is enlivened by a fantastic ongoing conversation of ideas, tutorials, and arguments online. I've tried to acknowledge individual developers and bloggers in each chapter, and there are too many to list here, but thanks to you all.

At Motorola, a number of managers and co-workers were supportive of my initial attempts to build Rails projects as well as the beginnings of this book. Special thanks to Greg Bell, Anne-Marie Jolie, MaryAnn Marks, Jay Marusich, Staszek Salik, Mike Wagner, and Michal Wieja.

Pathfinder has been amazingly supportive of this book, both in concept and in the amount of time spent. Thanks to Dietrich Kappe and Bernhard Kappe for the opportunity. Anthony Caliendo, Michael King, Jason Sendlebach, Alice Toth, and Lydia Tripp are all team members who have been supportive of me and this book. Thanks to all of you.

I'd like to acknowledge and thank Wally Dodge, who was my AP Computer Science instructor, and is as responsible as anybody for my choice of career.

I'm lucky to be part of an amazing and loving family, both immediate and extended. At the risk of angering everybody else, I'd like to especially acknowledge my godparents, Nancy and Richard Sher, and my cousin Dan Sher.

My parents, Donna and Donnie Rappin, have always enthusiastically supported me, no matter where I chose to go.

My wife, Erin, still and always the best part of my life, made it through this project with grace and humor. Thank you for everything.

My children, Emma and Elliot, are now old enough to read this for themselves. Hi! You are wonderful and amazing kids, and I love you both.

Contents

Contents

Contents

Contents

Contents

Introduction

First released to the public in 2004 after being developed to support the Basecamp project management application, Ruby on Rails promised nothing less than a revolution in the way web applications are constructed. With a strong grounding in the pragmatic ethic of avoiding repetition, the Rails way of supporting common conventions instead of complex options showed that there was a simpler way to build for the Web, and "my code is shorter than your configuration file" became the boast of the day.

In the intervening years. Rails has made friends and enemies, has been used to build some of the hottest web applications going, and has undergone several internal revolutions as the notion of what comprises Rails best practices continues to evolve. This book attempts to use the current best practices to show how to build a web application.

Who Should Read This Book

This book is intended for intermediate to advanced Rails programmers. It assumes that you already know Ruby, and have either read one of the many wonderful introductory books on Rails or have otherwise consumed some form of a Rails tutorial. In either case, you don't need me to tell you how to create a basic Rails application.

The focus of this book is on the step that comes after just being able to make Rails work. You've read the basic book, and now you've been asked to implement a real, live, web application. Suddenly you have all sorts of questions that weren't covered in the introductory material. How do I manage users and security? Is there an easy way to manage time zones or other internationalization issues? How does Rails expect me to organize a team of programmers and manage source issues? How do I automate common build tasks, and how do I deploy to a production server? What do I need to do to secure my site? How can I extend Rails to take advantage of the many wonderful things being done by the Rails programming community?

If you're interested in learning the answer to any of these questions, then this book is for you.

How This Book Is Structured

Over the course of this book, you'll build a single web application, and the ordering of the chapters is based on the growing needs of that application. However, the book has been structured so that individual chapters are as orthogonal as possible, and unless otherwise noted, you should not need to read the entire book to understand the concepts in a particular chapter.

There are two other things about the book's structure worth noting. Wherever possible, the code samples are presented in a test-first style, with a Rails unit or functional test documenting the expected behavior of the new code as written. The idea is to try and present the case for test-first development without a significant time cost, and also to present you with strategies for testing various kinds of Rails features.

Introduction

The Rails online community is an awesome and wonderful thing, full of enthusiastic developers sharing their knowledge and expertise with the community. Each chapter in this book includes a list of blogs, plugins, and/or other Rails web sites that are related to the topic at hand.

The book is organized into the following sixteen chapters and two appendixes:

Chapter 1, Building Resources — This chapter covers setting up the project and its initial resources using REST.

Chapter 2, Rails Source Control with Subversion — After a project is set up, it should be placed under source control immediately. Subversion is the Rails source control tool of choice and is the topic of this chapter.

Chapter 3, Adding Users — This chapter covers placing the concept of a user into the application, managing secure logins, performing e-mail authorization, and implementing CAPTCHA.

Chapter 4, Build Tools and Automation — Rake is a very handy tool for automating commonly performed actions. With those actions defined, it's a small step to create an environment where automated tests or metrics can be performed continually, as you learn in this chapter.

Chapter 5, Navigation and Social Networking — This chapter covers the basic elements of web application navigation, menus, tagging, search, and pagination.

Chapter 6, The Care and Feeding of Databases — This chapter discusses the use of other database tools besides the MySQL default, and adding more complex database relationships to the application. It also explores issues of database security.

Chapter 7, Testing Tools — This chapter introduces you to several different tools to improve your testing, including the use of RCov to measure testing, RSpec to specify behavior more directly, and methods for testing views and helpers.

Chapter 8, Rails-Driven JavaScript — This chapter describes how you can use Ruby and Rails to add Ajax and JavaScript to your application, including using RJS to create more complex JavaScript behavior and testing RJS output.

Chapter 9, Talking to the Web — This chapter shows you how to turn your application into a web services data producer, including how to create RSS feeds. It also describes how ActiveRecords turns a Rails application into a web services data consumer.

Chapter 10, Internationalizing Your Application — The World Wide Web encompasses many time zones and languages. This chapter covers managing time in Rails and using the Globalize plugin for internationalization.

Chapter 11, The Graphic Arts — This chapter describes how to install RMagick and other tools to enable graphics, as well as how to use Gruff and Sparklines to create charts.

Chapter 12, Deploying Your Application — This chapter discusses the current state-of-the-art in deploying Ruby applications using Capistrano to automate deployment tasks. It also covers the use of the Mongrel and other server tools to serve the application.

Chapter 13, Performance — This chapter shows you how to measure performance to find bottlenecks in your Rails application, and what to do when you find them.

Chapter 14, Going Meta — Metaprogramming, or writing code that writes or modifies code, is a nifty trick that Ruby handles deftly, and which is used to support some of the most dynamic features in Rails. Adding metaprogramming to an application can reduce duplicated code dramatically, as you learn in this chapter.

Chapter 15, Extending Rails with Plugins — This chapter gives you even more information on using Rails plugins, including how to create, test, and deploy a Rails plugin and use generators.

Chapter 16, Replacing Ruby Tools — This chapter covers using ERB replacements to define output and using JRuby to deploy your application in a Java Web Application server.

Appendix A, Things You Should Download—This appendix explains everything you should download to work with Ruby on Rails, including Ruby, Gems, Rails, and Subversion.

Appendix B, Web Frameworks Inspired by Rails—This appendix briefly describes web frameworks that have been influenced by Rails.

What You Need to Use This Book

This book assumes you are using Ruby version 1.8.6 and Rails 2.0.2. The examples in this book run against a MySQL database, and use the Mongrel web server. Instructions on installing the necessary software on Linux, Mac OS X, or Windows are contained in Appendix A.

Conventions

To help you get the most from the text and keep track of what's happening, a number of conventions are used throughout the book.

> **Boxes like this one hold important, not-to-be forgotten information that is directly relevant to the surrounding text.**

Tips, hints, tricks, and asides to the current discussion are offset and placed in italics like this.

As for styles in the text:

- ❏ New terms and important words are *highlighted* when they're introduced.
- ❏ Keyboard combinations are shown like this: Ctrl+A.
- ❏ Filenames, URLs, and code within the text looks like this: `persistence.properties`.
- ❏ Code is presented in two ways:

```
This is how most code in the book appears.
```

```
To call your attention to a specific line within code, it is highlighted like this.
```

Source Code

As you work through the examples in this book, you may choose either to type in all the code manually or to use the source code files that accompany the book. All of the source code used in this book is available for download at `www.wrox.com`. From this site, you can simply locate the book's title by using the Search box or by using one of the title lists, and then click the Download Code link on the book's detail page to obtain all the source code for the book.

Because many books have similar titles, you may find it easiest to search by ISBN. This book's ISBN is 978-0-470-22388-8.

After you download the code, just decompress it with your favorite compression tool. Alternately, you can go to the main Wrox code download page at `www.wrox.com/dynamic/books/download.aspx` to see the code available for this book and all other Wrox books.

Errata

We make every effort to ensure that there are no errors in the text or in the code. However, no one is perfect, and mistakes do occur. If you find an error in one of our books, such as a spelling mistake or faulty piece of code, we would be very grateful for your feedback. By sending in errata, you may save another reader hours of frustration and help us provide even higher-quality information.

To find the errata page for this book, go to `www.wrox.com` and locate the title using the Search box or one of the title lists. Then, on the book details page, click the Book Errata link. On this page, you can view all errata that has been submitted for this book and posted by Wrox editors. A complete book list, including links to each book's errata, is also available at `www.wrox.com/misc-pages/booklist.shtml`.

If you don't spot "your" error on the Book Errata page, go to `www.wrox.com/contact/techsupport .shtml` and complete the form there to send us the error you have found. We'll check the information and, if appropriate, post a message to the book's errata page and fix the problem in subsequent editions of the book.

p2p.wrox.com

For author and peer discussion, join the P2P forums at p2p.wrox.com. The forums are a Web-based system for you to post messages relating to Wrox books and related technologies, as well as to interact with other readers and technology users. The forums offer a subscription feature to e-mail you topics of interest of your choosing when new posts are made to the forums. Wrox authors, editors, other industry experts, and your fellow readers are present on these forums.

At http://p2p.wrox.com, you will find a number of different forums that will help you not only as you read this book, but also as you develop your own applications. To join the forums, just follow these steps:

1. Go to p2p.wrox.com and click the Register link.

2. Read the terms of use and click Agree.

3. Complete the required information to join as well as any optional information you wish to provide and click Submit.

4. You will receive an e-mail with information describing how to verify your account and complete the joining process.

    You can read messages in the forums without joining P2P, but in order to post your own messages, you must join.

After you join, you can post new messages and respond to messages other users post. You can read messages at any time on the Web. If you would like to have new messages from a particular forum e-mailed to you, click the Subscribe to this Forum icon by the forum name in the forum listing.

For more information about how to use the Wrox P2P, be sure to read the P2P FAQs for answers to questions about how the forum software works as well as many common questions specific to P2P and Wrox books. To read the FAQs, click the FAQ link on any P2P page.

1

Building Resources

Ruby on Rails is opinionated software. This doesn't mean that it's going to make fun of your haircut, or tell you what kind of car to drive. It does mean that Rails has definite ideas about how your web project should be structured, how it should interact with a database, how you should test, and even what kinds of tools you should use. Tasks that Rails feels that you should do often are easy, and tasks that Rails thinks should be rare are (usually) possible but more complicated. This works because the Rails team has done an exceptionally good job of deciding how web projects should work, and how they should not work.

Two important principles that Rails favors are especially useful when starting a new Rails project:

❑   *Representational State Transfer (REST)* is a relatively new mechanism for structuring a Rails application by organizing the application around resources, rather than pages.

❑   *Test Driven Development (TDD)* is an important part of ensuring the correctness and design of any software project, but Rails does a particularly good job of providing the developer with the tools needed for easy and powerful automated testing.

In this chapter, you will begin the construction of the Rails project that will carry you throughout the book. This will enable you to review the basic Rails functionality you should already be familiar with, but with an added emphasis on REST and TDD. At the end of this chapter, your Rails knowledge should be refreshed, state-of-the-art, and ready to go.

> *To run the examples throughout this book, a standard suite of applications is assumed to already be installed on your computer. The suite includes Ruby, Rails, MySQL, and Subversion. See Appendix A, "Things You Should Download," for details on how to install these tools.*

A Good Place to Start

The sample application that drives this book is called Soups OnLine, your Web 2.0 guide to all things hot and broth-y. As the site develops, it will have all sorts of modern web goodness, including an Ajax interface, social networking and content development, RSS syndication, and fancy graphics. For the moment, though, all it has is the standard Rails application structure, which you should see in your command window after you execute the following command:

```
rails -d mysql soupsonline
```

If you leave off the -d mysql, then your application will be created to use SQLite3, which is the new Rails default. The database can be changed later in developemnt. In response, Rails will create a standard application structure:

```
create
create   app/controllers
create   app/helpers
create   app/models

[... several creations skipped ...]

create   log/server.log
create   log/production.log
create   log/development.log
create   log/test.log
```

The examples in this book were written and tested against Ruby 1.8.6 and Rails 2.0.2. Ruby 1.9 has not been released as of this writing, but is expected shortly.

A Recipe for Recipes

There are two useful places to start when planning a Rails application:

❏   You can start from the front-end and move backwards by thinking about what actions or activities your users will perform in the site.

❏   You can start from the back-end and move forwards by thinking about what kind of data you will need to be storing.

The two directions feed back and forth on each other, of course, and there's no particularly correct way to go about site design. Rails is extremely good at supporting incremental development, so starting in one small place and gradually increasing functionality is a perfectly valid design process.

For the purposes of the book, I'd like to start with a brief description of user activities, but work in earnest with the initial data structure and administrative side, catching up with the user activities in future chapters. For me, at least, since Rails is so good at quick-and-easy data creation support, it feels more direct to start with that part, get some quick success under my belt, and then start designing the front end with some actual data to look at.

So, here's a quick description of user activities. Soups OnLine is intended to start as a recipe repository, where users can upload recipes, find recipes that match various categories or criteria, and comment on recipes. More advanced uses might include the capability to make and receive recommendations, information about various techniques or ingredients, and the capability to purchase equipment, ingredients, or even premade soup.

From the data perspective, the place to start is the recipe — that's the main unit of data that the users will be looking at. What's the data for a recipe? Pulling out my handy-dandy *Joy of Cooking* (Simon & Schuster), I see that a recipe consists of a title ("Cream of Cauliflower Soup"), a resulting amount ("About 6 cups"), a description ("This recipe is the blueprint for a multitude of vegetable soups . . ."), some ingredients ("¼ cup water or stock, 1 tablespoon unsalted butter"), and some directions ("Heat in a soup pot over medium-low heat . . .").

There are some interesting data representation questions right off the bat. To wit:

❑ Should the directions be a single text blob, or should each step have a separate entry?

❑ Should each ingredient be a single text string, or should the ingredients be structured with a quantity and the actual ingredient name?

❑ Is the ingredient list ordered?

❑ The *Joy of Cooking* is unusual in that it actually interpolates ingredients and directions, which is perhaps easier to read, and also enables lovely recipe visualizations such as the ones at the website www.cookingforengineers.com. Should you try to allow for that?

❑ Sometimes an ingredient may itself have a recipe. Many soup recipes start with a standard base stock, for example. How can you allow for that?

I find these decisions a lot easier to make with the understanding that they aren't permanent, and that the code base is quite malleable. Eventually, of course, there'll be the problem of potentially having to deal with a lot of data to migrate, but until then, here's how I think the site should start:

❑ Directions are a single text blob. There isn't really any data to them other than the text itself, and if you have a convention in data entry of using newlines to separate steps, it'll be easy enough to migrate should you choose to.

❑ There will be structured and ordered ingredient lists. Usually ingredients are given in a particular order for a reason. Adding the structure doesn't cost much at this point, and will enable some nice features later on (such as English-to-metric conversion). I also think that this one would be harder to migrate to the structured data if you don't start there — you'd have to write a simple parser to manage that.

❑ Interpolating ingredients and directions could be managed by adding directions to the ingredient data, but doing so adds some complexity to the user display, and I'm not ready to start with that. The idea of being able to do those shiny table visualizations is tempting, though. This is a possibility for change later on, although I suspect that it would be nearly impossible to extrapolate data from preexisting recipes.

Having ingredients themselves have recipes is a complication you don't need at this point. In case it's not clear, I should point out that I'm doing this planning in real time. As I write the draft of this, I haven't started the code yet, so I could yet turn out to be dead wrong on one of these assumptions, in which case you'll really see how suited Rails is for agile development.

Having done at least a minimum of design work, it's time to instantiate the data into the database. You're going to do that using the new-style REST resources with Rails.

The REST of the Story

I pledge right now that will be the only REST-related pun in the whole book (unless I think of a really good one later on).

REST is another one of those tortured software acronyms — it stands for REpresentational State Transfer. The basic idea dates back to the doctoral dissertation of Ray Fielding, written in 2000, although it only started gaining traction in the Rails world in early 2006, when a couple of different plugins allowed for a RESTful style within Rails. The functionality was rapidly moved to the Rails core and has just as quickly become a very commonly used practice, especially for standard Create, Read, Update, Delete (CRUD) style functionality.

What Is REST?

There are three different ways of thinking about REST as compared to a traditional Rails application:

❑ Pages versus resources

❑ Network protocols

❑ Rails features

You'll explore each of these in the following sections.

Pages versus Resources

The traditional view of data on the Web is action-oriented. A user performs an action on a page, usually by just accessing the page, but sometimes by sending data as well. The server responds with data, usually in HTML, but a pure web service is likely to send XML or JSON.

A RESTful application, in contrast, is viewed as a set of resources, each of which contains some data and exposes a set of functions to the Web. The core of these functions is made up of the standard CRUD actions, and the application programming interface (API) for the standard functions is supposed to be completely consistent between resources. A resource can also define additional actions for itself.

If this reminds you of the distinction between procedural programming and object-oriented programming (OOP), with REST resources playing the part of objects, well then you've got the gist. One difference is that using REST in Rails primarily changes the way in which the user accesses your data because it changes the URL structure of your site, but the data itself will be largely unaffected, whereas an object-oriented design does affect the way your data itself is structured.

Network Protocols

The signature feature of a REST-based web application is the use of HTTP access methods as critical data when determining what to do in response to a request. HTTP defines four different methods for requesting data (and eight methods overall). Many of us learned this fact in a beginning HTTP book or network course and promptly filed the information under "trivia that might win a bet someday, in a bizarre set of circumstances." Only two of these methods are in general use — nearly every server since the days of Mosaic has only used GET for getting information out of the server and POST for putting information into the server. In addition, most web applications used separate URLs for their GET and POST operations, even where it was technically feasible to share URLs. For example, the Java Servlet specification allows the same servlet to respond differently to a GET or POST, but all of the servlets I've written either defined one of the methods as a clone of the other, or only respond to one method, ignoring or failing if the other is invoked.

It turns out, though, that the HTTP protocol also defines PUT and DELETE. It's easy to understand DELETE, but it's not immediately clear what the original intention was for the distinction between PUT and POST — you'll see in a second the distinction REST and Rails make between them. A RESTful application uses all of these methods (often called *verbs*) as a meaningful part of the Web action. In other words, when confronted with a URL like http://www.soupsonline.com/recipes/1, a RESTful Rails application cannot determine what controller action to perform without knowing whether the request was a GET, DELETE, or PUT. A GET request would result in a show action, the DELETE request triggers the delete action, and the PUT request triggers the update action. In contrast, a traditional Rails application would have the controller action explicitly specified in the URL, ignoring the HTTP verb. The traditional URL might look like http://www.soupsonline.com/recipes/show/1 or http://www.soupsonline.com/recipes/update/1. (I realize that it's slightly absurd to refer to anything in Rails as traditional, but there isn't a better retronym for the non-REST applications.)

By now, you may have realized a contradiction that I've hand-waved my way past. If all the browsers handle only GET and POST, then how does a RESTful Rails application use PUT and DELETE? The Rails core team, like geniuses since time immemorial, is not going to let a little thing like the imperfection of the current state of browsers get in the way of a conceptually nifty idea like REST. When you ask Rails to create a PUT or DELETE link, it actually wraps the request inside a small POST form with a hidden field that Rails then decodes on the server end. In the happier RESTful future, servers will implement the complete HTTP specification, and Rails can dispense with the disguise and display its PUTs and DELETEs proudly.

Rails Features

Within Rails, you do not explicitly define a class called a Resource in the same way that you explicitly define Controller or Model classes — at least, not for resources controlled by the local Rails application (see Chapter 9 for how you might access resources from a remote server). A resource emerges from the interaction of a Controller and a Model, with some magic in the route-mapping gluing them together. Although Rails provides a REST resource generator that creates a tightly coupled Controller and Model, you could easily have two separate resources managing different facets of a model. Each resource would have a separate controller. For instance, if you had some kind of employee database, you could manage contact information and say, vacation days as separate resources with separate controllers, even though they are in the same model. As you'll see in just a few moments, you can also nest resources, designating one resource as the parent of another.

RESTful resources also bring along some helpful nuts-and-bolts functionality that makes them quite easy to deal with. The controller method respond_to was created for REST (although it can be used in any Rails controller), and makes it extremely easy to deliver your data in multiple formats. Continuing the description in the previous section, using respond_to, your application can return different data for the URL http://www.soupsonline.com/recipes/1.xml as compared to http://www.soupsonline.com/recipes/1.rss or even http://www.soupsonline.com/recipes/1.png.

A RESTful view can also use some logically named methods to generate the URL that you might use inside a `link_to` call in your view. Rather than fussing around with action parameters, or passing the object or ID you want to control, Rails will automatically respond to methods such as `recipe_path` or `edit_recipe_path` — assuming, of course, that you've defined a resource for recipes.

Why REST?

REST is elegant, and I think it's a logical progression of where the best-practices design of Rails applications has been heading since Rails was released. There's been a continual motion towards having more controllers, having thinner controllers with the real work done in the model, and enforcing consistency between controllers. REST provides a framework for moving that design style to the next level: lots of controllers, lots of activity possible with very little controller code, and absolute consistency for CRUD-style controllers. If you are the kind of web designer who likes to have the URL interface to your application be extremely crisp and concise — and many of us are — then REST will feel quite nice.

That said, you're going to see the biggest benefits from REST if your application is either implementing or consuming web services. The consistency of interfaces to REST resources, coupled with the almost trivial nature of converting an `ActiveRecord` object to an XML representation and back turns every Rails application into a potential web service, but if you aren't thinking of your application in those terms, it may not feel like that big of a win. Although you might try to think of your application as a potential service, it may open avenues of functionality that you haven't thought of before.

Even if you aren't providing a web service, pretty much every Rails application has to do some set of CRUD actions on its data. REST is a powerful mechanism for making that process even simpler. Again, though, REST isn't necessarily going to be much assistance in creating the fancy front-end of your application, but it will make the wiring easier to install, which will leave you more time to make that front-end even fancier.

Building Your First Resources

Earlier, you saw the initial design for Soups OnLine where two resources, recipe and ingredient, were described. It's time to put them in your application, using the Rails `generate` script. The action for the script is `scaffold`. (In versions of Rails prior to 2.0, it was called `scaffold_resource`.) The syntax is simple: the singular name of the resource, followed by pairs of the form `attribute:datatype` for each attribute you want initially placed in the resource.

The data-type portion of each pair can be any type available for use as a data type in a Rails migration: `binary`, `boolean`, `date`, `datetime`, `decimal`, `float`, `integer`, `string`, `text`, `time`, and `timestamp`.

There's no expectation that you have to have the attribute list correct up front (it can always be changed), but it should just be an easy place to start. The commands and responses look like this (for clarity, I've removed lines where Rails shows that a directory already exists):

```
$ ruby script/generate scaffold recipe title:string servings:string ↵
description:string directions:string

create  app/views/recipes
create  app/views/recipes/index.html.erb
```

```
create  app/views/recipes/show.html.erb
create  app/views/recipes/new.html.erb
create  app/views/recipes/edit.html.erb
create  app/views/layouts/recipes.html.erb
create  public/stylesheets/scaffold.css
create    app/models/recipe.rb
create    test/unit/recipe_test.rb
create    test/fixtures/recipes.yml
create    db/migrate
create    db/migrate/001_create_recipes.rb
create  app/controllers/recipes_controller.rb
create  test/functional/recipes_controller_test.rb
create  app/helpers/recipes_helper.rb
route   map.resources :recipes

$ ruby script/generate scaffold ingredient recipe_id:integer order_of:integer ↩
amount:float ingredient:string instruction:string unit:string

create  app/views/ingredients
create  app/views/ingredients/index.html.erb
create  app/views/ingredients/show.html.erb
create  app/views/ingredients/new.html.erb
create  app/views/ingredients/edit.html.erb
create  app/views/layouts/ingredients.html.erb
create    app/models/ingredient.rb
create    test/unit/ingredient_test.rb
create    test/fixtures/ingredients.yml
create    db/migrate/002_create_ingredients.rb
create  app/controllers/ingredients_controller.rb
create  test/functional/ingredients_controller_test.rb
create  app/helpers/ingredients_helper.rb
route   map.resources :ingredients
```

That's a lot of files for each scaffold, many of which will be familiar to you from traditional Rails code generation. You've got your controller object, views, the model class, a fixture file, and unit and functional tests. I'd like to focus some attention on items that are new or different.

Migrations

The generator script uses the attribute information provided to create Rails migration objects. Here's the one for Recipe, which you'll find in db/migrate/001_create_recipes.rb:

```
class CreateRecipes < ActiveRecord::Migration
  def self.up
    create_table :recipes do |t|
      t.string :title
      t.string :servings
      t.string :description
      t.string :directions
      t.timestamps
    end
  end
```

(continued)

(continued)

```
    def self.down
       drop_table :recipes
    end
  end
```

The `t.string` syntax is a Rails 2.0 method for spelling what would previously have been written `t.column :string`. The `timestamps` method adds the special Rails columns `created_at` and `updated_at`. The creation of the ingredient resource generates a similar migration at db/migrate/002_create_ingredients.rb.

Routes

The most important additions are the new routes added to the `routes.rb` file, which are the source of all the RESTful magic. As created by your two generators, the routes look like this:

```
  map.resources :ingredients
  map.resources :recipes
```

Standard Routes

The purpose of the `routes.rb` file is to control the conversion from an HTTP request to a Rails method call. Each of these `map.resources` lines causes Rails to associate URLs that start with the resource name to the resource for that controller, in this case /recipes would invoke the recipe controller. So far, it sounds similar to a traditional Rails route in :controller/:action/:id format. The difference is that the REST routes infer the action to call in the controller based on the HTTP method invoked. There are seven standard actions in a REST controller. The following table shows the standard interpretation of URLs and the HTTP methods that are used to describe the corresponding controller actions. Each controller action also has a path method, to be called inside views for `link_to` and form actions, as well as a URL method, which is called inside the controller when you need to redirect to a different action.

URL Called	HTTP Method	Controller Action	Path Method	URL Method
/recipes/1	GET	show	recipe_path(1)	recipe_url(1)
/recipes/1	PUT	update	recipe_path(1)	recipe_url(1)
/recipes/1	DELETE	destroy	recipe_path(1)	recipe_url(1)
/recipes	GET	index	recipes_path	recipes_url
/recipes	POST	create	recipes_path	recipes_path
/recipes/new	GET	new	new_recipe_path	new_recipe_url
/recipes/1/edit	GET	edit	edit_recipe_path(1)	edit_recipe_url(1)

When you call one of these path or URL methods with a PUT or DELETE HTTP method, you must make sure that the link_to or redirect call also contains the option :method => :delete or :method => :put to ensure that the URL is properly sent by Rails (link_to assumes GET; the form methods and link_to_remote assume POST). If you are using the standard HTTP method, there's a shortcut, where you just specify the object that is the target of the link:

```
link_to @recipe
```

You'll see examples of those calls when you examine the standard views that the generator has created.

Also, the methods that take an argument can take either an integer argument, in which case it's assumed to be the ID of the resource you are interested in, or they can take the resource object itself, in which case, the ID is extracted for use in the URL or path. They can also take the usual key/value pairs, which are converted to a query string for the request.

Nested Routes

You need to do a slight tweak of the routes to allow for the relationship between a recipe and its ingredients. As the design currently stands, there's a strict one-to-many relationship between recipes and ingredients, with an ingredient only being meaningful inside its specific recipe. To make your Rails routes reflect that relationship more accurately, the routes can be nested in routes.rb. Change your routes.rb file so that the resource lines are as follows:

```
map.resources :recipes do |recipes|
  recipes.resources :ingredients
end
```

With this nesting in place, Rails will generate similar routes for ingredients, but only with a recipe attached at the beginning of the URL. For example, the URL to call the index method for the ingredients in a recipe will be as follows:

```
/recipe/1/ingredients
```

And the URL for showing, updating, and deleting would look like this:

```
/recipe/1/ingredient/1
```

The named methods for a nested resource are similar to the parent-level methods listed previously, but they contain the parent resource name in the method, such as the following:

```
recipe_ingredient_url(@recipe, @ingredient)
```

```
edit_recipe_ingredient_url(@recipe, @ingredient)
```

The path-based methods are similar. Again, the methods can take either integer IDs or the actual resource objects. This naming convention is pretty clear when the nesting isn't very deep or when the variables are well named. But if you get into things like `user_address_street_house_room_url(x, y, z, a, b)`, it could get a little hairy. There are a couple of ways to clean those long method names up:

❏ The arguments to the URL or path method can be entered as key/value pairs:

```
recipe_ingredient_url(:recipe_id => @recipe, :id => @ingredient)
```

❏ For URLs, the `url_for` method can be used (remember to specify the HTTP method if needed):

```
url_for(@recipe, @ingredient)
```

Either choice should help tame unclear route method calls.

Customizing Resource Routes

The `resources` call in the `routes.rb` file can also be customized to adjust the behavior of the routes. The most common reason for doing this is to add your own actions to the resource. Each resource call provides three options for specifying custom actions. The `:member` option is for actions that apply to a specific resource, the `:collection` option is for actions on the entire list (like `index`), and the `:new` option applies to resources that have not yet been saved to the database. In each case, the value for each option is itself a hash. The keys of that hash are the method names, and the values are the HTTP verbs to be used when calling that method. So, if you wanted to add a print action to your recipes, it would look like this:

```
map.resources :recipes, :method => {:print => :get } do |recipes|
  recipes.resources :ingredients
end
```

The addition here of `:method => {:print => :get }` creates the new `print` action, and tells Rails that this action will be defined on a specific resource called via GET. The URL of this new action will be `/recipes/1/print`. (This is a change from older versions of Rails, where this used to be spelled `/recipes/1;print` — nobody really liked the semicolon syntax, and it tended to interfere with caching, so it was changed for Rails 2.0.)

The URL for a collection-based action would look like `/recipes/<action>`, and the URL for a new-based action would be `/recipes/new/<action>`.

What's more, you also get a URL and path method for the new action. In this case, they would be `print_recipe_path(@recipe)` and `print_recipe_url(@recipe)`.

The tricky thing about these custom routes is remembering to specify them. Unlike nearly everything else in Rails, a custom resource route needs to be specified twice: once in the controller itself, and then again in `routes.rb`. This is arguably a violation of one of Rails core design principles, namely Don't Repeat Yourself (DRY), and it's entirely possible that somebody clever will come along and clean this up at sometime in the future.

Like most of Rails, the standard names can be overridden if you like. In the case of a resource routing call, there are a few options to change standard naming. You can specify an arbitrary controller class to be the target of the resource with the `:controller` option. You can change the name of the controller within the URL (the `recipe` in `/recipe/1`) using the `:singular` option, and you can require a prefix to the URL with the `:path_prefix` option. The prefix passed to that option works just the same way as a traditional rails route — parts of the prefix specified as a Ruby symbol are converted to variables when the path is dereferenced. For example, if you wanted all recipes to be attached to a chef, you could add the option `:path_prefix => "/chef/:chef_name"`, and the show recipe URL, for example, would change to `/chef/juliachild/recipe/1`. Within the controller, the variable `params[:chef_name]` would be set to `juliachild`.

Controllers

The controller for each new resource contains seven actions, shown earlier in the table of standard routes. Each action is helpfully commented with the URLs that cause that action to be invoked. Each action is also set up by default to respond to both HTML and XML requests. Following are sections about the default controllers for the recipe resource with some comments.

Index

First up, the `index` method, which displays a list of all the recipes:

```
# GET /recipes
# GET /recipes.xml
def index
  @recipes = Recipe.find(:all)
  respond_to do |format|
    format.html # index.html.erb
    format.xml  { render :xml => @recipes }
  end
end
```

If you're familiar with traditional Rails, than the only new part here is the `respond_to` method, which is the REST mechanism that allows the same controller action to return different data based on the requested format.

Functionally what happens here is similar to a case expression — each potential format that the action might respond to is listed in the body of the `respond_to` block, and exactly one of them is performed based on the MIME type of the user request. In this case, if the URL request is `/recipes` or `/recipes.html`, then the `format.html` line is chosen. If the URL is `/recipes.xml`, then the `format.xml` line is chosen. Each type can have a block associated with it, which is executed when that type matches the user request. If there is no block associated with the type, then the Rails default action for dealing with that type is triggered. In the case of the `html` action, that would be the rendering of the matching `html.erb` view, `index.html.erb`. It has become customary to explicitly note that the format is being handled in a default manner with a comment naming the view file to be rendered.

Since this is one of those Ruby metaprogramming magic things, where it's not immediately clear what's happening behind the scenes, it's worth breaking the method down a little bit. The `respond_to` method comes in two forms. The one shown previously takes a block. Alternately, you could just pass a list of symbols corresponding to types (`:html, :js`). You would use the list version if every type on the list was handled via the default action for that type.

In the more typical case, the block is defined with a single argument. The argument is of a `Responder` class. Each line of the block calls a method on the responder object — in the previous code, those methods are `format.html` and `format.xml`. Each of these format methods takes an optional argument, which is also a block.

When the `respond_to` method is called, the outer block is invoked. Each format method is called, and does nothing unless the format method name matches the type of the request. (Metaprogramming fans should note that this is elegantly implemented using `method_missing`.) If the types match, then behavior associated with that type is invoked — either the block if one is explicitly passed or the default behavior if not.

The convention is to have nothing in your `respond_to` block except for the format calls, and nothing in the format calling blocks except the actual rendering call being made. This goes along with the general idea in Rails design that the controller should be as thin as possible, and that complex data processing should be handled in the model object.

The `respond_to` method adds a lot of flexibility to your Rails controller — adding XML data serialization or RSS feeds is nearly trivial. The syntax, I think, may still have some tweaking ahead of it — I'm not sure there's a lot of love for the way default behaviors are specified, and if the rendering is complex, the nested blocks can become hard to read.

Rails defines eight formats for you: `atom`, `html`, `ics`, `js`, `rss`, `text`, `xml`, and `yaml`. Just to be clear on this, `html` is used for ordinary browser output, `atom` and `rss` should be used for feeds, `xml` and `yaml` are used for object syndication, `ics` is the standard iCalendar format for calendar data, `text` is often used for simple serialization, and `js` is used either to serialize data via the JSON format or as the target of an Ajax call that would trigger JavaScript.

Adding your own formats is simple, assuming that the format has a MIME type. Suppose you wanted to allow a URL like `/recipes.png` to return some kind of graphical display of your recipe list. All you need to do is go into the `config/environment.rb` file and add the following line:

```
Mime::Type.register "image.png", :png
```

Now any `respond_to` block in your application will enable you to use `format.png` as a method.

Show

The default `show` method is nearly identical to the `index` method, except that it only takes a single recipe from the database, and renders the `show.html.erb` file.

```
# GET /recipes/1
# GET /recipes/1.xml
def show
  @recipe = Recipe.find(params[:id])
  respond_to do |format|
    format.html # show.html.erb
    format.xml  { render :xml => @recipe }
  end
end
```

The `render :xml => @recipe` method call creates an XML representation of the data object by making all of the attributes of the data object into subordinate tags of the XML (see Chapter 9 for more details).

New

The default `new` method is similar to `show`, except a new recipe object is created:

```
# GET /recipes/new
# GET /recipes/new.xml
def new
  @recipe = Recipe.new
  respond_to do |format|
    format.html # new.html.erb
    format.xml  { render :xml => @recipe }
  end
end
```

Edit

The default `edit` method is extremely simple because it does not have an XML representation defined, so the traditional Rails default behavior happens automatically, and a `respond_to` method is not needed. Here's an example:

```
# GET /recipes/1/edit
def edit
  @recipe = Recipe.find(params[:id])
end
```

Create

The `create` method is more complicated because it needs to output different information depending on whether the creation is successful. The new recipe object is created based on the incoming parameters, and then it is saved to the database. For example:

```
# POST /recipes
# POST /recipes.xml
def create
  @recipe = Recipe.new(params[:recipe])
  respond_to do |format|
    if @recipe.save
      flash[:notice] = 'Recipe was successfully created.'
      format.html { redirect_to(@recipe) }
      format.xml  { render :xml => @recipe,
                    :status => :created,
                    :location => @recipe }
    else
      format.html { render :action => "new" }
      format.xml  { render :xml => @recipe.errors,
                         :status => :unprocessable_entity }
    end
  end
end
```

I mentioned earlier that you could have code other than the format methods inside the `respond_to` block, and this example shows one reason why you might want to do that. The actual saving of the recipe takes place inside that block. If the `save` is successful, then the HTML response simply redirects to the `show` method. Rails infers that you want to show the object because the only argument to `redirect_to` is the object itself, and it uses REST routing to determine the unique URL for that object. The XML response returns the object as XML with a couple of extra headers containing additional information.

If the `save` is not successful, the HTML response is to show the new form again, and the XML response is to send the errors and status via XML.

In case you are wondering why the `create` method needs to support an XML format, the answer is to allow new objects to be created remotely via a separate web services client that might be dealing with your recipe server via XML.

Update

The `update` method is nearly identical to the `create` method, except that instead of creating a new recipe, it finds the existing recipe with the expected ID, and instead of calling `save`, it calls `update_attributes`. Oh, and the XML output is slightly different. The `update` method is as follows:

```
# PUT /recipes/1
# PUT /recipes/1.xml
def update
  @recipe = Recipe.find(params[:id])
  respond_to do |format|
    if @recipe.update_attributes(params[:recipe])
      flash[:notice] = 'Recipe was successfully updated.'
      format.html { redirect_to(@recipe) }
      format.xml  { head :ok }
    else
      format.html { render :action => "edit" }
      format.xml  { render :xml => @recipe.errors,
                      :status => :unprocessable_entity }
    end
  end
end
```

Delete

Finally, `delete`. The default method doesn't check for success or failure of `delete`; for an HTML request, it redirects to the index page via the `recipes_url` helper. An XML request gets a header signaling success. Here's an example of the `delete` method:

```
# DELETE /recipes/1
# DELETE /recipes/1.xml
def destroy
  @recipe = Recipe.find(params[:id])
  @recipe.destroy
```

```
    respond_to do |format|
      format.html { redirect_to(recipes_url) }
      format.xml  { head :ok }
    end
  end
```

Views

The views that are created by the generated script are largely similar to their non-REST counterparts, but I would like show the differences that come from using the RESTful URL features. In the edit.html.erb file, the form accesses its URL as follows

```
<% form_for(@recipe) do |f| %>
```

The form_for method merely takes the argument and automatically converts that to a PUT call to /recipes/1 (or whatever the id of the recipe is), which translates in the HTML source to this:

```
<form action="/recipes/1"
class="edit_recipe"
id="edit_recipe_1"
method="post">
<div style="margin:0;padding:0">
<input name="_method" type="hidden" value="put" />
```

Although this is implemented as a POST from the server point of view, Rails inserts the hidden field for _method with the value put to tell the Rails application to treat it as a PUT request and redirect to the update action.

At the bottom of the edit page, the link_to method for show uses the GET version of the default URL for the object, while the back link uses the named method for getting to the index action, as follows:

```
<%= link_to 'Show', @recipe %> |
<%= link_to 'Back', recipes_path %>
```

Similarly, from index.html.erb, it does this:

```
<%= link_to 'New recipe', new_recipe_path %>
```

And from show.html.erb, it does this:

```
<%= link_to 'Edit', edit_recipe_path(@recipe) %> |
<%= link_to 'Back', recipes_path %>
```

To clear up one quick issue, the .html.erb file-ending is a Rails 2.0 change. It was felt that .rhtml was not accurate because the file is actually an erb file, and the .html is there to denote what kind of file the erb file will be after it is processed.

Route Display

If you find yourself becoming confused by all the RESTful routing magic, as of Version 2.0, Rails provides a rake command, `routes`, that gives you a complete list of the routes that have been defined in your application (output has been truncated). For example:

```
$ rake routes

  recipes                  GET    /recipes
    {:controller=>"recipes", :action=>"index"}

  formatted_recipes        GET    /recipes.:format
    {:controller=>"recipes", :action=>"index"}

                           POST   /recipes
    {:controller=>"recipes", :action=>"create"}

                           POST   /recipes.:format
    {:controller=>"recipes", :action=>"create"}

  new_recipe               GET    /recipes/new
    {:controller=>"recipes", :action=>"new"}

  formatted_new_recipe     GET    /recipes/new.:format
    {:controller=>"recipes", :action=>"new"}

  edit_recipe              GET    /recipes/:id/edit
    {:controller=>"recipes", :action=>"edit"}

  formatted_edit_recipe    GET    /recipes/:id/edit.:format
    {:controller=>"recipes", :action=>"edit"}
```

It's a little tricky to see — you need some pretty long lines to lay this out, but the output is in four columns: the named method stem that is used to access the route (for example, `edit_recipe`, which can be the stem to `edit_recipe_path` or `edit_recipe_url`), the HTTP verb that triggers this call, the actual URL with symbols inserted, and then the controller and action called by the route.

Building Ingredients

Having now gotten a thorough tour of the new mechanisms that RESTful Rails provides by default, it's time for you to start writing some code and making this site come to life. The first task is to enable simple entry of a recipe, and allow the most recently entered recipes to be displayed on the user-centered front page, blog-style.

The following problems stand between you and that goal:

❑   The database schema and sample code as generated do not associate recipes and ingredients, so the forms that were created by the scaffold do not have a place to enter ingredient information.

❑ You changed the default routing after the scaffolds were generated, and therefore the ingredient forms, as generated, use invalid methods to create URLs.

❑ The basic index listing of recipes is useful from an administrative point of view, but it is not what you want to present to a user. In addition to the functional changes, you'll need it to be much nicer looking.

That list will take you through the end of this chapter. Time to build a webapp!

Setting Up Your Database

Most of the work of setting up the initial database was already done when you created the resources and generated migrations, but you still need to actually create the database instances. You'll need to go to the `database.yml` file first and adjust the database information for all three database environments — development, test, and production. If you are using MySQL (version 5.x, please) and the database is on your local development box, then you probably only need to put your root password into the file. (More complicated database setups are discussed in Chapter 6, "The Care and Feeding of Databases.")

> *A late change in Rails 2.0.2 has made SQLite3 the default database for new Rails projects. The examples in this book use MySQL for the database connections.*

Once that is done, you can use Rake to do all the database creation work, without touching your MySQL administration application. The first `rake` command (new in Rails 2.0) is this:

```
rake db:create:all
```

This command goes through your `database.yml` file and creates a database schema for each database listed for your local host.

Similarly, the `rake db:create` command creates only the development environment. The command creates empty database schemas. To populate the development environment with the tables and columns defined in the migration, enter the following command:

```
rake db:migrate
```

And to take that development environment and copy it to the test database, enter the following command:

```
rake db:test:prepare
```

This gives you all the database setup you need to get started.

Aligning Your Tests to the Nested Resource

I'm a firm believer in automated testing — unit, functional, and integration — so I love the fact that Rails includes such a complete test suite. It's very important to keep that suite current and running clean. I know that some of the tests will fail based on the routing changes that were made, but the first thing to do is get a sense of the damage with the following (this output has been modified slightly for readability):

```
$ rake
(in /Users/noel/Documents/Programming/ruby/soupsonline)

/usr/local/bin/ruby -Ilib:test
   "/usr/local/lib/ruby/gems/1.8/gems/rake-
   0.7.3/lib/rake/rake_test_loader.rb"
   "test/unit/ingredient_test.rb"
   "test/unit/recipe_test.rb"
Started
..
Finished in 0.327569 seconds.

2 tests, 2 assertions, 0 failures, 0 errors
/usr/local/bin/ruby -Ilib:test
   "/usr/local/lib/ruby/gems/1.8/gems/rake-
   0.7.3/lib/rake/rake_test_loader.rb"
   "test/functional/ingredients_controller_test.rb"
   "test/functional/recipes_controller_test.rb"
Loaded suite /usr/local/lib/ruby/gems/1.8/gems/rake-
   0.7.3/lib/rake/rake_test_loader
Started
EEEEEEE.......
Finished in 1.732989 seconds.
14 tests, 13 assertions, 0 failures, 7 errors
```

Looking at the errors, it seems that all the functional tests of the ingredients controller failed, as expected. The following section describes what you need to do to clean them up.

The Test Object

Rails sets up some test data in the `fixtures` directory, which can be loaded into your test directories to enable database-backed objects to work. By default, each controller test loads the fixtures for the data type the controller manages. However, now that the ingredients resource is subordinate to the recipe resource, the ingredients controller test also needs to load the recipe fixtures. This enables the controller to access recipe data during testing. Add the following line to `test/functional/ingredients_controller_test.rb`, right below where the ingredient fixture is loaded:

```
fixtures :recipes
```

Now, in the tests, there are two things that need to be fixed consistently throughout the test. Each individual test calls the `get`, `post`, or `put` helper method to simulate the HTTP call. Each and every one of those calls needs to add a parameter for the `recipe_id`. You can do this by adding the argument to each of the calls (remember to place a comma between hash arguments — for some reason I always forget that comma):

```
:recipe_id => 1
```

A couple of the tests also confirm that Rails redirects to the ingredient index listing, with a line like this:

```
assert_redirected_to ingredient_path(assigns(:ingredient))
```

This line no longer works because, now that ingredients are a nested resource, the pathnames are all defined in terms of a parent recipe. Change that line every time it appears to this:

```
assert_redirected_to
    recipe_ingredient_path(assigns(:recipe),
     assigns(:ingredient))
```

This changes the name of the helper method, and adds the recipe object to the arguments. The `assigns` method gives access to any instance attributes set in the controller action.

The Controller Object

Because you are going to be testing for it, you need to make sure that every controller method actually does assign a `@recipe` attribute. The best way to do that is with a before filter. The `before_filter` method allows you to specify a block or method that is performed before every controller action gets started. Add the following line to the beginning of the `IngredientController` class in `app/controllers/ingredient_controller.rb`:

```
before_filter :find_recipe
```

This specifies that the `find_recipe` method needs to be run before each controller action. To define that action, add the method to the end of the class as follows:

```
private

def find_recipe
  @recipe = Recipe.find(params[:recipe_id])
end
```

It's important that the method go after a `private` declaration; otherwise, a user could hit `/ingredients/find_recipe` from their browser, and invoke the `find_recipe` method, which would be undesirable. This mechanism ensures that every controller action will have a recipe defined, and you no longer need to worry about consistency. Readability can be an issue with filters, though, because it can sometimes be hard to track back into the filter method to see where attributes are defined. It helps to make smaller controllers where the filters are simple and clear. You'll see another common use of filters in Chapter 3, "Adding Users."

Next, you need to clean up the redirections. Two actions in this controller redirect to the show action using `redirect_to(@ingredient)`. Change those as follows:

```
redirect_to([@recipe, @ingredient])
```

The redirection method automatically handles the list of nested resource objects. The destroy action redirects to the list action, so you need to change that redirection as follows:

```
redirect_to(recipe_ingredients_url)
```

In this case, the controller automatically infers that it should use the @recipe attribute to generate the correct index path.

The Views

All you need to do to the view objects at this point is change the URLs for the forms and links. The form declaration in the edit and new views (in app/views/ingredients/edit.html.erb and app/views/ingredients/new.html.erb) should now read as follows:

```
<% form_for([@recipe, @ingredient]) do |f| %>
```

Again, this implicitly creates the correct URL from the two objects.

You also need to change the URL in the edit page (app/views/ingredients/edit.html.erb) as follows:

```
<%= link_to 'Show', [@recipe, @ingredient] %>
```

You make the same change to the URL on the index page (app/views/ingredients/index.html. erb), except in this case, ingredient is a loop variable, not an instance variable, so you don't include the @ sign.

Similarly, you need to change all the named routes by adding the prefix recipe_ to the method name and including the @recipe variable in the argument list. The link to the index page, accessed via the back link on several pages in app/views/ingredients should be changed to this:

```
<%= link_to 'Back', recipe_ingredients_path(@recipe) %>
```

You also need to make changes to the other named links. Here are some examples:

```
<%= link_to 'Edit', edit_recipe_ingredient_path(@recipe, @ingredient) %>
<%= link_to 'Destroy', [@recipe, ingredient],
    :confirm => 'Are you sure?', :method => :delete %>
<%= link_to 'New ingredient', new_recipe_ingredient_path(@recipe) %>
```

At this point, all your tests should run cleanly. If not, an error message will likely be displayed, showing you exactly which method name change you missed. When you make the analogous change in the edit view, note that the edit link in the index.html.erb page does not include the @ sign for the ingredient, as it is a loop variable, not an instance variable.

Rails Testing Tip

The default test runner text is fine as far as it goes, but sometimes it's not very easy to tell which methods have failed. If you include diagnostic print statements in your tests while debugging, it can be difficult to tell which output goes with which tests.

There are a few options for more useful test output. Most IDEs include some kind of graphical text runner, and over the past year or so, several Java IDEs have added Rails support — Aptana for Eclipse, NetBeans, and IntelliJ all have graphical Rails test runners. There are also a couple of available stand-alone GUI test runners, depending on the operating system you are running.

I've come to like a little gem called `turn`, which you can install and then place the line `require 'turn'` in your `test_helper.rb` file. It produces somewhat more useful and verbose test-runner output. The error message for each test is associated with that test, as is any diagnostic output. And if your command shell supports it, tests that pass are in green and tests that fail are in red. Here is some sample output:

```
IngredientsControllerTest
    test_should_create_ingredient PASS
    test_should_destroy_ingredient PASS
    test_should_get_edit PASS
    test_should_get_index PASS
    test_should_get_new PASS
    test_should_show_ingredient PASS
    test_should_update_ingredient PASS
RecipesControllerTest
    test_should_create_recipe PASS
    test_should_destroy_recipe PASS
    test_should_get_edit PASS
    test_should_get_index PASS
    test_should_get_new PASS
    test_should_show_recipe PASS
    test_should_update_recipe PASS

================================================================
    pass: 14,  fail: 0,  error: 0

    total: 14 tests with 25 assertions in 1.768561 seconds
================================================================
```

Because turn *changes the format of your text output, other plugins or tools that depend on the test output — most notably Autotest (see Chapter 7) — might have problems.*

Building a Recipe Editor

If you fire up the Rails server and look at the recipe input form, you'll see that at this point, it looks something like what is shown in Figure 1-1.

New recipe

Title

Servings

Description

Directions

(Create)

Back

Figure 1-1

While maintaining the proper amount of reverence to the tool that provided this form for free, it's easy to see that it won't do. Ingredients aren't listed, all the boxes are the wrong size, and basically the thing looks totally generic. Your punch list looks like this:

- ❏ Make the items that need longer data entry into text areas.
- ❏ Clean up the organization to look more like a finished recipe.
- ❏ Add ingredients to the recipe.

Naturally, you'll start by writing some tests.

Adding Ingredients

Test-Driven Development (TDD, sometimes also called Test-First Development) is a practice that first gained widespread attention as one of the core practices of Extreme Programming (or XP). Even if your programming is less extreme, writing automated tests is perhaps the best single way to ensure the quality and stability of your application over time. This is particularly true in Rails, because all kinds of testing goodness have been built into the framework, making powerful tests easy to write.

In this book, I'm going to try where possible to present working tests for the code samples as they are presented. The idea is to give you a sense of strategies for testing various parts of a Rails application, and to reinforce the idea that writing tests for all your Rails code is an achievable and desirable goal.

I'd like to start by reinforcing the previously created tests for the Recipe new form and the create method. For new, I'd like to confirm that the expected elements in the form actually exist, and for create, I'd like to confirm that when those elements are passed to the server, the expected recipe object is created. For both, I'd like to test the ingredient functionality.

Asserting HTML

To test the form, you'll use an extremely powerful feature of the Rails test environment called assert_ select, which allows you to test the structure of the HTML sent to the browser. Your first usage of assert_select just scratches the surface of what it can do. The following test is in tests/ functional/recipe_controller_test.rb:

```
def test_should_get_new
  get :new
  assert_response :success
  assert_select("form[action=?]", recipes_path) do
    assert_select "input[name *= title]"
    assert_select "input[name *= servings]"
    assert_select "textarea[name *= ingredient_string]"
    assert_select "textarea[name *= description]"
    assert_select "textarea[name *= directions]"
  end
end
```

The strategy in testing these forms is to verify the structure of the form. Writing tests for the visual aspects of the form is likely to be very brittle, especially this early in development, and would add a lot of cost in maintaining the test. However, no matter how it's displayed, the recipe form is likely to have some method for entering a title. You could test based on the CSS class of each form, if your design process was such that those names are likely to be stable. Then you could experiment with the visual display via the CSS file.

Each assert_select test contains a selector, and the job of the test is to validate whether the HTML output of the test has some text that matches the selector. This is roughly equivalent to a regular expression; however, the selectors are specifically structured for validating HTML output. Each selector can contain one or more wildcards denoted with a question mark, and the next argument to the method is a list of the values that would fill in those wildcard spots — similar to the way the find method works with SQL statements. The wildcard entries can either be strings or, if you are determined to make it work, regular expressions.

The first part of a selector element is the type of HTML tag that you are searching for. In the case of your first test, that's a form tag. Without any further adornment, that selector will match against all form tags in your returned HTML. You can then pass a second argument if it's a number or a range, and then the selector tests to see if the number of tags matches. The following tests would pass:

```
assert_select "form", 1
assert_select "form", 0..5
```

If the second argument is a string or regular expression, then the selector tests to see if there is a tag of that type whose contents either equal the string or match the regular expression.

The type tag can be augmented in several different ways. Putting a dot after it, as in `"form.title"`, checks to see if there's a `form` tag that is of the CSS class `title`. Putting a hash mark after the type `"form#form_1"` performs a similar test on the DOM ID of the tag. If you're familiar with CSS, you'll note this syntax is swiped directly from CSS selector syntax. If you add brackets to the type, then you are checking for an attribute that equals or nearly equals the value specified. The selector `"form[action=?]"` tests for the existence of a form tag whose action attribute matches the URL specified in the second argument. The equality test could also use the `*=` symbols, indicating that the attribute value contains the value being tested as a substring, so your test `"input[name *= title]"` would pass if there was an input tag whose name attribute contains the substring `"title"`. You can similarly use `^=` to test that the value begins with the string or `$=` to test if the value ends with the string.

You can do some further specifying with a number of defined pseudo-classes. Many of these allow you to choose a specific element from the list, such as `form:first-child`, `form:last-child`, `form:nth-child(n)`, and `form:nth-last-child(n)`, each of which matches only elements of that type that have the specified relationship with its parent element.

Finally, you can specify a relationship between two tags. Just putting one tag after the other, as in `"form input"`, matches `input` tags that are some kind of arbitrarily distant descendent of the `form` tag. Specifying those relationships can get a bit unwieldy, so you can nest the interior specification inside a block, as is done in the previous test method. Because of the nested block structure, the test only matches `input` tags that are inside a `form` tag. The specification can also be written `"form>input"`, in which case the `input` needs to be a direct child of the `form`. Alternately `"form + input"` indicates that the `input` tag is merely after the `form` tag in the document, and `"form ~ input"` would match the reverse case.

Add it all up, and your test is verifying the existence of a form tag that points to the create action. Inside that tag, you are testing for inputs with names that include "title" and "servings," and text areas that include the names "description" and "directions."

With the view as it is, these tests won't pass, because the view doesn't use `textarea` fields for data yet. Update the `app/views/recipes/new.html.erb` code as follows:

```erb
<% @title = "Enter a Recipe" %>
<%= error_messages_for :recipe %>
<% form_for(@recipe) do |f| %>
  <p>
    <b>Recipe Name:</b><br />
    <%= f.text_field :title, :class => "title", :size => 48 %>
  </p>
  <p>
    <b>Serving Size:</b>
    <%= f.text_field :servings, :class => "input", :size => 10  %>
  </p>
  <p>
    <b>Description (optional):</b><br />
```

```
   <%= f.text_area :description, :rows => 5, :cols => 55, :class => "input" %>
  </p>
  <p>
   <b>Ingredients:</b><br />
   <%= f.text_area :ingredient_string, :rows => 5, :cols => 55, :class => "input" %>
  </p>
  <p>
   <b>Directions:</b><br />
   <%= f.text_area :directions, :rows => 15, :cols => 55, :class => "input" %>
  </p>
  <p>
   <%= f.submit "Create", :class => "title" %>
  </p>
<% end %>
<%= link_to 'Back', recipes_path %>
```

There are a couple of changes. The fields that need more text now have text areas, things have been moved around a very little bit, and I've added CSS classes to the input fields that increase the size of the text being input (it bothers me when sites use very small text for user input).

The `:ingredient_string` *accessor used in the preceding form is described in the next section.*

Parsing Ingredients

The previous code listing included a bare text area for the user to enter ingredients. However, I'd still like to have the data enter the database with some structure that could enable some useful functionality later on, such as converting from English to metric units. Even so, I felt it was a little cruel to give the user a four-element form to fill out for each ingredient. So I wrote a small parser to convert strings like "2 cups carrots, diced" into ingredient objects. The basic test structure follows — put this code into the ingredient unit test class (`test/unit/ingredients.rb`):

```
def assert_parse(str, display_str, hash)
  expected = Ingredient.new(hash)
  actual = Ingredient.parse(str, recipes(:one), 1)
  assert_equal_ingredient(expected, actual)
  display_str ||= str
  assert_equal(display_str, actual.display_string)
end
```

The inputs are a string, a second string normalized for expected output, and a hash of expected values. One ingredient object is created from the hash, another is created from the string, and you test for equality. Then you test the display output string — if the input is `nil`, you assume the incoming string is the same as the outgoing string.

Chapter 1: Building Resources

The test cases I started with are described in the following table.

Case	Description
2 cups carrots, diced	The basic input structure
2 cups carrots	Basic input, minus the instructions
1 carrots, diced	Basic input, minus the unit
1 cup carrots	Singular unit
2.5 carrots, diced	A test to see whether decimal numbers are correctly handled
1/2 carrots, diced	A test to see that fractions are handled
1 1/2 carrots, diced	A test to see whether improper fractions are handled

Here's what the first two test cases look like in code (again, in `test/unit/ingredient_test.rb`):

```
def test_should_parse_basically
    assert_parse("2 cups carrots, diced", nil, :recipe_id => 1, :order_of => 1,
        :amount => 2, :unit => "cups", :ingredient => "carrots",
        :instruction => "diced")
  end

  def test_should_parse_without_instructions
    assert_parse("2 cups carrots", nil, :recipe_id => 1, :order_of => 1,
        :amount => 2, :unit => "cups", :ingredient => "carrots",
        :instruction => "")
  end
```

These test cases use the `assert_parse` method defined earlier to associate the test string with the expected features of the resulting ingredient. You should be able to define the remaining tests similarly.

There are, of course, other useful test cases that would make this more robust. Tests for proper error handling in deliberately odd conditions would also be nice. For right now, though, the previous test cases provide a sufficient level of complexity to serve as examples of how to do moderately complex processing on user data.

The way this worked in practice was that I wrote one test, made it work, and then refactored and simplified the code. I wrote the second test, which failed, and then fixed the code with another round of refactoring and code cleanup. By the time I finished the last test, the code was in pretty good shape. Here's a description of the code after that test.

I created a separate class for this called `IngredientParser`, and placed the code in a new file, `/app/models/ingredient_parser.rb`. The class starts like this:

```
class IngredientParser

  UNITS = %w{cups pounds ounces tablespoons teaspoons cans cloves}
```

```
    attr_accessor :result, :tokens, :state, :ingredient_words,
        :instruction_words

    def initialize(str, ingredient)
      @result = ingredient
      @tokens = str.split()
      @state = :amount
      @ingredient_words = []
      @instruction_words = []
    end

    def parse
      tokens.each do |token|
        consumed = self.send(state, token)
        redo unless consumed
      end
      result.ingredient = ingredient_words.join(" ")
      result.instruction = instruction_words.join(" ")
      result
    end
  end
```

The `parse` method is of the most interest. After splitting the input string into individual words, the class loops through each word, calling a method named by the current state. The states are intended to mimic the piece of data being read, so they start with :amount, because the expectation is that the numerical amount of the ingredient will start the line. Each `state` method returns `true` or `false`. If `false` is returned, then the loop is rerun with the same token (presumably a method that returns `false` will have changed the state of the system so that a different method can attempt to consume the token). After the parser runs out of tokens, it builds up the ingredient and instruction strings out of the lists that the parser has gathered.

The parser contains one method for each piece of data, starting with the amount of ingredient to be used, as follows:

```
    def amount(token)
      if token.index("/")
        numerator, denominator = token.split("/")
        fraction = Rational(numerator.to_i, denominator.to_i)
        amount = fraction.to_f
      elsif token.to_f > 0
        amount = token.to_f
      end
      result.amount += amount
      self.state = :unit
      true
    end
```

If the input token contains a slash, then the assumption is that the user has entered a fraction, and the string is split into two pieces and a Ruby rational object is created and then converted to a float (because the database stores the data as a float). Otherwise, if it's an integer or rational value, the number is taken as is. The number is added to the amount already in the result (because an improper fraction would come through this method in two separate pieces). The state is changed to :unit, and the method returns `true` to signify that the token has been consumed.

The unit method actually has provisions not to consume the token. If the token is numerical, the parser assumes it's a continuation of the amount, resets the state, and returns false so that the amount method will take a crack at the same token. For example:

```
def unit(token)
  if token.to_i > 0
    self.state = :amount
    return false
  end
  if UNITS.index(token) or UNITS.index(token.pluralize)
    result.unit = token.pluralize
    self.state = :ingredient
    return true
  else
    self.state = :ingredient
    return false
  end
end
```

If the token is not numerical, then it's checked against the list of known units maintained by the parser. If there's a match, then the token is consumed as the unit. If not, the token is not consumed. In either case, the parser moves on to the ingredient itself. Here's an example of how this works:

```
def ingredient(token)
  ingredient_words << token
  if token.ends_with?(",")
    ingredient_words[-1].chop!
    self.state = :instruction
  end
  true
end
```

The ingredient name is assumed to continue until the parser runs out of tokens, or until a token ends in a comma, as in "carrots, diced". Although none of the test cases expose it at this point, that's easily broken in the case where the ingredient is a list containing a comma. However, this error is handled gracefully by the parser, and is also rather straightforward for the enterer to correct, so I chose not to beef up the parser at this time.

Once you get past the comma, everything else is assumed to be part of the final instruction, as follows:

```
def instruction(token)
  instruction_words << token
  true
end
```

To use this, a class method in Ingredient sets the defaults and invokes the parser like this:

```
def self.parse(str, recipe = nil, order = nil)
  result = Ingredient.new(:recipe_id => recipe.id,
          :order_of => order, :ingredient => "",
```

```
                     :instruction => "", :unit => "", :amount => 0)
        parser = IngredientParser.new(str, result)
        parser.parse
    end
```

Finally, the `display_string` method of `Ingredient` makes sure everything is in a standard format as follows:

```
def display_string
    str = [amount_as_fraction, unit_inflected,
            ingredient_inflected].compact.join(" ")
    str += ", #{instruction}" unless instruction.blank?
    str
end
```

The `compact.join("")` construct gets rid of the unit if the unit is not set, and does so without putting an extra space in the output. The `amount_as_fraction` method converts the decimal amount to a fraction, matching the typical usage of cookbooks. (Although this may later be subject to localization, because metric cookbooks generally don't use fractions.) The inflected methods just ensure that the units and ingredients are the proper singular or plural case to match the amount — because "1 cups carrots" will just make the site look stupid.

Adding a Coat of Paint

At this point, I went to `www.freewebtemplates.com` and chose the canvass template, also available at `www.freecsstemplates.org/preview/canvass`. I wanted to spruce up the look of the site with something clean that didn't look like Generic Boring Business Site. The free templates on this site are generally licensed via Creative Commons (although if you use one, check the download to make sure). It's a good place to get ideas and to see how various CSS effects can be managed. Naturally, if you were doing a real commercial site, you'd probably want something more unique and original.

Integrating the template was straightforward. The template download has an HTML file, a CSS file, and a bunch of image files. I copied the image files into the application's `public/images` directory, and then took the CSS file and copied the entries into the preexisting `public/scaffold.css` file. Alternately, I could have just copied the entire file and added a link to it in the layout. Then I copied the body elements from the provided HTML file into the `app/layouts/recipes.html.erb` file so that the main content in the provided file was replaced by the `<%= yield %>` call that will tell Rails to include the content for the action. I also tweaked the text somewhat to make it work for Soups OnLine. Finally, I had to go back into the CSS file and change the relative references to image files (`images/img01.gif`) to absolute references (`/images/img01.gif`), so that they would be correctly found. The finished result is shown in Figure 1-2. The final layout and CSS files are a bit long and off-point to be included in the text here, but are available as part of the downloadable source code for this book.

Editing recipe

Recipe Name:

Grandma's Chicken Soup

Serving Size: 10

Description (optional):

A delicious soup

Ingredients:

2 cups chicken stock
1 3/4 carrots, sliced

Directions:

Pour the carrots over the chicken stock, heat and enjoy!

navigate

> Home
> Recipes
> Categories
> Authors
> Community
> Gear

categories

> 6/15: Chicken Stock
> 6/12: Cold Soup
> 6/9: Beef Stock

archives

> June 2007 *(2)*
> May 2007 *(31)*
> April 2007 *(30)*

Figure 1-2

Asserting Creation

Let's tighten up the remaining recipe controller tests while adding ingredient functionality. The test for creating a recipe asserts that the number of recipes changes, but it doesn't assert anything about the entered data. So, I added the following:

```
def test_should_create_recipe
  recipe_hash = { :title => "Grandma's Chicken Soup",
      :servings => "5 to 7",
      :description => "Good for what ails you",
      :ingredient_string =>
```

```
      "2 cups carrots, diced\n\n1/2 tablespoon salt\n\n1 1/3 cups stock",
          :directions => "Ask Grandma"}
      assert_difference('Recipe.count') do
        post :create, :recipe => recipe_hash
      end
      expected_recipe = Recipe.new(recipe_hash)
      new_recipe = Recipe.find(:all, :order => "id DESC", :limit => 1)[0]
      assert_equal(expected_recipe, new_recipe)
      assert_equal(3, new_recipe.ingredients.size)
      assert_redirected_to recipe_path(assigns(:recipe))
  end
```

In the new test, a hash with potential recipe data is defined, and sent to Rails via the post method. Then two recipes are compared, one created directly from the hash, and the other retrieved from the database where Rails put it (finding the recipe with the highest ID). The code then asserts that the two recipes are equal, and somewhat redundantly asserts that the new recipe has created three ingredients from the ingredients sent.

For that test to work, you also need to define equality for a recipe based on the values and not on the object ID. I created the following (rather ugly) unit test for for the recipe_test.rb file, and then the actual code for recipe.rb:

```
def test_should_be_equal
  hash = {:title => "recipe title",
    :description => "recipe description", :servings => 1,
    :directions => "do it", }
  recipe_expected = Recipe.new(hash)
  recipe_should_be_equal = Recipe.new(hash)
  assert_equal(recipe_expected, recipe_should_be_equal)
  recipe_different_title = Recipe.new(hash)
  recipe_different_title.title = "different title"
  assert_not_equal(recipe_expected, recipe_different_title)
  recipe_different_dirs = Recipe.new(hash)
  recipe_different_dirs.directions = "different directions"
  assert_not_equal(recipe_expected, recipe_different_dirs)
  recipe_different_description = Recipe.new(hash)
  recipe_different_description.description = "different description"
  assert_not_equal(recipe_expected, recipe_different_description)
  recipe_different_servings = Recipe.new(hash)
  recipe_different_servings.servings = "more than one"
  assert_not_equal(recipe_expected, recipe_different_servings)
end

def ==(other)
  self.title == other.title &&
      self.servings == other.servings &&
      self.description == other.description &&
      self.directions == other.directions
end
```

This might seem like overkill, to have a unit test for equality, but it took very little time to put together, and it makes me less concerned about the bane of the unit tester — the test that really is failing but incorrectly reports that it passed.

The data for the new ingredients comes in as a raw string via the ingredient text area. It's the responsibility of the recipe object to convert that string into the actual ingredient objects. Therefore, I created unit tests in `recipe_test.rb` to cover the ingredient-adding functionality. The first test merely asserts that ingredients in the recipe are always in the order denoted by their `order_of` attribute. To make this test meaningful, the ingredient fixtures are defined in the YAML file out of order, so the test really does check that the recipe object orders them, as you can see here:

```
def test_ingredients_should_be_in_order
  subject = Recipe.find(1)
  assert_equal([1, 2, 3],
      subject.ingredients.collect { |i| i.order_of })
end
```

Making the ingredients display in order is extremely easy. You just add this at the beginning of the `Recipe` class `recipe.rb` file:

```
has_many :ingredients, :order => "order_of ASC",
    :dependent => :destroy
```

The `ingredient.rb` file needs a corresponding `belongs_to :recipe` statement. The `:order` argument here is passed directly to the SQL database to order the ingredients when the database is queried for the related objects.

The test for the ingredient string takes an ingredient string and three expected ingredients, and compares the resulting ingredient list of the recipe with the expected ingredients. It goes in `recipe_test.rb` like this:

```
def test_ingredient_string_should_set_ingredients
  subject = Recipe.find(2)
  subject.ingredient_string =
    "2 cups carrots, diced\n\n1/2 tablespoon salt\n\n1 1/3 cups stock"
  assert_equal(3, subject.ingredients.count)
  expected_1 = Ingredient.new(:recipe_id => 2, :order_of => 1,
      :amount => 2, :unit => "cups", :ingredient => "carrots",
      :instruction => "diced")
  expected_2 = Ingredient.new(:recipe_id => 2, :order_of => 2,
      :amount => 0.5, :unit => "tablespoons", :ingredient => "salt",
      :instruction => "")
  expected_3 = Ingredient.new(:recipe_id => 2, :order_of => 3,
      :amount => 1.333, :unit => "cups", :ingredient => "stock",
      :instruction => "")
  assert_equal_ingredient(expected_1, subject.ingredients[0])
  assert_equal_ingredient(expected_2, subject.ingredients[1])
  assert_equal_ingredient(expected_3, subject.ingredients[2])
end
```

To make this work, the `Recipe` class is augmented with a getter and setter method for the attribute `ingredient_string` — this is the slightly unusual case where you want a getter and setter to do something genuinely different. The setter takes the string and converts it to ingredient objects, and the getter returns the recreated string:

```
def ingredient_string=(str)
  ingredient_strings = str.split("\n")
  order_of = 1
  ingredient_strings.each do |istr|
    next if istr.blank?
    ingredient = Ingredient.parse(istr, self, order_of)
    self.ingredients << ingredient
    order_of += 1
  end
  save
end

def ingredient_string
  ingredients.collect { |i| i.display_string}.join("\n")
end
```

At this point, the earlier test of the entire form should also pass.

The setter splits the strings on newline characters, and then parses each line, skipping blanks and managing the order count. When all the ingredients have been added, the recipe is saved to the database with the new ingredients. The getter gathers the display strings of all the ingredients into a single string.

Finishing up the testing of the basic controller features in `test/functional/recipe_controller_test.rb`, the edit and update tests are augmented as follows:

```
def test_should_get_edit
  get :edit, :id => 1
  assert_response :success
  assert_select("form[action=?]", recipe_path(1)) do
    assert_select "input[name *= title]"
    assert_select "input[name *= servings]"
    assert_select "textarea[name *= ingredient_string]"
    assert_select "textarea[name *= description]"
    assert_select "textarea[name *= directions]"
  end
end

def test_should_update_recipe
  put :update, :id => 1,
      :recipe => {:title => "Grandma's Chicken Soup"}
  assert_redirected_to recipe_path(assigns(:recipe))
  actual = Recipe.find(1)
  assert_equal("Grandma's Chicken Soup", actual.title)
  assert_equal("1", actual.servings)
end
```

The edit test is changed to be almost identical to the new test, the only difference being the form action itself. The easiest way to make this test pass is to take the form block from the `new.html.erb` file and put it in a partial file called `_form.html.erb`, and change the new and edit views to refer to it. The updated edit view would be as follows (the new view is similar):

```
<h1>Editing recipe</h1>
<%= error_messages_for :recipe %>
<%= render :partial => "form" %>
<%= link_to 'Show', @recipe %> |
<%= link_to 'Back', recipes_path %>
```

Short and sweet. If you are familiar with the traditional Rails model scaffolding, you know that the _ form partial was automatically created by that scaffold to be used in the edit and new forms. There is one slight difference. The older version had the actual beginning and ending of the form in the parent view, and only the insides in partial view. In the RESTful version, `@recipe` serves as a marker for the action in both cases, Rails automatically determines the URL action from the context. As a result, the form block can more easily be entirely contained in the partial view.

Adding a Little Ajax

At this point, the basic CRUD functionality works for recipes with ingredients. I'd like to add one little piece of in-place Ajax editing, allowing the user to do an in-place edit of the ingredients from the recipe show page. This will allow the user to switch from what is shown in Figure 1-3 to what is shown in Figure 1-4.

Grandma's Chicken Soup

Servings: 10

A delicious soup

Ingredients

2 cups chicken stock **Edit**
1 3/4 carrots, sliced **Edit**

Directions

Pour the carrots over the chicken stock, heat and enjoy!
Figure 1-3

Grandma's Chicken Soup

Servings: 10

A delicious soup

Ingredients

Amount	Unit	Ingredient	Directions	
2	cups	chicken stock		Update

Edit

1 3/4 carrots, sliced Edit

Directions

Pour the carrots over the chicken stock, heat and enjoy!

Figure 1-4

To allow Ajax to work in your Rails application, you must load the relevant JavaScript files by includ-ing the following line in the app/views.layouts/recipes.html.erb *file. Place the line in the HTML header.*

```
<%= javascript_include_tag :defaults %>
```

I find the best way to build in-place action like this is to build the action as a standalone first, and then incorporate it into the view where needed. I've made the design decision to leave the existing edit and update actions alone, and instead add new actions called remote_edit and remote_update. Here are the unit tests for them, in ingredient_controller_test.rb:

```
def test_should_get_remote_edit
    get :remote_edit, :id => 1, :recipe_id => 1
    assert_select("form[action=?]",
    remote_update_recipe_ingredient_path(1, 1)) do
      assert_select "input[name *= amount]"
      assert_select "input[name *= unit]"
      assert_select "input[name *= ingredient]"
      assert_select "input[name *= instruction]"
    end
  end

  def test_should_remote_update_ingredient
    put :remote_update, :id => 1, :ingredient => { :amount => 2 },
        :recipe_id => 1
    assert_equal "2 cups First Ingredient, Chopped", @response.body
  end
```

The tests are very similar to what you'd use for the normal edit and update, just with different URLs. The response for the update method is the ingredient display string, not a redirect to the show ingredient page, which enables the updated ingredient to be inserted back into place on the recipe page. In the interest of full disclosure among friends, I should reveal that I didn't actually develop this part strictly test-first — I played around with the layout within the recipe page a little bit before going back and writing the test.

Because this is a new action for a RESTful controller, new routes have to be added in the routes.rb file. Modify it as follows:

```
map.resources :recipes do |recipes|
  recipes.resources :ingredients,
      :member => {:remote_edit => :get, :remote_update => :put}
end
```

This creates a new remote_edit route that responds to GET, and a remote_update route that responds to PUT. Each of these routes gets a named method to refer to it: remote_edit_recipe_ingredient_path and remote_update_recipe_ingredient_path. Run the rake routes command for full details.

Both of these methods need controller methods and views. The controller methods are quite simple, and go in app/controller/ingredient_controller.rb as follows:

```
def remote_edit
   edit
end
```

You can't get much simpler than that. The remote_edit method uses the same method of getting its ingredient as edit does, so in the interest of avoiding cut and paste, I just call the other method directly. The next step would be another before_filter, which would make both methods empty.

There's also the following view for remote_edit, keeping things on as few lines as possible:

```
<% remote_form_for(@ingredient,
     :url => remote_update_recipe_ingredient_path(@recipe, @ingredient),
     :update => "ingredient_#{@ingredient.id}") do |f| %>
  <table>
    <tr>
      <th class="subtle">Amount</th>
      <th class="subtle">Unit</th>
      <th class="subtle">Ingredient</th>
      <th class="subtle">Directions</th>
    </tr>
    <tr>
      <td><%= f.text_field :amount, :size => "5" %></td>
      <td><%= f.text_field :unit, :size => "10" %></td>
      <td><%= f.text_field :ingredient, :size => "25" %></td>
      <td><%= f.text_field :instruction, :size => "15" %></td>
      <td><%= f.submit "Update" %></td>
    </tr>
  </table>
<% end %>
```

Notice the pathname in the result. This is `app/views/ingredients/remote_edit.html.erb`.

The following `remote_update` method in the ingredient controller is a simplification of `update` (for one thing, I'm not concerned here with responding in formats other than HTML):

```
def remote_update
  @ingredient = Ingredient.find(params[:id])
  if @ingredient.update_attributes(params[:ingredient])
    render(:layout => false)
  else
    render :text => "Error updating ingredient"
  end
end
```

The view for this method is simply this:

```
<%= h @ingredient.display_string %>
```

The only rendered output of this method is the display string of the newly constructed ingredient or an error message. The only reason it's in an `erb` file at all is to allow access to the `h` method to escape out HTML tags and prevent an injection attack.

Finally, the call to create this form has to be placed in the recipe `show.html.erb` file. Here's the relevant chunk:

```
<div class="ingredients">
  <h2>Ingredients</h2>
  <% for ingredient in @recipe.ingredients %>
    <div class="ingredient">
      <span id="ingredient_<%= ingredient.id %>">
        <%= h ingredient.display_string %>
      </span>
      <span class="subtle" id="edit_<%= ingredient.id %>">
        <%= link_to_remote "Edit",
              :url =>
                remote_edit_recipe_ingredient_path(@recipe, ingredient),
              :method => :get,
              :update => "ingredient_#{ingredient.id}"%>
      </span>
    </div>
  <% end %>
</div>
```

Watch out for the `:method` parameter of the `link_to_remote` call. By default, `link_to_remote` sends its request as a `POST`, and I already specified that `remote_edit` was a `GET`. Other than that, the `link_to_remote` call is typical. The URL to call is specified using the new name generated by the new route, and the DOM element to update is the preceding span containing the ingredient display string.

Resources

The primary source for the REST details in this chapter was the RESTful Rails tutorial, written by Ralf Wirdemann and Thomas Baustert and translated from the original German by Florian Görsdorf and Adam Groves. It's available at `www.b-simple.de/documents`. It's an excellent reference for the details of the Rails version of REST.

For more details on recipes in general, I reference *The Joy of Cooking* by Imra S. Rombauer, Marion Rombauer Becker, and Ethan Becker. The well-worn copy in my house was published by Scribner in 1997. I also recommend `www.cookingforengineers.com`, run by Michael Chu.

A full listing of all the `assert_select` codes can be found at `http://labnotes.org/svn/public/ruby/rails_plugins/assert_select/cheat/assert_select.html`, which is maintained by Assaf Arkin.

The CSS and text layout come from `www.freewebtemplates.com`.

Summary

In this chapter, you start with nothing and finish with the beginnings of a recipe-sharing website. The initial data design sets the pattern for the remainder of the development.

REST is a structure for organizing web pages by resource, with a common set of commands for accessing the basic Create, Read, Update, Delete (CRUD) functionality for each resource. REST also allows for URL patterns to be common from resource to resource, and depends on the specific HTTP method of the request to determine what action the server should take in response to a URL.

Rails supports REST by easily scaffolding the creation of a REST model and its associated controller. A single element in the `routes.rb` file specifies an entire suite of RESTful routes for the resource. These routes can be seen using the `rake routes` command. Resources can be nested, in which case the child resource URLs always contain an instance of the parent resource.

The basic application is augmented in this chapter with some server-side intelligence to make entering data easier for the user. An in-place editor is added using basic Ajax techniques, and unit and functional tests are written for all new code.

2

Rails Source Control with Subversion

Every software project needs to manage its source code. Developers on the project need to be able to find code within the project. Multiple people need to be able to work together on the project and see each other's work without accidentally overwriting it. And you need to make sure that nothing is ever, ever lost.

Rails provides a standard project layout, which helps with the first issue. For the second and third issues, you need to turn to a source control system. That system will allow each developer to retrieve code from a common repository and then return their changes to the repository. As soon as a developer has placed their changes back in the repository, other developers on the project can update their local copies of the code to see the changes. If two developers are working on the same file at the same time, the source control system manages the combination of the two pieces of work so that neither is lost. Using a source control system, you can recreate any past state of your application at any time.

Core Rails development (and most Rails plugin development) is performed using a version control system called *Subversion*, which has become the standard tool for many open-source projects. Because so much existing Rails development uses Subversion, you can get some benefits from using it in your own development. In this chapter, you'll learn how to set up your Rails project using Subversion, and how to use it to stay on the cutting edge of Rails development.

Subversive Control

Source control is the generic term for an application that manages a repository of source code being used by one or more developers. Such systems typically have three main purposes:

❑   Maintain a record of any and all changes made to the code base during its history, allowing the development team to precisely recreate the state of the code base at any point in time.

❏   Mediate changes between different developers such that changes made by one do not overwrite changes made by another, even if the two developers are working on the same file.

❏   Allow for easy distribution of the current state of the source code to your development team, or if you're managing an open-source project, to the entire world.

Most of the commonly used source control systems follow a client-server model. The server manages the central code repository, consisting of every revision of every file in the project. This data is maintained in some combination of a database and a regular file system. The server application is responsible for keeping track of all revisions to the code and mediating access to the files in the code base. Individual developers on the project interact with the code files via a client program that contacts the server for the up-to-date version of the code base, and sends changes back to the server to be integrated with the repository.

Source control systems differ from one another in the way they manage developer interaction. The paranoid style of source control attempts to prevent developer conflicts by allowing only one developer to have write access to a particular file at a time. You must explicitly check out and acquire a lock on the file before you can make changes. The person in the next cube over who also needs to make a change to that file must wait patiently (or more likely, impatiently) for you to *finish up already* and release the lock. To be fair, even the most paranoid of locking source control systems have provisions for allowing developers to work side by side. Most often this involves allowing each developer to use a custom branch of the repository to work in freely, forcing them to lock the common master branch only when the developer is ready to present the changes to the entire group.

Although restricting access to source files sounds sensible at first glance, like a lot of attempts to impose centralized structure on team development, the protection is often more trouble than it's worth. First and foremost, it places a barrier between the developer and the code. Having to take the step of explicitly gaining a lock on a file before you can edit it may seem minor, but it gets in the way surprisingly often, especially if you're making changes that affect multiple files. As a Rails developer, a significant change you make to your system could easily touch four or five files (model, view, controller, unit test, and functional test) without even getting complicated. By the time you need to update, say, 800 sample report files for your acceptance tests, you are ready to chuck the whole system out the window. (The author speaks from personal experience.) In addition, a locking system may require the developer to have network access to gain the lock.

And that assumes that everything goes smoothly. Sometimes you get Mike down the hall forgetting to check his files in before he flies off to the darkest Amazon for four weeks of R&R. Now nobody can get to those files, and you need to bring in one of your IT administrators to fix the locking permission. The IT administrators are rarely happy to do this. Issues like this make locking systems especially ill-suited to widely distributed open-source projects.

The hassle might be worth it if the locking actually prevented conflicts, but the sad fact is that it really doesn't. Any system that allows developers to have their own separate branches still allows simultaneous editing to the same file. Worse, by making it more time-consuming to merge back to the main branch, a locking system encourages developers to stay in their own sandbox as long as possible, increasing the possibility that there will be a conflict (and increasing the possibility that one developer or the other won't remember the details when the time comes to merge).

Resolving developer conflicts is a very risky thing. It's all too easy to inadvertently take the old version of both code and automated tests. Then you have old code that passes all the tests, and a change that was made and overwritten that might not be found for ages. The solution is to encourage developers to merge back to the common repository as frequently as possible, and the way to do that is to make dealing with the repository as simple and hassle-free as possible.

Which brings us to Subversion and its non-locking model of source control. In a Subversion system, each developer gets a *working copy* of the current state of the central repository. The developer is free to do whatever he or she wants with the files in the working copy. At some point, the developer *commits* the changes back to the repository. Then Subversion checks to see if any of the files have changed. If not, everything goes back to the mother ship, and other developers can see it when they next update. If there is a conflict that Subversion can't resolve, you must stop and resolve all the conflicts by hand before *any* of your changes are sent back to the repository. This prevents your changes from going into the system halfway — it's all or nothing. Notice that most of your work can be done offline, including adding new files to the repository. Subversion only needs to contact the server when you explicitly try to commit or update your system.

Although allowing free editing sounds like a recipe for chaos, in practice it works quite well. Because the system is easy to use, developers tend to commit changes frequently, minimizing the frequency and severity of code changes. Subversion is especially well-suited to distributed, open-source development. As a result, Subversion has become the clear standard for open-source projects. Because it's become so popular, there's a great deal of tool support, and many commonly used Rails editors and IDEs, such as TextMate and Eclipse/Aptana, support Subversion inside the tools themselves.

The Rails core team uses Subversion to manage the Rails code, and most Rails plugins are available via a Subversion server. Like many things in Rails, if you follow the convention of using Subversion on your own projects, you'll get some benefit in the quality of your interaction with Rails core code and plugins.

Even without the benefit of integration, it's still a good idea for any software project to be under source control, even one with just a single developer. The ability to remember and roll back to any arbitrary state in your code base is very useful, as are the frequent backups you'll get when you use a source control tool consistently. In addition, your source control system allows you to create branches from specific points in your system history. That enables you to continue making bug fixes on a 1.0 release, for example, without affecting the 2.0 release that you are working on simultaneously.

Instructions for installing Subversion are available in Appendix A, and I'm going to assume you've either already followed those directions or have Subversion previously installed on your system. In this chapter, you start by putting the Soups OnLine project under Subversion control. It's a very Rails-specific look at Subversion's features and how to apply them. The "Resources" section at the end of the chapter suggests general Subversion materials.

Normally, you'd perform the steps in this next section before you did any of the coding in Chapter 1. However, having the additional files and changes in your code isn't going to materially affect the steps you need to do to get your project under Subversion, and if there's one thing that's true about getting onto source control, it's better late than never.

Creating a Repository

Subversion keeps its information about your code in a database called a *repository*. To create one of those, find a nice, out-of the way spot on a hard drive somewhere. Ideally, this spot is on a remote server accessible over the network. The next-best case would be to store the repository on a remote hard drive. If neither option is available, then you can set up the repository on the same drive as your Rails project. In a team project, it's important that all team members have access to the repository.

Wherever you put the repository, the first step is to tell Subversion to create the repository with the svnadmin create command. Let's say that you've decided to put the Subversion repository on your local system at /usr/local/subversion. In that case, you can create your repository by entering the following commands:

```
$ cd /usr/local/subversion
$ svnadmin create ./soupsonline
```

Just to clarify, the command-line examples in this book should work under most flavors of Linux and under Mac OS X. Windows users will need to either use a Unix shell emulator like Cygwin or just flip the slashes around in the pathnames.

There won't be any text response in the command shell, but Subversion will have created the necessary files to manage an empty code repository in the directory /usr/local/subversion/soupsonline.

By convention, you need to set up three top-level subdirectories — trunk, tags, and branches — for each Subversion project. The trunk directory is for the current code base as it is being worked on live — the code for the project in this book will go in your trunk directory. A branch is an offshoot of your main code that is still receiving changes. A common branch scenario is to create a branch after a release of your software, and apply bug fixes to the branch without affecting the development of your trunk code. A tag is simply a snapshot of the code base at a particular point in time, with a friendly name and no expectation of further development. As far as Subversion is concerned, though, there is no difference between a tag and a branch — the distinction is solely in how they are treated administratively. Because of this, you'll sometimes see suggestions that the three-directory setup is a historical artifact, and that a different organization may be more manageable. However, for the moment, the three directories are the recommended standard, so this project will stick to that structure.

The svn mkdir command will create the directories inside the new repository. You can run this command as follows from anywhere on your file system (replace the <DIR> marker with the absolute path to the top level of your Subversion folder):

```
$ svn mkdir --message="standard project start" "file:///<DIR>/soupsonline/trunk"↵
  "file:///<DIR>/soupsonline/tags" "file:///<DIR>/soupsonline/branches"

Committed revision 1.
```

The new directories are being referred to as local file URLs rather than as remote pathnames (although Subversion will accept pathnames here as well). If you created your repository on a remote system, you would of course use an http:// or svn:// URL to the new directory depending on how the remote server was configured.

The `Committed revision 1.` response back from the Subversion server tells you that the change has been accepted, and now Subversion is tracking three directories.

At this point, you have an empty Subversion repository and a Rails application skeleton that don't know about each other's existence. It's time to introduce them.

Populating the New Repository

At the end of this section, the Rails application directory will be registered with Subversion as a working copy of the code stored in the Subversion repository. Subversion has an `import` command that is often used to place existing code trees into a Subversion repository. However, adding code to a Subversion repository via `import` does not associate the existing code tree with the Subversion repository. You'd still need to create a working copy of your code someplace else on your hard drive.

Checking Out and Adding Files

To allow your existing code tree to become your Subversion working copy, you need to start by checking out a copy of the (currently blank) repository directory. Open a command prompt at the top level of your new Rails application — the `soupsonline` directory — and type the following command:

```
$ svn checkout "file:///<dir>/soupsonline/trunk" .
Checked out revision 1.
```

This command does the following:

1. svn invokes the Subversion command line client.

2. checkout tells Subversion which command to actually run. In Subversion, all a checkout does is make a working copy from a location in a Subversion repository and place it in a location on the local hard drive.

3. The URL specifies the location of the repository.

4. The . specifies the destination location — in this case, the current directory.

In this case, the repository is still empty, so nothing is actually copied. However, Subversion has now noted that the remote and local file systems have been associated with one another. If you look at your Rails directory from the command line, you'll notice that a hidden .svn directory has been added — that's where Subversion stores its information.

If you are used to a stricter source-control system like Perforce or ClearCase, the use of the word "checkout" in this context may be confusing. In those systems, a checkout is an operation performed on an individual file to grant a developer exclusive, locked access to that file until the developer is done making changes. In Subversion, you do not need to lock a file before starting to make changes to it, and a checkout is a command performed on an entire area of the repository to give the developer a copy of those files to begin development.

With the repository checked out, you can now add your Rails files to it as follows:

```
$ svn add --force .
A          app
A          app/controllers
A          app/controllers/application.rb

[... A bunch of lines ...]

A          tmp/sockets
A          vendor
A          vendor/plugins
```

The add command, as you might expect, adds files to the Subversion repository, and the --force option causes Subversion to recursively descend through the file tree and add all subfolders and files, even those that might already be under source control.

What to Ignore

At this point, you are in good shape and could begin coding in earnest. However, there are a couple of details to take care of that will make your Subversion experience more pleasant. The basic rule of thumb for what files should be stored in a source control repository is that only files that are directly created by developers should be added. In general, you want to avoid adding files that are generated by the system — they take up unneeded room in the repository and add complexity to all your commits.

Within the Rails structure, this includes the log folder, the doc folder, and the tmp folder. At the moment, the only one of those folders that is populated is the log folder. Remove the existing files from the repository as follows:

```
$ svn revert log/*
Reverted 'log/development.log'
Reverted 'log/production.log'
Reverted 'log/server.log'
Reverted 'log/test.log'
```

The revert command takes the affected files out of the Subversion repository but leaves them in place locally. However, as it currently stands, Subversion will still know about the files in the log directory, and you might inadvertently add them at a later date. So you actually want to tell Subversion to pretend that the files in question don't even exist. You do this by setting a Subversion property on those files as follows:

```
$ svn propset svn:ignore "*.log" log
property 'svn:ignore' set on 'log'
```

This is the first of about three Subversion properties you'll encounter in this chapter. Subversion allows you to set any kind of property you want on files, but there are some pre-defined properties that have specific implications for Subversion's behavior. In this case, you're telling Subversion to ignore any file in the log subdirectory that ends in .log. Conveniently enough, that will keep Subversion from caring about anything that Rails logs. Even though you're executing this command locally, the property is set on the repository itself. Other developers who check out the repository will also have their log files ignored.

Similarly, you want Subversion to ignore the doc directory, because any documentation you place in there will be generated by rdoc. You also want it to ignore the tmp directory, because there's no point in putting temporary files in source control. Enter the following:

```
$ svn propset svn:ignore "*" doc
property 'svn:ignore' set on 'doc'
$ svn propset svn:ignore "*" tmp
property 'svn:ignore' set on 'tmp'
```

Later in the book, you'll find some other derived directories that you will want to have Subversion ignore.

Database Files in the Repository

There are a couple of other derived files that are worth addressing: the database setup file database.yml and the working schema file schema.rb. Although schema.rb is a generated file created by Rails during the database-migration process, no less a personage than David Heinemeier Hansson himself said that the file should be placed in source control anyway to allow somebody checking out the code for the first time to set the database up in one shot without walking through all the database migrations. Who am I to argue? You can leave schema.rb alone.

The issue with database.yml is a little bit different. Under normal circumstances, each developer will need to set up his or her own development environment pointing to his or her own local database with his or her own username and password. You certainly don't want every individual developer to be continually merging his or her database username and password up to source control and screwing up everybody else with the next update.

Now, for the purposes of this book, you could ignore the following — there's only one developer, and so the issue is less salient. However, there is a standard mechanism for managing this situation. You place a template version of the file in source control under a separate name, and remove and ignore the original file, as follows. Each developer is then expected to maintain their own local copy of the template.

```
$ cp config/database.yml config/database.yml.template
$ svn add config/database.yml.template
A         config/database.yml.template
$ svn revert config/database.yml
Reverted 'config/database.yml'
$ svn propset svn:ignore "database.yml" config
property 'svn:ignore' set on 'config'
```

Now, there's a database.yml.template in the Subversion repository, and everyone is free to copy that into database.yml and change it around to his or her heart's content because Subversion no longer cares about that file. One implication of this solution is that every checkout of the code will need to create a database.yml file before it can run. You'll need to pay particular attention to this when deploying your code to its runtime server.

Marking Executable Files

If your development team includes Windows developers as well as Linux or Mac OS X developers, you need to ensure that scripts intended to be executable have their file mode properly set on the UNIX-based operating systems. You do this by setting another Subversion property.

Within Rails, that's all the files inside the /script directory and its subdirectories, plus the dispatch files in the /public directory. The dispatch files are easy because they all have a common file name. You just do this:

```
$ svn propset svn:executable "*" public/dispatch.*
property 'svn:executable' set on 'public/dispatch.cgi'
property 'svn:executable' set on 'public/dispatch.fcgi'
property 'svn:executable' set on 'public/dispatch.rb'
```

Getting all the server files requires either some tedium to enter each of them separately, or some shell skills to get them all in one shot. Here's the whizzy UNIX way:

```
$ svn propset svn:executable "*" `find script -type f | grep -v '.svn'`
property 'svn:executable' set on 'script/about'
property 'svn:executable' set on 'script/breakpointer'
property 'svn:executable' set on 'script/console'
property 'svn:executable' set on 'script/destroy'
property 'svn:executable' set on 'script/generate'
property 'svn:executable' set on 'script/performance/benchmarker'
property 'svn:executable' set on 'script/performance/profiler'
property 'svn:executable' set on 'script/plugin'
property 'svn:executable' set on 'script/process/inspector'
property 'svn:executable' set on 'script/process/reaper'
property 'svn:executable' set on 'script/process/spawner'
property 'svn:executable' set on 'script/runner'
property 'svn:executable' set on 'script/server'
```

For those of you who are not twelfth-level UNIX gurus (I'm not, by the way), here's a quick explanation of what's going on here. find script -type f | grep -v '.svn' gives you a list of all files in the /script subdirectory and its subdirectories, which are actually files, not directories, and which are not hidden Subversion files. (If you try to do the more obvious svn propset svn:executable "*" script/*, Subversion will complain when it reaches the first subdirectory.) Those who are on Windows machines can either set the property on each of those individual files (boring), or write a short Ruby script to set the properties automatically.

Commiting Changes

Although you've made a number of changes to the local copy of the repository, none of them has actually been passed back to the mother ship yet. To get those changes back to the Subversion server, you need to commit them as follows:

```
$ svn commit -m "further project setup"
Adding          README
Adding          Rakefile
```

```
Adding          app

[... A lot of lines ...]

Adding          tmp/sockets
Adding          vendor
Adding          vendor/plugins
Transmitting file data
Committed revision 2.
```

The changes have now been sent back to the server, and other developers who check out or update their repositories will now see them.

Notice that Subversion tells you the status of all the files that are being changed before it actually transmits the file data at the end. Subversion uses an all-or-nothing model when your commit affects more than one file. The system validates that all the files you want to change are without conflict with other developer's changes. Only if all of your files are clear does Subversion send your changes to the client. This prevents the central repository from being placed in an inconsistent state caused by taking only part of a developer's change set.

The secret to successfully using Subversion in Agile Rails development is to commit often. Really often. Constantly. Nearly every time you create a new unit test and pass it, that's how often. In a tight, test-driven loop, that could easily mean committing changes every 15 minutes to half-hour. If you are used to a heavier-weight source control system, that may seem hideously unworkable, but in Subversion, a commit is a quick operation, especially if you perform it so often that you're sending only a few files back to the server at a time.

There are many benefits to continuous commits. Most obviously, it's almost impossible to lose significant amounts of work.

The Repository Life Cycle

Now that you have your repository, you need to keep it up to date. Any changes you make to your local copy of the code need to be registered back to the Subversion server before other developers can see it and the change can be assigned a revision tag.

Committing Normal Code Changes

Most of the time, the changes that you make to your code will simply involve changing text within an existing file. As you've seen, the svn commit command causes all of the changes in your local copy to be sent to the server. Subversion requires you to add a short message to the commit, describing the change by using the -m flag, as in svn commit -m "I fixed that really hairy bug. Hooray for me". If you don't include a descriptive message, Subversion will try to launch your system's default editor for you to type one in.

If you've lost track of the revisions you've made since your last commit, you can get a handy list by using the `svn status` command as follows:

```
$ svn status
?       edge_update.sh
?       soupsonline.tmproj
M       test/unit/ingredient_test.rb
M       test/functional/ingredients_controller_test.rb
M       test/functional/recipes_controller_test.rb
M       app/controllers/ingredients_controller.rb
M       app/views/recipes/show.html.erb
?       app/views/ingredients/remote_update.html.erb
M       app/views/ingredients/remote_edit.html.erb
?       db/schema.rb
X       vendor/rails
?       public/images/spacer.gif
?       public/images/img10.gif
?       public/images/img01.gif
?       public/images/img11.gif
?       public/images/img02.gif
?       public/images/img12.gif
?       public/images/img04.gif
?       public/images/img05.gif
?       public/images/img06.gif
?       public/images/img07.gif
?       public/images/img08.gif
?       public/images/img09.gif
?       public/images/img03.jpg
M       public/stylesheets/scaffold.css
```

Each file is prefixed by a character that describes that file's status. In this case, you have M, meaning the file has been modified; X, meaning the directory is part of an external definition; and ?, meaning the file is not under version control. You might also see A, D, or C, which mean the item is scheduled to be added, scheduled to be deleted, or currently in a conflict state, respectively.

The great thing about the `svn status` command is that all the data needed to run it is local to your copy — you don't have to be connected to the network to run the default version of the command. However, when you are connected to the network, you can get extra information by using the `--show-updates` option. When selected, Subversion connects to the server and puts an asterisk next to any file that has a more recent change on the server. Remember, if there is a more recent change, Subversion will not allow you to commit unless you update and resolve any conflicts.

Updates and Conflicts

You retrieve recent changes using the `svn update` command, which brings your working copy up-to-date with respect to the central repository. The output of the command is a list of all the files changed, each prefixed by a character that indicates what kind of change has been made.

The most common change character is U, meaning that there has been an update to a file that has not changed on the local copy. Other change types that do not affect local code are A and D, indicating that a file has been added or deleted.

If a file that you have changed locally has also changed on the repository, then you have one of two change types. If the two changes are in different parts of the file and do not affect each other, then the code is G for "merged." This means that Subversion has managed to integrate the two sets of changes on its own and the file should be in a valid state. But it's usually a good idea to run your test suite, just to be on the safe side.

If both you and somebody else on your project have made incompatible changes to the same part of a file, then the code is C, for "conflict." When Subversion detects a conflict, you will be prevented from committing your code back to the repository until you resolve the conflict.

To help resolve the conflict, Subversion does a couple of things that allow you to see the problem clearly. Subversion changes the file under conflict to mark where the conflict occurs. In addition, Subversion creates three complete alternate versions of the file, each with a new extension. They are as follows:

❏ .r<BASE REV #> is the file as it was before you started messing with it. The <BASE REV #> is set to the number of the Subversion revision that you started with. For example, if you were conflicted over the recipe_controller.rb file and your previous update was from revision 100, then this version would be recipe_controller.rb.r100.

❏ .r<HEAD REV #> is the file as it currently stands in the repository. The <HEAD REV #> is the most recent revision number, and will be the higher of the two numbers. Continuing the example from the previous bullet, this file might be recipe_controller.rb.r103.

❏ .mine is the file as you lovingly edited it (before Subversion gunked it up with markers to show the conflict).

These files give you three quick-and-easy ways to resolve the conflict. If you're convinced that your version contains the wisdom of the angels, and your coworker is deluded, take the .mine file, and copy it over the original file. If you think that your coworker is smarter than you, take the .rHEAD version and copy that one over the original. If you want to chuck the whole thing and start over, take the rBASE version.

If none of these options really fits, then there's no getting around it — you'll have to look at the original file with its markers. The file will look something like this:

```
def create
    @recipe = Recipe.new(params[:recipe])
    respond_to do |format|
      if @recipe.save
<<<<<<< .mine
        flash[:notice] = 'Recipe was spectacularly created.'
=======
        flash[:notice] = 'Recipe was wonderfully created.'
>>>>>>> .r103
        format.html { redirect_to(@recipe) }
        format.xml  { render :xml => @recipe,
            :status => :created, :location => @recipe }
      else
        format.html { render :action => "new" }
        format.xml  { render :xml => @recipe.errors,
            :status => :unprocessable_entity }
      end
    end
  end
```

In this case, you and your codeveloper are fighting over the adjective used to describe a successful recipe creation. (Well, I've seen bigger arguments over smaller things.)

Subversion alerts you to the location of the change by the three-part delimiter. The >> signs at the start indicate the beginning of the conflicted section, and the .mine at the end of that line tells you which revision is responsible for all the code between that line and the === line. All the code between the === line and the >>> line comes from the .r103 version of the file.

Now that you can see the two versions of the file side-by-side (or at least top-to-bottom), edit the file as needed to get it to the actual state you want. Be sure to remove the delimiters — the Ruby interpreter isn't going to like it if those stay in.

When the file is the way you want it (run your automated tests to confirm it), you tell Subversion that the conflict has been resolved with the command svn resolved <filename>, where the filename is the path to the file you just finished messing with. Subversion will note the resolution and delete the temporary files for you (be careful — you can't get them back once they are gone). When all conflicts are resolved, your commit will be allowed to proceed.

File-Level Changes

Subversion is not content only knowing about the changes you make within existing files. Subversion also wants to know about changes you make to the file structure itself.

When you add a new file to your Rails project, you must remember to register the change with Subversion using svn add <PATH>. The path can be a filename or a directory — if it's a directory, you get the contents of that directory and all its subdirectories added. The path can contain wildcard characters, which are interpreted normally. By itself, the add command updates only your local copy. The change is not passed to the central repository until your next commit.

Many of the files you add to Rails will be via the generate script. No matter what kind of thing you are generating, the script can always take the --svn option, which causes any file created by the generator to be automatically added to Subversion control. Again, a commit is needed for the change to be visible to the central repository.

To create an entire directory, use svn mkdir <PATH>. To remove a file, you use the command svn delete <PATH>. You can also copy and move files using svn copy <FROM> <TO> and svn move <FROM> <TO>. A move is identical to performing a copy followed by a deletion. At the risk of repeating myself, none of these takes full effect until the next commit.

Setting Up a Subversion Server with svnserve

Subversion works best in a team environment, and for the entire team to be able to see the repository, you need to be running it on a server. There are two reasonable options for setting up this server:

❑ The Subversion distribution comes with a program called svnserve, which provides for quick-and-easy setup of a repository server.

❏ You can use an Apache 2.x web server augmented with the mod_dav and mod_dav_svn modules. This setup is more complex, but it's also more feature-rich.

There's a third option, which is to run svnserve but allow access only via a Secure Shell (SSH) tunnel. This option is only recommended for networks that are already making heavy use of SSH, and will not be covered here.

The Subversion team recommends you avoid trying to run the repository over your file-sharing system as "local" to all developers. Doing so has significant security and stability risks.

The svnserve system is easy to set up and maintain, and is recommended as the simplest way to get your source control system up and running. It has two significant limitations — both security-related — that may prevent it from being used by your group. All network traffic to and from svnserve is in clear text — svnserve has no provision for encryption of code traffic. To use svnserve for sensitive data, the server should reside on a system that is accessible only inside a VPN or other mechanism for authenticating and encrypting traffic. Similarly, svnserve uses its own authentication system, and the passwords are stored in clear text on the server (although the password transfer is encrypted). As a more minor issue, svnserve does no logging. On the plus side, it usually outperforms the Apache solution.

The Apache solution fixes the issues with svnserve. You can use any authentication system that Apache supports, and you can use Apache to encrypt network traffic. In addition to logging, the Apache module also provides for Web-based repository browsing, which is useful. The Apache configuration is far more complex, and is well outside the scope of a book on Rails. (See the Subversion resources for more details.)

You can get svnserve running with the following command (it's recommended that you run this command under a user account that has access to the Subversion directories, and only the Subversion directories):

```
$svnserve -d -r /usr/local/subversion
```

Strictly speaking, both of the option flags are optional, but they are commonly used. The -d tag sets svnserve running as a background daemon. Under normal circumstances, you still need to keep the console window running for the server to stay up. The -r switch sets the root directory for client Subversion commands. In other words, all client URLs are resolved relative to this directory. Because this command sets up /usr/local/subversion as the Subversion root directory, users would access the Soups OnLine repository as:

```
svn://soupsonline
```

rather than

```
svn://usr/local/subversion/soupsonline
```

You can change the default host and port by using the options --listen-host and --listen-port. The default port is 3690. The -t and -i options prepare svnserve to be used over either an SSH tunnel (-t) or as a Unix inetd daemon (-i). These flags do not cause svnserve to be run those ways, but rather, they prepare svnserve to use stdin and stdout and to accept traffic as it comes in. See the Subversion documentation for more information about using inetd and SSH tunneling, or, for Windows users, running as a Windows service.

You can set up simple authentication for the svnserve server by modifying the conf/svnserv.conf file created in the repository (in other words, in /usr/local/subversion/soupsonline). Within that file are two commented-out options that are of interest: password-db and realm. The password-db option is the name of a file that contains the user information for this repository — typically that file is also placed in the conf directory. The realm option is an arbitrary label for the repository — it doesn't matter what it is, but it should be unique unless you have two repositories sharing a user file.

Two other options specify what different types of uses can do. The anon-access option specifies what an anonymous user can do. Valid values are read, write, and none (write access is assumed to include read access). The auth-access option specifies access for authorized users. The default is read for anonymous users, and write for authorized users. See the Subversion documentation if your access control needs are more complex than this.

The specified password file has the following simple format:

```
[users]
nrappin = bananamuffin
rlithgow = concrete
zpaleozogt = zot
```

It's just the user names and their clear text passwords.

That should be enough to get you started running Subversion for a team of developers. Now let's look at how Subversion manages the Rails ecosystem.

Living on the Edge

One of my favorite decisions that the core Rails team made when designing the Rails architecture was to allow each individual Rails project to easily maintain its own copy of Rails, thus making it trivial to have multiple projects require different versions of Rails. In particular, it's no trouble at all to have a new project use the cutting-edge version of Rails right off the trunk of the main Subversion repository, while every other project on your machine continues to use version 1.2.

Five Other Great Rails Architectural Decisions: A Subjective List

❑ The base idea that default behavior could govern 95 percent of relationships between database tables and objects, or between a URL, a method in the controller, and the view file that renders that method. If you've ever worked in a framework that made you spell all that out explicitly, time and time again, this feels like heaven.

❑ Having a separate database for tests, automatically populated by fixtures. This makes unit testing of complex data interactions not just possible, but easy and fun.

❑   Allowing access to raw SQL for powerful queries. I've tried the web-framework game in the past, and the temptation to wall off SQL is pretty strong. But SQL already exists, has tons of power and flexibility, and people already know it. No need to reinvent query languages.

❑   The ease of having a known public directory for images, JavaScript, CSS, and static text files. If you've ever played the game of "guess which directory the server thinks is the working directory," you'll appreciate this.

❑   The plugin architecture for allowing changes in the behavior of any Rails class, which allows incredible flexibility and allows new features to be tested as plugins before moving to the core.

Using a Specific Version of Rails

The current version of Rails under development and pre-release is usually called *Edge Rails*, in contrast to the official release versions, often called *Gem Rails.* There are a couple of different ways to ensure that your new project runs against a specific version of Rails, whether that version is Edge or a specific Gem version.

Using Subversion to Live on the Edge

Because the Soups OnLine project is being managed via Subversion, you'll use a Subversion-specific mechanism. Subversion enables you to specify that part of your project should be loaded from an external Subversion server — in this case, the Rails Subversion server. From your Soups OnLine top-level directory, run the following command:

```
$ svn propset svn:externals "rails http://dev.rubyonrails.org/svn/rails/↲
trunk/" vendor
property 'svn:externals' set on 'vendor'
```

This command tells Subversion that the `rails` directory of the specified Subversion server should be associated with the `vendor` directory of your Rails project. However, this command by itself does not give you the Edge Rails files. To do that, you need to update the directory as follows:

```
$ svn update vendor

Fetching external item into 'vendor/rails'
A    vendor/rails/cleanlogs.sh
A    vendor/rails/release.rb
A    vendor/rails/activeresource

[... An Oodle of files ...]

U   vendor/rails
Updated external to revision 7127.

Updated to revision 2.
```

At this point, not only will your project run using Edge Rails, but whenever you update your project, Subversion will automatically seek out the `dev.rubyonrails.org` server and update Rails for you.

However, there's now a slight discrepancy in your project. When you used the `rails` command to create the project, Edge Rails didn't exist on the system, so if there have been any changes to the Rails-generated project files since the Gem Rails version you used, you need to update your project to ensure you have the latest and greatest. Here's how:

```
$ rails .
      exists
      exists   app/controllers
      exists   app/helpers

[...  Stuff ...]

   identical  log/development.log
   identical  log/test.log
$ svn commit -m "updating Rails"
Sending        vendor

Committed revision 3.
```

If any files need to be changed, Rails will prompt you before changing them. However, if you've made custom changes to Rails system files, your modifications may be lost.

After you get started on your project, it's less feasible to update the Rails-created files every time there is a Rails update. Luckily, you probably won't need to do this often. Most of the Rails-created files are structural and don't change frequently. However, you should keep an eye on the Edge Rails changes and be prepared to update files if necessary. You might want to particularly keep an eye on changes to `vendor/rails/railties` — especially the JavaScript files in `vendor/rails/railties/html/javascripts` that are directly used as the JavaScript engines for your Rails application.

You can also use the handy rake task `rails:update` to keep your Rails project current with your Rails code base. The update task has the following three subtasks that can be called separately if you wish to update only part of your Rails project:

❑   `rails:update:configs` updates the `config/boot.rb` file.

❑   `rails:update:javascripts` updates all the JavaScript files.

❑   `rails:update:scripts` updates all the files in your scripts directory that perform Rails administrative tasks. Remember to specify any new files here as executable in Subversion if you're going back and forth between Windows and a Unix-based operating system.

Running `rails:update` is equivalent to running all three of these subtasks.

Specifying a Particular Version

By using Edge Rails, the Soups OnLine program will have access to the most up-to-the-moment ideas and brainstorms of Rails core programmers the world over. They have only to commit, and the code will show up in the project on the next update.

However, this is not always the best idea. Sometimes, a change to Edge Rails might affect an API call that you depend on in your application. Every now and then, a bug might sneak in to Edge Rails and make itself at home before it is noticed and fixed. Although you might be able to live with this instability for awhile during development, at some point you need to draw a line in the sand and define the Rails version that works for your project.

Staying within Subversion, you can respecify the property for your `vendor/rails` directory and use the `-r` option to specify a particular revision of Rails in the trunk. The revision number is specified in the output generated by Subversion when you update. The update shown in the previous section was to revision 7127. If you, for some reason, decided this was the most perfect version of Rails there ever could be and wanted this to be your application's Rails version forevermore, you would specify it by overwriting the `svn:externals` property with a new property as shown here:

```
$ svn propset svn:externals "rails -r 7127 http://dev.rubyonrails.org/↵
svn/rails/trunk/" vendor
property 'svn:externals' set on 'vendor'
```

Further updates to your project will no longer update the `vendor/rails` directory — you will have locked your local version of Rails to that particular revision.

Although it's nice to be able to specify an arbitrary Rails revision for your project, you are more likely to lock your version to one of the official Rails releases. This is a slightly different command because the Rails releases have been copied from the Rails trunk to their own branch. As of this writing, there are two releases available as stable branches: 1-1-stable and 1-2-stable. Accessing them is a simple matter of changing the externals command to point to the proper directory as follows:

```
$ svn propset svn:externals "rails http://dev.rubyonrails.org/↵
svn/rails/branches/1-1-stable/" vendor
```

or

```
$ svn propset svn:externals "rails http://dev.rubyonrails.org/↵
svn/rails/branches/1-2-stable/" vendor
```

Because these are branches, further updates are not expected, so you'll have the stability you need.

If you want a little more granularity, the `/tags` directory can reproduce any Rails release from 0.9.1 all the way through 2.0.2 and counting. The name of each follows the form `/tags/rel_2-0-2`.

Living on the Edge With Rake

If you're not using Subversion, or you just don't need the automatic updating feature, you can also specify your Rails version via the following simple `rake` task:

```
$ rake rails:freeze:edge
```

This will perform the same checkout of the current Edge Rails that setting the Subversion property and updating did in the last section. As previously mentioned, though, you'll no longer get automatic updates when you update your project. Running the command again will perform another checkout, overwriting your `vendor/rails/` directory with the newer version.

This mechanism also offers you the opportunity to specify a particular Rails revision to work against. To freeze your project to the same revision 7127 you loved from Subversion, issue the following command:

```
$ rake rails:freeze:edge REVISION=7127
```

There's no automatic mechanism in the `freeze` mechanism to manage branches. However, in the interest of preventing you from having to look it up, the following table lists the revision numbers for branches and tags that might be of interest.

Release	Revision
Release 1.1.6 Tag	4751
1.1 Stable Branch	6042
1.2 Stable Branch	7087
Release 1.2.6 Tag	8197
Release 2.0.2 Tag	8441

An advantage of using `rake` to manage your Edge Rails is that it's particularly easy to undo. The following command will empty your `vendor/rails` directory, effectively reverting you to whatever Rails version you have installed via RubyGems:

```
$ rake rails:unfreeze
```

Alternatively, you can copy the RubyGems version to your local project directory with the following command:

```
$ rake rails:freeze:gems
```

This is helpful if you want to freeze an existing Rails project before you update your system-wide RubyGems.

What's Up, RDoc?

One problem with developing against Edge Rails is that the online documentation repositories are no longer accurate. Luckily all the Rails documentation is generated automatically, and it's a snap to regenerate it locally for your purposes. You can do this with the following Rake command:

```
$rake doc:rails
```

However, if you'd like more control over the process, all you need to do is invoke the RDoc generator with some appropriate options. From the top-level directory of your Rails project, run the following command:

```
$ rdoc --op doc/apidocs/ -x test/ -x /railties/lib/rails_generator/↵
generators/components/controller/templates/controller.rb --all --↵
tab-width 2  --title 'Rails Edge API documentation'
```

This one will crank for as much as 5 to 10 minutes, depending on how powerful your computer is. The following table describes what you've done.

Command Option	Description
--op doc/apidocs	Creates an output directory. If an output directory already exists that RDoc doesn't recognize as an rdoc directory, it will halt.
-x test	Excludes the vendor/test directory. You can have more than one -x flag in the command if there are several things you don't want documented. The second flag, /railties/lib/rails_generator/generators/components/controller/templates/controller.rb, removes a file that is seriously weird syntactically and will hang RDoc.
--all	Include private methods in the output.
--tab-width 2	Set the tab width for the displayed source to 2. The default is 8.
--title	Sets the title of the web page.

When this command is complete, you'll have all your Rails API documentation in the doc/apidocs directory. There are a couple of potential advantages to running the rdoc command directly: customization and time. The rdoc command will regenerate Rails pages only when the source has changed; the rake command will redo the entire directory each time.

The rdoc output can be customized significantly. The following table describes some other useful options.

Command Option	Description
--exclude	Alias for -x.
--extension a=b	Handle document files ending in .a as if they ended in .b. This is useful if you have Ruby files with nonstandard extensions, the most common of which is probably .cgi.
--inline-source	Place the embedded source for documented methods in the documentation file itself. If not specified, the embedded source is placed in a pop-up window.
--line-numbers	Include line numbers in source code.
--quiet	Don't show the progress output.
--style url	Specify a CSS page for styles.
--template	Specify a directory containing rdoc template files.

When you find a set of options you like, it's probably a good idea to store the command in a shell script so that you can easily run it again whenever you update. RDoc will only update documentation for files that have changed, so subsequent documentation updates should go much more quickly.

Resources

The most important Subversion resource is the book *Version Control with Subversion*, originally published by O'Reilly, and available online at `http://svnbook.read-bean.com`. The print book was published in 2004, and the online version is more current (a second edition of the print book should be out shortly).

François Beausoleil's blog post at `http://blog.teksol.info/2006/03/09/subversion-primer-for-rails-projects` was an important resource for me when I was learning about Subversion and Rails. It's in the comments to this post that David Heinemeier Hansson recommends versioning `schema.rb`.

There are a number of resources for managing Edge Rails. The official Rails wiki page on the subject is at `http://wiki.rubyonrails.org/rails/pages/EdgeRails`. The page is a little flaky though — it includes a link to an older version of itself, among other things. Another blog post on the subject is by Tim Lucas at `www.sitepoint.com/blogs/2006/07/11/installing-and-managing-edge-rails`.

Summary

Source control is critical to the functioning of a successful software team, and the overwhelming majority of public Rails projects use a tool called Subversion to manage their code repository. Subversion enables multiple developers to freely work on the same files, manages conflicts, and ensures that any save point in the life of the system can be recreated.

After a Subversion repository is created, your Rails project can be added to the repository, although certain files, such as log files, should be set to be explicitly ignored. It's easy to save your changes back to the repository frequently. If one of the files you changed has been updated by another developer, you'll be required to issue an `svn update` command to see the changes. Subversion tries to merge the two changes, but if both of you were working on the same part of the file, there may be conflicts that need to be manually resolved. After you have committed your code, other developers can see it by performing their own updates.

Subversion includes a program called `svnserve` that enables you to easily set up a server that is available to your entire team.

Subversion is the easiest (but not the only) way to keep your project aligned with the latest Rails code, known as Edge Rails.

3

Adding Users

You can't have a community website without users. Users set the tone for your site, commenting in forums, adding information, noticing mistakes, giving reviews, rating, and tagging. At the same time, allowing user accounts opens your site to spam, data risks, session capturing risks, and so on. Proper management of your user data can make your site resistant to common user permission and security issues.

In this chapter, you add users to Soups OnLine. First, you create user accounts and see how to prevent automated accounts from gunking up your database. Then, you add user authentication and session management to your Rails controllers. And finally, you examine user roles and how to implement them.

Creating Users

Before a user is anything else, from the Rails perspective, it's just another resource with a model, a controller, and several views. The user can be created as a RESTful resource:

```
$ ruby script/generate scaffold --svn user username:string first_name:string
last_name:string email:string encrypted_password:string salt:string
```

As before, a number of files are created, including a migration and a new route in the routes.rb file. If you are doing these examples in order, Rails may prompt you to override the scaffold .css file. Don't do that — you've already made changes to that file that you don't want to lose. A way to avoid this issue would be to move the additions to a separate CSS file and include that file in the layout header.

The use of the --svn option will add all the newly created files to the Subversion repository. Obviously, you can leave that option off if you aren't using Subversion. If you are using Subversion but forget to use --svn, the quickest way to add all the files is to use the command svn add * --force. However, that command will add to the repository every file within your local working copy that isn't already known to Subversion, so use it with caution.

This is a minimal definition of a user: just a username, a full name, an email address, a password that will be stored in an encrypted state, and some salt (a random string encrypted with the password to make it harder to guess). I decided that the initial conception of a user in this application will allow for creating, editing, and commenting on recipes. Other user information that you might need for, say, selling things, can be added later.

Before you actually run the migration that will update the database with the new user table, you should make one addition. To associate each recipe with a user, the recipe table needs a `user_id` column. So, add the following lines to the newly created migration, which should be at `db/migrations/003_create_users.rb`. The completed migration should look like this (highlighted lines need to be added by you):

```ruby
class CreateUsers < ActiveRecord::Migration
  def self.up
    create_table :users do |t|
      t.string :username
      t.string :first_name
      t.string :last_name
      t.string :email
      t.string :encrypted_password
      t.string :salt
      t.timestamps
    end

    add_column :recipes, :user_id, :integer

  end

  def self.down
    drop_table :users
    remove_column :recipes, :user_id
  end
end
```

Run the migration with the rake `db:migrate` command. Also, head into the recipe model at `app/models/recipe.rb`, and add the line `belongs_to :user`. Then go to the new user model `app/models/user.rb` and add the line `has_many :recipes`.

With everything set up, it's time to manage the first line of security in your application — the user password.

User Creation Form

First off, you'll edit the Rails-provided resource code to display the users as needed. To get the new user views to display in the same layout that you put together in Chapter 1, you need to add the following line to the top of the `UserController` in `app/controllers/user_controller.rb`:

```ruby
layout "recipes"
```

This will ensure that the UserController looks to the recipes.html.erb layout file when generating HTML output for its actions, and keeps you from having to maintain multiple layout files.

There are a couple of somewhat quibbly things you should do. For instance, the listing from the index page contains all data for each user, including the encrypted password and salt. The security team probably won't be too happy about that, so go into the view file and remove those lines from the table header and the display loop, so that only the username, first and last names, and email are being displayed. The changed /app/views/users/index.html.erb file should look like this:

```erb
<% @title = "Users" %>

<table>
  <tr>
    <th>Username</th>
    <th>Firstname</th>
    <th>Lastname</th>
    <th>Email</th>
  </tr>

<% for user in @users %>
  <tr>
    <td><%=h user.username %></td>
    <td><%=h user.first_name %></td>
    <td><%=h user.last_name %></td>
    <td><%=h user.email %></td>
    <td><%= link_to 'Show', user %></td>
    <td><%= link_to 'Edit', edit_user_path(user) %></td>
    <td><%= link_to 'Destroy', user, :confirm => 'Are you sure?', :method => :delete %></td>
  </tr>
<% end %>
</table>

<br />

<%= link_to 'New user', new_user_path %>
```

While you're at it, the display is probably much more useful if it's alphabetized, so change the first line of the index method in the user controller. The method, in app/controllers/users_controller.rb, should look like this:

```ruby
def index
  @users = User.find(:all, :order => "username ASC")
  respond_to do |format|
    format.html # index.html.erb
    format.xml  { render :xml => @users }
  end
end
```

Before you make some changes to the user entry form, it's best to combine the common new and edit forms into a _form partial view template, the way you did for recipes back in Chapter 1. The form also contains entries for encrypted password and salt, when you actually just want a masked entry for passwords. Plus, you'll want the user to confirm the password and email address. Eventually, the view code should look like this:

```
<% form_for(@user) do |f| %>
  <table>
    <tr>
      <td class="tdheader">First Name:</td>
      <td class="tdheader">Last Name:</td>

    </tr>
    <tr>


      <td><%= f.text_field :last_name, :size => 20 %></td>
      <td><%= f.text_field :first_name, :size => 15  %></td>
    </tr>
  <table>
    <tr>
      <td class="tdheader">User Name:</td>
      <td><%= f.text_field :username, :size => 15 %></td>
    </tr>
    <tr>
      <td class="tdheader">Email Address:</td>
      <td><%= f.text_field :email %></td>
    </tr>
    <tr>
      <td class="tdheader">Confirm Email:</td>
      <td><%= f.text_field :email_confirmation %></td>
    </tr>
    <tr>
      <td class="tdheader">Password:</td>
      <td><%= f.password_field :password, :size => 10 %></td>
    </tr>
    <tr>
      <td class="tdheader">Confirm:</td>
      <td><%= f.password_field :password_confirmation,
          :size => 10 %></td>
    </tr>
  </table>

  <p>
    <%= f.submit "Create" %>
  </p>
<% end %>
```

For that form to work, you need to add some attributes to the user object for the items in the form that are not in the database — the clear-text password, and the confirmation fields for the password and email address. In about a page or so, you'll need to actually create explicit getter and setter methods for the password. But for now, just add the validations that you'll need for user objects to app/models/user.rb, like this:

```
class User < ActiveRecord::Base
  has_many :recipes
  attr_accessor :email_confirmation, :password_confirmation, :password
  validates_presence_of :username, :email
```

```
    validates_uniqueness_of :username
    validates_confirmation_of :email, :password
    validates_length_of :password, :minimum => 6
end
```

You could add a validation on the format of the user-entered email messages, but I don't think that's worth the effort at the moment. The `validates_confirmation_of` method assumes the convention of having two fields named `something` and `something_confirmation`, and tests for their equality before saving the model object.

How much you test these validations is something of a judgment call—because they are part of Rails Core, the validations probably don't need to be pounded extra hard. It is, however, indisputable that the new validations are breaking some of the default tests because the blank forms that are being sent to the new and update tests do not pass these validations. You need to add sample data that will pass the validations in `test/unit/user_test.rb`, as follows:

```
def user_form
  {:username => "kermit", :firstname => "Kermit",
   :lastname => "the Frog", :email => "kermit@frogs.net",
    :email_confirmation => "kermit@frogs.net",
     :password => "iheartpigs", :password_confirmation => "iheartpigs"}
end

def test_should_create_user
  assert_difference('User.count') do
    post :create, :user => user_form
  end
  assert_redirected_to user_path(assigns(:user))
end
```

Change the `test_should_update_user test` to also pass the `user_form` result to its method call, and the tests will pass. The resulting form, shown in Figure 3-1, has a slightly different layout than the default.

Enter New User

First Name	**Last Name**
[_____]	[_____]

User Name: [_____]

Email Address: [_____]

Confirm Email: [_____]

Password: [_____]

Confirm: [_____]

(Create)

Back

Figure 3-1

Not that you asked, but I much prefer the tabular layout for form data than the default layout with the caption above the text field. It's more compact and easier to scan.

Refactoring Forms Using A FormBuilder

Take another look at the code in that form view in the previous section. One thing you should notice is that the pattern of having a table row where the first cell is a caption and the second cell is a form element is repeated over and over. Not only does that make for a lot of unnecessary and error-prone repetition, but all the extra elements make for a lot of clutter and hard-to-read code.

I have to say, I'm familiar with a number of web frameworks that depend on some kind of code or HTML template, and the problem with nearly all of them is that complex code in the view or template becomes difficult to lay out, read, and maintain. Part of this is due to the fact that the code and the HTML have two distinct, intertwined structures, each with its own indentation and layout needs, and these two structures work together only barely. Other frameworks depend on building all the HTML tags programmatically, which can also be difficult to manage in complex cases.

One of the strengths of Ruby on Rails, especially when compared to systems which came before, is an awareness of this problem of structuring views. Rails provides a number of ways to move complex, repetitive code to places where it can be easily consolidated and managed. Throughout the book, you'll take a look at some of these features as they become useful to the project. Right now, it's time to look at custom form builders.

The Rails `FormBuilder` class is passed to a `form_for` block within a view (in the previous code, it's the class of the object named `f`). The `FormBuilder` class defines the instance methods used for the helpers such as `text_field` and `password_field`. Because `FormBuilder` is just an ordinary Ruby class, there's nothing stopping you from creating a custom subclass of `FormBuilder` that does whatever you want it to do with each helper method. All you need to do is tell the `form_for` method to use your builder instead of the default, which you do by passing a `:builder => CustomClassName` argument to the `form_for` call.

To build the custom form builder, you need a way to inject HTML into the output of the template from the builder code. You do this by using the `@template` instance variable, created by Rails, and referring to the code template currently being evaluated. The `@template` object has an instance method, `content_tag`, which takes the name of an HTML tag, a hash of the tag's attributes, and a block that resolves to the content inside the tag. The result of the `content_tag` call can then be placed in the template output.

Now, in planning out what this custom form builder is going to do, it's hard not to notice the pattern: calling `text_field` should result in a table row with a caption and the text field, and calling `password_field` should result in a table row with a caption and the password field. On the other hand, a `select` call should result in a table row with a caption and the select field. You could write each of those methods individually, but even if they all called a common general method, there's still a certain amount of repetition. Instead, I recommend writing all the similar methods at once using Ruby's metaprogramming capabilities, particularly the `define_method` method.

I'm going to present the first part of the code for the custom builder, and explain it. (A complete description of Ruby metaprogramming in general and define_method in particular is included in Chapter 14.) To begin, place the following class in models/tabular_form_builder.rb:

```ruby
class TabularFormBuilder < ActionView::Helpers::FormBuilder

  def self.build_tabular_field(method_name)
    define_method(method_name) do | attribute, *args |
      options = args[0] || {}
      caption = options[:caption] || attribute.to_s.humanize
      caption_class = options[:caption_class] || "tdheader"
      options.delete(:caption)
      options.delete(:caption_class)
      @template.content_tag("tr") do
        @template.content_tag("td", :class => caption_class) do
          "#{caption}"
        end +
        @template.content_tag("td") do
          super(attribute, options)
        end
      end
    end
  end

  field_helpers.each do | method_name |
    build_tabular_field(method_name)
  end
end
```

Like a lot of Ruby metaprogramming code, this looks a little strange at first. The basic structure is to define a class method called build_tabular_field. This method is called with a single argument, and the effect of calling that method is to create an instance method whose name is that single argument. So calling build_tabular_field(:text_area) creates the instance method TabularFormBuilder .text_area.

The magic happens in the define_method call, which takes as an argument the name that will be used to call the new method and then a block. The arguments to the block will be the argument list for the new method, and the body of the block is the body of the new method. You may be familiar with metaprogramming by awkwardly building up a string that would be evaluated to create a dynamic program. Due to the nature of Ruby blocks, you don't have to do that — you can just write ordinary Ruby code in the block part of define_method, and the block automatically becomes the body of the newly created dynamic method. What does that block do inside define_method? First, it pulls an options hash out of the args list — given the way that the field helpers are called, the options hash will always be the second argument if it exists. However, you can't define a default value in a block argument list the way you can in a method argument list, so the *args notation is a somewhat awkward compromise between the normal call list of a field helper and the allowed semantics of a Ruby block.

From the options, the text and CSS class of the caption cell are retrieved. If they are not there, the text defaults to a humanized conversion of the attribute name, and the CSS class defaults to tdheader. The two new fields need to get removed from the options hash; otherwise, Rails will put them in the attribute lists of the table cells you're going to build, which would be a little annoying.

After that, a `tr` cell is created with a block that contains two `td` cells — notice the critically important plus sign between the two `td` cell blocks. Each `content_tag` call returns a string, and you have to be sure that the `tr` cell contents are the two `td` cells concatenated together. (If you leave off the plus sign, only the second cell will be included in the row, because it would be the last value of the block expression.) The first `td` cell contains only a string with the previously determined caption. The second cell actually calls `super`, which is the default `FormBuilder` rendering of a text field, password field, or whatever. The result is just placed in the second table cell.

The loop that comes after the `build_tabular_field` method is raw code — it's part of the class but not inside any method. That code is evaluated when the class is loaded, and it calls `build_tabular_field` once for each known field helper in the `field_helper` list. This should cleanly create all the methods needed for the new field helper to be a drop-in replacement for an existing field helper.

However, it turns out that `submit` is not in the `field_helper` list. Plus, it's probably useful to have a general method to put an arbitrary row into the field table. Add the following two methods to the `TabularFormBuilder` class:

```
def submit(caption, args={})
  row(super(caption, args))
end

def row(content)
  @template.content_tag("tr") do
    @template.content_tag("td", :colspan => 2) do
      "#{content}"
    end
  end
end
```

This completes a simple form builder, but as you may have noticed, it creates all the `tr` and `td` tags but not the surrounding table. This can be done with some ordinary helper methods placed in `application_helper.rb`. Creating the helper method has the secondary advantage of encapsulating the `form_for` method with the builder argument, so you won't have to repeat that typing either. Add the following to `application_helper.rb`:

```
def convert_args(builder_class, args)
  options = args.last.is_a?(Hash) ? args.pop : {}
  options = options.merge(:builder => builder_class)
  args = (args << options)
end

def table_form_for(name, *args, &proc)
  concat("<table>", proc.binding)
  form_for(name, *convert_args(TabularFormBuilder, args), &proc)
  concat("</table>", proc.binding)
end
```

The `table_form_for` method should look straightforward — it uses `concat` (a standard way to inject code into the template from a handler method with a block) to surround the `form_for` call with `table` tags. The `convert_args` method, on the other hand, probably looks a little weird to you. The problem here is that `form_for` can be called with its `options` hash as the second argument, after the object being displayed in the form, or as the third argument, after the model class and the object. The `convert_args` method just makes sure that you add the builder argument to the actual hash, taking advantage of the fact that you know it's always the last argument.

One oddity about this code snippet is that it places the `form` tag inside the `table` tag. Technically, this is legal HTML, but it sure looks weird to my eyes.

With the helper in place, it's time for my favorite part — the actual new form under the custom form builder. The following code is an exact, drop-in replacement for the previous view code with all the `tr` and `td` tags:

```
<% table_form_for @user do |f| %>
    <%= f.text_field :first_name, :size => 15, :class => "input" %>
    <%= f.text_field :last_name, :size => 20, :class => "input" %>
    <%= f.text_field :username, :size => 15, :class => "input" %>
    <%= f.text_field :email, :class => "input" %>
    <%= f.text_field :email_confirmation, :class => "input" %>
    <%= f.password_field :password, :size => 10, :class => "input" %>
    <%= f.password_field :password_confirmation, :size => 10,
        :class => "input" %>
    <%= f.submit "Create" %>
<% end %>
```

Now that's more like it. With the extraneous table tags moved to the table builder, it's much easier to see exactly what the form defines. This code will be much easier to maintain going forward.

This form will get the user data into the system. The next step is to scramble the passwords before you save them.

Storing Encrypted Passwords

Storing user passwords in the database as clear text is a security risk, because anybody who had access to your database would instantly be able to steal any user's login. And although that's not necessarily a big deal on this little recipe site, in general allowing people's passwords to leak is A Bad Thing. Among the many advantages of encrypting passwords in the database is that not even you can get to the password data, which is a nice thing to be able to say to your users.

If you aren't familiar with encryption and passwords, then the inclusion of a user data attribute called `salt` probably raised an eyebrow. I know that this is a recipe site but actually including salt in the user database seems a bit . . . literal.

You are going to use one of Rails built-in cryptographic modules to create a hash from the user password. Although the hash uniquely matches one specific password, it's computationally impossible (or at least computationally infeasible) to recreate the original password. By saving the hash instead of the password, you can still use the hash to validate against the original password, but a malicious miscreant who got a hold of the hash would not be able to recreate the password to perform a fake login.

Salt is a cryptographic term for a random or semi-random sequence that is input to a cryptographic algorithm along with the message to be encrypted. In this case, each user will have his or her own unique salt sequence, and you will append the salt to the password before sending it to the hash algorithm.

Using a salt sequence as part of the encryption method has a few benefits. Because the salt effectively increases the length of the password, it makes cracking the code that much harder, especially if the salt contains characters that are not valid in the password itself. The salt is unique for each user, so even if somebody was able to crack one password with some kind of brute-force lookup, that single crack would give no leverage in an attempt to crack the next password — even two users with the same password would have different salt, and therefore different hashed passwords.

The exact method you use to generate the salt is arbitrary. You want something that is guaranteed unique, but has a random component. The length probably doesn't matter a whole bunch, but it should probably be at least the length of the password. I'm going to go with the following, placed in the user object at `app/models/user.rb`:

```
def mine_the_salt
    self.salt = "#{id}_#{Standards.random_string(10)}"
end
```

To support that method, I also created some external utilities. In a `app/models/extensions.rb` file, I placed this:

```
class Array
  def pick_at_random
      self.rand
  end
end

class Standards

  def self.random_string(len)
     (1..len).collect {Standards.alphanumeric_characters.pick_at_random}.join
  end

  def self.alphanumeric_characters
     ("A".."Z").to_a + ("a".."z").to_a + ("0".."9").to_a
  end

end
```

The method `self.alphanumeric_characters` creates an array with all the alphanumeric characters. The method `self.random_string` creates an array of 10 characters, each chosen at random from the alphanumeric array. (The range object at the beginning of that line serves as a counter.) The method in the user class concatenates the user's ID with the randomly generated characters.

Then you need to place the line `require 'extensions'` at the very top of the `models/user.rb` file, before the class statement, or at the bottom of the `config/extensions.rb` file to make these new methods available.

The `pick_at_random` method uses a feature which enables existing classes to be reopened so you can add new methods. I also created a `Standards` class. Right now, it just has two methods, which define the array of alphanumeric characters and the random string, but I wouldn't be surprised if this grew some other standard elements.

Although it's difficult to test the salt completely because of its random component, the following test ensures that the non-random pieces of the salt are properly generated:

```
def test_salt_mining
  salt = users(:one).mine_the_salt
  assert_equal 12, salt.length
  assert_equal "1_", salt[0..1]
end
```

To test the random component, you could change the pick_at_random during the test to spit out known sequences of pretend random numbers for testing. This process is called "mocking" and is described more fully in Chapter 7. That's not a lot of work, and if you were doing a game or something where various actions were being triggered by chance, it would be worth it. But here, because all you really care about is that the sequence is random, it's not an effort that's necessary.

With the salt in place, you can now create an encrypted password. Add the following private method to the user model:

```
def encrypt_a_password(plaintext, salt)
  salted_password = Digest::SHA256.hexdigest(plaintext + salt)
end
```

And then, still within `app/models/user.rb`, remove `password` from the attribute accessor list and add the explicit getter and setter methods. This turns `password` into an implicit property — it's effectively a front-end for the encrypted password and salt methods that will actually go into the database. Here's what you need to add:

```
def password
  @password
end

def password=(new_password)
  @password = new_password
  mine_the_salt
  self.encrypted_password = encrypt_a_password(new_password, salt)
end
```

The setter method will generally be called by Rails when it processes a new or updated user via the entry form, so you know the password is at least five characters long. The setter sets the non-database password property, and then sets the salt and encrypted password attributes using the methods already described. When the user object is saved to the database, the salt and encrypted password are saved, and that's what is retrieved when the time comes to authenticate a user.

The unit test for this validates the password setter, the salt, and the password:

```
def test_passwords
  user = users(:one)
  user.password = "banana"
  user.save
  assert_not_equal user.encrypted_password, "banana"
```

(continued)

(continued)

```
        assert_equal 12, user.salt.length
        assert_equal "1_", user.salt[0..1]
        assert user.validate_password("banana")
        assert !user.validate_password("apple")
        pass = User.find_by_username_and_password("ktf", "banana")
        assert_not_nil(pass)
        nope = User.find_by_username_and_password("ktf", "apple")
        assert_nil(nope)
    end
```

Validation comes in two flavors, the first is an instance method that takes the clear-text password, performs the same encryption with the user's salt, and tests it against the encrypted password already in the database:

```
    def validate_password(clear_password)
      encrypt_a_password(clear_password, salt) == encrypted_password
    end
```

I also wrote a class method that takes a username and password, and returns the user object if there is a user that validates that password, returning `nil` otherwise. The method name is a derivation of the other special find methods:

```
    def self.find_by_username_and_password(username, password)
      user_to_validate = self.find_by_username(username)
      return unless (user_to_validate and
          user_to_validate.validate_password(password))
      user_to_validate
    end
```

At this point, all tests pass, and you have a working user resource with encrypted passwords. Commit your changes to Subversion.

What about OpenID?

OpenID is an attempt to provide Web users with a single user ID and password that can be accepted by multiple sites. The basic idea is that any website can choose to authenticate its user logins against the OpenID provider using a standard API. There is a Ruby gem and associated Rails plugin to connect to an OpenID provider; the plugin is available at `http://agilewebdevelopment.com/plugins/openidauthentication`.

Authentication

Now that you're creating new users and storing their passwords securely, the next step is to allow the user to log in. This involves setting up two new actions in the user controller — login and logout — and setting up partial views to display the login form and logout link.

The Routes

Because you are adding new actions to the RESTful user controller, the place to start is in the `routes.rb` file. Change the entry for users to this:

```
map.resources :users, :new => {:login => :post},
    :member => {:logout => :get}
```

This line adds a new action for `login`, which operates on a new or unsaved user object, and another action for `logout`, which operates on a single existing user object. The `login` action is a POST, because data is being sent to the server, and `logout` is a GET, which I suppose is arguable but seemed the best choice because no additional data besides the user ID is being sent to the server.

The most commonly used RESTful plugin for authentication, called restful_authentication, does this a bit differently. It creates a Sessions controller where the login method is `Sessions#create` *and logout is* `Sessions#delete`. *There's certainly value in maintaining REST consistency, but there's not a whole lot of practical difference between the two designs, unless you have other uses for a Sessions controller.*

The Tests

The user tests for password management have already been written. Here are the controller tests for successful login, unsuccessful login, and logout, which are defined in `test/functional/users_controller_test.rb`:

```ruby
def test_should_login_succesfully
  post :login, :user => {:username => "ktf", :password => "qwerty"}
  assert_response :success
  assert_equal 1, session[:user_id]
  assert_template "users/_already_logged_in"
end

def test_should_not_login_on_bad_credentials
  post :login, :user => {:username => "ktf", :password => "banana"}
  assert_response :success
  assert_nil session[:user_id]
  assert_template "users/_login"
end

def test_should_logout
  post :login, :user => {:username => "ktf", :password => "qwerty"}
  assert_equal 1, session[:user_id]
  get :logout, :id => 1
  assert_response :success
  assert_template "users/_login"
  assert_nil session[:user_id]
end
```

There's sort of a chicken-and-egg problem with testing a login. You need to have a valid user object in your `test/fixtures/users.yml` fixture file, but that valid user object needs to have an encrypted password as it's stored in the database. In other words, it needs to look like this:

```
one:
  id: 1
  username: ktf
  first_name: Kermit
  last_name: The Frog
  email: kermit@frogs.net
  encrypted_password: 242e401c23ec2612fce9bf19ce3816c77c283d75126c0d5ee0e06897a89a300e
  salt: "_aq0TcTITNE"
  created_at: 2007-07-15 10:54:32
  updated_at: 2007-07-15 10:54:32
  is_active: false
```

Just using the password field, and expecting Rails to use the user object to create the encrypted field as though it was entered via a form will not work — Rails loads the fixtures to the database directly, without mediation by the ActiveRecord object. What I did was create a user using the actual interface developed in the previous section, and copied that user's salt and encrypted password to the fixture file. This works, but it's less than elegant. You could also use the console to create a user object and generate a valid salt and encrypted password.

A successful login will store the current user ID in the session object at `session[:user_id]`. Because the session object is usually stored on the server and the user can never manipulate it directly, the session is a reasonably secure place to store user data, although it's a good idea to clear out old sessions to prevent them from living forever. This means that users will have to log in again if they leave the site and come back. Later in the chapter, you'll see a mechanism for securely allowing persistent logins.

In the logout test, you prime the session object by simulating a successful login first, asserting that the login was successful, and then logging out to observe the change. You can also see that there will be two partial templates defined: one displayed with the login form, and the other displayed if the user is already logged in.

The Controller

The login code goes in the user controller, `app/controllers/users_controller.rb`, and starts by calling the `User.find_by_username_and_password` method defined earlier. Here's the code:

```
def login
  @user = User.find_by_username_and_password(params[:user][:username],
      params[:user][:password])
  if @user
    session[:user_id] = @user.id
    render :partial => "already_logged_in"
  else
    flash[:login_message] = "Login failed"
    @user = User.new
    render :partial => "login"
  end
end
```

The user find method either returns the successfully matched user object, or it returns `nil`. If there's an actual user created, the ID is placed in the session, and the partial for a user who is logged in is rendered. If the method returns `nil`, a message is put in the flash text for eventual display, and the `@user` attribute is set to a new, empty user object.

There are a couple of design decisions to be made here. The rendering of just partial templates, and the insistence that the `@user` variable have a non-nil value, will make more sense when you see how the login form is integrated into the site.

Return a Vague Error Message

When you're returning an error message from a failed login, it's tempting to differentiate between "unknown username" and "invalid password." This is generally considered a bad idea, because a malicious user can use this message to verify that a username is actually in the system database, making the job of cracking a username/password pair that much easier.

Despite this, you'll still see systems, even successful web applications, that will make that distinction on a failed login. And I have to say, as a benevolent web user who has dozens of logins on dozens of sites, I appreciate the consideration because it makes my guessing what I was thinking of six months ago when I created that site account that much easier.

But I still would send the vague error message to a user on any site I developed.

The logout action is even simpler. It depends on the following `load_user` method, which you need to place in `app/controllers/application.rb`, because other controllers will want it:

```
def load_user
  @user = User.find_by_id(session[:user_id]) || User.new
end
```

Right now, the method either creates a user object from the ID stored in the session, or it creates a blank user object and assigns that to the `@user` variable. Next, you define the `logout` method like this:

```
def logout
  load_user
  flash[:login_message] = "Logged out"
  if @user.id == session[:user_id]
    session[:user_id] = nil
    @user = User.new
    render :partial => "login"
  else
    render :partial => "already_logged_in"
  end
end
```

All this does is reset the session and the @user object to default values, and then renders the login partial. One security issue to note here is that because logout is a RESTful action, it is called with a user ID. Because you have the ID used to make the call, you might as well ensure that the user ID from the call actually matches the user ID in the session before performing the logout. It's a good habit to get into — validating that the attributes passed via a URL are what you expect before performing an action— although in this case, it's admittedly hard to see what serious security breach could actually occur.

The Views

The form for logging in and logging out is going to be part of the common layout. In keeping with Rails best practice, it's implemented as a helper method that redirects to the proper partial template based on the user status, although as you saw previously, explicitly calling login or logout bypasses that helper and displays the correct partial template directly from the controller.

Within the layout file app/views/layouts/recipes.html.erb, add the following highlighted code:

```
<div id="sidebar">
    <ul>
        <li id="login">
                <h2 class="bg2">Login</h2>
                <%= render_login_div %>
        </li>
        <li id="menu" class="bg6">
```

This creates an element in the sidebar, and calls a helper method named render_login_div. Place that method in app/helpers/application_helpers.rb as follows:

```
def is_logged_in?
  return false unless @user && session[:user_id]
  not @user.username.blank?
end

def render_login_div(&proc)
  content_tag("div", :id => "login_form") do
    if flash[:login_message]
      content_tag("div", "#{flash[:login_message]}", :id => "notice")
    end
    if is_logged_in?
      render :partial => "/users/already_logged_in"
    else
      render :partial => "/users/login"
    end
  end
end
```

What you want is for a div element with the id login_form to be created, and to display either the login form or the "already logged in" message depending on whether the user is already logged in. This code assumes that the @user object will already exist. To ensure that, add a before_filter to the recipe controller, calling the load_user method you just saw, like this:

```
before_filter :load_user
```

To actually generate the HTML text, you'll use your old friend `content_tag`, last seen supporting metaprogramming in the form builder. The `div` is created, the flash message is added if needed, and then the `if` logic redirects the rendering code.

Because the common elements and the display logic have been placed in the helper, both of the view files are quite simple. That's the point. Pure Ruby code in the helper method is much better situated to manage complexity than the mixed HTML and Ruby code of the `.erb` file.

The login form uses the table form builder, and is rather simple. This is `app/views/user/login.html.erb`:

```
<% remote_table_form_for(@user, :url => login_new_user_url,
     :update => "login_form") do |f| %>
  <table>
    <%= f.text_field :username, :size => 10,
          :caption_class => "subtle" %>
    <%= f.password_field :password, :size => 10,
          :caption_class => "subtle" %>
    <%= f.submit "Log In", :class => "subtle" %>
    <%= f.row link_to("New User?", new_user_url, :class => "subtle") %>
  </table>
<% end %>
```

It's an Ajax remote form, meaning that it will update a specific element within the page — in this case the `login_form` element that the helper method created to enclose the form. You define the `remote_table_form_for` helper method in `app/helpers/application_helper.rb` (it's analogous to the one you defined earlier for non-Ajax form creation):

```
def remote_table_form_for(name, *args, &proc)
  remote_form_for(name, *convert_args(TabularFormBuilder, args),
      &proc)
end
```

There is one difference between the regular and Ajax versions, though. Remember when I said that the regular version put the `form` tag inside the `table` tag? It turns out that this has no functional affect on a regular form, but at least one browser can't handle it in an Ajax form — for some reason it refuses to match the attributes to the form. So, in the best tradition of web programming, you can work around unexpected browser behavior by putting the `table` tags inside the actual `form_for` block, which organizes things more in line with browser expectations.

Other than that, the form is simple, using the features of the custom form builder to remove the clutter. The generic `row` mechanism is used to add a non-form element link to create a new user.

After a successful login, display the active user's name and the logout option. This is the `_already_logged_in.html.rb` partial:

```
<div>
  You are logged in as <%= @user.full_name %>.
</div>
<div>
```

(continued)

(continued)

```
<%= link_to_remote "Log Out", {:url => logout_user_url(@user),
        :method => :get,
        :update => "login_form"},
        :class => "subtle" %>
</div>
```

The result is two displays in the sidebar. Figure 3-2 shows the first display, for the login form.

Username noelrap

Password ••••••

(Log In)

New User?

Figure 3-2

Then, once the user has logged in, he'll see the second display, shown in Figure 3-3.

You are logged in as
Noel Rappin.
Log Out
Figure 3-3

Using Authentication

Now that the user has to authenticate, there are some features that should be limited. For example, only a user who has logged in should be able to enter a recipe, and only the user who initially entered the recipe should be able to edit it. After writing the code so far, adding these features is almost staggeringly simple.

Put the following methods in `application_helper.rb`:

```
def if_is_current_user(user_id)
  yield if is_logged_in? and user_id == @user.id
end

def if_is_logged_in
  yield if is_logged_in?
end
```

Both of these methods are *block helpers* — helper methods that expect to be called with a block of the ERB template as an argument. In these cases, you are using the helper to remove the conditional logic from the view template. There are a couple of advantages to doing this, the simplest of which is basic Don't Repeat Yourself (DRY) — if the logic changes or gets more complex, then the code needs to be touched only in one place. Also, the named helper method will generally be better at revealing intent than the `if` statement.

Each of the helper methods executes the block only if the conditional is true. This means that the HTML or ERB code inside the block is only printed to the response if the condition is true.

The first place you'll want to use these helpers is in the recipe listing. The new recipe link should be available only if the user has logged in, and the actions should be available only if the user is actually responsible for that recipe. Here's what the new code in `app/views/recipes/index.html.erb` looks like, with a couple of other cosmetic changes:

```
<% @title = "Recipes" %>
<table width="75%">
  <tr><th>Title</th></tr>
  <% for recipe in @recipes %>
    <tr>
      <td><%= link_to(h(recipe.title), recipe) %></td>
      <% if_is_current_user recipe.user_id do %>
        <td><%= link_to 'Edit', edit_recipe_path(recipe) %></td>
        <td>
          <%= link_to 'Destroy', recipe, :confirm => 'Are you sure?',
                  :method => :delete %>
        </td>
      <% end %>
    </tr>
  <% end %>
</table>
<br />
<% if_is_logged_in do %>
  <%= link_to 'New recipe', new_recipe_path %>
<% end %>
```

Each block helper is used in this view, and these helpers are used just the same as any other method that takes a block, except that in this case, the blocks are composed of arbitrary ERB text placed between the do and end statements. Like an `if` or `for` statement, the helper blocks take the `<%` execute marker and not the `<%=` execute and print marker.

The other place where a user can edit is in the recipe show page, where you allowed the inline change to an ingredient. That also needs a guard clause around it. Here's the relevant part of that view:

```
<div class="ingredients">
  <h2>Ingredients</h2>
  <% for ingredient in @recipe.ingredients %>
    <div class="ingredient">
      <span id="ingredient_<%= ingredient.id %>">
        <%= h ingredient.display_string %>
      </span>
```

(continued)

77

(continued)

```
<% if_is_current_user @recipe.user_id do %>
    <span class="subtle" id="edit_<%= ingredient.id %>">
        <%= link_to_remote "Edit",
                :url => remote_edit_recipe_ingredient_path(
                    @recipe, ingredient),
                :method => :get,
                :update => "ingredient_#{ingredient.id}"%>
    </span>
<% end %>
        </div>
    <% end %>
</div>
```

Again, the block helper ensures that the edit field will display only if the current user is actually the owner of the recipe.

Adding User Roles

I realize that this security model is a little simplified. At the very least, you'd want an administrator level that could edit any recipe, and you might also want some kind of friend or group access. One mechanism for adding role-based access to your Rails application is by using the plugin simple_access_control, which works with the custom authentication system built in to Soups OnLine. The plugin is available via the following:

```
$ script/plugin install -x
http://mabs29.googlecode.com/svn/trunk/plugins/simple_access_control
```

For the plugin to be of use, there are basically three requirements:

1. The user class must respond to a `roles` method. The mechanism recommended by the plugin is to create a roles database table with a single column, using the following in a migration:

```
create_table "roles", :force => true do |t|
   t.column "title", :string
end
```

2. Have a many-to-many relationship between the User model and the Role model, which involves creating a standard join table for `roles_models`. That's overkill for Soups OnLine, where there are probably only two or three levels of access and a user would exclusively belong to one of them. This being Rails, you could achieve roughly the same effect by adding a role attribute to the users table and doing something like this:

```
def roles
  [Role.new(role)]
end
```

3. And then, elsewhere, define the following:

```
Class Role
  attr_accessor :title
  def intialize(role)
```

```
      @title = role
    end
  end
```

There are also two methods that need to be accessible in your controllers, generally by being in the application.rb file. The method current_user needs to return the user object that is current in the session, and the method logged_in? needs to return true or false based on whether a user is currently logged in (if you are using the restful_authentication plugin, those methods are defined for you by that plugin). That functionality exists in the system, but under different names. The following changes should go into application.rb:

```
def current_user
  load_user
end

def logged_in?
  user = load_user
  return false unless user && session[:user_id]
  not user.username.blank?
end
```

With that accomplished, the plugin allows you to set access rules at either the controller level or around specific blocks of view code. At the controller level, there is a new method, access_rule, that looks like this:

```
access_rule "user", :only => [:index, :show]
```

The first argument is the role being measured up for the rule. You can allow the same rule to apply to multiple roles by using a pseudo-Boolean syntax, "user || admin". The :only parameter is a list of all controller actions that should be accessible to a user who has that role. If a user has multiple roles, that user has access to any controller action accessible to any of those roles. If there are no rules defined for a specific role, it is assumed to have access to all actions.

If the user attempts to access an action he or she does not have access to, the plugin redirects the call to a permission_denied method, which you need to define either in each controller or in application .rb. The typical behavior of this method is to put an alert message in the flash, and redirect the user someplace harmless. You should also end the user's session as a security measure. There's also a permission_granted callback method should you have some specific action to take when the user is allowed to do something (for example, logging).

Within a view, you have access to the following restrict_to helper method, which takes an access rule and a block:

```
<% restrict_to 'admin' do %>
  <%= link_to "Edit", edit_recipe_url(@recipe) %>
<% end %>
```

The block is executed only if the current user has one of the roles listed in the rule. A related method, has_permission?, takes a rule as an argument and returns a Boolean suitable for use in if statements or clauses.

Bot Protection via Authorization Email

One of the most serious security issues facing any kind of social content site is the issue of bots and spam. This involves fake user accounts being set up for no other reason than to post spam messages to your unsuspecting little site. There are a few methods available to help protect your site. This section and the next discuss two popular mechanisms for ensuring that there is a real person behind every new account created for Soups OnLine. Neither of these mechanisms is perfect, and either could be defeated by a determined spammer. But they are both enough of a hurdle to make attacking your site less inviting, when there are so many other easy sites to exploit.

The first mechanism is the authorization email, and is very popular for mailing lists and other kinds of forums. When users create a new account, they are sent an email with a special URL. They need to retrieve the email and open the URL in their browser to validate the account. Although, in theory, this is defeatable by anybody willing to automatically read and parse the email, in practice this seems to be rarely done.

The main piece of data you need to implement this is some kind of token. Exactly what doesn't matter much as long as it's random enough not to be guessable. You need to associate the token with a newly created user account so that when the token comes back to the server, you know which user account to unlock.

Generating the Model and Migration

The token will be implemented as a simple Rails model. It doesn't need to be a full-fledged resource because you don't need the entire suite of CRUD methods in a web-based interface. The other alternative would be to make the token a column in the user table, but I think the token concept will be useful in enough contexts that it warrants its own table. Here's the simple token model:

```
$  ruby script/generate model token

    exists  app/models/
    exists  test/unit/
    exists  test/fixtures/
    create  app/models/token.rb
    create  test/unit/token_test.rb
    create  test/fixtures/tokens.yml
    exists  db/migrate
    create  db/migrate/004_create_tokens.rb
```

The token class needs a string for the actual token, and you'll give it an integer link to a user ID. You'll also define an optional string for a value, which won't be used here, but which will be used later on. The token should also have a time at which it ceases to be valid. For this to work, the user class also needs a flag to specify whether the account is actually active. Place the follwing text in db/migrate/004_create_tokens.rb:

```
class CreateTokens < ActiveRecord::Migration
  def self.up
    create_table :tokens do |t|
      t.string :token
      t.integer :user_id
```

```
      t.string :value
      t.datetime :expires_at
      t.timestamps
    end

    add_column :users, :is_active, :boolean
  end

  def self.down
    drop_table :tokens
    remove_column :users, :is_active
  end
end
```

This will need a new action in the user controller called `activate`. Again, this needs a new RESTful route, so you define the action as follows:

```
map.resources :users, :new => {:login => :post},
       :member => {:logout => :get, :activate => :get}
```

Test First

The flow of control here is that a new user will have the `is_active` column set to `false`, but that a token will be placed in the tokens table with an expiration date two days in the future. The controller test covering that functionality looks like this, in `test/functional/users_controller_test.rb`:

```
def test_should_create_user
  assert_difference('User.count') do
    post :create, :user => user_form
  end
  assert !assigns(:user).is_active
  tokens = Token.find_all_by_user_id(assigns(:user).id)
  assert_equal 1, tokens.size
  assert_equal 2, (tokens[0].expires_at - Date.today)
  assert_redirected_to user_path(assigns(:user))
end
```

To pass this test, you need to change the `create` action of the user controller as follows (the new lines are highlighted):

```
def create
  @user = User.new(params[:user])
  @user.is_active = false
  respond_to do |format|
    if @user.save
      flash[:notice] = 'User was successfully created.'

      Token.create_email_token(@user)
      format.html { redirect_to(@user) }
      format.xml  { render :xml => @user, :status => :created,
         :location => @user }
    else
```

(continued)

(continued)

```
        format.html { render :action => "new" }
        format.xml  { render :xml => @user.errors,
            :status => :unprocessable_entity }
      end
    end
  end
```

The actual token is created in the `token` class method in `app/model/token.rb`, like this:

```
def self.create_email_token(user)
  Token.create(:user_id => user.id,
      :token => Standards.random_string(25),
      :expires_at => DateTime.now + 2)
end
```

Notice that I've also factored the functionality of creating a random string, used earlier in creating the salt for the user to a common method. The new token has the user ID, a random string for a value, and an expiration date two days in the future.

The `activate` method will activate the user if the `user_id` and the `token` match the entry in the database, and if the token has not expired. That's one test for success, and failure tests for an incorrect user ID, incorrect token, and expired token. All four of the tests have the same basic skeleton, so you should factor that out to a common method. Place the following in `test/functional/users_controller_test.rb`:

```
def assert_token_test(user_id, token, should_be_valid,
    should_be_deleted, date_offset=2)
  Token.create(:user_id => 1, :token => "qwerty",
      :expires_at => Date.today + date_offset)
  get :activate, :id => user_id, :token => token
  assert_equal should_be_valid, assigns(:is_valid)
  user = User.find(1)
  assert_equal should_be_valid, user.is_active
  tokens = Token.find_all_by_user_id(1)
  assert_equal should_be_deleted, tokens.empty?
end
```

This test pre-creates a token, and then simulates a GET request to attempt an activation from the given user ID and token. The test then checks to see if the user valid state has been changed appropriately and that the token is consumed if expected. The four individual tests then become simple one-liners that call that assert function, like this:

```
def test_should_activate_successfully
  assert_token_test(1, "qwerty", true, true)
end

def test_should_not_activate_wrong_user
  assert_token_test(2, "qwerty", false, false)
end

def test_should_not_activate_wrong_token
  assert_token_test(1, "banana", false, false)
```

```
  end

def test_should_not_activate_timed_out
  assert_token_test(1, "qwerty", false, true, -90)
end
```

The successful test passes the correct user ID and token, and asserts that the user should be valid and the token should be consumed. The next two tests send an incorrect token challenge — the user should still be invalid, and the token should remain. The final test shows the result of testing against an expired token — it is invalid, and the token is also consumed.

Controller Logic

The `activate` controller method in `app/controllers/users_controller./rb` turns out to be simple — as usual, the heavy lifting is placed in a model:

```
def activate
  find_user
  @is_valid = Token.is_valid_for_user(@user, params[:token])
  @user.update_attributes(:is_active => @is_valid)
end

private

def find_user
  @user = User.find(params[:id])
end
```

The controller simply asks the token class if the request is valid, and updates the user object appropriately, the change made via `update_attributes` is immediately saved to the database.

The main logic is placed in the token class, `app/models/token.rb`, as you can see here:

```
def self.is_valid_for_user(user, incoming_token)
  actual_token = Token.find_by_user_id(user.id)
  return false unless actual_token
  time_valid = actual_token.expires_at > Time.now
  token_valid = actual_token.token == incoming_token
  is_valid = time_valid && token_valid
  actual_token.destroy if token_valid
  is_valid
end
```

A quick note — this wasn't quite as clean when I first wrote it, I had all the logic in the controller and it was a bit convoluted. Moving the logic to the model class cleaned up both the logic and the controller response.

The validation method checks to see if there is a token for the requested user — if not, the method is done immediately. Then the method confirms that the token codes match and the token has not expired. If the token codes match, the token is removed from the database, and the result of the validity test is returned.

At this point, all the tests should pass. Wait a moment while I commit my changes to Subversion.

Sending the Email

With the logic in place, now you need to handle the actual sending of the email. For this to work, you need to set the mail settings as appropriate for your system. For most cases, the development default of SMTP will work just fine, but you may need to set the `config.action_mailer.server_settings` object in the `environment.rb` file as follows:

```
ActionMailer::Base.server_settings = {
  :address => "<SMTP HOSTNAME -- default is localhost>",
  :domain => "<DOMAIN OF SMTP HOST>",
  :port =>[{[SPACE]}]<SMTP PORT -- default is 25>
}
```

In addition, if your SMTP host requires authentication, you need to set `:user_name` and `:password` options, as well as an `:authentication` option that is `:cram_md5`, `:login`, or `:plain`.

The email will be managed via a Rails `ActionMailer` object, which you first need to generate, like this:

```
$ ruby script/generate mailer AuthorizationMailer authorize
```

This generates a new mailer with a single command that it recognizes, `authorize`. The `ActionMailer` object is something like a hybrid between a model and a controller. It's stored with the other models, but the mailer gets its own subdirectory under `/app/views` along with the other controllers, where the templates used to actually define the email are stored. The mailer is invoked from a controller object, and data passed to the mailer is merged with the template to create the body of the email. Headers for the email are handled by the instance method of the mailer called with the invocation.

The test for the mailer will be part of the creation test in the `users_controller_test.rb` file. Add the following lines to the `setup` method to allow other tests to track emails:

```
def setup
  @controller = UsersController.new
  @request    = ActionController::TestRequest.new
  @response   = ActionController::TestResponse.new
  @emails = ActionMailer::Base.deliveries
  @emails.clear
end
```

The new test looks like this:

```
def test_should_create_user
  assert_difference('User.count') do
    post :create, :user => user_form
  end
  assert !assigns(:user).is_active
  tokens = Token.find_all_by_user_id(assigns(:user).id)
  assert_equal 1, tokens.size
  assert_equal 2, (tokens[0].expires_at.to_date - Date.today)
  assert_redirected_to user_path(assigns(:user))
  assert_equal 1, @emails.size
```

```
    sent_email = @emails[0]
    assert_not_nil sent_email.body.index(
        "users/#{assigns(:user).id}/activate?token=#{tokens[0].token}")
end
```

The last three lines test that an email was actually generated and that its body contains the URL fragment that will direct the user to the activation page.

Rails also generated a unit test for the mailer itself, but you don't want it. It compares the generated email against a text file. It's a nice scaffolding for a golden output test, but it will also be very fragile, breaking every time the text of the email template changes. So go into /test/unit/authorizaition_ mailer_test.rb and disable it by commenting out the assert_equal line in the sample test method.

The generate script created a default set of values in the action mailer object itself, but those values aren't going to be suitable for your purposes. So, rewrite the authorize method as follows:

```
def authorize(user, token)
    @subject     = 'Welcome to Soups OnLine'
    @body        = {:user => user, :token => token}
    @recipients  = user.email
    @from        = 'admin@soupsonline.com'
    @sent_on     = Time.now
    @headers     = {}
end
```

Most of these instance variables should be more or less self-explanatory. The @body variable contains a hash of values that become instance variables in the actual mail template. The @recipient value can be either a single value string or multiple values as a list.

Rails also created a blank template in /app/views/authorization_mailer/authorize.erb. The exact text doesn't quite matter, but the gist should go like this:

```
Dear <%= @user.first_name %>,

Thank you for signing on to Soups OnLine. In order to activate your account, please
follow the URL below by clicking on it or by pasting the URL into your browser.

<%= url_for(:controller => 'users', :action => 'activate',
    :id => @user.id, :token => @token.token) %>
See you soon,

Soups OnLine
```

With that done, actually generating the email involves adding a single line to the if-successful clause of the UserController#create method. The new line is highlighted here:

```
        flash[:notice] = 'User was successfully created.'
        session[:user_id] = @user.id
        token = Token.create_email_token(@user)
        AuthorizationMailer.deliver_authorize(@user, token)
        format.html { redirect_to(@user) }
        format.xml  { render :xml => @user, :status => :created,
            :location => @user }
```

85

The `deliver_authorize` call tells Rails to invoke the `AuthorizationMailer` using the `authorize` method, and then deliver the email right away. In contrast, you could choose `create_authorize`, which would return the email as a Rails object, allowing it to be delivered later. The user and token objects are passed to the authorization mail object, and then to the template to be included in the email body.

That should pass the tests you've created. The only remaining piece is to add something to the `/app/views/users/activate.html.erb` file to display a success or failure message to the user after the activation attempt. For example:

```
<div>
   Congratulations on successfully activating your account!  Enjoy
</div>
```

CAPTCHA

The other commonly used mechanism for preventing spambots from taking over your system is those blurry, transmogrified letters and numbers. The generic name for those things is CAPTCHA, which stands for *Completely Automated Public Turing test to tell Computers and Humans Apart* (which is not only one of the most tortured acronyms you'll ever see, but is, according to Wikipedia, a registered trademark of Carnegie Mellon University).

Now, I am of two minds about the familiar CAPTCHA images. On the one hand, it's true that a good implementation is difficult, if not impossible, for bots to crack. On the other hand, CAPTCHA images are not at all accessible to visually impaired users, which under certain circumstances might have legal consequences for your site. Even for users with normal sight, these images can still be awkward and are somewhat mistake-prone. In addition, users hate them.

What I'm going to do is present a simple CAPTCHA system that presents a text-based addition problem for the user to solve, such as "What is three plus the number of days in a week plus the number of fingers on a hand?" I'll leave it up to you to decide whether that is more or less irritating to a user than a fuzzy image. I'm pretty sure, though, that it will be more usable for a visually impaired user. It will use the existing token mechanism to store and validate user input. It's not a full-protection CAPTCHA — in fact, according to the somewhat sneering tone of the Wikipedia article, it's not a true CAPTCHA at all — but it should keep the riff-raff out, and it's a mechanism for discussing the issues involved. Later, I'll point out a few existing Rails plugins that can do more traditional CAPTCHA, if you expect to have determined spammers targeting your site.

Creating a Test-Driven CAPTCHA Object

The implementation of the simple CAPTCHA will be a Ruby class, `MathCaptcha`, that you can place in `app/models/math_captcha.rb`. You will also add a `test/unit/math_captcha_test.rb` file to the unit test directory. The functionality of the CAPTCHA object is pretty basic — it needs to generate a random sequence of operands, determine their sum, and convert them to a string for output.

Some Rails developers think that applications and models should be strictly limited to `ActiveRecord` subclasses, in which case, the `MathCaptcha` object could be placed either in the `lib` directory or in a

new application subdirectory such as `app/utilities`. *Alternately, the MathCaptcha could be developed as a plugin. (See Chapter 15 for more details.)*

You'll need to place three unit tests in the `math_capcha_test.rb` file. The first test generates a list of operands:

```
require File.dirname(__FILE__) + '/../test_helper'

class MathCaptchaTest < Test::Unit::TestCase

  def setup
    @captcha = MathCaptcha.new
  end

  def test_should_generate_list
    @captcha.generate_operands(3)
    assert_equal 3, @captcha.operands.size
    @captcha.random_stream = [1, 3, 5]
    @captcha.generate_operands(3)
    assert_equal [1, 3, 5], @captcha.operands
    assert_equal 9, @captcha.sum
  end
```

The only unusual thing about this test is that I chose to give the actual CAPTCHA object a `random_stream` attribute that allows me to inject fake-random numbers to the object to test the result of a particular sequence of random numbers on the object. I find this mechanism to be much more manageable than using `srand` to specify the random number seed. Another option would be to split the functionality into two methods: one method that generates a random number and then calls the other method with that argument, and then in the unit tests, you call the second method with a prepared argument. In any case, I recommend that you have some way to specify random inputs for testing.

Test two verifies that the CAPTCHA can generate multiple string representations of the same operation, as follows:

```
def test_string_representation
    assert_equal (["7", "seven", "the number of days in a week"],
        MathCaptcha::OPTIONS[7])
    @captcha.random_stream = [1, 3, 5, 0, 0, 0]
    @captcha.generate_operands(3)
    assert_equal "What is 1 plus 3 plus 5?", @captcha.display_string
    @captcha.random_stream = [1, 3, 5, 1, 1, 1]
    @captcha.generate_operands(3)
    assert_equal "What is one plus three plus five?",
        @captcha.display_string
  end
```

Test three verifies that the CAPTCHA generates a token object and places it in the database, like this:

```
def test_token
    @captcha.random_stream = [1, 3, 5, 1, 1, 1]
    @captcha.generate_operands(3)
    assert_difference('Token.count') do
```

(continued)

(continued)

```
        @captcha.generate_token
        assert_equal 9, @captcha.token.value
      end
    end

  end
```

CAPTCHA Object Implementation

The `MathCaptcha` class will have three attributes: `operands`, which will represent the actual list of numbers to be added; `random_stream`, which will house the random numbers and be used for testing; and `token`, which will hold the token object associated with this CAPTCHA. The skeleton of the class looks like this:

```
require 'extensions'
class MathCaptcha
  attr_accessor :operands, :random_stream, :token
end
```

I suppose it should go without saying, but the remaining methods in this section will go inside that class definition. I just think that it will be easier to explain the code piece by piece rather than in a larger code dump.

The first unit test involves generating a random list of attributes and knowing their correct sum:

```
def initialize
  self.random_stream = []
end

def generate_operands(size)
  self.operands = (1..size).collect { get_random }
end

def get_random(max=21)
  result = random_stream.shift
  if result then result else rand(max) end
end
```

To generate the operands, I used the same range and collection trick previously used for the randomized token strings — this method allows for an arbitrary length of math sentence, although I suppose using less than two operands is kind of pointless. The `get_random` method is the hook for preset random streams. If a preset array exists, then the first value in that array is taken and used; otherwise, the system random function is used. The operands are random values between 0 and 20.

The sum of the operands is a simple one-line call to the already generated array:

```
def sum
  operands.sum
end
```

The second test involves turning the math sentence into a string. The data structure here is a class constant called OPTIONS, a section of which looks like this:

```
OPTIONS = [
    ["0", "zero", "nothing", "the number of legs on a fish"],
    ["1", "one", "the number of thumbs in a hand"],
    ["2", "two", "the number of feet a person has"],
    ["3", "three", "the number of sides in a triangle"],
```

I trust you get the idea. To create the display string, the object chooses one of the synonyms for each number at random, and pieces them together into a sentence, like this:

```
def display_string
    operand_string = operands.collect { |o|
        string_for_operand(o) }.join(" plus ")
    "What is #{operand_string}?"
end

def string_for_operand(operand)
    opts = OPTIONS[operand]
    opts[get_random(opts.size)]
end
```

As is so often the case when you're manipulating lists, the collect-and-join combination is your friend. It enables the array to be converted to the data string in a single line of code that can then be slotted in the sentence skeleton. Also notice that the string_for_operand method uses the same get_random hook, which allows the unit test to validate specific combinations of the number options.

Finally, the CAPTCHA object needs to create a unique token. You want to do this because one of the ways in which CAPTCHA systems are subverted is by breaking the code on either the filename used for the image or a hidden field used within the form to identify the CAPTCHA being used. Because this CAPTCHA will use the token mechanism to create a one-off random string unrelated to the value of the CAPTCHA, that line of attack should be defended against. The token is defined as follows:

```
def generate_token
    self.token = Token.create(:value => sum,
        :token => Standards.random_string(25),
        :expires_at => DateTime.now + 2)
end
```

Of course, this is not really an industrial-strength CAPTCHA, and it's not out of the question that a determined spammer could parse the string. The most likely weakness of this system, however, is probably the fact that there are relatively few possible answers — because you'll use this with three operands, there are only 61 possibilities. A mechanism could easily cycle through them on the same CAPTCHA, or could just guess and accept the 1.6-percent success rate. That would require a spammer to be deliberately targeting your site, of course. Some of these vulnerabilities can be mitigated during deployment by restricting repeated access from the same site.

It's not part of the test, but you will need a constructor for this object to use during deployment. It should create the operands and generate the token, as follows:

```
def self.create(operand_count, random_stream = [])
  result = MathCaptcha.new
  result.random_stream = random_stream
  result.generate_operands(operand_count)
  result.generate_token
  result
end
```

I named the method `create` rather than `new`, to conform to the Rails convention that `create` is used to denote class methods that save something to the database — in this case, the token. At the moment, there's no need for a specific method that would just generate the operands and tokens and would not save the tokens to the database.

Deploying the CAPTCHA

The CAPTCHA needs to be deployed as part of the new user form and validated on user creation. It's probably also a good idea to put it in the recipe form and validate new recipe creation, lest spammers get one legitimate login and pummel the site with recipes for "Get Rich Quick with Penny Stocks Soup." The testing and implementation of the two are nearly parallel, so I'll only show the recipe side here.

I placed the following two common testing methods in `test_helper.rb`:

```
def create_mock_captcha_token(token, value)
  Token.create(:token => token, :value => value,
      :expires_at => Date.today + 2)
end

def assert_captcha
  created_token = assigns(:captcha).token
  saved_token = Token.find_by_value(assigns(:captcha).sum)
  assert_equal created_token.token, saved_token.token
end
```

The first method creates a fake token for a mythical CAPTCHA so that user input can be validated against it. The second method asserts that a token has been created by a CAPTCHA object, and that it has the expected value.

Now the actual tests need to be created. The test for `new` needs to validate that the CAPTCHA is created and that the form elements are placed in the form. This needs to be placed in `recipes_controller_test.rb`, with the new lines highlighted here:

```
def test_should_get_new
  get :new
  assert_response :success
  assert_captcha
  assert_select("form[action=?]", recipes_path) do
```

```
            assert_select "input[name *= title]"
            assert_select "input[name *= servings]"
            assert_select "textarea[name *= ingredient_string]"
            assert_select "textarea[name *= description]"
            assert_select "textarea[name *= directions]"
            assert_select "input[name *= captcha_value]"
            assert_select "input[name *= token]"
        end
    end
```

The test for create needs to add the valid CAPTCHA data, and a new test needs to be added to test correct behavior when invalid CAPTCHA data is presented. The existing `create` test has new lines that are highlighted in the following code:

```
        def test_should_create_recipe
          create_mock_captcha_token("fred", "3")
          recipe_hash = { :title => "Grandma's Chicken Soup",
              :servings => "5 to 7",
              :description => "Good for what ails you",
              :ingredient_string =>
                  "2 cups carrots, diced\n\n1/2 tablespoon salt\n\n
                  1 1/3 cups stock",
              :directions => "Ask Grandma"}
          assert_difference('Recipe.count') do
              post :create, :recipe => recipe_hash, :token => "fred",
                  :captcha_value => "3"
          end
          expected_recipe = Recipe.new(recipe_hash)
          new_recipe = Recipe.find(:all, :order => "id DESC", :limit => 1)[0]
          assert_equal(expected_recipe, new_recipe)
          assert_equal(3, new_recipe.ingredients.size)
          assert_redirected_to recipe_path(assigns(:recipe))
        end
```

And the new test looks like this:

```
        def test_should_not_create_recipe_without_captcha
          create_mock_captcha_token("fred", "3")
          old_size = Recipe.count
          recipe_hash = { :title => "Grandma's Chicken Soup",
              :servings => "5 to 7",
              :description => "Good for what ails you",
              :ingredient_string => "2 cups carrots, diced",
              :directions => "Ask Grandma"}
          post :create, :recipe => recipe_hash, :token => "fred",
              :captcha_value => "5"
          new_size = Recipe.count
          assert_equal old_size, new_size
        end
```

Passing these tests involves slight changes to the new and create methods of the recipes controller to use the CAPTCHA data that you have already created. The change to new is as simple adding the highlighted line in the following code):

```
def new
  @recipe = Recipe.new
  @captcha = MathCaptcha.create(3)
  respond_to do |format|
    format.html # new.html.erb
    format.xml  { render :xml => @recipe }
  end
end
```

The create change is a little more involved (but only a little). You check to see if the CAPTCHA is valid before allowing the new recipe to be in the database. Otherwise, the code redirects back to the form — but because @recipe has the user-entered data in it, the user will not have to reenter all the recipe data. Note the following highlighted code:

```
def create
  @recipe = Recipe.new(params[:recipe])
  if Token.is_valid_captcha(params[:token], params[:captcha_value])
    saved = @recipe.save
  else
    @recipe.destroy
    flash[:notice] = 'Sorry, you answered the robot question
          incorrectly, please try again.'
    saved = false
  end
  respond_to do |format|
    if saved
      flash[:notice] = 'Recipe was successfully created.'
      format.html { redirect_to(@recipe) }
      format.xml  { render :xml => @recipe, :status => :created, :location =>
@recipe }
    else
      format.html { render :action => "new" }
      format.xml  { render :xml => @recipe.errors, :status => :unprocessable_
entity }
    end
  end
end
```

This code depends on the following method of the Token class in app/models/token.rb to determine if the token and the incoming CAPTCHA value really do match:

```
def self.is_valid_captcha(token, incoming_value)
  actual_token = Token.find_by_token(token)
  return false unless actual_token
  actual_token.destroy
  actual_token.is_valid?(token, incoming_value)
end
```

This method finds the token by its random token value and asserts that the incoming value matches the calculated value stored with the token. No matter what happens, the token is removed from the database, so the same token cannot be exploited twice.

The user's controller has extremely similar changes.

I also created a view to display the CAPTCHA inside a form block. I placed it in `app/views/math_captcha/_math_captcha.html.erb`. It puts the token in a hidden field, and gives the user a space to enter his answer, as follows:

```
<tr>
  <td colspan="2">
    We regret the inconvenience, but we need you to answer the
    following question to prove that you are not a robot.
  </td>
</tr>
<input type="hidden" name="token" value="<%= @captcha.token.token %>">
<tr>
  <td colspan="2">
    <%= @captcha.display_string %>
  </td>
</tr>
<tr>
  <td class="tdheader">Answer (as digits):</td>
  <td>
    <input class="input" type="text" name="captcha_value" size="5">
  </td>
</tr>
```

The fields are inside table elements to allow them to coexist with the tabular form builder used in the user form. To insert this partial template in the new recipes form, it just needs to have the following table around it:

```
<% if @captcha %>
  <table>
    <%= render :partial => "math_captcha/math_captcha" %>
  </table>
<% end %>
```

The end product puts the new form elements at the bottom of each form, as shown in Figure 3-4.

We regret the inconvenience, but we need you to answer the following question to prove that you are not a robot.

What is the number of sides in a square plus eight plus the number of sides in a hexagon?

Answer (as digits): [   ]

Create

Figure 3-4

That's not quite the end of the story. There are some more elaborate features on the server side that can help security. You can keep track of how long it takes the user to fill out the form, and only accept forms that are completed within a certain length of time, such as 30 seconds. You can block a given requester IP from performing more than a few CAPTCHA checks in a certain amount of time.

If you want the next level of protection, there are some image-based CAPTCHA plugins for Rails (which you can find at the websites listed in the "Resources" section later in this chapter).

Sessions and Cookies

Allowing the user to log in once and stay logged on between sessions is a convenience offered by many websites. Typically the persistent login is managed via a cookie stored in the user's browser. This introduces a significant security risk. The cookie is just a text file coming from an untrusted source and could easily have been copied, tampered with, or otherwise spoofed. Because the cookie is being used in lieu of a normal username and password challenge, this opens a huge potential hole in your system, should somebody get a hold of a valid login cookie.

Your strategy for dealing with persistent logins and cookies needs to isolate the data sent over the cookie from other data in the system, and to mitigate the potential damage from a misused login cookie. As with most security features, the exact cost-benefit tradeoff depends on the specifics of your site, how valuable the data on the site is, and how much inconvenience your users will stand in the name of security.

Persistent Login Cookie Strategies

Here are some specific features that a persistent login system using cookies should have:

❑ Never send real data. You should never send a user's actual username, let alone his actual password. I'd even avoid sending the hashed password. The value sent to the cookie should have no relationship to any other piece of user information in the system. Having that value should give a malicious user no leverage toward calculating other user data.

❑ Just like cookies in the supermarket, login cookies should come with an expiration date. Exactly how far in advance that date should be is something you need to decide for your site. GMail uses a two-week expiration period, for example. Whatever period you choose, the important thing is that the expiration date is managed on the server, not the client. The client date is too easy to forge.

❑ Login cookies should be consumed and regenerated after being used successfully. This minimizes the amount of time a cookie can be used maliciously — as soon as the real user logs in, the old cookie is no longer accepted.

❑ Depending on the structure of your site, it may make sense to restrict user privileges if the user has come into the site via a cookie. For example, a user may be allowed to see their personal data from a cookie, but then might be challenged for a password before being allowed to edit it. This has the potential to be irritating to a user — on the other hand, it proivdes stronger protection against the misuse of cookies.

Persistent Login Mechanism — Test First

I'm going to show an example of a persistent login structure using the token mechanism already created, which fulfils the first three of the aforementioned features.

The life cycle of a cookie starts on a successful username/password login or new user creation, when a new cookie is created for that user. Later, when a page on the site is hit and there is no user session in place, the system will look for the cookie to validate a login. After an attempted validation, the cookie will be consumed and replaced by a new cookie with a different token. When a user logs out, the token should also be consumed.

To test the creation and destruction of the cookie, I added some assertions to the existing user controller test methods in `test/functional/user_controller.rb`. The login that is successfully tested gets an assertion that a cookie has been created:

```
assert_not_nil cookies["token"]
```

An unsuccessful login method gets an assertion that a cookie has *not* been created:

```
assert cookies["token"] = []
```

I should mention that, unlike almost every other hash-like object in Rails, the `cookies` object for functional testing does not automatically convert between symbols and strings.

The logout test adds both of those assertions — the assertion that a cookie has been created after the mock login, and the assertion that it has been destroyed after the logout. The destroy test gets a similar change, as you can see in the new lines highlighted in the following code:

```
def test_should_destroy_user
  post :login, :user => {:username => "ktf", :password => "qwerty"}
  assert_not_nil cookies["token"]
  assert_difference('User.count', -1) do
    delete :destroy, :id => 1
  end
  assert_redirected_to users_path
  assert cookies["token"] = []
  assert_nil session[:user_id]
end
```

Finally, the `assert_token_test` method used to manage the activation process should also generate a cookie if the user validates successfully. This is shown in the highlighted lines in the following code:

```
def assert_token_test(user_id, token, should_be_valid,
    should_be_deleted, date_offset=2)
  Token.create(:user_id => 1, :token => "qwerty", :value => "email",
    :expires_at => Date.today + date_offset)
  get :activate, :id => user_id, :token => token
  assert_equal should_be_valid, assigns(:is_valid)
  user = User.find(1)
  assert_equal should_be_valid, user.is_active
```

(continued)

(continued)

```
        tokens = Token.find_all_by_user_id_and_value(1, "email")
      assert_equal should_be_deleted, tokens.empty?
      if should_be_valid
        assert_not_nil cookies["token"]
      else
        assert cookies["token"] = []
      end
    end
```

I also changed the generated activation codes in `app/models/token.rb` slightly so they can be distinguished from the cookie-generated tokens, as you can see here:

```
def self.create_email_token(user)
  Token.create(:user_id => user.id, :token => Standards.random_string(25),
      :value => "email", :expires_at => DateTime.now + 2)
end

def self.create_cookie_token(user)
  Token.create(:user_id => user.id, :token => Standards.random_string(50),
      :expires_at => 14.days.from_now, :value => "cookie")
end
```

Finally, you need a test to ensure that a cookie coming from the user browser can actually be validated as a login. In the following `test/functional/users_controller_test.rb` code, there's one common method, then the use of the method for a successful login, and another method for an unsuccessful login:

```
def assert_cookie_login(expected_correct, token=nil)
  post :login, :user => {:username => "ktf", :password => "qwerty"}
  token1 = cookies["token"]
  assert_not_nil cookies["token"]
  assert_equal 1, session[:user_id]
  session[:user_id] = nil
  @request.cookies["token"] = (token || cookies["token"])
  get :index
  assert_equal expected_correct, session[:user_id]
  token1
end

def test_should_login_with_cookie
  token = assert_cookie_login(1)
  assert_not_equal(token, cookies["token"])
end

def test_should_not_login_with_bad_cookie
  assert_cookie_login(nil, "bananamuffin")
  assert_equal([], cookies["token"])
end
```

The common test starts with a successful login, which generates a cookie, and then sets the session user id to `nil`, simulating the end of a browser session. Then you add a cookie to the request — either with a specified incorrect token, or with the token that was created from the original login. At this point, any request to the system should read the cookie and put the user ID in the session object. The test arbitrarily chooses the index page, and then validates that the session ID is the expected value — the user ID if the test is successful, or `nil` if it is not. The test also checks to see if the cookie is correctly consumed, and replaced by a new token if the login was successful.

Cookie Life Cycle

To pass these tests and add the persistent login, you should start by adding the following two methods to the `application.rb` file for functionality that will be used in more than one action of the controller:

```
def set_user_cookie
  cookies[:token] = Token.create_cookie_token(@user).token
end

def remove_user
  session[:user_id] = nil
  cookies.delete :token
end
```

The first method creates a token based on the current user ID, saves it to the database, and writes the cookie. The second method zaps the user from the session object and from the client cookie.

The `set_user_cookie` method is called in two places. First, it is called in `app/controllers/user_controller.rb` as follows when the user successfully activates a cookie via email:

```
def activate
  find_user
  @is_valid = Token.is_valid_for_user(@user, params[:token])
  @user.update_attributes(:is_active => @is_valid)
  set_user_cookie if @is_valid
end
```

The method is also called on any successful login, as follows:

```
def login
  @user = User.find_by_username_and_password(params[:user][:username],
      params[:user][:password])
  if @user
    session[:user_id] = @user.id
    set_user_cookie
    render :partial => "already_logged_in"
  else
    flash[:login_message] = "Login failed"
    @user = User.new
    render :partial => "login"
  end
end
```

The cookie is deleted when the user logs out, like this:

```
def logout
  load_user
  flash[:login_message] = "Logged out"
  if @user.id == session[:user_id]
    @user = User.new
    remove_user
    render :partial => "login"
  else
    render :partial => "already_logged_in"
  end
end
```

The cookie is also deleted if the active user is destroyed somehow, as follows:

```
def destroy
  find_user
  @user.destroy
  remove_user if session[:user_id] == @user.id
  respond_to do |format|
    format.html { redirect_to(users_url) }
    format.xml  { head :ok }
  end
end
```

Validating Login Cookies

The actual check for a valid cookie for login is done in the same load_user method used earlier to put the user ID into the session object. Now, the code adds a test to look for a cookie. Because this method gets called from all controllers, it's placed in application.rb as follows:

```
def load_user
  @user = User.find_by_id(session[:user_id])
  return if @user
  @user = Token.validate_login_from_token(cookies[:token])
  if @user
    session[:user_id] = @user.id
    set_user_cookie
  else
    cookies.delete :token
    @user = User.new
  end
  @user
end
```

The code extends the options for where to find the current user. The first option is to try to find the user in the session object. If there's no user there, then the code asks the Token class to validate the cookie from the browser as a login. If it can do that, then the new user ID is added to the session and a new cookie is generated. If that doesn't work, the same default behavior of creating a blank dummy user is called, and the cookie is removed from the user's stash.

The Token class now needs to validate the cookie. This method is similar to the two previous Token class methods already created:

```
def self.validate_login_from_token(token)
    return false unless token
    actual_token = Token.find_by_token(token)
    return false unless actual_token
    valid = actual_token.expires_at > Time.now
    user = if valid then User.find(actual_token.user_id) else nil end
    actual_token.destroy
    user
end
```

The incoming token is the value of the user cookie. If there is no user cookie, the method returns false immediately. Otherwise, the method tries to find a matching token from the database, again returning false if one is not found. If the token has not expired, then the user matching that token's user ID is found. The token is removed from the database as a security precaution, and the user object is returned.

This gives three separate Token class methods with a very similar structure, which is a strong hint that some refactoring is in order. The mechanism I tried first was to move some of the common logic to token instance methods to simplify the logic in the class methods. This gives the following redefinition of the Token class, which I think is a little easier to read:

```
require 'extensions'
class Token < ActiveRecord::Base

  belongs_to :user

  def self.create_email_token(user)
    Token.create(:user_id => user.id, :token =>
        Standards.random_string(25),
        :value => "email", :expires_at => DateTime.now + 2)
  end

  def self.create_cookie_token(user)
    Token.create(:user_id => user.id, :token =>
        Standards.random_string(50),
        :expires_at => 14.days.from_now, :value => "cookie")
  end

  def self.is_valid_for_user(user, incoming_token)
    actual_token = Token.find_by_user_id(user.id)
    return false unless actual_token
    actual_token.destroy if actual_token.token_is?(incoming_token)
    actual_token.is_valid?(incoming_token, "email")
  end

  def self.is_valid_captcha(token, incoming_value)
    actual_token = Token.find_by_token(token)
    return false unless actual_token
    actual_token.destroy
```

(continued)

(continued)

```
      actual_token.is_valid?(token, incoming_value)
    end

    def self.validate_login_from_token(incoming_token)
      return false unless incoming_token
      token = Token.find_by_token(incoming_token)
      return false unless token
      user = if !token.is_expired? then token.user else nil end
      token.destroy
      user
    end

    def is_expired?
      expires_at < Time.now
    end

    def token_is?(expected_token)
      token == expected_token
    end

    def value_is?(expected_value)
      value == expected_value
    end

    def is_valid?(expected_token, expected_value)
      !is_expired? && token_is?(expected_token) &&
          value_is?(expected_value)
    end

  end
```

Resources

The new standard plugin for user authentication is Restful Authentication, by Rick Olson, which you can install from `http://svn.techno-weenie.net/projects/plugins/restful_authentication`. It provides a slightly different design for the same basic login, password management, and cookie functionality as discussed in this chapter. It's quite easy to incorporate the plugin into your application.

Bernie Thompson has a guide to getting started with OpenID at `http://leancode.com/openid-for-rails`.

For general insight on Rails security issues, check out `www.rorsecurity.info`, a blog by Heiko Webers. Be sure to look at the security checklist at `www.rorsecurity.info/ruby-on-rails-security-cheatsheet` or the similar one at `www.quarkruby.com/2007/9/20/ruby-on-rails-security-guide` for extensive details on locking down your Rails application.

There are several different plugins that manage CAPTCHA tests. The implementation shown in this chapter was inspired by a description of the BrainBuster plugin by Rob Sanheim, available at `http://code.google.com/p/robsanheim/wiki/BrainBuster`. There's also a Ruby gem called

Turing (`http://turing.rubyforge.org`) and a plugin called CAPTCHA (`http://sargon .interinter.net/validates_captcha`) that do image-based CAPTCHA and depend on ImageMagick (see Chapter 11). And there's also Simple Captcha (`http://agilewebdevelopment .com/plugins/simple_captcha`).

Summary

Managing user authentication is a critical security task for many web applications. In Rails, a user is basically managed like its other resources. The user's password should be stored in the database in an encrypted state, and the encryption should be augmented with a random salt. Rails validations can be used to verify the confirmation of the password in the form.

Form builders can be used to automate the repetitive aspects of maintaining a common form layout across your application. The login and logout actions can be managed as part of a separate RESTful controller or as part of the user's controller.

After the user authentication is built in, some simple helper methods enable you to specify blocks of code as accessible only by users who have logged in. You can also use the simple_access_control plugin to define more specialized access control. A token system can be used to support authorization via email.

CAPTCHA is a test designed to prevent automated responses from messing up the system. A traditional image can be used, or you can create a system based on any kind of logic problem that might be difficult for a computer system to parse. The same token system can help support the CAPTCHA security.

Cookies are used to provide authentication that persists beyond a single user session. However, you must be careful not to introduce security issues with this method of access.

4

Build Tools and Automation

Automation is critically important to the success of an ongoing project. As the project continues, you will accumulate task after task — things that need to be done over and over again to keep the project running smoothly. These include cleanup tasks to remove unneeded files or database entries. Depending on the project, you may have to build tasks for compiling or interpreting files in advance. You'll have deployment tasks, to move your program from the development environments to your production servers.

These tasks need to be done repeatedly and they need to be done accurately, which makes them prime targets for automation. And so, for decades, programmers have defined repetitive tasks in various kinds of make files, named, of course, after the original Unix make program — the granddaddy of all programs used to define build tasks.

The key element of a make-like system is the capability to define tasks as being dependent on other tasks. For example, a testing task might depend on a database setup task running first. Or a deployment task might depend on a clean rebuild of the entire project completed successfully before deployment can begin. The complexity of a make system comes not just from defining the tasks themselves, but also from defining the dependency relationships between tasks.

The classic make application is often considered to have a difficult-to-read syntax, and is still most widely used within Unix and C development worlds. Other programming communities have developed other tools. Many Java projects use Ant, which has an XML-based syntax for defining tasks and dependencies. However, Ant files also have a tendency to become unwieldy as they get more complex over time. (As software guru Martin Fowler said, "Until we tried it, I thought XML would be a good syntax for build files.")

Most Ruby projects now use Rake (Ruby Make), which uses Ruby's flexible syntax to combine a readable dependency syntax with the full power of Ruby in defining tasks. When you use Rake in your Rails project, you also have full use of your Rails environment, including your ActiveRecord models, which is nice. Rails comes with a large number of predefined tasks (some of which you've seen already) that perform a number of useful tasks. You can, of course, write your own tasks specific to your own project.

When you can run your build tasks automatically, you can run them all the time. This is especially useful for compilation and test tasks. Continuous integration has proven to be so useful, that a number of tools have been developed specifically to enable your Rake-based project to run its tests automatically on a regular basis.

Another tool called Capistrano has emerged to support the complex job of deploying a Rails application to multiple production servers. Capistrano extends Rake to support transferring files and ensuring consistency among deployment servers. Capistrano will be more fully discussed in Chapter 12.

What Rake Can Do for You

Before talking about how you can write custom Rake tasks to support your project, you should take a look at the variety of Rake tasks that have already been created. These cover a wide variety of tasks, including database support, documentation support, annotation support, and test support. Use the following command line to see a list of defined Rake tasks :

```
rake -T
```

The output of this command is a list of the defined Rake tasks with their descriptions as entered in the rakefile.

The following sections describe the tasks in the standard Rails rakefile. There's a good chance that there's a task in here that you didn't know about that will save you time on your projects. Each group of tasks has a table, and any further comments about these tasks are included after the table.

Rake Database Tasks

Most of the Rake tasks defined by Rails concern the database, in part to provide a common command line shortcut for database features that would otherwise take a significant amount of scripting, and which might differ depending on the exact database being used.

The first set of tasks, described in the following table, deals with creating a database or setting it to the current schema. A couple of methods of dumping the schema to a text file are also supported. The colon is the namespace delimiter in Rake, and all the database tasks start with db:.

Task	Description
db:abort_if_pending_migrations	Used as a dependent task, stops Rake if there is an unperformed database migration. Specifically used to prevent tests from running.
db:create	Creates one database, the one defined in the database .yml file for the default environment defined in environment.rb.
db:create:all	Creates all the databases defined in database.yml.
db:drop	Removes one database according to the same rule as db:create.
db:fixtures:identify	Takes one argument and finds a fixture with that label.
db:fixtures:load	Takes the fixtures defined in /test/fixtures and loads them into the current database. This is useful for seeding the development database with test data. It also takes the optional argument FIXTURES=fix1, fix2, which limits the load to specific tables.
db:migrate	Runs the necessary migrations to bring the current database to the current schema version. It takes an optional argument VERSION=version if you want to bring the current database to a version other than the current schema.
db:migrate:redo	A shortcut for rolling back the database one version and re-performing the most recent migration.
db:migrate:reset	Similar to db:migrate but completely drops the current database and runs through all migrations, rather than just performing the incremental changes. The VERSION=version argument will cause the process to stop at a specific version that is not current.
db:reset	Drops and recreates the current database
db:rollback	Rolls back the current migration. Use the argument STEP=x to indicate the number of steps backward.
db:schema:dump	Creates the schema.rb file for defining the current schema. This file can be loaded into a different database via Ruby and ActiveRecord without going through the list of migrations.
db:schema:load	Loads the schema.rb file created by db:schema:dump.
db:structure:dump	Outputs the current database structure to /db/ development_structure.sql, as an SQL script. (The filename will change based on the current Rails environment type.)

The second batch of database items handles sessions. These items, which are described in the next table, are useful only if you are storing your session data in the database via the ActiveRecord session object (discussed in Chapter 13).

Task	Description
db:sessions:clear	Empties out the session table.
db:sessions:create	Creates a session table, enabling the storage of session data as an ActiveRecord object.

Another set of database tasks manage the test database, enabling you to easily recreate the development schema in the test database. As you can see in the following table, these tasks use different methods to divine the structure of the development database, although in practice there should be little difference between them.

Task	Description
db:test:clone	Creates a test database from the result of a db:schema:dump on the current database.
db:test:clone_structure	Creates a test database from the result of a db:structure:dump on the current database.
db:test:prepare	Creates a test database based on whichever format schema file has already been created.
db:test:purge	Recreates the test database with no data.

Finally, there are a few database tasks that just output potentially useful information about the current database. The following table describes these tasks.

Task	Description
db:charset	Returns the character set being used by the current database (utf8, for example).
db:collation	Collation is the sorting algorithm used for ordering strings in the database — colloquially, you'd call it alphabetical order, but Unicode doesn't necessarily have an alphabet.
db:version	Returns the current version number of your schema, as used by migrations.

Rake Documentation Tasks

Rake has a series of predefined tasks that simplify the process of running RDoc on various portions of your project, as described in the following table. The normal behavior of RDoc is to regenerate HTML files only for source files that have changed since the last time RDoc was run. To regenerate the entire part of the project in question, use the `doc:clobber` tasks to remove the documentation.

Task	Description
doc:app	Runs RDoc on the files in your application, specifically the contents of the `/app` and `/lib` directories. Documentation is placed in `/doc/app`.
doc:clobber_app	Removes all files in `/doc/app`.
doc:clobber_rails	Removes all files in `/doc/api`.
doc:clobber_plugins	Removes all files in `/doc/plugins`.
doc:plugins	Runs RDoc on all plugins in `/vendor/plugins`. Documentation is placed in `/doc/plugins`.
doc:rails	Runs RDoc on a Rails installation in `/vendor/rails`, if one exists. Documentation is placed in `/doc/api`.
doc:reapp	Equivalent to `doc:clobber_app` followed by `doc:app`.
doc:rerails	Equivalent to `doc:clobber_rails` followed by `doc:rails`.

Rails also automatically generates tasks of the form `doc:plugins:<plugin name>` for each plugin in the `/vendor/plugins` directory. This task generates the RDoc documentation for just that single plugin.

Rake Testing Tasks

If you're developing your Rails project using Test Driven Development (TDD), then you're going to use the Rake tasks described in the following table most often.

Task	Description
test	Runs all the automated tests defined in your project. This is equivalent to running `test:functionals`, `test:integration`, and `test:units`. It is also the default task run if you call Rake with no task declared.
test:functionals	Runs all the test classes defined in `test/functional`. The specific pattern being matched is `test/functional/**/*_test.rb`.
test:integration	Runs all the test classes defined in `test/integration`. The specific pattern being matched is `test/integration/**/*_test.rb`.
test:plugins	Runs all the tests for all plugins in `/vendor/plugins`. The specific pattern being matched is `vendor/plugins/*/**/test/**/*_test.rb`. An optional `PLUGIN=plugin` argument runs tests on just the specific plugin, meaning the pattern changes to `vendor/plugins/<plugin>/test/**/*_test.rb`. These tests are not run as part of the default test task.
test:recent	Runs tests for any file modified in the last 10 minutes. This means any file in the `/test` directory, plus the unit test for any modified `/app/model` and the functional test for any modified `/app/controller`. Integration tests are not run from this task. Dependencies on other test files are not detected.
test:uncommitted	Runs tests for any file modified since the last Subversion checkin. This task works only if you are using Subversion. Unit tests are run for any changed model files, and functional tests are run for any changed controller files. As I'm reading the current source, it looks like changed test files are not run unless the associated model or controller has also changed.
test:units	Runs all the tests defined in `test/unit`, matching the pattern `test/unit/**/*_test.rb`.

Rake Cleanup Tasks

Rake defines a few tasks to clean up temporary files, as described in the following table. These are guaranteed to be a little bit easier than the Unix command line, or wandering through Windows Explorer dragging files to the Recycle Bin.

Task	Description
log:clear	Resets all files in /log/log* to empty.
tmp:cache:clear	Empties the cache files in the /tmp/cache directory.
tmp:clear	Equivalent to tmp:cache:clear, tmp:session:clear, and temp:sockets:clear. As I write this, tmp:pids:clear is not included in this task.
tmp:create	Recreates the three directories /tmp/cache, /tmp/sessions/, and /tmp/sockets.
tmp:pids:clear	Empties the /tmp/pids directory.
tmp:sessions:clear	Empties the session files in /tmp/sessions.
tmp:sockets:clear	Empties the /tmp/sockets directory.

Rake Rails Tasks

Some of this was touched on in Chapter 2, but Rake defines a few tasks (described in the following table) to allow you to manage the specific version of Rails being used by your project, especially in cases where you expect Rails to change (if you are using Edge) or to differ from one project to the next. The update tasks are useful if you are on Edge and Rails has made a change to the underlying common scripts that were copied to your project space, such as the boot file or the JavaScript libraries.

Task	Description
rails:freeze:edge	Freezes your project to a specific version of Rails, by loading it via Subversion to the /vendor/rails directory. By default, this task uses the current head of the Rails source tree. The optional REVISION=# argument chooses a specific revision number, and the optional TAG=tag argument freezes to a specific tag. The svn Subversion client must be available for this command to work, although the rest of your project need not be managed with Subversion. This command overrides any external declaration being used to keep /vendor/rails up to date with Edge Rails, as described in Chapter 2.
rails:freeze:gems	Freezes your project to a specific version of Rails by unpacking the Rails gems installed with Ruby and placing them in the /vendor/rails directory. This does not affect any non-Rails gems you may have installed.
rails:unfreeze	Undoes a freeze command through the simple mechanism of clearing the /vendor/rails directory.

Table continued on following page

Task	Description
`rails:update`	Equivalent to `rails:update:configs`, `rails:update:javascripts`, and `rails:update:scripts`.
`rails:update:configs`	Updates the `/config/boot.rb` file to the version currently defined by the version of Rails used by the project.
`rails:update:javas-cript`	Updates the public JavaScript (such as the effects and prototype files) to the version defined by the current Rails.
`rails:update:scripts`	Updates the contents of the project `/scripts` directory based on the currently defined version of Rails.

Other Rake Tasks

The following table describes the Rake tasks that don't fit in the previous categories.

Task	Description
`notes`	Equivalent to `notes:fixme`, `notes:optimize`, and `notes:todo`.
`notes:fixme`	Outputs a list of all comments that start with the notation FIXME.
`notes:optimize`	Outputs a list of all comments that start with the notation OPTIMIZE.
`notes:todo`	Outputs a list of all comments that start with the notation TODO.
`routes`	Outputs a list of all defined URL routes. (See Chapter 1 for sample output.)
`stats`	Outputs a list of statistics about the code in the project.

The output of the `notes` commands is a series of entries like this:

```
app/controllers/recipes_controller.rb:
  * [  6] [TODO] Something cool
```

That's the filename, followed by one line for each note. The line consists of the line number, the tag for the comment, and the rest of the comment.

The stats command outputs basic metrics information. At this point, the stats for Soups OnLine look like this:

```
+----------------------+-------+-------+---------+---------+-----+-------+
| Name                 | Lines |   LOC | Classes | Methods | M/C | LOC/M |
+----------------------+-------+-------+---------+---------+-----+-------+
| Controllers          |   366 |   278 |       4 |      31 |   7 |     6 |
| Helpers              |    89 |    75 |       1 |      10 |  10 |     5 |
| Models               |   346 |   283 |       9 |      41 |   4 |     4 |
| Libraries            |     0 |     0 |       0 |       0 |   0 |     0 |
| Components           |     0 |     0 |       0 |       0 |   0 |     0 |
| Integration tests    |     0 |     0 |       0 |       0 |   0 |     0 |
| Functional tests     |   347 |   295 |       6 |      43 |   7 |     4 |
| Unit tests           |   220 |   184 |       6 |      22 |   3 |     6 |
+----------------------+-------+-------+---------+---------+-----+-------+
| Total                |  1368 |  1115 |      26 |     147 |   5 |     5 |
+----------------------+-------+-------+---------+---------+-----+-------+
    Code LOC: 636      Test LOC: 479      Code to Test Ratio: 1:0.8
```

What You Can Do for Rake

No matter how complete the predefined Rake tasks are, there are always going to be tasks specific to your project that you are going to want to automate. Because Rake is just Ruby, it's not hard to write new tasks. And as you might expect, Rails provides a couple of features to make it easy to integrate your custom Rake tasks with your entire Rails project.

The first is autoloading. Any file placed in the /lib/tasks directory and ending with the extension .rake will automatically be loaded when Rake is invoked. This means that you will be able to access your tasks from the same command line invocation of rake as the preexisting tasks, and also that your tasks will be included in the common listing for rake -T. Not only does this allow you to integrate your custom tasks, but it also facilitates keeping the rakefiles under control, because you can group related tasks into their own files.

The second feature is complete access to the Rails environment, including being able to use your ActiveRecord models in your Rake tasks and getting all the nice database connections for free.

A Simple Rake Task

To show you what a typical Rake task looks like, I chose a pretty basic one from the Rails distribution — the log:clear task, which resets all the log files. You can look at the source for all the Rails tasks in vendor/rails/railties/lib/tasks. Here's what log:clear looks like -- the task is named :clear inside a namepsace called :log:

```
namespace :log do
  desc "Truncates all *.log files in log/ to zero bytes"
  task :clear do
    FileList["log/*.log"].each do |log_file|
      f = File.open(log_file, "w")
      f.close
    end
  end
end
```

Although it might be difficult to believe at first, this is 100-percent valid Ruby — or at least, 100-percent valid Ruby plus the added extra methods namespace, desc, and task, all of which are defined by Rake. Rake takes advantage of Ruby's flexible syntax to make ordinary method calls look like system keywords. This is often called a *Domain-specific language* or *DSL*, generically defined as a small language specifically designed for a single task. However, if you want to argue that Rake isn't really a language unto itself, and is more like a fancy API, I'm not going to press the point. No matter what you call it, the end result is a readable, logically structured piece of code to define tasks.

The most important of the methods defined by Rake is task. In the simple form shown here, task takes two arguments, the first of which is a symbol and is the name of the task, and the second of which is a block defining the task. The block is really just more Ruby code, although you'll frequently want to use some Rake-defined helper features. In this task, the block uses one of those features: the file list.

A FileList is just a Ruby class that overrides the array lookup [] operator as a class method, resulting in the somewhat unusual syntax shown in the previous code listing. The FileList creation line could also be written as FileList.new("log/*.log"). In either case, the argument to the file list is one or more glob patterns and the result is an array-like object that contains a list of existing filenames that match the pattern. The file list object is lazy, and doesn't actually evaluate the pattern until it's asked to. In this case, the object is asked to evaluate immediately, when it encounters the each call, which declares another block to be called with each matching filename as an argument. The inner block just opens each file for writing and immediately closes it, neatly erasing all the existing content in the file, while leaving the file intact. In case it's not clear, the base directory of the Rake task is the top-level Rails directory of your project, no matter where the rakefile is actually defined.

The other two special methods manage some logistics. The desc method takes a single string argument and attaches that argument as a documentation string to the next defined task — the string argument is displayed when rake -T is called. The namespace method takes a symbol argument that names the space and a block argument that contains some subset of a rakefile. This provides you with a namespace that serves as a common prefix used to access the tasks defined inside the namespace and that differentiates them from tasks in other namespaces. As a result, the task defined in this code block would be accessed as log:clear, using the namespace around the task as a prefix, rather than just as clear.

Another use of file lists is to specify the set of files to be managed by the default Rake tasks clean and clobber. The clean task is supposed to remove temporary files that might have been explicitly created during builds, and clobber is supposed to remove all gunk that isn't part of the project, no matter how it got there. You can use a file list to define which files should be removed when rake clean or rake clobber is invoked. Each task depends on a constant file list defined in your rakefile with an uppercase name. Here's how to define the file list for clean:

```
CLEAN = FileList['.tmp']
```

The file list for clobber is defined similarly.

Tasks with Dependencies

Although it's undeniably nifty to be able to define tasks with a special syntax and have them converted into a convenient command line utility, so far you haven't seen Rake do anything that you couldn't do almost as easily with plain vanilla Ruby scripts.

The true genius of Rake, and the primary functionality of build files in general, is the ability to enforce task dependencies. This means that you can define a task as being dependent on any number of other arbitrary tasks. Then, any time you run the dependent task, all of the tasks on which it depends are also automatically invoked. Of course, those tasks may themselves be dependent on still other tasks, and the entire task dependency tree is planned out by Rake before any tasks are started.

Build tasks have these kinds of dependencies all over the place — run is dependent on compile, which is dependent on cleanup. Deploy is dependent on test, which is dependent on compile, which is dependent on setup. Having to manage all these relationships manually in your code is a pain, which is why even somewhat awkward build systems like make and Ant can give you huge time savings. An elegant build file system like Rake is even more useful.

Here is a simple example based on the short task described earlier. Suppose you want to institute some kind of logging archive system instead of just clearing logs. To keep this on the simple side, the archive system will consist of copying the log files to an external location, and putting a timestamp in the file names. This implies two tasks, one of which does the copying, and one of which resets the existing files to zero-length. Translated to Rake, it looks like the following code — put this in `lib/cleanup.rake`:

```ruby
namespace :cleanup do

  desc "Timestamp and copy all log files"
  task :archive do
    timestamp = Time.now.strftime('%y_%m_%d_%H_%M_%S')
    FileList["log/*.log"].each do |log_file|
      FileUtils.copy_file(log_file, "#{log_file}.#{timestamp}")
    end
  end

  desc "Truncates all *.log files in log/ to zero bytes"
  task :clear => :archive do
    FileList["log/*.log"].each do |log_file|
      f = File.open(log_file, "w")
      f.close
    end
  end

end
```

The `:archive` task is similar to the log task shown previously, but I did want to point out the Ruby `FileUtils` module, which provides the basic file manipulation functionality that you'd expect from, say, a Unix command line.

The `:clear` task is identical to the previous version of the log task, except for moving it into a different name space, and changing the declaration to `task :clear => :archive`. This declaration defines the

:clear task as being dependent on :archive to run. If you want to define a task with multiple dependencies, then you declare them as an array, like this:

```
Task :clear => [:archive, :email_notification] do
```

If it becomes important, the dependent tasks are evaluated in order. The first task in the list is evaluated (which may include that task's dependencies), then the second task, and so on. Only after all the dependencies have been evaluated is the actual task itself executed. Rake prevents a task from being executed twice, even if it's in the dependency tree multiple times.

Now, with these tasks defined, the rake -T command will display them as follows:

```
rake cleanup:archive         # Timestamp and copy all log files
rake cleanup:clear           # Truncates all *.log files in log/ to zero bytes
```

Running rake cleanup:clear will invoke the archive behavior, and then the clear behavior.

Another useful feature of Rake is that it is extraordinarily flexible about where you declare the dependencies for the task. Task dependencies can be declared separately from the task body. Dependencies can even be declared for the same task in multiple places throughout the rakefile — all the dependencies are merged into a master list when the rakefile is interpreted, and all the dependencies are tracked. So, the clear task in the previous code could have been written like this:

```
desc "Truncates all *.log files in log/ to zero bytes"
task :clear do
  FileList["log/*.log"].each do |log_file|
    f = File.open(log_file, "w")
    f.close
  end
end

task :clear => :archive
```

In fact, copying the entire log:clear task into the custom namespace was not the best way to keep the code maintainable. You can just add the dependency to the existing task from within the custom file — you do need to get around the namespace issue, though. Here's how:

```
namespace :cleanup do

  desc "Timestamp and copy all log files"
  task :archive do
    timestamp = Time.now.strftime('%y_%m_%d_%H_%M_%S')
    FileList["log/*.log"].each do |log_file|
      FileUtils.copy_file(log_file, "#{log_file}.#{timestamp}")
    end
  end
end

task "log:clear" => "cleanup:archive"
```

The extra dependency had to be done outside the namespace to allow the two different namespace prefixes to be properly resolved. At this point, running the existing `log:clear` task will trigger the custom `cleanup:archive` task.

You can, and often will, have `rake` tasks that have no body of their own, but simply consist of a list of dependency tasks that you want to group together. Here's an example from one of the standard Rails rakefiles, `tmp:clear`:

```
desc "Clear session, cache, and socket files from tmp/"
task :clear => [ "tmp:sessions:clear", "tmp:cache:clear", "tmp:sockets:clear"]
```

The `tmp:clear` task doesn't do anything on its own. It just ensures that the three component clear tasks are called.

Like all of Ruby's freedoms, the capability to specify dependencies willy-nilly should be used judiciously, so that you don't lose all ability to predict what will happen when you call a task in your rakefile. Rake itself can help you out, though — calling `rake -P` gives you a list of all tasks with their immediate dependencies. At this very moment, that output basically reads as follows:

```
rake log:clear
    cleanup:archive
```

File Tasks

There is another mechanism for defining tasks in Rake, based explicitly on transforming files, and called, conveniently enough, a *file task* (programmers and their silly names). The file task model is extremely similar to the classic makefile syntax for compilation. Because compilation is not part of the standard Rails workflow, you may not use file task syntax very often, but it's a very powerful way to manage a certain type of file-transformation task.

Continuing with the theme of dealing with log files, suppose that you wanted to convert your log files into HTML for display in some kind of web-based administration tool. The initial core of that tool might be a Rake task like this:

```
file "log/development.html" => "log/development.log" do |task|
  LogConverter.convert(:input => task.prerequisites[0], :output => task.name)
end
```

`LogConverter`, by the way, is a fictional log file to a HTML generator that is driving this example — it doesn't really exist, so this example won't work as written. You can see from this example that the syntax of a file task is relatively similar to the syntax of a regular task. The task name is the file that is going to be created, and the dependency list contains the files that are going to be used as the input. Within the task body, the attribute `name` of the task object contains the string name of the task, which is to say, the output file, and the attribute `prerequisites` contains an array of the input files.

The input files may themselves have Rake tasks defined for them, in which case those tasks are resolved first just as any other dependant task would be managed. This would be the case, for example, in a typical C compilation structure, where the actual application might consist of linking several libraries together, and each library might need to be compiled from several different source files.

The task listed in the previous code listing would be invoked as `rakelog/development.html`, which is something of a mouthful, so it's not uncommon to define a regular task as a wrapper around the file task like this:

```
task :convert_log => "log/development.html"
```

Then `rake convert_log` will invoke the file task.

"Ah," you say, "that's nice if there's only one log file, but there might be several, and I certainly don't want to track them all individually." Luckily, you don't have to — you can use a `FileList` and the fact that Rake allows dependencies to be created flexibly.

The exact mechanism depends slightly on whether you want all the input files to be grouped into one output file or not. If so, you can build up the dependencies in the loop, and then define the actual task after the loop. For example:

```
FileList["log/*.log"].each do |log_file|
  file "log/development.html" => log_file
end

file "log/development.html" do |t|
  LogConverter.convert(:input => t.prerequisites, :output => t.name)
end

task :convert_logs => "log/develpment.html"
```

Inside the `each` loop, the output file task gains a new dependency for each element of the list. The body of the task is defined only after the loop is complete, but all the prerequisites remain defined. Again, there's a wrapper task to make the calling easier.

If each log file is going to a different output file, then each output file needs a separate task created from the list, and the dependencies are managed by the wrapper task. You can create each file task dynamically as follows:

```
FileList["log/*.log"] each do |log_file|
  outfile = log_file.split(".")[0] + ".html"
  file outfile => log_file do |t|
    LogConverter.convert(:input => t.prerequisites, :output => t.name)
  end
  task :convert_logs => outfile
end
```

Using Rails in Rake

Giving your Rake task access to your ActiveRecord objects or other classes defined in your Rails project is absurdly simple — just create a dependency to the task `:environment`. That was easy, right?

Here's a modest example. In Chapter 3, you made a lot of use of the `Token` class, which expires after a set period of time. Although tokens are often deleted on usage, it is possible from the definition of the class as written that a token would be created, never used, and would just hang around clogging up the database forever. It sure would be nice to have some kind of automated task that would check the database to see if there were any expired tokens and remove them. Luckily, it's not very much work. Put this in any lib/*.rake file:

```
desc "Remove old tokens from the database"
task :tokens => :environment do
  old_tokens = Token.find(:all, :conditions => ["expires_at < ?", Time.now])
  old_tokens.each { |token| token.destroy }
end
```

The code here should be straightforward Ruby and ActiveRecord. The only Rails-specific feature is the addition of the :environment task to ensure that Rails is loaded.

The find call could have been written differently:

```
old_tokens = Token.find(:all).select { |token| token.is_expired? }
```

Now that's a hair more readable and already uses written model functionality. However, the second version is likely to be significantly slower because it will cause the database to return all Token records before filtering, whereas the first version does the filtering in the database itself.

Testing Rake Tasks

I've broken somewhat with precedent in this section, because I have not presented test-first automated tests for the Rake tasks I've defined. The unfortunate fact is most developers don't write tests for their build scripts, even in projects that are otherwise well tested. (Yes, I speak from experience.) Many of the tasks you're going to put in your Rake script are going to be important, though, and it would be useful to at least leave open the option of testing them. Here are a couple of strategies that will help you test your Rake files.

Direct Testing

One strategy is to actually dynamically load your rakefile and call Rake from inside the unit test. There's a trick or two to doing this successfully. The code to test the Token clean up task that you just wrote looks like this (you can put this file in test/unit/rake_test.rb):

```
require File.dirname(__FILE__) + '/../test_helper'
require 'rake'

class RakeTest < Test::Unit::TestCase
  fixtures :tokens

  def setup
    @rake = Rake::Application.new
    Rake.application = @rake
    @rake.load File.dirname(__FILE__) + '/../../lib/tasks/cleanup.rake'
    @rake.load File.dirname(__FILE__) +
               '/../../vendor/rails/railties/lib/tasks/misc.rake'
  end

  def teardown
    Rake.application = nil
  end
```

(continued)

(continued)

```
    def test_token_cleanup
      assert_difference('Token.count', -2) do
        @rake["cleanup:tokens"].invoke
      end
    end
  end
end
```

Thanks to Nick Sieger and his blog at `http://blog.nicksieger.com` *for hints on successfully testing the Rake task.*

Let's look at this code one step at a time. After requiring the Rails `test_helper` file, you also need to require Rake itself. Then you use the `setup` and `teardown` features of the RubyUnit test framework. In the setup, you create a new instance of a Rake `Application` class. The Rake application object is an attribute of the main `Rake` class, which is a Singleton-like object that manages all the Rake functionality, so you need to register the application to the Rake class.

The application object can then load the `cleanup.rake` file from its location in your project's `/lib/tasks` directory. In addition, you also need to load all the Rake files from all the tasks you'll need in the dependency tree. In this case, the only task needed is the `environment` task, which is defined in the Rails `lib/tasks` directory. This is where the testing gets somewhat brittle. For one thing, you need to know which Rails rakefiles contain the tasks you need. The task also becomes dependent on using Rails in the `/vendor/rails` directory. Both of these potential issues can be mitigated. You can use the `RAILS_ROOT` constant to determine where Rails is located. From there, you could load all the `.rake` files, which would decrease maintenance time and potentially increase the run time. Then you undo it all in the `teardown` method by setting the application attribute back to `nil`.

The application object can be treated as a hash-like object where the keys are the names of the loaded tasks and the values are the tasks themselves, which can then be invoked using the conveniently named `invoke` method. The test uses the `assert_difference` block method to determine that two of the fixtures loaded are removed by the Rake task called inside the block.

When the test passes, add the file to Subversion and commit it.

Indirect Testing

Testing the Rake task directly is a useful mechanism, and the best way to test the interaction between a Rake task and the tasks it depends on. However, it involves the overhead of loading the Rake environment (and in this case, loading Rails within Rake), which could make for slower or harder-to-maintain tests. Also, many Rake tests interact with portions of the system with a complexity that may be hard to recreate in a test environment.

When dealing with a structure in your project that is hard to test directly, a common strategy is to put as much code as possible in a regular object or structure and make the hard-to-test layer as thin as possible. For example, Rails views are difficult to test precisely without making the tests fragile, which is one reason why the push is always to move the code logic to a helper or to the model.

In the case of Rake, this would also involve writing the bulk of the code for your tasks in a helper method or class, and then just calling that class from within Rake. Now, the two line token cleanup might not be the best way to show off this mechanism, but the cleanup functionality could easily be placed in the `Token` model class like this:

```
def self.cleanup_expired
  old_tokens = Token.find(:all, :conditions => ["expires_at < ?", Time.now])
  old_tokens.each { |token| token.destroy }
end
```

This method could be tested with a simple method in the `test/unit/token_test.rb` unit test suite, without going through the rigmarole of loading in Rake. For example:

```
def test_token_cleanup
  assert_difference('Token.count', -2) do
    Token.cleanup_expired
  end
end
```

And the Rake task would just be this:

```
desc "Remove old tokens from the database"
task :tokens => :environment do
  Token.cleanup_expired
end
```

This tests every part of the functionality except the last mile of whether it works within the Rake environment. For a task with complex logic that doesn't depend on Rake very much, this could well be a good tradeoff.

Continuous Integration

So far, I've been talking about automating build tasks in the sense of allowing complex tasks to be repeated at will with a single command. Although this is very cool and useful, it would be even more useful if complex tasks could be repeated automatically without any manual intervention. The two tools in this section allow you to do just that.

Fully automatic build tasks are most notably used for running tests and for deployment. For now, the focus is on testing. (Deployment will be covered in a future chapter.) A fully automated test tool continually runs your project's test suite whenever it detects a change. Several continuous test tools aimed at Ruby or Rails have been created, and it's not clear as of this writing that any one of them has established itself as the best and brightest. One tool, ZenTest, runs best locally on the developer's machine, while another, CruiseControl.rb, is designed to be placed either on a local machine or a common build server.

ZenTest

ZenTest is a Ruby testing utility that has a number of interesting features, including the capability to automatically create stub tests for methods in your project, and some utilities for improving the output and structure of your Rails tests. The feature under discussion here is called Autotest, and it's a nice way to continuously run automated tests on your development box.

ZenTest is distributed as a Ruby gem. To get it, try the following:

```
gem install ZenTest
```

Depending on your operating system, you may have to run this as `sudo`. Also, you may be prompted to download a couple of dependencies. After ZenTest is installed, move to your project's root directory, and type the following command:

```
$ autotest
```

All the tests in your suite will run, but when the run is over, the program will not exit — instead, it will sit and wait. While Autotest is running, anytime you save a file within your Rails project, Autotest will re-trigger all or part of your test suite.

When you have failing tests, Autotest will try to run the failing test files first, and then move to running the entire test suite only after those tests pass. This is very convenient, allowing you to focus on only the small number of failing tests. When your tests are passing, Autotest will try to run the the associated tests when you save a file -- saving a test file will rerun that test class, saving a model or controller will run the associated test file. Also, because Autotest does not have to reload the Ruby interpreter every time it reruns the tests, it runs the tests more quickly. At any time, you can type Control+C in the Autotest console to rerun the entire test suite. Press Control+C twice to exit out of Autotest.

Autotest does not use the Rake test tasks to identify what tests are available. Instead, it uses its own mechanism to determine what tests need to be run (this is noticeable because unlike the default Rake task, Autotest runs all tests in alphabetical order, regardless of whether they are unit or functional tests). However, Autotest does know the structure of Rails programs, and as long as you aren't modifying the predefined Rake test tasks, you should be okay. However, Autotest's management of fixtures appears to be slightly different than the default Rake tasks, and as a result, you might have some issues if your various tests load different sets of fixtures — you can have tests pass in Autotest and fail in Rake, and vice versa. Most of the issues seem to be resolvable if you load all the fixtures in your `test/test_helper.rb` file, ensuring that every test has the same set of fixtures.

If you do get into trouble, Autotest allows you to modify its default behavior through the use of an `.autotest` configuration file in your home directory. Using this file, you can specify arbitrary blocks of Ruby code to run at different points in the Autotest cycle.

The basic structure of the blocks that you might place in your `.autotest` file is as follows:

```
Autotest.add_hook :run do |at|
   ## your code here
end
```

`:run` is the name of the type of hook — in this case indicating behavior to be performed before a test run. Possible hooks are `:all_good`, `:green`, `:initialize`, `:interrupt`, `:ran_command`, `:reset`, `:run`, `:red`, `:run_command`, and `:quit`.

CruiseControl.rb

CruiseControl.rb is the Ruby and Rails version of the highly popular Java-based CruiseControl tool by ThoughtWorks. CruiseControl.rb is much simpler to set up than its Java brother, but it also more strongly encourages a specific project structure. Specifically, CruiseControl.rb requires you to use Subversion, and it's easier to set up if you happen to have a project where the default Rake task runs your complete test suite. And since you just happen to have one of those, it's time to give it a whirl.

Setting up CruiseControl.rb is pretty simple. Head to `http://cruisecontrolrb.thoughtworks.com`, download using the provided link, and unpack the archive file someplace useful. To associate your project with CruiseControl.rb, you need to open a command line on the top directory of the unpacked archive, and run the following command:

```
$ ./cruise add soupsonline --url svn://<hostname>/soupsonline/trunk
```

Generically, of course, the argument after the `--url` is the URL you use to specify the location of your Subversion repository. Remember to include `/trunk`; otherwise, nothing will work right. If you are using CruseControl locally, rather than on a remote server, the URL can be a file URL such as this:

```
$ ./cruise add soupsonline -- url file:///usr/local/subversion/soupsonline/trunk
```

At this point, CruiseControl will checkout the project from the server, and then attempt to run the default Rake task of the project once.

In your case, this will initially fail, because of the way I told you to set up your project in Subversion. Specifically, you did not include a `database.yml` file because of the possibility that different developers would need different database setups. However, without a `database.yml` file, Rails will not run. To fix this, head for the `<cruise_home>/projects/soupsonline/work` directory, which is the top directory of the project checkout. Then head to the `config` directory, and copy the `database.yml.template` file, renaming it `database.yml`.

Then you can start the CruiseControl server back from your command line with the following:

```
$ ./cruise start
```

From a web browser, enter the URL `http://localhost:3333`, and you'll see something like what's shown in Figure 4-1.

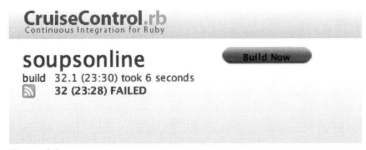

Figure 4-1

Click the Build Now button to trigger another build. This one should be successful. (As you can see, the screen shot was actually taken after I triggered the successful build, which took six seconds. The failed build after the initial checkout is numbered 32, matching the subversion revision number. I saved the database file without a subversion checkin, which triggered a passing build numbered 32.1.)

When the CruiseControl server is running, it will query the Subversion repository every 30 seconds — a default that you can change. If it detects a commit, it will perform a new checkout, run the test task and report the results in the web application. (You can also configure email and RSS reporting.) CruiseControl will see only the files that have already been committed, so it's a good way to ensure that you haven't forgotten to add files to your repository. Note the difference between Autotest, which runs on every save, and CruiseControl, which runs on every commit. Autotest is more of an individual tool, whereas CruiseControl is designed to support teams of developers.

> *As of this writing, CruseControl is incompatable with Ruby 1.8.6 due to a known bug in Ruby that causes CruiseControl to never report failure from a failed unit test. This issue should be patched by the time you read this. CruiseControl does work with Ruby 1.8.4 and 1.8.5.*

From this main display, you can trigger another build, or use an RSS feed that will contain build information. Clicking on either the successful or unsuccessful build note reveals more information about the test, as shown in Figure 4-2.

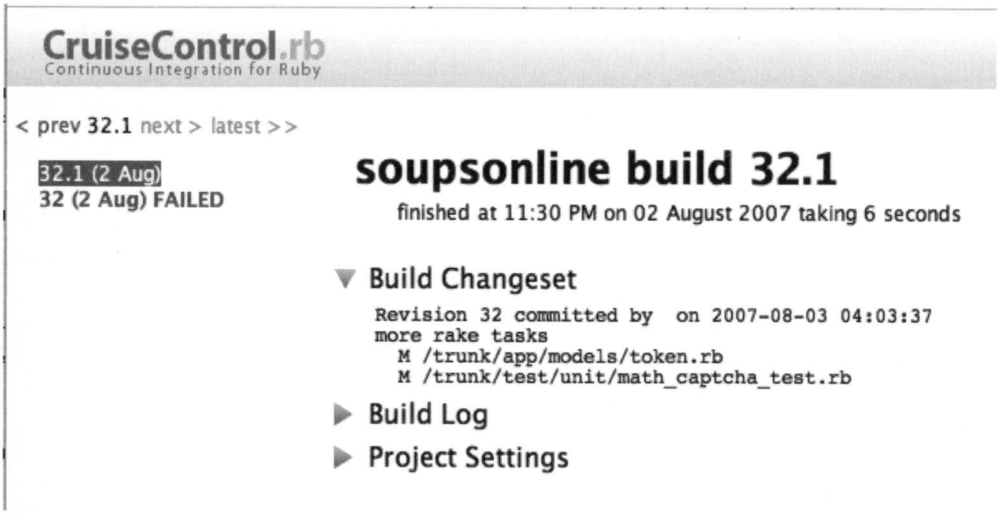

CruiseControl.rb
Continuous Integration for Ruby

< prev **32.1** next > latest >>

32.1 (2 Aug)
32 (2 Aug) FAILED

soupsonline build 32.1

finished at 11:30 PM on 02 August 2007 taking 6 seconds

▼ **Build Changeset**

Revision 32 committed by   on 2007-08-03 04:03:37
more rake tasks
  M /trunk/app/models/token.rb
  M /trunk/test/unit/math_captcha_test.rb

▶ **Build Log**

▶ **Project Settings**

Figure 4-2

The project settings enable you to change the default Rake task run to start a build, or to avoid Rake altogether and designate a shell command to run instead. The build log has the messages that would go to the Rails testing log for that build.

Typically, you wouldn't put CruiseControl on a development machine. You'd be more likely to put it on a central server (possibly the same machine that has the repository), and it would be used to provide quick feedback on how various developer's changes interact. Even if you are on your own, however, the continual build functionality is useful to provide a record of your development history.

Resources

Rake documentation is online at `http://rake.rubyforge.org`. This link shows you the RDoc, and additional tutorials are linked from there. A very good tutorial and description of why Rake is so nice compared to other build languages (such as Ant) are available at `http://martinfowler.com/articles/rake.html`.

Autotest is part of the ZenTest suite. What documentation there is can be found at `www.zenspider.com/ZSS/Products/ZenTest`. This site also includes some other test tools that are mentioned in Chapter 7.

Mac users who use the Growl notification utility should know that Autotest can send Growl messages — just include `require autotest/growl` in your `.autotest` file. More information on customizing that window is available at `http://blog.codefront.net/2007/04/01/get-your-testing-results-via-growl-notifications` by Chu Yeow and `http://blog.internautdesign.com/2006/11/12/autotest-growl-goodness` by David Lowenfels.

Full documentation on CruiseControl.rb is available at `http://cruisecontrolrb.thoughtworks.com/documentation/docs`.

Summary

Automated build tasks are very important to the success of a project. The Ruby tool for defining and running these tasks is Rake. Rake creates a structure for defining tasks that are dependent on other tasks. Rails augments Rake by defining several tasks for managing tests, the database, documentation, and Rails versioning.

You can also define your own Rake tasks and have them be visible at the command line with the predefined Rails tasks. Rake syntax is Ruby with a few special methods that create a domain-specific language for task definition. With a little bit of additional structure, you can also add unit tests to cover your Rake tasks.

Continuous integration tools run your tests on every save or commit. The Autotest utility runs the test suite locally, and CruiseControl.rb is designed to run the test suite on a remote server.

## 5

Navigation and Social Networking

When you last looked at the Soups OnLine application, you had just added user logins. However, you haven't actually given the users very much to do besides create an account and add and edit their own recipes. Right now, the users have no way to browse the site or find recipes based on ingredients or keywords. It also would be nice if users could provide feedback on recipes and see the feedback that other users have left.

Menus and Sidebars

The simple tab-like menu or sidebar is the most common user interface element on the Web. In this section, you'll see how to create a simple menu using some HTML and Rails-supported logic.

Single-Level Menus

Rails, unsurprisingly, has some built-in-support for the logic needed to manage a menu list. The logic involved is to simply display a link to another page unless that page is the active page, in which case do something else — usually display the text without the actual link. The Rails method is link_to_unless_current, and you use it in a menu something like this:

```
<li>
  <%= link_to_unless_current "Home",
    {:controller => "recipes", :action => "home"} %>
</li>
<li>
  <%= link_to_unless_current "Recipes",
    {:controller => "recipes", :action => "index"} %>
</li>
```

(continued)

(continued)

```
<li>
  <%= link_to_unless_current "Categories",
    {:controller => "recipes", :action => "categories"} %>
</li>
<li>
  <%= link_to_unless_current "Authors",
    {:controller => "recipes", :action => "authors"} %>
</li>
<li>
  <%= link_to_unless_current "Community",
    {:controller => "recipes", :action => "community"} %>
</li>
<li>
  <%= link_to_unless_current "Gear",
    {:controller => "gear", :action => "index"} %>
</li>
```

This is a drop-in replacement for the Navigate sidebar in the `recipes.html.erb` layout file. Because you're going to want this to become rather generic, put this code in a partial — I call mine `app/views/shared/_navigation_sidebar.html.erb`. Then you can drop in the call from the layout file like this:

```
<li id="menu" class="bg6">
  <h2 class="bg1">Navigate</h2>
  <ul>
    <%= render :partial => "/shared/navigation_sidebar" %>
  </ul>
</li>
```

Functionally, this is identical to the list that was there before, except that the active page will no longer be displayed as a link. (I would show you this in a screenshot, but given the current color and display scheme, the distinction wouldn't really play in black and white.)

This code works, but it's pretty ugly and repetitive. What you really want is to make this data-driven, storing the link data somewhere, and then looping over it to create the menu. The obvious first question is how to define the data structure. This being Rails, the obvious first answer would be to save the links as ActiveRecord models and store them in the database. I'm going to look past that first answer in this case, though. The data model for the links isn't very complex, and more to the point, it isn't going to change very often. At this point, I think ActiveRecord would be overkill. If I had a much more complex data structure, I might consider it — especially if I felt that I was going to need online link-editing functionality (which I don't in this case).

You do need to put the data somewhere in some kind of structure, though. The data that needs to be saved includes the order in which the captions appear in the menu and the set of URL options associated with each caption. You could store the data as a list of lists, or a hash and a list, but at some point it's just easier to encapsulate it into a couple of objects.

You will need one object to represent the items. I put this in `app/models/menu_sidebar.rb` as follows (although `lib/menu_sidebar.rb` is also a reasonable location):

```ruby
class MenuSidebarItem

  attr_accessor :caption, :option_hash

  def initialize(caption, option_hash = {})
    @caption = caption
    @option_hash = option_hash
  end

end
```

Then I put another object for the sidebar as a whole in the same file, like this:

```ruby
class MenuSidebar

  attr_accessor :items

  def self.load_from_list(list_items)
    sidebar = MenuSidebar.new
    list_items.each do | caption, options |
      sidebar.append_link(caption, options)
    end
    sidebar
  end

  def initialize
    @items = []
  end

  def append_link(caption, url_option_hash = {})
    items << MenuSidebarItem.new(caption, url_option_hash)
  end

end
```

I've got no tests on this yet, on the somewhat dubious grounds that the objects aren't doing anything interesting yet beyond holding data. (Well, the collection object is loading objects, but more on that in a moment.)

This transforms the clunky menu sidebar view into the somewhat more elegant loop shown here:

```erb
<% menu_sidebar.items.each do |item| %>
  <li><%= link_to_unless_current item.caption, item.option_hash %></li>
<% end %>
```

That's a lot better, but it does beg the question of where to store the data. A first pass might be to put the data in a helper method that creates the sidebar, in app/helpers/application_helper.rb:

```ruby
def menu_sidebar
  MenuSidebar.load_from_list([
    ["Home", {:controller => "recipes", :action => "home"}],
    ["Recipes", {:controller => "recipes", :action => "index"}],
    ["Categories", {:controller => "recipes", :action => "categories"}],
    ["Authors", {:controller => "recipes", :action => "authors"}],
    ["Community", {:controller => "recipes", :action => "community"}],
    ["Gear", {:controller => "gear", :action => "index"}]
    ])
end
```

There are basically two problems with this — first is that it's kind of ugly to put data inside the helper, and second and more importantly is that it's a performance issue because the sidebar item is being recreated on every page hit. You're going to want to cache the item somewhere.

One way to address the data inside the helper is to move the data to an external file. Fortunately, there is an external file format already blessed as part of the Rails family. Here's the menu data as a YAML file, which I placed in `config/menu.yml`:

```
-
  - Home
  - controller: recipes
    action: home

-
  - Recipes
  - controller: recipes
    action: index

-
  - Categories
  - controller: recipies
    action: categories

-
  - Authors
  - controller: recipes
    action: authors

-
  - Community
  - controller: recipes
    action: community

-
  - Gear
  - controller: gear
    action: index
```

This YAML file resolves to the exact same data structure as the list shown previously, and at least in my opinion, it's going to be a little easier to maintain long-term. For those of you who are not fully versed in the wonders of YAML, the dashes indicate lists, a colon indicates a key/value pair, and the indentation indicates structure. In this case, it's a nested list, where each menu item has an inner list consisting of a caption and then the key/value pairs of the URL option hash. Again, look at the Ruby list in the previous example to get a sense of the YAML-to-Ruby translation.

This is not the only way to specify a YAML file for this data. Specifically, it's not what you would get if you dumped the `MenuSidebar` object directly to YAML — doing that would add a fair amount of YAML structure to the file to fully describe the MenuSidebar Ruby object, which would make it a little bit harder to maintain. However, the format I used does require the YAML file to be parsed to create the Rails data structure. Luckily, that's not very difficult — in `app/models/menu_sidebar.rb`, add the following class method to the `MenuSidebar` class:

```
def self.load_from_yaml(filename)
  result = MenuSidebar.new
  File.open(filename) do |f|
    YAML.load(f).each do |item_data|
      result.append_link(*item_data)
    end
  end
  result
end
```

The helper method in `app/helpers/application_helper.rb` must now be changed to this:

```
def menu_sidebar
  MenuSidebar.load_from_yaml(File.join(RAILS_ROOT, 'config', 'menu.yml'))
end
```

With this code in place, the menu item corresponding to the currently active page will show up as plain text, and all the others will show up as a list. That's fine, but you probably also want to actively call attention to the current page, or make its display distinctive somehow. Rails allows you to override the default behavior of `link_to_unless_current` by passing in a block to be executed when the page is current. A simple change would be to place the text in a custom CSS class. The `app/views/shared/_navigation_sidebar` partial would look like this:

```
<% menu_sidebar.items.each do |item| %>
  <li>
    <%= link_to_unless_current item.caption, item.option_hash do |name|
      content_tag :span, name, :class => "current_item"
    end %>
  </li>
<% end %>
```

The punctuation on that block call may seem a little counterintuitive. It's somewhat atypical in that the entire function being called with the block argument is actually inside a single ERB output tag containing the entire block. It's more common to have the block start and end lines inside ERB `evaluate` tags and have the body of the block be outside those tags — in the typical case, the contents of the block are meant to be evaluated by ERB. Because the entire goal of the `link_to_unless_current` method is to return a string as part of the response output, and the block just defines the alternate string to be displayed, enclosing the entire call in the output tags is the cleanest way to get everything to work right. Personally, I'm never quite sure of the best way to lay this out — should the `end` command line up with the beginning of the output tag of the line that starts the block (as shown here), or should it line up with the actual start of the method call, as it would in a regular Ruby layout? If the contents of the block were to get at all complicated, I would move the whole thing to a helper file, and just call the helper here.

The block argument for `link_to_unless_current` is shown here taking a single argument, `name`, which is the name being displayed (and is the first argument to the outside call). There's a second form of the block that takes the same argument list as the outside call, which you can use if you want to do something more complex with the data — the method will correctly interpret the arguments based on whether you pass one argument to the block or more than one.

For this example to actually change the presentation of the display, you also need to define a CSS class for `current_item` in your `scaffold.css` file. What to do there is up to you. I opted for the following simple color change to red for the link:

```
.current_item {
  color: #f00;
}
```

Figure 5-1 shows the ultimate result, albeit in black-and-white. Remember that not all of these links have been defined yet, so they don't all go to actual parts of the site.

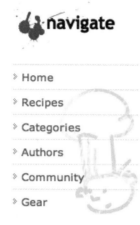

Figure 5-1

Object Cache

There's one performance problem with the code as presented. The YAML file is being reloaded and reparsed on every page load. Because the exact same `MenuSidebar` object is being created each time, this seems to be redundant. One way to avoid this problem is to cache the `MenuSidebar` object after it is created. The unit test that needs to be created in `test/unit/menu_sidebar_test.rb` for this functionality is as follows:

```
require File.dirname(__FILE__) + '/../test_helper'
require 'menu_sidebar'

class MenuSidebarTest < Test::Unit::TestCase

  def test_load_from_yaml
    file = File.dirname(__FILE__) + '/../fixtures/menu.yml'
    assert_equal(0, MenuSidebar.cache.size)
    menu = MenuSidebar.load_from_yaml(file)
    assert_equal(6, menu.items.size)
    assert_equal(1, MenuSidebar.cache.size)
    assert_equal(file, MenuSidebar.cache.keys[0])
    assert_equal(6, MenuSidebar.cache.values[0].items.size)
```

```
        menu = MenuSidebar.load_from_yaml(file)
        assert_equal(1, MenuSidebar.cache.size)
    end

end
```

You will need to copy the menu.yml file to the test/fixtures directory so that you can run tests against it and the tests won't break when you change the actual application menu.

In this test, don't actually try to load the menu.yml file using the standard test fixtures helper. That won't work because Rails will assume that there is a menus table in the database and try to load the fixture to the database — but there isn't a menus table. Just load the file in the actual test.

The test first asserts that the cache is empty, and then that the menu YAML file loads. After the load, the test verifies that the cache now has one element, whose key is the filename the menu was loaded from, and whose value is the MenuSidebar object. Finally, the test loads the file again and verifies that the cache has not grown.

To implement this cache, you can use a nice feature of Ruby where a Hash can be declared with a block argument. The block argument takes two arguments: the hash itself and a key. The block is then invoked any time there is an attempt to get the value of a hash key that does not exist. The typical behavior within this block is to return a default value and optionally populate the hash with that default value. In this case, the key will be the filename, and the block will read in the YAML file and place it in the hash. A second call to the hash will just return the menu object without reloading the file. Here's the relevant section of menu_sidebar.rb:

```ruby
@@cache = Hash.new do |hash, filename|
  hash[filename] = MenuSidebar.read_from_yaml(filename)
end

def self.cache
  @@cache
end

def self.read_from_yaml(filename)
  result = MenuSidebar.new
  File.open(filename) do |f|
    YAML.load(f).each do |item_data|
      result.append_link(*item_data)
    end
  end
  result
end

def self.load_from_yaml(filename)
  @@cache[filename]
end
```

The code now separates the read_from_yaml behavior away from the load_from_yaml method. The preexisting load_from_yaml method now just does a lookup in the new @@cache class variable. The call to actually read the YAML file is now in the block declared when the @@cache is defined. With this caching in place, performance of the menu system will improve.

Tagging

One of the key elements of Web 2.0 is the concept of *tagging*, giving each item in your database an arbitrary number of keyword tags and using those tags to structure the user's interface to the data. Allowing users to tag items allows for a richer categorization of the data, and doesn't restrict items to just a single category. From the perspective of a user browsing the data, tags allow for a quick way to find related items quickly.

Installing the Acts As Taggable Plugin

From Rails, tagging is managed with a plugin named Acts As Taggable On Steroids, or AATOS. (Why the name? Because it's a replacement for a previously created Acts As Taggable plugin — apparently you need to inject illegal substances to improve your tag plugins these days.) Anyway, the AATOS plugin provides support for adding tags to an arbitrary ActiveRecord model in your project.

To start using AATOS, you need to first install the plugin. Most Rails plugins are distributed via a Subversion server, which you can load into your project, or if you are also using Subversion to manage your project, you can add the plugin site as an external site (in the same way that Edge Rails is added as an external site). The standard Rails mechanism for installing a plugin is the provided `plugin install` script. Installing AATOS via this command looks like this:

```
$ ruby script/plugin install
-x http://svn.viney.net.nz/things/rails/plugins/acts_as_taggable_on_steroids
```

The URL is the address of the Subversion server for the plugin. The `-x` option adds the plugin to your local Subversion repository as an external site — if you don't need that feature, just remove the `-x`. Running this command will add a bunch of files to the `vendor/plugins/acts_as_taggable_on_steroids` directory.

To start using the plugin, you first need to make some changes to your database schema. The plugin will automatically generate a migration file if you ask it nicely with the following command:

```
$ ruby script/generate acts_as_taggable_migration
```

The migration sets up one table for the tags themselves and another table to manage the association between the tags and another `ActiveRecord` object, like this:

```
class ActsAsTaggableMigration < ActiveRecord::Migration
  def self.up
    create_table :tags do |t|
      t.column :name, :string
    end

    create_table :taggings do |t|
      t.column :tag_id, :integer
      t.column :taggable_id, :integer
      t.column :taggable_type, :string
      t.column :created_at, :datetime
    end

    add_index :taggings, :tag_id
```

```
        add_index :taggings, [:taggable_id, :taggable_type]
    end

    def self.down
      drop_table :taggings
      drop_table :tags
    end
  end
```

A tag is simply a string. The association uniquely identifies an external object via the combination of taggable_type, representing the class name of the object, and taggable_id, representing its ID number, this is a standard Rails mechanism that will be discussed in Chapter 6. Run the migration using rake db:migrate to apply the changes to your development database.

Applying Tags to a Model

After the migration has been applied, adding tags to any model is quite easy. To declare the ActiveRecord model as taggable, call the method acts_as_taggable at the top of the class, right along the place where you declare database relationships:

```
class Recipe < ActiveRecord::Base

  acts_as_taggable
  has_many :ingredients, :order => "order_of ASC", :dependent => :destroy
  belongs_to :user

  #
  # rest of class definition
  #
end
```

Basic Tag API

Declaring the model as taggable gives you a simple API to set, change, and search for tags. The following unit test, added to recipe_test.rb, shows the expected behavior:

```
def test_is_taggable
  recipe = Recipe.find(1)
  assert recipe.tag_list.blank?
  recipe.tag_list = "yummy, vegetarian"
  recipe.save
  assert !recipe.tag_list.blank?
  recipe.tag_list.remove "yummy"
  assert_equal("vegetarian", recipe.tag_list.to_s)
  recipe.tag_list.add("french")
  assert_equal("vegetarian, french", recipe.tag_list.to_s)
  recipe.save
  should_be_recipe = Recipe.find_tagged_with("vegetarian")
  assert_equal(1, should_be_recipe[0].id)
  should_also_be_recipe = Recipe.find_tagged_with("vegetarian, French",
      :match_all => true)
  assert_equal(1, should_also_be_recipe[0].id)
end
```

The basic attribute for handling tags is `tag_list`, generated by the plugin declaration, which is an instance of the plugin class `TagList`. You will rarely deal with `tag_list` directly — all of your interaction with this attribute is via string objects, which are parsed or generated by the `TagList` object for communication with the outside world.

For example, in the test, the tag list is created by setting `tag_list` to "yummy, vegetarian". Internally, the taggable plugin parses the list and converts it to two tags. The default delimiter is a comma, but you can change that by setting the class attribute `Tag.delimiter`. So the following line of code in `config/environment.rb` would set the tag delimiter to a space:

```
Tag.delimiter = " "
```

When the ActiveRecord is saved to the database, the taggable plugin manages the tags. It saves two tags to the database, and associates them with the recipe instance. The `tag_list` has relatively few methods of its own, but you can query to see if the list is blank, and you can add and remove tags from the list as shown — the test removes `yummy` and replaces it with `French`.

Retrieving recipes based on their tags is achieved via the `find_tagged_with` method defined by the plugin. The argument to the record is a string of all the tags you are trying to match, separated by the current tag delimiter. So `Recipe.find_tagged_with("vegetarian")` returns a list with a single recipe object. If you include more than one tag in the argument list, then the default behavior is to return any object that contains any of the tags — a logical OR search. If you want the search to match only recipes that contain all the tags in the argument list, then you must also pass the `:match_all => true` argument, as the next-to-last line of the previous test does.

Caching Tags

The AATOS program does a nice job of seamlessly integrating tagging across your ActiveRecord models. One potential problem in a production environment is the performance of a tag search, because the search has to go through several joins to make everything work. You can improve performance by caching the tag lists for each object. The plugin makes this relatively simple. To get the ball rolling, you create the following migration:

```
$ ruby script/generate migration cache_tags
```

This creates an empty migration file, which Rails will name `db/migrate/006_cache_tags.rb`. Within that file, add a column to any ActiveRecord model that contains tags you want to cache. For example:

```
class CacheTags < ActiveRecord::Migration
  def self.up
    add_column :recipes, :cached_tag_list, :string
  end

  def self.down
    remove_column :recipes, :cached_tag_list
  end
end
```

After the migration is written, you need to run `rake db:migrate` to apply the change to the database.

The default name for the list of cached tags is, oddly enough, `cached_tag_list`. If, for some reason, that name offends you or conflicts with an existing name in your project, you may use any arbitrary name you'd like. If you do choose to get creative with the naming, you need to add the following line in your `ActiveRecord` class telling the plugin what column name you've chosen:

```
set_cached_tag_list_column_name "YOUR NAME HERE"
```

No matter which name you choose, the plugin will use a cached list if one is available. The cache will automatically be updated whenever the `tag_list` attribute is modified or the `TagList` add and remove methods are called. If you have some need to get fancy and manipulate the tag list manually you can update the cached version by calling the instance method `save_cached_tag_list`.

Tags and the User Interface

To complete the addition of tags to the Soups OnLine user experience, you need a way for the tags to get into the data in the first place, as well as a way for the prospective user to see and browse tags.

Entering Tag Data

At this point, it's actually very little additional work to get the tags into the database. Because the taggable plugin manages the `tag_list` attribute for setting and saving, all the rest of the code needs to do is get the tag list value to the appropriate place for ActiveRecord to be able to manage it.

Simply add the following command to the `/view/recipes/form.html.erb` file (I put mine right before the CAPTCHA clause):

```
<p>
  <b>Tags:</b> (separate tags with a comma) <br />
  <%= f.text_field :tag_list, :class => "input", :size => 55 %>
</p>
```

And amazingly, that does it. You do not need to change the controller at all — just adding the element to the form will automatically cause it to be saved correctly. To prove this with a functional test, modify the `test_should_create_recipe` test in `test/funcitonals/recipes_controller_test.rb` to pass a tag list into the controller, and test that the tag list is preserved in the created recipe:

```
def test_should_create_recipe
  create_mock_captcha_token("fred", "3")
  recipe_hash = { :title => "Grandma's Chicken Soup",
      :user_id => 1,
      :servings => "5 to 7",
      :description => "Good for what ails you",
      :ingredient_string =>
"2 cups carrots, diced\n\n1/2 tablespoon salt\n\n1 1/3 cups stock",
      :directions => "Ask Grandma",
      :tag_list => "yummy, chickeny"}
    ### ... already existing tests that we don't need to duplicate ...
    assert_equal("yummy, chickeny", new_recipe.tag_list.to_s)
  end
```

Showing Tag Detail Data

After the tag list is entered, you probably also want to display it in the detail listing for each recipe. For a nice Web 2.0 social kind of site, you'll also want to give users the chance to edit tags for any recipe, even ones they didn't actually upload.

To enable editing tags from the detail page, start by adding the following code to the show.html.erb file for recipes. Putting this chunk right below the title display is as good a place as any:

```
<p>
  Tags:
  <%= render :partial => "show_tags" %>
</p>
```

The rendering of the tag listing goes in a partial because it has a little bit of logic, and it's going to be called again on the other side of this process. The partial goes in app/views/recipes/_show_tags .html.erb, and looks like this:

```
<span id="tags">
  <%= h @recipe.tag_list.to_s %>
  <% if_is_logged_in do %>
    <%= link_to_remote "Edit", :url => remote_tag_edit_recipe_path(@recipe),
        :method => :get, :update => "tags" %>
  <% end %>
</span>
```

This code is similar to the code you wrote back in Chapter 1 to support in-place editing of ingredients. You'll notice that this partial has some minimal security to prevent tags from being changed willy-nilly: the user has to be logged in to edit tags. The Ajax remote link calls a path that hasn't been defined yet. This requires the addition of the following two routes in the routes.rb file, in place of the existing block of routes for map.resources :recipes:

```
map.resources :recipes,
    :member => {:remote_tag_edit => :get, :remote_tag_update => :put }  do |recipes|
        recipes.resources :ingredients,
            :member => {:remote_edit => :get, :remote_update => :put}
    end
```

Again, notice that similar to the ingredient change, both edit and update routes are needed. The controller code for both of them is simple — just add the following to app/controller/recipes_ controller.rb:

```
def remote_tag_edit
  edit
  render(:layout => false)
end

def remote_tag_update
  @recipe = Recipe.find(params[:id])
  if @recipe.update_attributes(params[:recipe])
    render(:partial => "show_tags")
  else
    render :text => "Error updating tags"
  end
end
```

The remote tag edit controller just grabs the `@recipe` from the incoming `id` parameter, and renders its view without a layout. The remote tag update controller updates the attributes based on the incoming parameters and renders the `show_tags` partial defined previously or an error message.

The edit form just defines a one-element form, with just the tag list. This goes in a new partial named `app/views/recipes/_remote_tag_edit.erb`:

```
<% remote_form_for(@recipe,
    :url => remote_tag_update_recipe_path(@recipe),
    :update => "tags") do |f| %>
  <%= f.text_field :tag_list, :size => "50" %>
<% end %>
```

ActiveRecord and the taggable plugin collaborate again to ensure that the `tag_list` is correctly dropped into the database.

One limitation of the data structure created by this plugin is that the tag list is common to all users — there's no way for a user to create a private set of tags. To do that within the plugin structure, you'd need to have a join table associating users with recipes on a many-to-many basis, and allowing each of those join elements to have a tag list.

Viewing Tags

Now that the tag data is in the database, one example of using that information would be allowing the user to see recipes based on the tag. This section shows you how to make a simple list display based on the tag; the next section shows you one way to allow the user to browse tag data; and later in the chapter, you'll see how to integrate this with the site's search capabilities.

When talking about RESTful resources and controllers in Chapter 1, I mentioned that a RESTful resource does not necessarily have to correspond to an actual model in the system. The category resource will be the first example in the Soups OnLine application of such a resource. Rather than stuff the controller actions for displaying categories into the recipe controller, it's considered better practice to create a separate controller that just manages category information. In this case, the `index` method would be used to display the tag cloud of all categories, and the `show` method would be used to display the details for a specific category. All you need to do to create the resource is add the following line to `config/routes.rb`:

```
map.resources :categories
```

Let's start with functional tests. Create the file `test/functionals/categories_controller_test.rb` and start it off like so:

```
require File.dirname(__FILE__) + '/../test_helper'
require 'categories_controller'

# Re-raise errors caught by the controller.
class CategoriesController; def rescue_action(e) raise e end; end

class CategoriesControllerTest < Test::Unit::TestCase
```

(continued)

(continued)

```
fixtures :recipes


def setup
  @controller = CategoriesController.new
  @request    = ActionController::TestRequest.new
  @response   = ActionController::TestResponse.new
end

def test_should_show_categories
  recipe_1 = Recipe.find(1)
  recipe_1.tag_list = "yummy, vegetarian"
  recipe_1.save
  get :show, :id => "yummy"
  assert_equal(1, assigns(:recipes).size)
  assert_equal("Soup One", assigns(:recipes)[0].title)
end
```

The test sets the tags for the recipe with an ID of 1, as specified in the fixture data, and saves it. Then it calls the new controller method and asserts that one recipe is in the list, and it matches that recipe with the tag under consideration.

I chose to update the tag list in the test itself, rather than in the fixture, for no particular reason except that I felt the intent of the test would be clearer if the tag list was set close to the assertion that's testing it. Also, I'm not explicitly testing the view output, largely because it is quite straightforward. You should, however, add a test to make sure nothing crashes if no category is specified in the request, so, in the same file, add this:

```
def test_should_show_categories_empty_call
  recipe_1 = Recipe.find(1)
  recipe_1.tag_list = "yummy, vegetarian"
  recipe_1.save
  get :category
  assert_equal(0, assigns(:recipes).size)
end
```

The implementation of this method is actually much shorter than the test. Most of the work is done by the `find_tagged_with` method discussed previously in this chapter. Create a file called app/controllers/categories_controller.rb, and start it off with the following `show` method:

```
class CategoryController < ApplicationController
  layout "recipes"
  before_filter :load_user

  def show
    @category = params[:id] ||= ""
    @recipes = Recipe.find_tagged_with(@category)
    respond_to do |format|
```

```
        format.html #default
        format.xml { render :xml => @recipes}
      end
    end
end
```

A request for all recipes in a specific category strikes me as a very reasonable potential remote call, so the controller method allows an XML request. A view page is also needed. Place the following at app/views/categories/show.html.erb:

```
<% @title = "Recipes in category #{@category}" %>

<div>
  There
  <%= pluralize @recipes.size, "is, "are" %>
  <%= @recipes.size %>
  <%= pluralize @recipes.size, "result" %>.
</div>

<ul>
  <% for recipe in @recipes %>
    <li><%= link_to(h(recipe.title), recipe) %></li>
  <% end %>
</ul>
```

The only thing to say about this is that the string block at the top uses a built-in helper method called pluralize, which pluralizes a word if the passed quantity is not equal to 1 (using the Rails built-in inflectors). So the singular message is "There is 1 result," but the plural message would be "There are 12 results."

Tag Cloud Calculation

Tag data for an entire site is often displayed in a tag cloud, an alphabetical list of tags, with more frequently used tags displayed larger, bolder, or in brighter colors. Usually, the tags in the list are also links to a listing of all the elements in the data set that contain that tag. With the acts_as_taggable_on_steroids plugin, all the data needed to create your very own recipe tag cloud is available, although you will have to do a bit of data massaging.

There are three steps to creating the tag cloud:

1. Gather a list of tags and their frequency.

2. Convert the frequency counts to some kind of Cascading Style Sheets (CSS) style based on their relative magnitudes.

3. Create a view to display the tags in their styles.

The tag cloud calculations are generic, rather than something specific about recipes, so I'm going to create a class in app/models called TagCloud to house the calculations. The unit test for step 1 goes in test/unit/tag_cloud_test.rb. It sets up the existing recipe fixtures with some tag data, and then validates the hash structure as follows:

```
require File.dirname(__FILE__) + '/../test_helper'

class TagCloudTest < Test::Unit::TestCase
  fixtures :recipes
  fixtures :ingredients

  def calculator
    TagCloud.new(Recipe, 7)
  end

  def test_should_get_tag_counts
    recipe_one = Recipe.find(1)
    recipe_one.tag_list = "yummy, chicken"
    recipe_one.save
    recipe_two = Recipe.find(2)
    recipe_two.tag_list = "yummy, beef"
    recipe_two.save
    counts = calculator.tag_count_hash
    assert_equal(3, counts.size)
    assert_equal(2, counts["yummy"])
    assert_equal(1, counts["chicken"])
    assert_equal(1, counts["beef"])
  end
end
```

The `TagCloud` calculator, as declared in the `calculator` method, takes the taggable class itself as an argument, along with the number of buckets.

Getting the correct information into the hash uses two features of the taggable plugin. The `tag_counts` method, which is added to each class declared to act as taggable, returns the set of tags defined by all the elements in that class. Despite the name, the `tag_counts` method in this plugin doesn't actually return the counts; instead, each tag that is returned has a `counts` attribute to retrieve that information. So the method to return the hash with all tags and their counts is a class method in `tag_cloud.rb`. It simply walks the list of tags and retrieves their counts.

Here's the beginning of the `TagCloud` class to implement the `tag_count_hash` function — notice that the taggable class is coming in as an instance variable, and that variable is being used to call class methods of that class:

```
class TagCloud

  attr_reader :taggable_class, :num_of_buckets

  def initialize(taggable_class, num_of_buckets)
    @taggable_class = taggable_class
    @num_of_buckets = num_of_buckets
  end

  def tag_count_hash
    result = Hash.new
```

```
      taggable_class.tag_counts.each do |tag|
        result[tag.name] = tag.count
      end
      result
    end
```

The `tag_counts` method of the taggable class actually takes several options that can filter the list of tags that is returned in the list. The most interesting option for our purposes is `:limit`, which takes an integer, and is the maximum number of tags to place in the cloud. You'd probably also want to use that in conjuction with `:order => "tags.count DESC"` to ensure that the tags with the highest frequency are included in the cloud. You can also use the `:at_least` and `:at_most` options to filter based on the raw frequency count, and the `:start_at` and `:end_at` options can limit the number of tags returned based on the time each tag was created, which you'd most likely use to create a cloud of recent additions. A more elaborate implementation of the tag cloud would allow those options to be specified when the calculator is created.

The next step is to take those raw counts and split them into buckets that can each have a different CSS style when rendered. There are several design-level decisions that could be made about the cloud display at this point. Should the tags go into discrete buckets, or should the size differences between the tags be continuous? If elements go into discrete buckets, how many should there be? How much size difference should there be between buckets, and should boldface or color also be used to distinguish between the tags.

In the interest of relative simplicity, I've implemented this cloud with seven buckets differentiated by size alone, and created seven CSS styles to manage the buckets. I placed them in `public/stylesheets/scaffold.css` like this:

```
.tag_cloud_bucket_1 { font-size: 75%; }
.tag_cloud_bucket_2 { font-size: 100%; }
.tag_cloud_bucket_3 { font-size: 125%; }
.tag_cloud_bucket_4 { font-size: 150%; }
.tag_cloud_bucket_5 { font-size: 175%; }
.tag_cloud_bucket_6 { font-size: 200%; }
.tag_cloud_bucket_7 { font-size: 225%; }
```

I really wanted the median bucket number to have the normal font size of 100%. But as a practical matter, if the default text size is about 12 points, it's hard to go much below 75% of that, which would be 9 points, and still have it be at all legible. The linear increase between buckets should be pretty noticeable to the user.

The tag cloud class will add a method to convert the tag count hash you just created to a hash where the key is the tag and the value is the bucket number. The following unit test for this class is careful to test the boundary conditions around the end of buckets, because off-by-one errors are common in this kind of numerical algorithm:

```
def test_should_bucketize_tags
  raw_counts = {"a" => 1, "b" => 5, "c" => 10, "d" => 11, "e" => 59, "f" => 70}
  expected = {"a" => 1, "b" => 1, "c" => 1, "d" => 2, "e" => 6, "f" => 7}
  actual = calculator.assign_tag_cloud_buckets(raw_counts)
  expected.each do |key, value|
    assert_equal(value, actual[key],
          "key #{key}, expected [#{value}], got [#{actual[key]}]")
  end
end
```

Because the algorithm uses the minimum and maximum values of the counts to determine the buckets, the boundaries of the entire data set are always tested, no matter what range was picked. However, there does need to be some special handling when all the tags have the same count value. The most reasonable thing to do in that case would be to put all the tags in the middle bucket, as in the following unit test:

```
def test_should_bucketize_tags_no_dif
  actual = calculator.assign_tag_cloud_buckets({"a" => 1, "b" => 1})
  expected = {"a" => 4, "b" => 4}
  expected.each do |key, value|
    assert_equal(value, actual[key],
        "key #{key}, expected [#{value}], got [#{actual[key]}]")
  end
end
```

Now you need a method to determine the minimum and maximum values of the range, and another method to calculate the actual bucket for each tag. Put the following bucket-assignment code in the `TagCloud` class:

```
def assign_tag_cloud_buckets(tag_counts)
  result = Hash.new
  min = tag_counts.values.min
  max = tag_counts.values.max
  tag_counts.each do |tag, count|
    result[tag] = bucket_from_range(count, min, max)
  end
  result
end
```

The bucket calculation should return a median value within the number of buckets if the minimum and maximum values of the range are identical. Otherwise, it should pass the calculation off to the actual linear interpolation calculation. Here's how to make that happen:

```
def bucket_from_range(count, min, max)
  return (num_of_buckets / 2).floor + 1 if min == max
  linear_bucket(count, min, max)
end

def linear_bucket(count, min, max)
  return 1 if count == min
  spread = max - min
  ((count - min) * 1.0 / spread * num_of_buckets).ceil
end
```

If the count in question is the minimum value, then you get the first bucket. Otherwise, the count is compared to the spread of values and the number of buckets to return the bucket count.

Finally, you need to put it all together with a method that unifies both parts of the calculation. Add the following to the `TagCloud` class:

```
def self.calculate(taggable_class, num_of_buckets=7)
  calculator = TagCloud.new(taggable_class, num_of_buckets)
  calculator.assign_tag_cloud_buckets(calculator.tag_count_hash)
end
```

Tag Count Display

Now it's time to add the `index` method to the categories controller. The functional test for this is simple, and is mostly there to catch syntax errors, as most of the complex calculation is already under unit test:

```
def test_should_show_tag_cloud
  recipe_1 = Recipe.find(1)
  recipe_1.tag_list = "yummy, vegetarian"
  recipe_1.save
  get :tag_cloud
  assert_response :success
end
```

Next, you define the controller method to call the `TagCloud` object, and create a sorted list of the tags themselves. Add this method to `app/controllers/categories_controller.rb`:

```
def index
  @tag_cloud = TagCloud.calculate(Recipe)
  @tag_counts = TagCloud.tag_counts(Recipe)
  @tags = @tag_cloud.keys.sort
end
```

Again, the idea is to have a thin controller object, with the calculation offloaded into models and helper classes wherever possible.

The ERB view for the tag cloud takes the list and the bucket hash to create the actual cloud (by this time, that view is also pretty thin). Add this to `app/views/categories/index.html.erb`:

```
<% @title = "Recipe Tag Cloud" %>

<div class="tag_cloud_whole">
  <% @tags.each do |tag| %>
    <%= link_to tag, category_recipes_path(:category => tag),
        :class => "tag_cloud_bucket_#{@tag_cloud[tag]}"%>
  <% end %>
</div>
```

The `link_to` call makes every tag link to the category display for that tag. The CSS class is built from the `tag_cloud_bucket` constant used in the CSS file, and the number of the bucket as calculated by the tag cloud calculator.

Figure 5-2 shows the end result, at least with the current state of my production database.

Recipe Tag Cloud

banana carrots chicken **grandma** yummy

Figure 5-2

Searching

If the success of Google proves anything about how to structure information, it's that it doesn't matter how you structure information if your search algorithm is good enough. The difficulty is to create a search system that will catch all the results relevant to the search request without overwhelming the user with irrelevant matches. You also need to present the results to users in such a way that they can tell which results are relevant and which are spurious.

Within Rails, the goal is to search the ActiveRecord objects based on text input that might match one or more fields of the record. For the main text box, you want an unstructured match against multiple fields. You can then provide an advanced search form to specify particular fields to use for the match. This section describes two useful methods for handling a search. One method uses SQL queries. It's simple, and requires nothing beyond the existing ActiveRecord find mechanism. However, it doesn't easily distinguish the importance of the match, and it's hard to add support for Boolean logic in the search.

The second, more complex method uses the Ferret text-indexing tool to support a full-text search. Ferret scores each match based on importance, plus it allows a rich language for logic within the query. However, it requires a Ruby gem, a Rails plugin, and some additional files to support the indexes.

Both methods may have performance issues in high-traffic production sites.

Searching with SQL

The simple mechanism for text search using SQL is to include the LIKE operator in the condition of your SQL query. The operator needs to be augmented slightly to allow for partial matches and case-insensitive matching. You also want the match to work whether the word is in the title, the description, the directions, or the ingredient list (although you may want to allow the user to create a more advanced search that only looks at a subset of the fields).

The LIKE operator normally is of the form `title LIKE <pattern>`. The pattern is typically a string that includes one or more wildcards. The clause is true if the entire text of the column string matches the pattern, so if there are no wildcards, then the behavior is identical to using the `equals` operator.

There are two separate wildcards that are defined, one of which is used more often. The one you'll use less often is a simple underscore (_), which matches any single character, so `title like 'ba_'` would match bar and bat, but not ball or balloon. You will more commonly use the percent sign (%), which matches zero or more characters. So `title like 'ba%'` would match all those words. Using a string with percent signs on both sides is the common SQL idiom to test for an included substring; so `title like '%ba%'` would match all of the preceding words plus things like lumbar and debacle.

The test suite to validate this search method consists of a common test, a set of test strings, and then a test for the non-match conditions. To make the testing a little more straightforward, all the tests are expected to match against the same fixture in the recipe fixtures.

The actual test calls the method under test, validates that only one response is found, and that the response is the expected recipe. Place these tests in `test/unit/recipe_test.rb`:

```
def assert_expected_match(string)
  results = Recipe.find_text_like(string)
```

```
    assert_equal(1, results.size, "Error testing #{string}")
    assert_equal(Recipe.find(1).title, results[0].title)
  end
```

The list of test cases consists of words from the title, description, directions, ingredients, and tag list, plus a test for case-insensitivity and one for partial word matching:

```
def test_expected_matches
  tests = %w{Soup ou sOUP Scrumptious drink First}
  tests.each do |test|
    assert_expected_match(test)
  end
end
```

The handle error suite consists of a word that has no matches, an empty string, and `nil`:

```
def test_text_search_no_match
  tests = ["gazorgenplatz", "", nil]
  tests.each do |test|
    assert Recipe.find_text_like(test).empty?
  end
end
```

Making these tests pass involves adding the `find_text_like` method to the `Recipe` class in app/models/recipe.rb, and a similar method to the `Ingredient` class in app/models/ingredient.rb. Here's the `Recipe` method:

```
def self.find_text_like(search)
  return [] if search.blank?
  fields = ["title", "description", "directions", "cached_tag_list"]
  conditions = [fields.collect { |field| "#{field} LIKE ?"}.join(" or ")]
  fields.each { conditions << "%#{search}%" }
  recipes = Recipe.find(:all, :conditions => conditions, :order => "title ASC")
  recipes += Ingredient.find_recipes_with_text_like(search)
  recipes.uniq.sort_by { |recipe| recipe.title }
end
```

The structure here is designed to make it easy to add new fields without duplicated code effort — it's actually only a refactoring or so away from being completely generic and applicable to any arbitrary class. The first line gets you out of the code immediately if the search is blank, avoiding any sort of null testing on the search parameter later in the code.

The next three lines build up the conditions list. Normally, you'd pass the `find` method a parameter something like this:

```
:conditions => ["title LIKE ? or description LIKE ? ", "%#{search}%", "%#{search}%"]
```

But building up that list manually in the code is kind of ugly, and involves duplication of effort. So the method builds the list programmatically. First, all the LIKE clauses are created in a list and joined by an `or` operator. Then for each column mentioned in the list, the search term is appended to the list. After the list is built, it's included in the `find` call. Because of the way Rails magically handles strings and quotation marks in an ActiveRecord `find` call, the percent signs are included in the string part of the condition list, and not in the actual condition clause. If you try to do something like `["title like '%?%'", "banana"]`, the quotation marks will not be added properly, and you'll get an SQL syntax error.

That `find` call will take care of matches within the recipe fields, but not ones within the ingredients. You could handle this by messing around with SQL joins, but I usually find that to be a frustrating activity, especially because you are sort of going against the grain by explicitly specifying joins within Rails. Instead, I set up a simplified text find to search the ingredient field in the ingredients table — making an executive decision that the code does not need to do a text search against the directions that say whether the carrots are chopped or diced. This code goes in the `Ingredient` class:

```
def self.find_recipes_with_text_like(search)
    ingredients = Ingredient.find(:all,
        :conditions => ["ingredient LIKE ?", "%#{search}%"],
        :select => "distinct recipe_id")
    ingredients.collect { |i| i.recipe }
end
```

This method returns a list of recipe objects. The only oddity here is the use of the `:select` option to limit the return values to just the `recipe_id` values and to use `SELECT DISTINCT` to return each individual recipe only once.

After the ingredient code is called, the method needs to combine, de-duplicate, and sort the data before everything is returned.

Using SQL as your text search engine has a couple of advantages. It's fairly simple. Because it does not depend on any external plugins or features, it's rather portable to production servers you might not control. The code is not necessarily portable between database engines, though — the code here is written for MySQL, which performs a `LIKE` operation on a case-insensitive basis. Other databases do `LIKE` operations with case-sensitivity, so porting this code to one of those databases would require converting both the search string and the database text to a common case. The performance might be a bit spotty — especially if you have to normalize the case (caching the normalized versions in the database itself would be a big performance win here). Other disadvantages include missing features, such as support for more complex logic in the search strings. (Some databases, including MySQL, support complex logic strings in the search calls, but there's no SQL standard for the feature.) The SQL results are not given any kind of relevance, and you are merely sorting them by title.

Searching with Ferret

If you're doing any kind of complex text search in your application, then you want an engine that actually supports complex text search. You want a Ferret. Ferret, in this context is a Ruby port of the popular Java search engine Lucene, and with the help of a snazzy Rails plugin, supporting Ferret-based searches in your Rails application is pretty straightforward.

Installing Ferret

To integrate Ferret with your Rails application, you need two things. The first is Ferret itself, available as a Ruby gem. Type the following command:

```
gem install ferret
```

You'll get prompted for a version based on your platform. (Windows has a separate binary download.) This is a gem that may need to compile some C code, so the C compiler for your environment needs to be available (see Appendix A for more details).

The second installation is a Rails plugin called Acts as Ferret. Although you can install `acts_as_ferret` as a gem (`gem install acts_as_ferret`), that's probably not the best course of action (for one thing, you need to explicitly `require 'acts_as_ferret'` in your Rails project. You are probably better off grabbing the plugin as a Rails plugin, like this:

```
$ ruby script/plugin install -x ↵
svn://projects.jkraemer.net/acts_as_ferret/tags/stable/acts_as_ferret
```

If you don't want to maintain the plugin as a Subversion external repository, then leave off the `-x` option.

Turning Your Model into a Ferret

Ferret's functionality, at least as far as this project is concerned at the moment, is similar enough to the SQL experiment that the unit tests are almost identical — they just call a different search method. The only difference is the partial match test: ou in the previous test suite. Ferret indexes on full words or short phrases only, and does not do generic matching of parts of words. All the other tests will work, including the case-insensitivity test.

Each ActiveRecord class that you want to be indexable by Ferret needs to be registered using the `acts_as_ferret` method call. The arguments to this call define the parameters of the indexing. For the `Recipe` class, you can use the following:

```
acts_as_ferret :fields => [:title, :description, :directions,
    :tag_list, :ingredient_string], :remote => false
```

The `:fields` argument specifies the list of fields that Ferret will index for this class. An immediate difference from the SQL search is that the list of fields here is not limited to actual database fields. Both `tag_list` and `ingredient_string` are derived attributes — `tag_list` is from the taggable plugin, and `ingredient_string` is the list of ingredients created for the detail display. As long as the attribute returns a string, Ferret will happily include it in the index. This is great for your applications, because it means that two of the more hack-like elements of the SQL solution — using the cached version of the tag list, and having to separately search the ingredient table — completely vanish. (Although, I did get some strange behavior when there were recipes with blank tag lists in the test database.) The `:remote` argument specfies that the index files will be managed by the local Rails server. If the argument is `true` (the default), then the index will be managed by an external Distributed Ruby (DRb) server. Using DRb is preferred for production servers.

Ferret will now create an index for the objects in this class. By default, the index is stored under the main directory for your project in `index/<environment>/<class>`, so the test index for the `Recipe` class will go to `index/test/recipe`. This default can be changed when you call `acts_as_ferret` by passing the `:index_dir` key argument with the directory name of your choice.

Once the class is declared to be Ferret-acting, all the actual search work is done by Ferret. The new search method just calls Ferret via the `find_by_contents` method, although you do need to filter out `nil` search strings, as follows:

```
def self.find_text(search, options = {})
  return [] if search.blank?
  Recipe.find_by_contents(search, options = {})
end
```

A couple of things about this method may be unexpected. The return value for this method is technically not an array, but an Acts as Ferret `SearchResult` class. The only difference as far as you are concerned is that the search result object also has a `total_hits` accessor. All other array methods are treated normally, but if you're doing something weird with explicit typing somewhere, it might not work (so cut that out).

Why, you might ask, does the result array need a `total_hits` attribute when it presumably has a perfectly good `size` method to contain the same information? Glad you asked, because that brings us to the second unexpected thing about this method call, at least compared to ActiveRecord `find` methods. By default, `find_by_contents` limits the results to the first 10 results. To change this behavior, `find_by_contents` offers some options that affect pagination, similar to the SQL commands. The `:limit` option governs the number of results returned, and the `:offset` option governs where in the list the first option returned will be — as opposed to the previous method, which just passes the options along to the actual `find_by_contents` method. Use `:limit => :all` to guarantee that you get all the matching results in the index. As you'll see in a second, this functionality can be used to paginate the Ferret results when displayed.

Ferret allows you several more advanced search operators. A particularly useful one is OR as in *this* OR *that* (the keywords must be capitalized), which allows for matches with objects that contain any of the search terms. You can also use the NOT keyword to exclude objects with a particular term, as in `chicken NOT grandma` (if you'd like to go outside the family for some soup). If you want to limit the search to a particular field, then the syntax is `fieldname:search` term, as in `title:chicken`. Elements can be prefixed with a + (for include) or a - (for exclude) as another way of performing Boolean searches. Ferret will also use the * and ? characters as wildcards with the traditional meanings that the * matches zero or more characters and ? matches exactly one character. The only limitation is that you cannot start a search term with a wildcard character. Finally, you can test for what's called a fuzzy search (translated as "something kind of like this") by putting a tilde at the end of the term — for example, `grandma~` might help you catch some of the alternate folksier spellings.

More Data on Ferret Fields

You might have a follow-up question: what exactly are the items sorted by? The sort is based on a *ferret score*, which is a number between 1 and 0 that is supposed to measure which found item is most valuable based on how many times the search string exists, the length of the string, where the match is, and such. To a certain extent, you can adjust this metric if you know that some fields are more important than others. To do this, specify each field with a `boost` attribute when it's declared, as follows:

```
acts_as_ferret :fields => {
  :title => { :boost => 10 },
  :description => { :boost => 4 },
  :directions => { :boost => 2 },
  :tag_list => { :boost => 8 },
  :ingredient_string => { :boost => 5 }
}, :remote => false
```

The `:fields` argument is now a hash instead of an array. The actual fields to be indexed are the keys, and each field now has its own hash of options where a boost value is specified. There's no particular meaning to the magnitude of the boost values, except in their relationship to the values on the other fields — meaning that if you specify a boost value for one field, you probably should specify it for all the fields to make sure you have the relationships you think you have. The boost values adjust the ferret-score calculations but do not totally rewire them — it's still possible for a match only in the directions field to beat out a match in the title field if the directions match is deemed to be really, really relevant.

By default, the Ferret index contains only the index itself, and not the actual data for each object — Ferret queries the database for the objects after it determines the needed IDs from the index. However, Ferret does provide a couple of ways to avoid hitting the database for all the data on each matching object.

One option is to replace the call to `find_by_contents` with `find_id_by_contents`. You might expect this method to return a list of just the IDs of each matching instance. You'd be wrong. You actually get a list of hashes, with each hash containing three keys: `:id`, which holds the ID of the instance in question; `:model`, which contains the class name of the model (`Recipe`, in this case); and `:score`, which is the Ferret score for the match.

You are then free to do anything you want with those results. Most likely you'll want to iterate over them, which `find_id_by_contents` supports by taking an optional block argument that is evaluated for each result returned. If, for some reason, you wanted a slower version of `find_by_contents`, you could mimic it like this:

```
matches = []
Recipe.find_id_by_contents("banana") do |match|
  matches << Recipe.find(match[:id])
end
```

If you've got the hard drive space for it, there's another way. You can tell Ferret to store the instance data in the index itself. This can be done on a field-by-field basis by giving each field a `:store => :yes` attribute like this:

```
acts_as_ferret :fields => {
    :title => { :boost => 10, :store => :yes },
    :description => { :boost => 4, :store => :yes },
    :directions => { :boost => 2, :store => :yes },
    :tag_list => { :boost => 8, :store => :yes },
    :ingredient_string => { :boost => 5, :store => :yes }
  }, :remote => false
```

Then, when you call `find_by_contents`, you can specify fields that should be managed lazily, meaning from the index, rather than from the database. Here's how:

```
def self.find_text(search, options = {})
  return [] if search.blank?
  options[:lazy] = [:title, :description, :directions, :tag_list,
      :ingredient_string]
  Recipe.find_by_contents(search, options)
end
```

Assuming you have the space to store the data, specifying all your fields as stored and lazy will result in a text query that doesn't hit the database at all, which could have significant performance implications. Storing something locally is necessary to use the Ferret highlighting feature, so you might store locally even if you don't want to use the lazy search option.

Viewing the Search Results

Setting up a view for the search results lets you see the highlighting features of the Acts as Ferret plugin. Here are some tests for the `Recipe` controller. I put the following method in `test/test_helper.rb` to set up tags for recipes in the fixture list:

```
def setup_recipe_tags
  recipe = Recipe.find(1)
  assert recipe.tag_list.blank?
  recipe.tag_list = "yummy, vegetarian"
  recipe.save
  recipe = Recipe.find(2)
  recipe.tag_list = "yuckky, beef"
  recipe.save
end
```

The following functional tests, which need to be added to `test/functional/recipes_controller_test.rb`, ensure successful execution, and that a search with a blank string is redirected to the index list:

```
def test_should_search
  setup_recipe_tags
  post :search, :search => "scrumptious"
  assert_response :success
  assert_equal(1, assigns(:recipes).total_hits)
  assert_equal("scrumptious", assigns(:search))
end

def test_should_search_blank
  setup_recipe_tags
  post :search, :search => ""
  assert_redirected_to recipes_path
end
```

The code in the actual recipe controller (`app/controllers/recipes_controller.rb`) is not complicated and mostly redirects to the `Recipe` search you just wrote:

```
def search
  @search = params[:search]
  if @search.blank?
    redirect_to recipes_url
  else
    @recipes = Recipe.find_text(@search, :limit => :all)
    respond_to do |format|
      format.html #default
      format.xml { render :xml, @recipes }
    end
  end
end
```

It would also be a reasonable design decision to place the search in its own RESTful controller, in which case this method would be `SearchesController#show`.

This takes you to the view, which is basically a loop around the `@recipes` variable, but it shows off the beginning of the highlight functionality. This code goes in `app/views/recipes/search.html.erb`:

```erb
<% @title = "Search Results: #{h @search}" %>

<p>
  Your search matched <%= @recipes.total_hits %>
  <%= pluralize @recipes.total_hits, "recipe" %>
</p>

<% @recipes.each do |recipe| %>
  <div id="search_<%= recipe.id %>">
    <% text = recipe.highlight @search, :field => :title,
      :pre_tag => "<strong>", :post_tag => "</strong>" %>
    <%= link_to text, recipe %>
  </div>
  <div>
    <%= recipe.highlight @search, :field => :description,
      :pre_tag => "<strong>", :post_tag => "</strong>"%>
  </div>
  <br/ >
<% end %>
```

The Acts as Ferret plugin adds a `highlight` instance method to its classes. The `highlight` method performs the task of emphasizing the search term within the display. The first argument to the method is the search term to be highlighted. Then come several optional arguments. The `:field` argument specifies which field to return. If it is not specified, then all fields in the instance will be shown. This is rarely what you want. By default, the `highlight` method surrounds the matches with an `<em>` tag, which italicizes the text in most browsers. If you want something else instead, use the `:pre_tag` and `:post_tag` to specify the surrounding tag.

More advanced use of the highlight method allows you to show just snippets of longer text (such as a news article or a web page). There are three options that govern this behavior. The `:num_exerpts` option, which defaults to 2, allows you to set how many excerpts would be chosen from a longer text. The `:excerpt_length` option, which defaults to 150, controls the length of the excerpt in characters, with the actual matched text displayed in the middle. If you use the default behaviors for both of these options, text fields shorter than 150 characters will be displayed in their entirety. Finally, the `:ellipsis` behavior allows you to swap out the ASCII ellipsis character used by default with something more Unicode-friendly. Overall, this highlight behavior is much more powerful and flexible than the helper provided within Rails proper, which doesn't handle the multiple snippets.

At this point, the search can be invoked via the URL `recipes/search?search=param`. You can insert this into the `app/views/layouts/recipes.html.erb` layout file with the following simple form:

```erb
<li id="search">
  <h2 class="bg2">Search</h2>
  <% form_tag :action => "search" do %>
    <%= text_field_tag :search, "", :size => 10 %>
    <%= submit_tag "Go" %>
  <% end %>
</li>
```

When the form is submitted, the `search` method of the recipes controller will be invoked.

Pagination

If you've used Google, you've seen pagination in action. The first 25 or so search hits are displayed, followed by some navigation to allow you to move between pages. On the back end, the server knows what page you are looking for and serves up the correct set of results for that page.

In the Rails 1.*x* days, pagination was a helper method and part of the Rails core. But it turned out that a lot of people didn't much care for the implementation, and the pagination helper was removed from Rails 2.0 as part of the general shedding of non-core functionality. There's no clear market leader in its place, but there are a couple of plugin contenders worth looking at. Keep an eye out for new developments in this space.

will_paginate

The first contender is the will_paginate plugin available from the folks at Err Free consulting. You can get the plugin from here:

```
$ ruby script/plugin install svn://errtheblog.com/svn/plugins/will_paginate
```

This plugin allows you to use the paginate method in any place where you would use the method find(:all). Here is an example of the simplest use of this method:

```
@recipes = Recipe.paginate(:page => params[:page])
```

The page option tells the plugin which page of data to retrieve, and must be specified on each call to paginate. The default is to put 30 items on the page. If your class responds to a per_page class method, the results of that method are used, so you can specify that as follows:

```
def self.per_page
  10
end
```

Any options you send to paginate are preserved and passed the underlying find method, so you can also use any find options, such as condition or the like. You can even emulate the dynamic find versions like this:

```
@recipes = Recipe.paginate_by_title("Chicken Soup", :page => 1)
```

On the view side, you can get the paginate navigation, which allows the user to select a different page. You do this by simply including the helper method will_paginate with the object returned from the paginate call, like this:

```
<%= will_paginate @recipes %>
```

The helper method uses metadata placed inside the array-like paginate result to determine what page is being displayed and what URL to use to get different pages. It assumes that future pages will come from the same controller action, using the :page parameter, and it reloads the page entire screen when a different page is requested. All the elements of the pagination output have CSS classes, so the final look can be customized to your needs.

paginating_find

The other contender is the paginating_find plugin, by Alex Wolfe. This plugin is available at

```
$ ruby script/plugin install http://svn.cardboardrocket.com/paginating_find
```

With this plugin installed, all your find commands behave exactly as normal, unless you pass them a special :page parameter. The :page parameter is itself a hash that takes options for page size and current page. For example:

```
@recipes = find(:all, :page => {:size => 25, :current => 2})
```

The :size parameter defaults to 10, and the :current parameter defaults to the first page. If you know the exact number of records that will be found, you can pass that in the :page hash as :count. If this is specified, the plugin doesn't have to go to the database to calculate the number of total records, which is a potential performance boost.

Because this is just piggybacking on the regular find behavior, anything that you can do in a regular find method can be done in a method that includes pagination.

This plugin also includes enough metadata in the returned object that the view pagination can be managed with a single helper, as in this example:

```
<%= paginating_links @recipes %>
```

Again, this can be customized with CSS.

I've used both plugins with fairly similar results. Neither manages Ajax out of the box, but adapting the helpers to use Ajax calls is not tremendously complex. Because both plugins use the base find method as their core, they can have difficulty interacting with other plugins that use their own search mechanisms — such as the find_with_tags or find_by_contents method described previously in this chapter. The worst-case workaround for that is to have the other method return a list of IDs and filter that list during pagination, but that has negative performance implications.

Resources

For another way to create navigation links, as well as some nice-looking tabbed navigations, take a look at the Widgets plugin from SeeSaw at www.seesaw.it/en/toolbox/widgets. A mechanism for using pure CSS to create menus was created by Eric Meyer and can be found at http://meyerweb.com/eric/css/edge/menus/demo.html.

The home of Acts As Taggable On Steroids (AATOS) is http://agilewebdevelopment.com/plugins/acts_as_taggable_on_steroids. The implementation of the tag cloud in this chapter was partially inspired by Juixe TechKnow's version at www.juixe.com/techknow/index.php/2006/07/15/acts-as-taggable-tag-cloud.

Gregg Pollack and Jason Seifer of Rails Envy have a great tutorial on the Acts as Ferret plugin at www.railsenvy.com/2007/2/19/acts-as-ferret-tutorial. (Also check out their parodies of the "I'm A

Mac" ads.) The MySQL full-text searching referenced in this chapter is explained in more detail in the MySQL documentation at `http://dev.mysql.com/doc/refman/5.1/en/fulltext-search.html`.

The will_paginate plugin lives at `http://errtheblog.com/post/4791`, and you can find paginating_find at `http://cardboardrocket.com/pages/paginating_find`. A quick helper method to integrate will_paginate and acts_as_ferret can be found at `http://opensoul.org/2007/8/17/acts_as_ferret-will_paginate`.

Summary

Rails has a number of facilities, both built-in and via plugin, for supporting navigation and information architecture of your application. It's straightforward to build a sidebar using some basic Ruby data structures and the Rails helper method `link_to_unless_current`.

Tagging is a very popular way to allow flexible and user-centric organization. In Rails, the recommended way of managing tagging is via the Acts As Taggable On Steroids (AATOS) plugin, which creates an ActiveRecord structure for associating tags with any ActiveRecord object. The plugin manages the basic data association, and you can easily add more complex calculations to display tag clouds or other fancy representations of your tags.

Search can be handled on your site via pure SQL, which is simple but does not allow for easy inclusion of Boolean logic or weighted queries. MySQL has such a facility, but it's not portable between databases. The Ferret gem and the Rails plugin Acts As Ferret can be used to add full-text indexing and searching to your site.

Pagination was removed from the Rails 2.0 core, but two simple plugins offer similar functionality to add pagination to your application: will_paginate and paginating_find.

6

The Care and Feeding of Databases

One of the best features of Rails is that it protects you from many of the most irritating details of working with relational databases. For most purposes, you don't need to remember the command line syntax, unusual GUI viewer, departures from the SQL standard, or other maintenance quirks because you sit comfortably behind the shield of Rails protective abstractions.

Databases, however, are subtle and powerful, and you cannot escape their awesome might for long. There are a few situations in which a Rails developer might have to display an unusual knowledge of the details of the underlying database. One of those situations is when you are forced to use a preexisting legacy database.

Opinionated framework that it is, Rails has certain expectations about the naming and structure of database tables. It assumes, for example, that each table has a single primary key and that the name of that primary key is id. Similarly, Rails assumes that a foreign key for a relationship has a predictable name based on the table being linked to. Those conventions enable a Rails developer to consistently understand the structure of the model objects based on the database schema and vice versa.

All of which works great if you are in a position to create and maintain your own database schema. But that is often not the case. Sometimes you're brought into a project and the data already exists, and other existing projects depend on the schema, so you can't change it to bring it in line with Rails standards.

If you are in a situation where you have an existing database schema to work with, you need to decide how to manage it. Depending on the exact nature of your project, you might be able to try one or more different options. You'll need to decide whether to split your application into two databases — one that is created by Rails and uses Rails conventions, and the other for the existing legacy system — or leave the entire system in the legacy schema and extend it as needed. Migrating all the data from the existing schema to a Rails database might also be an option.

All these solutions have pros and cons. Migrating all data to a Rails database is the smoothest for Rails development, but requires the development and maintenance of a separate migration application. Also, if the migration is applied frequently and affects a lot of data, this could have implications for caching and other tasks that require stable object relationships. Leaving the legacy database alone is probably best where the legacy database has a consistent naming convention of a kind that Rails can be readily adapted to follow. If not, then every table is going to need special-case treatment, which can be error prone. Splitting the database is a good choice if the legacy database is legitimately a subset of the entire application (such as a preexisting user mailing list database), or if you have hopes of seeing the Rails code assimilate the existing data, Borg-like, one table at a time. On the down side, much of ActiveRecord is written assuming a single source of data — the second source of data is excluded from some of Rails' best tricks. Personally, unless the existing database has a very good naming convention, I tend to favor creating a second database with Rails defaults for models that may arise during a project's lifecycle. I think it's less painful to deal with two database systems then to have no Rails convention in the project at all. Your mileage may, of course, vary.

Don't panic. Rails has tools that will allow it to manage the data in the legacy system with almost the same ease that you've come to expect. There are four issues to manage: connecting to the database in the first place, managing whatever weird naming conventions Fred in IT came up with, allowing for ActiveRecord relationships, and managing testing against the new schema.

Plugging In to Your Legacy

For the purposes of having something concrete to wrap your head around, let's assume that Soups OnLine has secured a strategic coup: the ability to deliver information from Ingredientopedia, the world's leading online source of information about the kind of ingredients that one might use in, say, a soup. Sadly, due to the sort of contrivance that involves armies of fictional lawyers, Soups OnLine has to use the existing database as-is, and is not free to migrate the schema to something useful. So you're stuck with a database schema that looks, in part, like this (a naming convention only a database admin could love):

```
CREATE TABLE `ingredientopedia`.`the_ingredient_table` (
  `ingredient_id` INTEGER AUTO_INCREMENT,
  `ingredient_name` VARCHAR(255),
  `ingredient_description` VARCHAR(4000),
  `ingredient_nutritional_info` VARCHAR(4000),
  `ingredient_category_id` INTEGER,
  PRIMARY KEY (`ingredient_id`)
)
CHARACTER SET utf8;
```

To get Rails to open this database, you need to adjust the `database.yml` file to add three more database environments: one for each Rails environment. You can use the YAML merge feature to make the declaration more compact, like this:

```
ingredient: &ingredient
  adapter: mysql
  username: root
  password:
  socket: /tmp/mysql.sock
```

```
ingredient_development:
  database: ingredientopedia_development
  <<: *ingredient

ingredient_production:
  database: ingredientopedia_production
  <<: *ingredient

ingredient_test:
  database: ingredientopedia_test
  <<: *ingredient
```

The basic unit of a YAML file is a key/value pair of the form `key: value`. Several key/value pairs can be indented under a common parent like this:

```
parent:
  key: value
  other_key: other_value
```

Now all of the key/value pairs are bundled into a hash named `parent`.

The `&ingredient` marker is YAML syntax that takes a symbolic name internal to the YAML file and assigns it to the entire data structure — in this case, the `ingredient` line and all its indented children. The symbolic name does not need to be the same as the attribute name for the hash. After the symbolic name is assigned, the hash can be referred to using that name. The `<<: *ingredient` syntax tells the YAML parser to take any key/value pairs that are defined in the hash using the symbolic name and merge them into the hash currently being defined. So, in this example, the common values for all the legacy databases are defined only once, and then merged into each environment database in turn.

> *Windows users will have to change the socket line to the valid Windows path or alternatively replace the socket line with* `hostname: localhost`.

The declaration sticks to the `development, production, test` naming structure, which will enable Rails to ensure that any ActiveRecord object you point at the legacy database maintains the standard separation between the three environments.

What you'd like is to be able to manage the data in the legacy database using ActiveRecord just as though the database has been created using Rails conventions. Add a `test/unit/ingredient_data_test.rb` file, and start with the following test:

```
require File.dirname(__FILE__) + '/../test_helper'

class IngredientDataTest < Test::Unit::TestCase

  def teardown
    super
    IngredientData.delete_all
  end

  def test_should_load_and_save
    subject = IngredientData.new
    subject.id = 2
```

(continued)

(continued)

```
      subject.name = "Carrot"
      subject.description = "Orange and crunchy."
      subject.save
      saved_subject = IngredientData.find(2)
      assert_equal(2, saved_subject.id)
      assert_equal("Carrot", saved_subject.name)
      assert_equal("Orange and crunchy.", saved_subject.description)
    end

  end
```

This test simply creates an instance of the new legacy ActiveRecord object, sets some of its values, saves it, and verifies that the values persist. For a database table that was created by Rails, this test would barely need to be run, because this is core ActiveRecord functionality.

However, in this case, the ActiveRecord class does not have a name based on the table name (you wouldn't want a class named `TheIngredientTable`, and `Ingredient` is already taken). Additionally, the test strips the common `ingredient_` prefix off of each column in the table. Also notice that the test needs to explicitly delete the item from the database — Rails test loading won't do it by default because the legacy test database is not the known test database to be scrubbed.

Creating the connection is best managed through an abstract parent class for all tables that would connect to the same the legacy database (even though you've only seen one so far, there might be others in the future). To manage this connection, you need to explicitly perform the `ActiveRecord` `establish_connection` method call that would otherwise be handled explicitly.

Create a file in `app/models` called `ingredient_base.rb` and fill it with the following snippet:

```
class IngredientBase < ActiveRecord::Base
  self.abstract_class = true
  establish_connection "ingredient_#{RAILS_ENV}"
end
```

The first line of this snippet just tells Rails that `IngredientBase` is abstract, which in this context means that it doesn't have a database table of its own, so Rails shouldn't go looking for one. The second line tells Rails that `IngredientBase` and all its subclasses don't connect to the expected database, but instead connect to one of the new ingredient databases previously specified. The database it connects to depends on what environment the code is in, which is how you can preserve the standard three-headed development, production, and test database structure.

Naming Unconventionally

ActiveRecord has a few useful class-level attributes that enable you to change the default relationship between table names and class names, and the default primary key names. You can't use them in this case, because they are class-level, and would apply to all ActiveRecord classes in the project, even the ones that have already been created against the traditional Rails database. However, it's worth listing them here (which I've done in the following table) because under somewhat different project parameters, they are very useful. Typically, you'd put these changes in your `environent.rb` file.

Attribute	Description
pluralize_tablenames	Defaults to true. If your database schema uses the singular form of the table name instead of the plural, set this value to false.
primary_key_prefix_type	Specifies common behavior for primary key names where the table name is used as part of the key. If the key names are of the form recipeid, this field should have the value :table_name. If the key names are of the form recipe_id, this field should have the value :table_name_with_underscore. The default is nil.
table_name_prefix	A common string at the beginning of each table name. For example, you could use the_.
table_name_suffix	A common string at the end of each table name. For example, you could use _table.

Because you can't use these defaults, the new IngredientData class needs to specify the table name and primary key name explicitly. Create an app/models/ingredient_data.rb file, and start with this:

```ruby
class IngredientData < IngredientBase

  set_table_name "the_ingredient_table"
  set_primary_key "ingredient_id"
end
```

It would be nice if columns analogous to table_name_prefix had a name prefix and suffix that could be used to automatically strip that annoying ingredient_ from each column. One doesn't exist, so you should write one. Put the following code in IngredientBase:

```ruby
def self.column_prefix(prefix)
  self.column_names.each do |each|
    next unless each.starts_with? prefix
    method_name = each[prefix.size..-1]
    define_method :"#{method_name}" do
      read_attribute(:"#{each}")
    end

    define_method :"#{method_name}=" do |new_val|
      write_attribute(:"#{each}", new_val)
    end
  end
end
```

This uses a number of ActiveRecord and Ruby features to dynamically create new accessor methods for each column in the database. First, it uses the ActiveRecord column_names function to get a list of column names. Looping over them, any column name that does not begin with the prefix is ignored. For those column names that are of interest, the code calculates the prefix-less name and goes through two calls to Ruby's `define_method` metaprogramming method. The first one uses the method name and calls the ActiveRecord `read_attribute` for the real column name, and the second uses the method name and an equals sign (the standard setter syntax) and calls ActiveRecord `write_attribute`.

Call this method by including a third line to the `IngredientData` class:

```
class IngredientData < IngredientBase

  set_table_name "the_ingredient_table"
  set_primary_key "ingredient_id"
  column_prefix "ingredient_"

end
```

The net effect is to create a parallel set of accessors, both getters like id, name, description, and setters like id=, name=, description=. The existing set of accessors does not go away, so if you are determined to use `ingredient_description`, it is still available.

At this point, the test will pass, and you've created an ActiveRecord connection to a legacy database.

Testing a Legacy Database with Fixtures

As previously mentioned, when you go against Rails defaults by adding a legacy database, you lose some of Rails automatic generation magic. One thing that becomes a little bit harder is using fixtures in your unit and automated tests. The standard `fixtures` method call (which technically is a class method added by Rails to the `TestUnit` class) assumes that it will be working with the database defined for the `test` environment. Your secondary database, defined as `ingredient_test`, is somewhat out of luck. Fortunately, there is a workaround that allows you to have all the functionality of Rails fixtures, and most, if not all, of the convenience that you have when working in a Rails database.

Among the conveniences you give up are the nice little Rake tasks that automatically prepare your test database based on the schema of the development database. You'll need to go in manually to create the test database. You might want to invest the time to create a shell script and/or a Rake task to create your legacy database automatically. Usually that's going to be something like this:

```
mysql legacy_database < schema.sql
```

If you do declare this as a Rake task, you can add it as a dependency to the existing `test:prepare` style tasks like this:

```
namespace :db do
  namespace :test do
    task :legacy_prepare do
      sh my_load_test_script
    end

    task :prepare => :legacy_prepare
  end
end
```

Put something like that in your `lib/tasks` directory, and the Rake `db:test:prepare` task should now include preparing the legacy test database.

With that done, here's the test that you want to have pass — The fixture needs to be put in a YAML file in `test/fixtures/the_ingredient_table.yml`:

```
one:
  ingredient_id: 1
  ingredient_name: bananas
  ingredient_description: yellow and squishy
  ingredient_nutritional_info: high in potassium
  ingredient_category_id: 1
```

To ensure that this gets loaded into the database by the Rails test functionality, define the following:

```
def test_should_read_fixture
  from_db = IngredientData.find(1)
  assert_equal "bananas", from_db.name
end
```

Most of the functionality that you are going to add to support this fixture is pretty general, so I recommend putting it in `test_helper.rb`, so that future legacy classes in this database can take advantage of the code.

The first step is to associate the YAML file with the actual ActiveRecord class. Rails seems to be happier if the YAML file is named to match the actual table name in the database; however, that table name is not what you used for the model class. That's easy enough to manage, though, because Rails provides a hook to override the default naming convention. Put this in `test/test_helper.rb`:

```
def self.set_fixture_classes
  set_fixture_class :the_ingredient_table => IngredientData
end
```

The `set_fixture_class` method takes in a hash, which you can build through the usual Ruby syntax of passing a series of key/value pairs. In this case, the key is a symbol matching the table name and, therefore, the name of the YAML file; and the value is the name of the ActiveRecord model you created to hold that data. As you add more classes from the legacy database, add the association to this method, and call the `set_fixture_classes` method at the top of any test that needs the legacy fixtures. This will be much easier to manage than trying to set only the fixture data being used in each particular class (especially because the error message if you forget to set the class is a little on the cryptic side).

Because you can no longer use the `fixtures` class method to load fixtures, you now need to explicitly load the fixtures in the `setup` method of your test class. In the `ingredient_data_class`, the `setup` and `teardown` should look like the following, with the `set_fixture_classes` call included:

```
set_fixture_classes

def setup
  load_external_fixtures :the_ingredient_table
end
```

(continued)

(continued)

```
def teardown
  super
  cleanup IngredientData
end
```

Okay, that's not very much help so far, because these methods are just calling the general methods from `test_helper.rb`. So now, you'll define those methods. First up, the `load` method:

```
def fixture_dir
  File.join(RAILS_ROOT, 'test', 'fixtures')
end

def load_external_fixtures(*table_names)
  Fixtures.create_fixtures(fixture_dir, table_names) do
    IngredientBase.connection
  end
end
```

What this code is doing is explicitly forcing the fixture loading process. The input is a list of the table names, which can be strings or symbols (the Rails method will convert). The block argument should return the actual connection to be used to store the database data loaded from the fixtures — it should match the connection that the ActiveRecord model class is expecting.

The main gotcha here has to do with foreign key constraints, when you are loading fixture data from multiple tables and the legacy database has foreign keys declared. If that's the case, then the fixtures need to be placed in order, with the dependent table that contains the foreign key constraint going last. In this case, I placed a column in the ingredient data for `category_id`. If I was also loading a category table, and there was a foreign key constraint on `the_ingredient_table`, then the category fixture would need to be loaded first. If you don't do this in the right order, then you'll get constraint violation errors when you try to load the fixtures. (See the "Foreign Keys: Threat or Menace?" sidebar for some more chatter about Rails and foreign key constraints.)

In a legacy database, you don't get the data automatically pre-loaded, and you don't get it automatically cleaned up, either. So you need to define the following method:

```
def cleanup(*classes)
  classes.each do |klass|
    klass.delete_all
  end
end
```

In this case, the argument is a series of actual ActiveRecord classes, and the method cheerfully demolishes all the data. The ordering of the classes is also important in this method — you need to delete the data in the opposite order in which they were created. Again, doing the deletion in the wrong order will cause a constraint violation error.

At this point, the unit test will pass. Rails correctly puts the data from the fixtures into the test database for retrieval. You might have noticed, though, that I did not include a test featuring one of the nice helper methods that Rails normally creates for accessing fixture data without hitting the database, like `recipes(:one)`. Sadly, as far as I can tell, doing fixtures explicitly this way bypasses the normal process of creating those methods. So to get at the data in the fixtures, you need to do a database find as shown in the original test.

If you really want to see the actual fixture data, Rails does store it in the `Fixtures` class. It's a bit of a pain to get it out though — it's nearly 10 whole lines of Ruby code, which you can place in `test/test_helper.rb`:

```ruby
def external_fixture(table, id)
  table = table.to_s
  id = id.to_s
  Fixtures.all_loaded_fixtures.each do |tablename, fixtures|
    next unless tablename == table
    fixtures.each do |fix_id, fixture|
      return fixture.to_hash if fix_id == id
    end
  end
  nil
end
```

The `Fixtures` class stores the fixtures in a series of nested lists. The top level is an array, each member of which is a two-element array: the first element is the table name, and the second element is the data. The data is stored similarly: each fixture is stored as a two-element list, the first element being the identifier for the fixture in the YAML file, and the second element being the fixture object. The data looks like this for the sample case:

```ruby
["the_ingredient_table", [["one", #<Fixture:0x25df348 @fixture={"ingredient_id"=>1,
"ingredient_category_id"=>1, "ingredient_nutritional_info"=>"high in potassium",
"ingredient_description"=>"yellow and squishy", "ingredient_name"=>"bananas"},
@class_name="TheIngredientTable">]]]
```

All the `helper` method does is walk through the data until it gets a match for the `tablename` and `fixture` identifier, and then it returns that fixture as a hash. You can also convert the hash into an ActiveRecord class, but the hash itself should be good enough for most purposes.

There's one more issue that you might need to be aware of. There are some reported cases where Rails mistranslates data back and forth between the legacy database. If you are having this problem, you might need to explicitly set the ActiveRecord connection in your setup, and then revert it in your teardown method, like this:

```ruby
def setup
    ActiveRecord::Base.connection = IngredientBase.connection
    load_external_fixtures :the_ingredient_table
  end

def teardown
    super
    ActiveRecord::Base.establish_connection("#{RAILS_ENV}")
    cleanup IngredientData
  end
```

Foreign Keys: Threat or Menace?

One of the points of contention between Rails and its critics is the relative lack of support in Rails for the strong foreign key constraints used in most databases to ensure referential integrity between tables. Among other issues, there's no nifty syntax for defining foreign keys in a Rails migration (although there's a plugin if you need the feature). Also, the ordering of fixture loads as shown in the legacy database section is not supported natively by the Rails `fixture` method.

Rails impresario David Heinemeier Hansson is on record as saying that foreign keys are unnecessary in a Rails database, because Rails handles the referential integrity needs through its own relationship definitions and does so in a richer, database-independent way. Longtime database developers are, let's say, skeptical.

Just to get a sense of the issues, here are some of the pros and cons of using foreign keys in your system.

In Favor of Foreign Keys

❑ Using foreign keys, you ensure that your data will always be in a valid state.

❑ Foreign keys do not require you to use Rails to get referential integrity. This is important if other scripts or applications will write to the database.

❑ If the database administrators at your company find out that you're doing a production database without constraints, they may come after you in your sleep. Longtime database admins see this as a train wreck waiting to happen.

In Favor of The Rails Way

❑ Foreign key syntax and behavior differs among databases. Rails is database-independent.

❑ Often, strict foreign key constraints prevent you from doing things to the data that you actually want or need to do. (You may, for instance, legitimately need to keep an orphaned record around for a while.)

❑ During testing, a full set of foreign key constraints can force you to load a number of extra fixtures not needed for a unit test to satisfy the constraints.

❑ Rails taxonomy of relationships is richer and closer to the programmer's intent than the database foreign key.

My tendency so far has been to trust Rails where possible and add constraints when a problem develops—which is rarely, at least for me.

Building a Relationship across Multiple Databases

At this point, you've successfully integrated the data from the external Ingredientopedia database into Soups OnLine. The next thing you're probably going to want to do with the data is allow the preexisting ingredient objects to have a Rails-mediated relationship with the external `IngredientData` table. Trying to create this relationship exposes another way in which you leave the reservation when trying to support a legacy database alongside the Rails database.

Normally, Rails manages a many-to-many relationship through a series of SQL `JOIN` calls to the database that retrieve the related data. The problem, of course, is that SQL does not have the magical powers needed to join two tables from two separate databases. However, with a little bit of extra plumbing behind the scenes, it is possible to make the relationship across the database-divide almost as transparent as a typical Rails relationship.

> *This section applies only to Rails relationships that rely on SQL* `JOIN`, *which is to say* `:has_and_belongs_to_many` *and* `:has_many` `:through`. *One-to-one relationships like* `:belongs_to` *and* `:has_one` *do not use* `JOIN` *calls and can be managed seamlessly by Rails across multiple databases.*

The key to making the join relationships work across multiple databases is to place a proxy table in the Rails database that maps to items in the legacy database. Items in the Rails database can participate in many-to-many relationships with the proxy object, which then acts like the actual legacy object.

Defining the Functionality

Let's assume that the ingredient definitions in the Ingredientopedia don't quite map directly to the ingredients that you might put in soup. Perhaps there are some general-level ingredients like "vegetables" or "legumes" that might require you to map multiple data pieces to one Soups OnLine ingredient, and vice versa. In this case, you'll create an `IngredientDataProxy` class that will join with the existing `IngredientData` and `Ingredient` tables.

As usual, unit tests help define exactly what the functionality should be. These are all in the `ingredient_data_test.rb` file:

```
## at the top of the file
fixtures :ingredients
fixtures :ingredient_data_join
fixtures :ingredient_data_proxies

## at the end of the file
def test_proxy_should_be_there
  proxy = IngredientDataProxy.find(1)
  assert_equal("bananas", proxy.ingredient_data.name)
end

def test_ingredient_should_relate_to_data
  ingredient = Ingredient.find(1)
  assert_equal(2, ingredient.ingredient_data.size)
  data = ingredient.ingredient_data[0]
```

(continued)

(continued)

```
    assert_equal("plantains", data.name)
    data.name = "pita chips"
    data.save
    saved = IngredientData.find(data.id)
    assert_equal("pita chips", saved.name)
  end

  def test_data_should_relate_to_ingredient
    data = IngredientData.find(1)
    assert_equal(1, data.ingredient_data_proxy.id)
    assert_equal(1, data.ingredients.size)
    assert_equal("First Ingredient", data.ingredients[0].ingredient)
  end
```

For the test to work, you need to load in data from traditional Rails fixtures. Because these fixtures are from the existing Rails database, they can be loaded the standard way. (I realize that you haven't seen all of those database tables yet.) The ingredient fixture file already exists. Create an `ingredient_data_proxies.yml` file with the following proxy objects:

```
one:
  id: 1
  ingredient_data_id: 1
  created_at: 2007-08-22 09:38:18
  updated_at: 2007-08-22 09:38:18

two:
  id: 2
  ingredient_data_id: 2
  created_at: 2007-08-22 09:38:18
  updated_at: 2007-08-22 09:38:18
```

Also create the `ingredient_data_join.yml` file, which manages the join table between ingredients and the proxy data as follows:

```
one:
  ingredient_id: 1
  ingredient_data_proxy_id: 1

two:
  ingredient_id: 1
  ingredient_data_proxy_id: 2
```

The first test merely asserts that the proxy objects are created and associate with their legacy `IngredientData` objects as expected. The second test verifies that an ingredient can find its associated `IngredientData` object, and can manipulate that object using the expected Rails attributes, including the ability to change and save the data object. The third test checks the relationship the other way around — that is, it verifies that the `IngredientData` object can reach its associated `Ingredients`. (You don't have to test for write and save features in this direction because the `IngredientData` object is getting an actual `Ingredient` object, whereas the `Ingredient` object may just be getting a proxy to the `IngredientData`.)

Creating the Proxy Model

To get this to work, you need to create the proxy object. This object will live in the Rails database and point to objects in the legacy database. To begin, type the following:

```
$ ruby script/generate model --svn ingredient_data_proxy
```

This generation creates a new migration to define the proxy data table, which is quite simple. The migration also needs to create the join table that will be used for the relationship between ingredients and data. Here's the migration:

```
class CreateIngredientDataProxies < ActiveRecord::Migration
  def self.up
    create_table :ingredient_data_proxies do |t|
      t.integer :ingredient_data_id
      t.timestamps
    end

    create_table :ingredient_data_join, :id => false do |t|
      t.integer :ingredient_id
      t.integer :ingredient_data_proxy_id
    end
  end

  def self.down
    drop_table :ingredient_data_proxies
    drop_table :ingredient_data_join
  end
end
```

The only elements in the proxy table are the local ID of the proxy object and the remote ID of the object in the legacy table — you can think of this as basically managing a join across the two databases. The migration also creates the actual join table (you can tell it's a join table because of the `:id => false` argument). Somewhat reluctantly, I departed from the Rails default naming convention for the join table — it's easy enough to work around, and I felt that `ingredient_data_proxies_ingredients` might be a touch awkward.

Invoke `rake db:migrate` to load the changes to the existing database.

Making Connections

Now, the relationship information has to be added to all three involved classes. First, in `Ingredient`, the connection looks like this:

```
has_and_belongs_to_many :ingredient_data_proxy,
    :join_table => :ingredient_data_join
```

This declaration defines the relationship with the non-standard proxy class as the target, and the non-standard join table name.

From the `IngredientDataProxy` side, the declaration looks like this:

```
has_and_belongs_to_many :ingredients, :join_table => :ingredient_data_join
```

It's basically the same declaration, the class name for ingredients is standard and doesn't need to be specified.

The other half of the connection is between `IngredientDataProxy` and the actual `IngredientData` class. From the proxy side, there's nothing at all unusual about it — remember, `belongs_to` relationships aren't affected by the database separation. It's just this::

```
belongs_to :ingredient_data
```

The relationship declaration in `IngredientData` is also standard:

```
has_one :ingredient_data_proxy
```

At this point, both `Ingredient` and `IngredientData` have accessors populated with a bunch of `IngredientDataProxy` objects. However, you don't want to deal with proxy objects — you want to the real deal. In both cases, you need to write accessors with the expected names to go through the proxy object and get the other half of the connections.

From the `IngredientData` object, you call your single proxy to get its list of ingredients like this:

```
def ingredients
  ingredient_data_proxy.ingredients
end
```

On the flip side, from the `ingredient` object, you call your multiple proxies and ask each of them for its remote data object, like this:

```
def ingredient_data
  ingredient_data_proxy.collect {|data| data.ingredient_data}
end
```

With all the connections in place, the tests will pass, and the legacy ingredient information is now accessible to your application.

Alternate Data Access Mechanism

One thing that might bother you about the previous solution is that, when gathering the data objects, the `Ingredient` object walks through the entire list and creates a new list. If there are lots of data objects, this might cause unnecessary performance problems. Given the parameters of the Soups OnLine application as I defined them, it's unlikely to be a serious problem. However, there are circumstances where it would be beneficial to continue to deal with the legacy object through the proxy, so I want to show you how that might be done.

The basic goal here is to use Ruby metaprogramming to create accessors in the proxy object that shadow the ones in the remote object. Then, the proxy object can be manipulated as if it was the legacy object itself. Here's the code for an abstract `Proxy` object that does this metaprogramming (it goes in `app/models/remote_data_proxy.rb`):

```
class RemoteDataProxy < ActiveRecord::Base
  self.abstract_class = true

  class_inheritable_accessor :proxy_object
  class_inheritable_accessor :read_only

  def self.set_proxy_object(obj)
    self.proxy_object = obj
  end

  def self.create_proxy_accessors(class_to_proxy, options = {})
    prefix = options[:prefix] ||= ''
    class_to_proxy.column_names.each do |each|
      next unless each.starts_with? prefix
      method_name = each["ingredient_".size..-1]
      define_method :"#{method_name}" do
        send(:"#{proxy_object}").send(:"#{each}")
      end

      next if read_only
      define_method :"#{method_name}=" do |new_val|
        send(:"#{proxy_object}").send(:"#{each}=", new_val)
      end
    end
  end

  def save
    super
    send(:"#{proxy_object}").save unless read_only
  end

end
```

You start by declaring this an abstract class so that Rails doesn't go looking for a `remote_data_proxies` table in your database. The `class_inheritable_accessor` method is a Rails add-on to the Ruby core. It provides a get and set method for a class attribute, which allows each subclass to maintain its own value for the attribute. The code also aliases one of the setter methods for a slightly cleaner look when called from a subclass.

The attributes themselves define what accessor is used at the instance level to access the object being proxied, and whether the connection to the remote object is read-only.

The meat of the code is the `create_proxy_accessors` method, which is similar to the method you put in `IngredientBase` earlier in this chapter. It takes the class being proxied and an optional prefix, and creates new accessors for all attributes in that class. If the proxy is supposed to be read-only, it skips creating setter methods. Finally, `save` is overridden to save the remote object if the proxy allows write changes.

To use this class, some changes need to be made to `IngredientDataProxy` and `Ingredient`. First, you need to make `IngredientDataProxy` a subclass of `RemoteProxy`, and then make the appropriate data calls:

```
class IngredientDataProxy < RemoteDataProxy

  belongs_to :ingredient_data
  has_and_belongs_to_many :ingredients, :join_table => :ingredient_data_join

  set_proxy_object :ingredient_data
  create_proxy_accessors(IngredientData, :prefix => "ingredient_")

end
```

Then change the definition of the relationship in `Ingredient` as follows:

```
has_and_belongs_to_many :ingredient_data,
      :class_name => "IngredientDataProxy",
      :join_table => :ingredient_data_join
```

With these changes in place, the proxy objects themselves are placed in the `ingredient_data` accessor (the class name of the connection has to be changed to accommodate this). At this point, the tests will work again — calling `ingredient.ingredient_data` will return proxy objects, which will pass the accessor write and reads back to the remote data object.

Why Be Normal?

The database software that most Rails programs use — MySQL, PostgreSQL, and Oracle — all belong to a database structure known as a *relational database*, in contrast to a flat database, (such as a CSV text file), a hierarchical database (such as an XML structure), or an object-oriented database (such as . . . well, nothing you've probably ever heard of, but like the Loch Ness Monster, you do hear about sightings of OO databases from time to time).

A Little Bit of Theory

Although databases may seem like one of the most pragmatic of all software, in fact, there's a huge amount of theory behind the structure and design of relational databases — although, to be fair, a true database purist would argue that none of the popular databases that call themselves relational actually adhere to the strict relational model. Be that as it may, much of the theory of relational database design is concerned with various kinds of *normalization*. A full discussion of all the various flavors of normalization (Wikipedia lists a solid nine named forms) is beyond the scope of this book (and frankly, I think it may be beyond my humble ability to comprehend).

However, the basic idea behind normalization is simple enough: use the structure of the database to ensure database integrity. In general, this involves keeping unrelated data in separate tables such that data is not duplicated. In your classic Order/Customer database, for example, an un-normalized database might include customer information such as name or address inside the order table, where it might potentially be duplicated if one customer is repeated in multiple orders. A normalized database would put the customer information in its own table, where it would be referenced via a foreign key in the order table. An even more normalized database might separate various parts of the customer information, such as phone number or address, into their own separate tables.

A normalized database has a number of beneficial features. Because duplicated data is frowned on, the database size is smaller (often a lot smaller) than an un-normalized version. Most relational databases offer mechanisms, such as foreign key constraints, that are used with normalized database structures to ensure database integrity.

However, there are some costs to using a fully normalized database. The most important one for our purposes is that the more complex the normalized structure is, the more expensive it is to read from a database (although, depending on the structure, a write operation can actually be cheaper because data in other tables would not need to be rewritten). If you've ever tried to run a database query that tries to join more than two tables at a time, you know that it can become painful quite quickly. Even though Rails tries to be smart about managing lookups to joined tables, there's no getting around some kind of speed hit when you try to do a join.

Relational databases arose among a series of constraints. Data storage was much more expensive, for example. And in many back-end systems, the savings from not having to write a customer address multiple times, for example, made up for the increased cost of reading an order.

These conditions do not apply to most modern web applications. Database storage is pretty cheap, megabyte for megabyte, and bandwidth and server CPU time is much more likely to be a bottleneck for your application. In addition, for many web applications, data is read far more often than it is written. Think of a blog database, for example — or Flickr, or Twitter.

In this context, normalization might be too much of a good thing. If you are having database-speed problems with your normalized relational database, one thing to consider is a little denormalization. For our purpose, denormalizing a database amounts to caching foreign data within a column of a table that is using it. You've already seen one example in this book — the way the `acts_as_taggable` plugin allows you to cache the tag string within the table being tagged. Now, you'll implement it on your own data.

A Little Bit of Practice

Before starting, it's important to emphasize that this kind of performance optimization should only be undertaken towards the end of a product cycle, when you actually have data suggesting that there's a slowdown in accessing the data. (In Chapter 13 you'll learn more about how you might gather that data.) Any kind of caching tends to make development more complicated, which in turn makes testing and debugging that much more difficult.

That said, the Soups OnLine database schema includes an association that would certainly be the kind of thing you'd expect denormalizing to speed up. I speak, of course, of the association between recipes and ingredients, where the recipe displays the ingredients not just through a join relationship, but also through some further processing on the ingredient data to convert it to a string. If the ingredients change rarely, as you might expect, then denormalizing the ingredient string back to the recipe table could potentially have a large savings.

The first design decision is exactly when to create the cached version of the string. I decided to create it lazily as part of the process of requesting the ingredient string for the first time. The advantage of a lazy construction here is that it sidesteps the complication of exactly when during the creation of the recipe to create the cache. A poorer design choice would be to put the cache command in the controller for creation or editing of a recipe. That's a poorer choice because there's no reason why the controller should know or care whether the recipe is caching ingredients or not.

The test looks like this (in `recipe_test.rb`):

```
def test_should_cache_ingredient_string
  subject = Recipe.find(1)
  assert subject.cached_ingredient_string.blank?
  subject.ingredient_string
  assert_equal(subject.ingredient_string, subject.cached_ingredient_string)
  string_1 = "1 1/2 cups First Ingredient, Chopped"
  string_2 = "1 1/2 cups Second Ingredient, Sliced"
  string_3 = "1 1/2 cups Third Ingredient, Diced"
  assert_equal("#{string_1}\n#{string_2}\n#{string_3}",
      subject.cached_ingredient_string)
end
```

Create a recipe, and then verify that the cached string starts out blank. Then create the ingredient string and verify that it matches the ingredient string. For good measure, verify that the string actually matches a known literal (the first test feels a little tautological for me to be completely comfortable with it).

This test will need a database migration to add the new column. The file name should be `db/migrate/008_add_ingredient_cache.rb` and should include the following:

```
class AddIngredientCache < ActiveRecord::Migration
  def self.up
    add_column :recipes, :cached_ingredient_string, :string
  end

  def self.down
    remove_column :recipes, :cached_ingredient_string
  end
end
```

After running the migration and updating the test database, the model code change turns out to be a slight change to the `ingredient_string` method in `recipe.rb`. This change is as follows:

```
def cache_ingredient_string
  self.cached_ingredient_string = ingredients.collect do |i|
    i.display_string
  end.join("\n")
end

def ingredient_string
  cache_ingredient_string if self.cached_ingredient_string.blank?
  self.cached_ingredient_string
end
```

The actual `ingredient_string` method creates the cache version if needed. When the cached version is in place, that version will be sent out without bothering to look at the actual ingredients.

That's all well and good, but it doesn't cover the case where an ingredient is edited after the cached string is created — the cached string needs to be changed. This is much easier if you assume that the cache will update only when the ingredient is actually saved. This makes sense because it's unlikely that unsaved ingredient changes are going to linger in memory, and it's harder to update the cache on the attribute set, and even harder to guarantee that Rails isn't going to have more than one copy of the recipe instance floating around.

Here's the unit test for `test/unit/recipe_test.rb`:

```
def test_should_cache_ingredient_string_if_ingredient_changes
  first_ingredient = Ingredient.find(1)
  subject = first_ingredient.recipe
  first_ingredient.ingredient = "bananas"
  first_ingredient.save
  string_1 = "1 1/2 cups bananas, Chopped"
  string_2 = "1 1/2 cups Second Ingredient, Sliced"
  string_3 = "1 1/2 cups Third Ingredient, Diced"
  assert_equal("#{string_1}\n#{string_2}\n#{string_3}",
      subject.cached_ingredient_string)
  first_ingredient.ingredient = "carrots"
  string_1_new = "1 1/2 cups carrots, Chopped"
  assert_equal("#{string_1}\n#{string_2}\n#{string_3}",
      subject.cached_ingredient_string)
end
```

This one is a tiny bit more involved. It starts by creating the ingredient and taking not of its recipe. The test then changes the ingredient, saves it, and tests that the cached string has changed as expected. The process is then repeated, mostly for good measure. The somewhat odd dodge in the second line to get the recipe from the ingredient rather than vice versa seems to protect against ActiveRecord creating a second recipe object (although it's not immediately clear to me whether that's an artifact of the test environment or not).

ActiveRecord Callbacks

To make this test pass, you're going to use the *callback* feature of ActiveRecord, which allows you to specify arbitrary code to be run before or after a validation, creation, or save. The following line toward the top of `ingredient.rb` will get the ball rolling:

```
after_save :update_recipe_cache
```

The `after_save` here is the name of the callback that, surprisingly enough, denotes code that is called after the ActiveRecord is saved. There are actually 14 callbacks. For new objects, the sequence is as follows:

```
before_validation_on_create
after_validation_on_create
before_create
after_create
```

For existing objects, the possibilities are these:

```
before_validation_on_update
after_validation_on_update
before_update
after_update
```

All objects, new or existing, respond to this:

```
before_validation
after_validation
before_save
after_save
before_destroy
after_destroy
```

In general, any validation that returns `false` cancels any further activity. This means that having the `before_save` method return `false` cancels the save operation.

Although you can actually define a method with one of the callbacks as a name, it's more common to use a declaration-style version with a semantically meaningful symbol, as shown at the beginning of this section. You can define more than one symbol for each callback, in which case they are all called in the order that they are declared.

The definition of the actual method is simple, and just calls the existing feature of the recipe object. Here's that method:

```
def update_recipe_cache
   recipe.cache_ingredient_string unless recipe.nil?
end
```

The `unless` clause protects against data integrity problems. The hook after the save is used to ensure that the ingredient data is actually stored in the database, in case ActiveRecord decides it needs to look there when creating the recipe string (although that might lead to a very short time period where the recipe object is out of synch with the database). Another option might just be to clear the cached string on the recipe object (`recipe.cache_ingredient_string = "" unless recipe.nil?`), and force the recipe object to recreate it when needed. That minimizes the chance of data being out of synch at the cost of another database lookup later on.

This discussion should give you the sense that adding this kind of caching to your application is not without cost, and issues of maintaining data integrity need to be addressed. The callback mechanism is a very powerful way to automatically add behavior to your objects that you might otherwise have to specify manual or by overriding methods of `ActiveRecord::Base`.

Unit tests will pass at this point.

A Common Case

There is one common case where Rails provides a preexisting hook to cache a value. It's fairly common to need to get a count of child objects in a one-to-many relationship. It's a little simplistic, but can be handy. What you need to do is augment the `belongs_to` side of the relationship with an option. Let's assume this is working on recipes and ingredients, although I'm not actually going to implement it, because it's not necessary. The `belongs_to` line in ingredient would change to this:

```
belongs_to :recipe, :counter_cache => true
```

In addition, a column named `ingredient_count` needs to be added to the recipes table. If you'd rather give the column a different name, pass that name as a string as the argument to `:counter_cache` instead of `true`.

Now Rails will automatically track the count of ingredients in the recipe object, so it can be retrieved without an additional database call. For this to work properly, all changes to the ingredient count need to go through ActiveRecord. If the database is changed outside Rails, the caching will fall out of sync.

Polymorphic Associations

Sometimes you'll have an ActiveRecord class with a relationship that could apply to objects in multiple classes. Tagging is an example you've already seen, where the tag class might relate to any ActiveRecord model in your system. Or, in a business system, an address table might relate to either a supplier or a customer, each of which has its own separate table. In SoupsOn Line, you might use a rating system where both recipes and users have ratings. Rails makes setting up this kind of relationship reasonably straightforward.

You need to have some kind of common name for whatever feature all the different classes on the receiving end of the relationship might have in common — something like "taggable" or "addressable" or "rateable." This is something vaguely like a Java interface. Unlike Java, Rails doesn't create anything like a class with that kind of actual existence in the code. The name you choose for this relationship is completely up to you, but you do have to be consistent. For this example, you'll create a `Rating` class, and use `ratable` for the interface. Enter the following to begin:

```
$ ruby script/generate model rating --svn
```

From the `Rating` side, you declare the relationship in terms of the arbitrary interface name, as follows:

```
class Rating < ActiveRecord::Base
  belongs_to :ratable, :polymorphic => true
end
```

Thanks to the `:polymorphic` option, this will work even though there is no `Ratable` class. On the other side of the relationship, the `:as` option signifies the polymorphic behavior. Add the following to both `User` and `Recipe`:

```
has_many :ratings, :as => :ratable
```

And boom — it works. Both `User` and `Recipe` will have ratings attributes.

Well, you do have to do the migration first. Create `db/migrate/009_create_ratings.rb` and enter the following, with a `rake db:migrate` when you're done:

```
class CreateRatings < ActiveRecord::Migration
  def self.up
    create_table :ratings do |t|
      t.integer :rating
      t.integer :ratable_id
      t.string  :ratable_type
      t.timestamps
    end
  end

  def self.down
    drop_table :ratings
  end
end
```

The magic is in the `ratable_id` and `ratable_type` columns, which will hold the foreign information. The `id` column is, of course, just what you'd have in a normal relationship. The `type` column, as you might expect, will hold enough information about the class of the object on the other side for Rails to be able to recreate it properly when the association is used.

If you want to create a polymorphic `has_many :through` relationship, you need to set the `:source` option on the side of the `has_many` that cannot infer the correct table from the information it has. This prevents Rails from searching for a table using the interface name.

Database Refresher

Let's close out this chapter with a brief look at some important Rails database security and integrity features. Although these features may already be familiar to you, they are important enough to be touched on here. Three of the most critical needs of the database system are preventing SQL injection attacks by preventing arbitrary user-uploaded statements from being executed, preventing partial data from being saved to the database, and preventing users from getting access to resources that don't belong to them.

Preventing SQL Injection with the Power of Find

A SQL injection attack occurs when user input from, say, a search box is allowed to execute freely on the server side. A malicious user could place an SQL statement into the search box like:

```
'); DROP DATABASE soupsonline_production
```

If that statement is actually executed — well, hopefully you have a recent backup handy. Luckily, it's relatively straightforward to ensure that the user code is not executed, the basic idea is to ensure the user input is treated as a string (or converted to the non-string data type), and that any single quote marks are escaped to prevent the user from being able to break out from the string.

Rails automatically sanitizes data sent to the database when it is the data argument of a `find` method or a `find_by` method, or where the data is part of the ? interpolation of the `:conditions` argument to a `find` method. In other words, all of the following are safe:

```
Recipe.find("banana") ## string will be converted to ID of 0
Recipe.find_by_name("NASTY DELETE STATEMENT")   ## string will be escaped
Recipe.find(:all, :conditions => ["name > ?", params[:name]])
```

Rails does not sanitize data if it's just part of the string in a conditions method, so don't do this:

```
Recipe.find(:all, :conditions => "name = #{params[:name]}" ### NOOOOOOO!!
```

In this case, the string interpolation is handled by Ruby, and Rails never gets the chance to be smart about it.

It's also worth pointing out that the bare `find` method is smart enough to handle an array argument, but not a range argument. For example:

```
Recipe.find([1, 2]) ## converts to SELECT * FROM recipes where id in (1, 2)
Recipe.find(1..2) ### error
```

Using Transactions

Transactions are the standard relational database mechanism for maintaining data integrity when several database operations are related to each other. The basic idea is that you explicitly enter a transaction block, and then any error that occurs while actions are performed inside the block automatically causes the database to roll back to its pre-transaction state. The canonical example is a bank transfer, where you want both the withdrawal and the deposit to occur together, or not at all.

Rails automatically places both `save` and `destroy` calls inside a transaction so that any associated objects are saved or destroyed within the transaction block. This covers the most common use of transactions; however, you'll still need to use them manually from time to time. The `transaction` method is invoked as a class method of ActiveRecord, like this:

```
begin
  Recipe.transaction do
    recipe1.save
    recipe2.save
  end
rescue Exception => e
  return false
end
```

You need the `begin/rescue/end` block if you want to handle any exception thrown in the transaction block. Rails will propagate the exception.

The important thing to note here is that any change you make to the ActiveRecord objects in memory inside the transaction block will still hold even if the transaction rolls back the database. (There used to be a mechanism to include the ActiveRecord objects in the transaction as well, but it was deprecated in the Rails 1.2 timeframe.)

The other notable limitation is that a transaction will not work across database connections. The transaction block in the previous example is not limited to just recipes — any ActiveRecord object managed in that database can be included in the transaction. However, items in the legacy database cannot. The best workaround at the moment is to nest the two transactions as follows:

```
begin
  Ingredient.transaction do
    IngredientData.transaction do
      #stuff
    end
    #after stuff
  end
rescue Exception => e
  return false
end
```

This solution may work in some cases, but not in all. Specifically, a failure of `Ingredient` after the internal transaction has already closed will not trigger a rollback of the closed internal transaction. A full implementation of this feature is considered outside the scope of ActiveRecord.

Preventing Data Hijacking with Associations

Imagine a system that has more secretive data than a recipe site — medical information, for example. A naïve implementation of a method to show records by user might look like this:

```
def show
  @user = current_user
  @record = Record.find(params[:id])
end
```

The problem with this is that there is no mechanism for ensuring that the record being found actually belongs to the current user. In this case, a malicious user might start manually changing the ID in the URL to see records of other users. Although you could do some logical checking for the association after you search for it, it's much easier to just use the features added to associations by Rails.

Although the result of an association in Rails may seem like a simple record or array, in fact, it's an association object that can respond to `find` methods. For example:

```
def show
  @user = current_user
  @record = @user.records.find(params[:id])
end
```

In this case, calling `find` on the user/records association implicitly limits the scope of the search to record objects that actually belong to the user.

This feature has obvious security benefits, and it has some nice code cleanup effects. You can also define your own methods on the association. For example, in this hypothetical User class, you could write the following:

```
has_many :recipes do
  def most_recent
    find(:all, :order => "date DESC", :limit => 10)
  end
end
```

Now that method can be called as follows:

```
@user.recipes.most_recent
```

Notice that this is a call on a user instance and not on the User class.

Resources

There are not all that many specific external resources to point to in this chapter.

Much of the discussion of using legacy databases was fueled by two articles in the Rails wiki, `http://wiki.rubyonrails.org/rails/pages/HowtoUseMultipleDatabases` and `http://wiki.rubyonrails.org/rails/pages/HowtoUseMultipleDatabasesWithFixtures`. In addition, there's a discussion of using proxy objects for covering legacy databases in *Rails Recipes* by Chad Fowler (Pragmatic Bookshelf, 2006).

If there's a funny side to SQL injection, it's in the incomparable XKCD strip at `http://xkcd.com/327`.

Summary

Rails has exceptional support for managing databases, although there are times when you still need to manage the underlying database directly. One such case is a legacy database that does not conform to Rails naming conventions. There's a little bit of up-front work, but you can gain nearly all the Rails benefits when working with a legacy database, including associations, testing, and database fixtures.

To improve database performance, you can denormalize certain fields of the database, essentially caching some derived information in your database tables. This mechanism is easy to implement using ActiveRecord callbacks, which allow you to specify arbitrary code to be automatically executed at various points of the ActiveRecord lifecycle.

You can create polymorphic relationships, in which the other end of the relationship could be a member of multiple classes. This is implemented by using a multiple foreign key to represent the ID and type of the foreign object.

Rails provides basic functionality to prevent SQL injection attacks, take advantage of database transactions, and automatically restrict a find call within an association.

7

Testing Tools

In this book, I've put testing front and center for the simple reason that I believe that automated testing is a critically important method for ensuring both code quality and long-term code maintainability. So far, I've focused on Ruby's standard Test::Unit structure as the primary tool in the testing toolkit. And while Test::Unit is a very important part of automated testing, it's far from the only tool you should be using to ensure that your Rails application is fully and completely tested.

In this chapter, you'll fill out your toolkit a bit and examine why each new tool is vital to your being a test-driven developer. You'll see how to measure the amount of code that is touched by your tests, and how you can use mock objects to improve your code and reach otherwise-difficult-to-cover parts of the code. Then you'll look at some tools for behavior-driven testing, a technique that uses mock objects extensively. Finally, you'll see a way to separate controller and view tests in Rails.

Test Driven

Writing automated tests as a standard part of the development process first gained wide prominence as one of the Extreme Programming core practices. The idea is frequently mischaracterized or misapplied, however, and partially as a result, the practice formally known as *Test-First Programming* is now more frequently called *Test-Driven Development* (*TDD*).

The TDD process comprises the following three steps, which are repeated over and over until your application is complete:

1. Write a simple test specifying something that your program does not currently do. If this step is taking more than a couple of minutes, you are either trying to do too much or your application structure is too complex. This test should fail because you have not yet added the new feature to the system. Run the test to ensure that the test fails.

2. Write simple code that causes the test to pass. The important thing here is to not get caught up in trying to predict what you will need to do to pass the next test. Focus on passing the current test.

3. Refactor. It's likely that the code changes added in either step 1 or step 2 have led to code duplication or some other kind of ugliness. Clean it up right here and now, and make sure the tests pass. Then it's time to move on to the next test.

For the examples in this book, I tend to just show the initial test and final code, and not show the details of the refactorings done to clean up the code. In some cases, I present a series of tests together — even though the code was, in fact, generated one test at a time.

You'll see some mild differences of opinion on exactly how simple to make the code that you add in step 2 of the process. Some coders go so far as to start with just a constant — meaning that if the test has this assertion:

```
assert_equal(7, x.foo)
```

then you should start with this:

```
def foo
  return 7
end
```

If `foo` is not a constant method, then you're supposed to write another test to trigger a failure, and eventually it should become easier to write the actual method than to keep juggling constants. In my opinion, this is usually a bit much (although it rarely takes long to cycle through), and my step two is along the lines of "the simplest thing that could actually be an implementation for this function" or maybe "the simplest thing that would work if I didn't know exactly what the test input would be." Generally, you will also want to write explicit test cases for potential error conditions such as nil or blank arguments.

It's very important not to skip the refactoring step — that's the design part. Doing refactoring after each testing step keeps the cleanup small and manageable, and reduces the chance that you will have to do a large-scale cleanup later on.

Follow the process and, at least in theory, your application will always have 100-percent test coverage, and will always be roughly as simple as possible. These are both worthwhile goals for your application — an application written using TDD should be much easier to modify and maintain moving forward.

TDD is, first and foremost, a software design methodology. The fact that it gives you automated test coverage can help you feel confident about the quality and functionality of your code. However, developer-written, automated tests are not in and of themselves a complete testing solution. In particular, the value of the developer tests is limited by the developers' understanding of the problem. In other words, a developer unit test can only test that the program is doing what the developer expects, not that the expectation is itself correct. To test the real-world correctness of the program, you need to do a separate round of automatic or manual acceptance testing.

Covering It All

When you're trying to determine the quality of a set of unit tests, the most basic question you need to ask yourself is whether the tests actually fully exercise the code being tested — a metric known as *code coverage*. Code coverage is the simple percentage of the application code that is executed when the test suite is run. Coverage can be computed based on the number of lines in the code or by the number of branch paths through the code. Although you could get in a nice programmer-minutia kind of argument over which is the One True Way of measuring coverage, the fact is that in your Rails applications, the goal is complete 100-percent coverage. (Actually, I've started to shoot for 100 percent two ways: 100-percent coverage of the models from the unit tests alone, and 100 percent for the application as a whole from the entire test suite.) The details of the measuring metric are not really that important.

Obviously, coverage in and of itself does not guarantee test quality — for instance, the tests might cover everything but never have any assertions, which only verifies that the program runs without crashing (and in fairness, there are times when that's a perfectly valid test). Lack of coverage pretty much ensures that the test suite is in some trouble — the parts of your application that are missing tests often contain problem code. However, if you are confident that your test writers can consistently and competently create tests that are actually doing something reasonable, then the code-coverage percentage is a decent ballpark measurement of test quality.

Installing rcov

rcov is the standard Rails tool for measuring test coverage. It is not shipped by default with Rails, but you can install it in one of two ways. If you don't have access to a C compiler on your development machine, you can install rcov as a RubyGem as follows:

```
$ gem install rcov
```

As with some of the other gems you've seen, you may be prompted for a separate version between Windows and non-Windows operating systems.

If you have some kind of C compiler on your machine (meaning pretty much any serious Linux distribution, Mac OS X with Xcode installed, or Windows with the Microsoft free command-line compiler), you should install rcov with its native extension. The rcov project claims that using the native extension gives you a speedup factor of 100, which certainly seems worth typing an extra command to install the extension.

To get the extension, download a tarball from `http://eigenclass.org/hiki.rb?rcov`. Unpack the tarball, go to the new directory, and run the following `setup` command to compile the extension:

```
$ ruby setup.rb
```

If you are on a Windows machine without the compiler, and you're running one of the standard Windows Ruby distributions, the `http://eigenclass.org/hiki.rb?rcov` page also has a link for a precompiled Windows extension and how to install it.

To specifically integrate rcov with Rails, you need to install the `rails_rcov` plugin:

```
$ ruby ./script/plugin install -x http://svn.codahale.com/rails_rcov
```

As with other plugins you've installed, remove the -x if you aren't on Subversion. This particular plugin merely contains a single Rake file, so there's not much to worry about either way.

Using rcov and Rails

The rails_rcov plugin adds several Rake tasks to your repertoire. For each type of Rails test (unit, functional, and integration), the plugin adds an rcov task, which generates rcov data, and a clobber task, which clears the data. The new tasks are named as extensions of the exising test types, of the form test:units:rcov and test:units:clobber.

These Rake tasks are useful, but incomplete. Each of them runs the Rails test suite of its type and produces a coverage report, with highlights sent to standard output. The file output from the tasks goes to the <rails root>/coverage directory, and you're going to want to tell your Subversion repository to ignore files in that directory because you probably don't want to have all your coverage data loaded into your repository. (You'll have to add the directory itself to tell Subversion to ignore its contents.)

Though it may be interesting to know specifically what coverage your functional tests are getting, you also want to know about your entire test suite as a group. Unfortunately, there's no task for the rcov plugin to aggregate the data out of the box. (The plugin documentation erroneously states that there is such a task, but it lies — or at least it did when I was writing this, though things may have changed since then.) Fortunately, it's not at all hard to whip up your own Rake task for the occasion. The following example puts a slight gloss on a version presented on the rcov website. Place this in lib/tasks/coverage.rake:

```
require 'rcov/rcovtask'

namespace :test do
  namespace :coverage do
    desc "Delete aggregate coverage data."
    task(:clean) do
      rm_rf "data/coverage"
      rm_f "data/coverage.data"
    end
  end

  test_types = %w[unit functional integration]

  desc 'Aggregate code coverage for unit, functional and integration tests'
  task :coverage => "test:coverage:clean"

  tests_to_run = test_types.select do |type|
    FileList["test/#{type}/**/*_test.rb"].size > 0
  end

  tests_to_run.each do |target|
    namespace :coverage do
      Rcov::RcovTask.new(target) do |t|
        t.libs << "test"
        t.test_files = FileList["test/#{target}/**/*_test.rb"]
        t.verbose = true
        t.rcov_opts << '--rails --aggregate data/coverage.data'
        if target == tests_to_run[-1]
          t.output_dir = "data/coverage"
        else
```

```
            t.rcov_opts << '--no-html'
        end
      end
    end
    task :coverage => "test:coverage:#{target}"
  end

  end
```

This file adds two tasks — test:coverage:clean and test:coverage — which build rcov tasks programmatically and place the final output in coverage/complete. The keys to this are the --aggregate and --no-html options. Aggregating causes a common data file to be placed in coverage .data and added to by each separate task (which will cause rcov to go a bit slower, so I hope you managed to get the native extension installed). Ordinarily, this would cause each task to have the data for that task combined with all the tasks previously run. Because that doesn't seem particularly useful, I use the --no-html option for all but the final test, which is then saved to the coverage/complete directory.

Running the test:coverage task causes all three unit test sub-suites to run, with both their normal output and a text overview of the data. A slew of HTML files are placed in test:coverage. The first one you'll take a look at in this discussion is the index.html file, which should be similar to what's shown in Figure 7-1.

C0 code coverage information

Generated on Tue Aug 28 09:51:49 -0500 2007 with rcov 0.8.0

Name	Total lines	Lines of code	Total coverage	Code coverage
TOTAL	1120	894	93.0%	91.5%
app/controllers/application.rb	31	23	100.0%	100.0%
app/controllers/category_controller.rb	19	16	100.0%	100.0%
app/controllers/ingredients_controller.rb	101	76	94.2%	78.9%
app/controllers/recipes_controller.rb	121	94	86.8%	83.0%
app/controllers/users_controller.rb	136	109	92.6%	90.8%
app/helpers/application_helper.rb	55	44	96.4%	95.5%
app/helpers/category_helper.rb	2	2	100.0%	100.0%
app/helpers/ingredients_helper.rb	2	2	100.0%	100.0%
app/helpers/recipes_helper.rb	2	2	100.0%	100.0%
app/helpers/tabular_form_builder.rb	37	32	100.0%	100.0%
app/helpers/users_helper.rb	2	2	100.0%	100.0%
app/models/authorization_mailer.rb	11	10	100.0%	100.0%
app/models/extensions.rb	23	15	100.0%	100.0%
app/models/ingredient.rb	65	53	100.0%	100.0%
app/models/ingredient_base.rb	18	16	100.0%	100.0%
app/models/ingredient_data.rb	13	9	100.0%	100.0%
app/models/ingredient_data_proxy.rb	9	4	100.0%	100.0%
app/models/ingredient_parser.rb	67	58	100.0%	100.0%
app/models/math_captcha.rb	71	60	100.0%	100.0%
app/models/menu_sidebar.rb	60	45	90.0%	86.7%
app/models/rating.rb	3	3	100.0%	100.0%
app/models/recipe.rb	66	57	95.5%	94.7%
app/models/remote_data_proxy.rb	33	27	33.3%	25.9%
app/models/tag_cloud.rb	44	36	100.0%	100.0%
app/models/token.rb	60	48	95.0%	93.8%
app/models/user.rb	49	36	100.0%	100.0%
lib/tasks/cleanup.rake	20	15	100.0%	100.0%

Figure 7-1

The output lists the source files in your Rake project. For each file, it lists total lines and lines of code. The difference is that the Total lines column includes comments and `def` and `end` lines, while the Lines of code column includes only executable lines. For each metric, there's an estimated percentage of the lines that have been executed at least once during the test suite. (rcov can generate a total count of how many times each line has been hit, but that information is less useful for the current purpose.) A source file that is not touched at all by test code does not show up in the list, so make sure all the files you expect to see are actually there.

Each row is one source file and links to more information about coverage within that file. Figure 7-2 shows a snippet from `ingredients_controller.rb` that shows one of the uncovered segments.

```
42    end
43
44    # POST /ingredients
45    # POST /ingredients.xml
46    def create
47      @ingredient = Ingredient.new(params[:ingredient])
48      respond_to do |format|
49        if @ingredient.save
50          flash[:notice] = 'Ingredient was successfully created.'
51          format.html { redirect_to([@recipe, @ingredient]) }
52          format.xml  { render :xml => @ingredient, :status => :created, :location => @ingredient }
53        else
54          format.html { render :action => "new" }
55          format.xml  { render :xml => @ingredient.errors, :status => :unprocessable_entity }
56        end
57      end
58    end
59
```

Figure 7-2

I'm not sure how well that shows up in black and white, but the `else` clause of this method is highlighted in red to indicate that the test suite did not cover that particular branch of the code. rcov does an impressive amount of analysis on the Rails interpreter's output to gather this data, but it's not always 100-percent correct. In this example, the fact that the `respond_to` inner blocks are all done on one line is masking the fact that there is not actually a test that renders XML for this method. It's also a little weird that the end lines for the `respond_to` block and the method both show as uncovered — I'm not sure that's actually meaningful.

The goal for your Rails project should be to run at 100-percent coverage all the time. This is feasible in Rails partially due to the flexibility of Ruby. When you are at 100-percent coverage with good tests, you have a tremendously strong safety net to support you as you add new features, fix bugs, and refactor your application. Verifying that you haven't introduced new bugs is just a single test-run away at all times.

As you can see from the preceding snapshot (which is the current state of the Soups OnLine code as I write the initial draft of this chapter), the project is already extremely close to 100-percent code coverage. And this is just the result of using Rails scaffolding and the TDD practices shown in this book. The one major coverage hole is the proxy object which was developed as an option in the last chapter. There are no method creator calls for the proxy base class in the current code base, so that class is not being exercised by the test cases — which is not really a problem at the moment (and in a real code base, would be cause to remove the unused code).

Most of the uncovered cases are the error cases of various create and update methods, as shown in the previous screenshot. (I also seem to have forgotten to write controller tests for the Ajax tag edit forms.) To test for a save failure, you need to set up a test scenario where a save would fail. The most obvious way to do that is to try to save an object that fails either Rails validation or database constraints.

There's only one problem. As currently set up, `Recipe` has no database constraints or Rails validations. Although I could probably come up with one or two plausible objects to add (or do something weird like try to save a 10,000-character title and blow up the field), it sure seems like there should be an easier way.

And so there is.

Mock Testing

Mock object testing involves the use of fake objects as stand-ins for your real objects to support automated testing. Traditionally, this technique allows testing in systems involving databases, network connections, or some other relationship that would be difficult or impossible to set up for real in the test context. Over time, the technique has also proven useful in helping to verify program behavior and to focus testing.

Mock testing is one of those areas where anyone who has put together a toolkit has come up with a slightly different naming structure than everybody else. I'm following Martin Fowler's usage from the article "Mocks Aren't Stubs" (see the "References" section at the end of the chapter). Much like a stunt double, a *test double* is any object used as a stand-in for the real thing during testing. A *stub* is a fake object or method set up during the test to return a preset value without performing the real calculation. A *mock* is also set up to return a preset value, but a true mock has the additional capability to track what calls have been made to the mock object and, more importantly, to automatically validate that the calls match expectations that are created during test setup.

Now, the wonderful thing about doing mock object testing in Rails is that the mock tools can leverage the extensive Rails metaprogramming capabilities to turn ordinary, preexisting objects and classes into stubs or mocks. This is in contrast to, say, the Java mock object tools, which tend to do fancy things with Java interfaces or classloaders to create mock object that are proxies to the original object, but which are different from the original object in ways that can cause difficulties during testing.

Because Ruby makes creating mocks and stubs so easy, you gain some very nice testing flexibility. An example that's relevant to the current predicament is that you can create an ActiveRecord model from your project that behaves exactly like every other ActiveRecord model in the system, except that it captures attempts to save and returns a value without actually contacting the database.

Using FlexMock

There are three or four different Rails packages for doing mock object testing. They all seem to have similar features, so I'm only going to discuss one of them here. The package is called FlexMock, and it was created by Jim Weirich (who is also the person responsible for Rake). FlexMock is distributed as a Ruby gem so you install it via a typical `gem` command, like this:

```
$ sudo gem install flexmock
```

To use FlexMock in your test suite, put the following `require` line at the top of each test script that will need mocks (and if it's going to be used frequently, put it in `test_helper.rb`):

```
require 'flexmock/test_unit'
```

Now you're ready to mock.

I'm going to show you the specific mock test I used to reach one uncovered part of the code base, and then walk you through how that test might be extended and how other stubs and mocks might be created.

The uncovered code was the `else` clause in this method from `recipes_controller.rb`, as highlighted in the following code:

```
def update
    @recipe = Recipe.find(params[:id])

    respond_to do |format|
      if @recipe.update_attributes(params[:recipe])
        flash[:notice] = 'Recipe was successfully updated.'
        format.html { redirect_to(@recipe) }
        format.xml  { head :ok }
      else
        format.html { render :action => "edit" }
        format.xml  { render :xml => @recipe.errors,
          :status => :unprocessable_entity }
      end
    end
  end
```

To reach the uncovered part of the code, a test must fail the `update_attributes` call. However, as mentioned previously, setting up an error condition for a recipe is not immediately obvious because the `Recipe` class doesn't do any validation to speak of. Rather than tie your head in knots trying to create a failure case, it's much easier to just impose a failure case on the system. Place this in `test/fixture/recipes_controller_test.rb`:

```
def test_should_fail_update
    flexmock(Recipe).new_instances.should_receive(
        :update_attributes). and_return(false)
    put :update, :id => 1, :recipe => {:title => "Grandma's Chicken Soup"}
    assert_template('edit')
    actual = Recipe.find(1)
    assert_not_equal("Grandma's Chicken Soup", actual.title)
    assert_equal("1", actual.servings)
  end
```

The key line of code here, obviously, is the first line. Let's break it down, piece by piece:

❑   `flexmock(Recipe)` — Creates a new test double (in this case, it's a stub). The `flexmock` method takes a number of different options that I'll get to in a moment. In this case, `flexmock` is being called with a real, live Ruby object as an argument, namely the `Recipe` class. The goal in this case is to build mock behavior around the real object.

❏ new_instances — This is a method on the mock object proxy. It is only valid in the case where the object being mocked is actually a class object. When this is called, FlexMock applies any further specifications to all new instances of the class being mocked — in other words, it overrides the behavior of calls to new. As a result, any ActiveRecord recipe object created in the call — including the object that will get created in the controller method to be updated — will be augmented with the mock behavior. This means that objects already created and stored as fixtures will not have the new behavior, but the same objects loaded back out of the database and into ActiveRecord models will. This method call (along with most of the similar methods in FlexMock) returns a special object that records all the various expectations to allow the constraints to be chained as they are in this example.

❏ should_receive(:update_attributes) — Now the test is actually starting to specify behavior of the stub objects. This method call alerts FlexMock to the idea that you want to do something with the update_attributes call, but does not yet specify exactly what that behavior will be. The should_receive method can take an arbitrary number of symbol arguments, each of which represents a method that will be stubbed or mocked according to the same specification.

❏ and_return(:false) — The line of code ends with the actual behavior specification. FlexMock will now cause any call to update_attributes to return false instantly without hitting the database, passing Go, or collecting 200 dollars. This method has a lot of flexibility. You can pass in several values, in which case FlexMock will return them one by one on each new call to the mocked method — if there are more classes than values, the last value is used again and again. You can also pass in a block, which takes in all the arguments to the actual method and enables you to perform arbitrary manipulation to determine the mock return value.

This test passes as-is because it was added to increase coverage and targeted at a specific branch of the code. The flexmock statement leads off the test, and then the normal functional test controller method is invoked. The difference is that when the controller method goes to call update_attributes, the FlexMock system intercepts the call and returns false, as specified. The controller interprets this as a failure, and walks down the error branch of the method, enabling the test to validate that the controller behaves as expected under error.

This is a simple and elegant way to test for failure conditions or other conditions that might be difficult to specify explicitly in the object model. Add tests similar to this for the other error clauses that weren't previously covered, and 100-percent test coverage not far away. (For the record, it took me about an hour and a half to get to 100-percent coverage from this test, and that included finding one genuine bug, taking a stab at reincorporating the proxy object, and some rather silly confusion because I had two tests with the same name.)

Specifying Stubs

FlexMock is nothing if not flexible in the way it allows you to create its proxy objects. The preceding mock test is written against a class object and applies to all new instances. Another option is to create a real instance, and then specify stub methods on the object, like this:

```
soup = Recipe.new
flexmock(soup).should_receive(:ingredients).and_return([])
```

Where the method name and return value can be expressed as a simple key/value pair, FlexMock offers the following shortcut for the second line:

```
flexmock(soup, :ingredients => [])
```

This is shorter, but it's a bit further from being a readable English sentence. You can, of course, pass in multiple key/value pairs, and you can also do this in multiple lines. For example:

```
flexmock(soup)
flexmock(soup).should_receive(:ingredients).and_return([])
```

Or you can do this as a block, as in the following example:

```
flexmock(soup) do |soup|
   soup.should_receive(:ingredients).and_return([])
end
```

You can also create a complete fake object that isn't associated with an existing class, just by passing a string or symbol to `flexmock`. For example:

```
flexmock("banana")
flexmock("banana").should_receive(:do_something) and_return(3)
flexmock("banana", :do_something => 3)
flexmock(:do_something => 3)
```

The second and third lines are identical in effect. The last line is almost identical, but it doesn't give the stub object an individual name.

If, for some reason, you want to add stub or mock methods to a string, you need to do something slightly tricky because the default would be to treat the string as the name of a new mock, as in the first line of the preceding example. To actually add stub methods to a string or symbol, use the :base option like this:

```
flexmock(:base, "string_to_mock")
```

You can also make the first argument the symbol :safe. A FlexMock object in normal mode adds a few methods to the real object's namespace, most notably `should_receive`, and `new_instance`. This is a problem if methods by those names already exist in the object. In safe mode, FlexMock does not add those methods. Therefore, to add expectations to a safe-mode mock object, you must do so inside a block such as this:

```
flexmock(:safe, soup) do |mock|
   mock.should_receive(:ingredients).and_return([])
end
```

This works because the proxy object used within the block will have the FlexMock `should_receive` method, but when the proxy object is used outside the block, it will not have that method added.

All of these chains return the internal FlexMock expectation object, not the mock itself (this supports the chaining of the method). To get the actual mock back, end the chain with the following `mock` call:

```
mock = flexmock(Recipe).should_receive(:save).mock
```

Finally, the following FlexMock mechanism is specifically designed to play nicely with ActiveRecord:

```
require 'flexmock/activerecord'
mock = flexmodel(Recipe) do |mock|
   # arbitrary mock stuff
end
```

Using the `flexmodel` form gives you a stub object with a few predefined ActiveRecord style methods — `class`, `id`, `is_a?`, `errors`, `new_record?`, and `to_params` — which return simple stub versions of the real methods. `id` returns a unique identifier, `isa?` and `class` match the real class, and so on.

Mock Expectations

All of the FlexMock functionality you've seen so far actually creates stubs — objects that can receive messages and return values, but don't have any provision yet to validate behavior. FlexMock has a series of methods that can be chained onto an expectation declaration to add validations.

There are three general types of expectations that can be added to a stubbed method to turn it into a mock. You can add an expectation about the number of times the method will be called using one of the following modifiers:

- ❏   `never`
- ❏   `zero_or_more_times`
- ❏   `once`
- ❏   `twice`
- ❏   `times(n)`

By default, the test for each of these is that the method is called exactly that number of times (except, of course, for `zero_or_more_times`). Any of these methods can be prefixed by the method `at_least` or `at_most`. For example:

```
should_receive(:update_attributes).at_most.once.and_return(false)
```

These modifiers appear after the `should_receive` call and before the `and_return` call. They can be chained, as in `at_least.once.at_most.times(3)`.

Updating the initial test with the preceding decoration still results in a test that validates. The `at_most` call is needed here because although the ActiveRecord object created in the controller gets an `update_attributes` call, the ActiveRecord object created in the fourth line of the test does not. All `Recipe` objects get the same specification, and the test will fail with a message that looks like this:

```
in mock 'flexmock(Recipe)': method 'update_attributes(*args)' called incorrect
number of times.
```

Notice that the error message does not specify which instance of `Recipe` has the problem. Validation failures are somewhat easier to diagnose if the mock object is based on a single instance rather than the class.

You can also specify what arguments should be passed to the mock call, using the
with(*Argument1*, *Argument2* ...) specifier method. The argument list you put in the expectation is
matched against the argument list when called. Objects are matched using eq, with two exceptions. If
you pass in a class name, any instance of that class is a valid entry, as shown here:

```
foo.should_receive(:thing).with(String, Integer) #thing("hi", 2) is valid
```

You can also pass in a regular expression (regex) as an argument, in which case the real arguments are
valid if they match the expression (FlexMock converts the arguments to strings before comparing). If you
actually want to validate against a literal class or regex, you can do that with the form
with(eq(ClassName)).

The third kind of validation you can have a FlexMock object perform pertains to the order in which the
real calls to the method are made. If you use the ordered decorator, FlexMock validates the order of the
actual calls, such that all methods specified as ordered are invoked in the same order as they are
specified. So, the following specification:

```
flexmock(toast) do |mock|
   mock.should_receive(:toast_bread).ordered
   mock.should_receive(:spread_butter).ordered
end
```

considers this to be valid:

```
toast.toast_bread
toast.go_to_fridge
toast.spread_butter
```

The presence of the non-ordered go_to_fridge method does not affect the validation.

The ordered method can take a single argument, which is a symbol representing a group. A number of
consecutive methods can be decorated with the same group name. This changes the behavior of the
validation slightly. Methods within the group can be called in any order. However, all methods specified
before the named group must be called first, and all methods specified after the group must be called
later. Here's an example:

```
flexmock(toast) do |mock|
   mock.should_receive(:toast_bread).ordered
   mock.should_receive(:go_to_fridge).ordered(:passing_time)
   mock.should_receive(:look_at_clock).ordered(:passing_time)
   mock.should_receive(:pace).ordered(:passing_time)
   mock.should_receive(:spread_butter).ordered
end
```

Here, go_to_fridge, look_at_clock, and pace can be invoked in any order, as long as toast_bread
is before any of them and spread_butter is after all of them.

Mock objects are very useful for validating hard-to-reach parts of your application, and are also good for
focusing unit tests on the particular part of the application under test. Following that thought to its
logical conclusion leads you to a slightly different paradigm of unit testing.

Behavior-Driven Design

One thing you may have noticed about shifting to mock object validation is that it alters the very nature of the kinds of testing that you perform in your unit tests. Traditional unit tests, which perform most of their validation via assertions, are testing the *state* of the application. A mock object test, which is validating the calls made during the test against a predefined expectation, is testing the *behavior* of the application. The behavioral test is, at least potentially, more readily capable of separating the intended behavior of the program from the specific implementation being used.

Advocates of the flavor of automated test development called *Behavior-Driven Design* (BDD) attempt to move the test design closer to the problem space than to the implementation space, in part by designing the BDD tool sets so that tests can be specified in an idiom that is closer to natural language. BDD toolkits make extensive use of mock objects both as a way to specify the problem domain and as a way to separate individual unit tests from each other. Using traditional TDD tests, a change in a low-level method can cause multiple tests to break. A BDD advocate would argue that the fact that a single code change can trigger multiple test failures means that the tests are not truly unit tests, but in fact are integration tests, although at a very small scale. Where a TDD style of testing might use mock objects only in cases where the real object is unavailable or awkward, a BDD style uses mocks more aggressively to separate the method under test from the rest of the system.

This section provides an overview of RSpec, the most popular BDD test package for Ruby. RSpec has very nice integration with Rails, including the capability to separately test controllers, views, and helper methods.

Loading RSpec

RSpec is available as both a Ruby gem (`gem install rspec`) and as a Rails plugin. For use within Rails, grab both the RSpec plugin and the RSpec Rails plugin like this:

```
ruby script/plugin install -x svn://rubyforge.org/var/svn/rspec/tags/CURRENT/rspec
ruby script/plugin install -x ↵
svn://rubyforge.org/var/svn/rspec/tags/CURRENT/rspec_on_rails
```

As usual, if you don't want to install RSpec as external to your Subversion server, you can remove the `-x` option.

Windows users also need to install a gem called `win32console` for RSpec to work properly.

After RSpec has been installed, you need to run the following generator to set up RSpec directories and files:

```
ruby script/generate rspec
```

This command's primary purpose is to create the `spec` subdirectory under your top-level Rails directory, which it populates with a `spec_helper.rb` file, analogous to the standard `test_helper.rb` file. It also creates a couple of scripts, and some other files that you don't need to deal with right now. The command does not, however, set up the RSpec subdirectories that the Rails naming convention will expect. You'll need to do that manually.

RSpec uses a Rails naming convention that is similar to the conventions already in place. The following table shows this convention by providing sample names.

Test Type	Example Name
Controller test	`spec/controllers/recipe_controller_spec.rb`
Helper test	`spec/helpers/recipes_helper_spec.rb`
Model test	`spec/models/recipe_spec.rb`
View test	`spec/views/recipe/new_spec.rb`

For the purposes of this section, you'll be manually creating the spec files because the model, view, controller, and helper files have already been generated. If you are starting from scratch with RSync, some custom generators have been defined: `rspec_controller`, `rspec_model`, and `rspec_scaffold`. Their behavior is identical to the preexisting controllers — they all take the same arguments. The only difference is the creation of RSpec stub test files in the spec directory, rather than Test::Unit files in the test directory.

You can run all your RSpec specifications with the command `rake spec`. If you only want to run one of the subsuites, use a more specific command such as `rake spec:models`. Subtasks exist for `controllers`, `helpers`, `models`, `plugins`, and `views`. If you have rcov installed, then any of these commands can also have `:rcov` added onto it, and a coverage report will be generated. However, even though RSpec has tests for view templates, rcov will not give a coverage report for the ERB template files. In Rails 2.0, the default rake task will run both unit tests in the test directory and RSpec specifications in the spec directory.

Writing RSpec Specs

An RSpec spec file contains one or more behaviors, each of which contains one or more examples. Notice that the naming conventions already set up the idea of how RSpec differs from Test::Unit — "behavior" and "example" are talking about the tests in terms of functionality and intention, whereas "test" and "assertion" are associated with implementation. An RSpec behavior is roughly equivalent to a Test::Unit class, although you are much more likely to see multiple behaviors in a single spec file than multiple classes in a Test::Unit class file.

The method for declaring a behavior is `describe`, and the method for declaring an example is `it`. The skeleton outline of a spec file looks like this:

```
describe Foo do
  it "should not crash when I call it" do
    # do something testable here
  end
end
```

Notice that the example is described with a natural language string rather than a method name.

Within a behavior, you can specify initial conditions and cleanup using the `before` and `after` methods. These methods take two modifiers. The default is `:each`, which signifies that the associated block should be run before or after each individual example, just like a `setup` or `teardown` method in Test::Unit. The other alternative is `:all`, which signifies that the block should be run at the very beginning of the behavior before all the examples, or at the very end after all the examples. You may declare multiple `before` and `after` blocks with the same modifier, and all of the blocks will be executed at the appropriate time.

Any methods you declare inside a behavior using the normal Ruby `def` syntax can be accessed from any example within the behavior, so you can still write custom verifiers or common helper methods.

Also, although examples normally take a block, you can temporarily put an example in with just the string and no block. For example:

```
it "should do something that hasn't been implemented yet"
```

RSpec will interpret this test as pending, and will report the number of pending tests separate from the number of passing or failing tests.

You can take that one step further and account for those instances in which you know a test is failing and don't care, but would like to know when the test starts passing. The general form is this:

```
it "should fix this silly bug" do
  pending("this is Bob's problem") do
    #specify the failing test here
  end
end
```

In this case, RSpec will run the code inside the pending block. If it fails, the test will still report as pending, but if it succeeds you'll get an expectation failure that essentially tells you the test no longer fails and doesn't need to be pending.

Writing Model Tests

Over the next few sections, you'll see some examples of RSpec specifications based on Test::Unit tests that have already been written. The goal is not to completely redo the tests that have already been written, but rather to see some examples of how RSpec tests work, and note how they differ from a Test::Unit test. Let's start with the models.

For these tests to work, the ingredient and recipe YAML files need to be copied from test/fixtures to spec/fixtures. The following RSpec is from the file `spec/models/recipe_spec.rb`:

```
require File.dirname(__FILE__) + '/../spec_helper'

describe Recipe, "basic test suite" do
  fixtures :recipes
  fixtures :ingredients

  it "should have ingredients in order" do
    subject = Recipe.find(1)
    subject.ingredients.collect { |i| i.order_of }.should == [1, 2, 3]
  end
end
```

This is an almost direct translation of a unit test from Chapter 1. The `describe` block sets up the behavior (there's no `before` or `after` code in this behavior yet). The `it` block sets up a specific expectation — in this case, the expectation that ingredient strings will always be ordered.

The `should` method (and its sibling `should_not`) is the key to testing state in RSpec. It's used here with an `==` modifier after it, in which case it performs what is essentially a straightforward assertion test with the right-side value being the expected case, and the left-side value (the object being passed the `should` message) being the actual value.

You can put other things after a `should` message. In particular, any message of the form `be_<something>` is automatically translated by RSpec to the predicate `<something>?`. Because `nil?` is defined for all objects, you can always test `should be_nil` or `should_not be_nil`. Within a Rails project, you can always test `should be_blank`; arrays can be tested for `should be_empty`; and so on. If you think it reads better, you can use `be_a` or `be_an` as the prefix. Also, RSpec is smart enough to adjust for have/has, so `should have_key` for a hash will test against the `has_key?` predicate. Remember that this trick works only against methods that are defined with the question mark in the name, even though you don't type the question mark in RSpec.

The first test is actually pretty similar to the original unit test, but the next one shows more of the difference between RSpec and Test::Unit. Way back in Chapter 1, you wrote a bunch of tests to validate the code that parsed a string like `"2 cups of carrots, chopped"` into an `Ingredient` object. And then there was also a test to validate that a recipe could take a number of those strings and convert them into a list of ingredients. The RSpec version of the recipe test looks like this:

```
it "should split ingredient strings into separate lines" do
    Ingredient.should_receive(:parse).exactly(3).times.and_return do |s, rec, ord|
        Ingredient.new(:recipe_id => rec.id, :order_of => ord, :amount => 2,
            :ingredient => ord)
    end
    subject = Recipe.find(2)
    subject.ingredient_string =
        "2 cups carrots, diced\n\n1/2 tablespoon salt\n\n1 1/3 cups stock"
    subject.ingredients.count.should == 3
    subject.ingredients.collect { |i| i.order_of }.should == [1, 2, 3]
    subject.ingredients.collect { |i| i.ingredient }.should == %w[1 2 3]
end
```

There are two components to the test. The recipe object is given a string with three ingredients and two blank lines. The recipe is supposed to ignore the blank lines and cause the other lines to be parsed.

In the Test::Unit version of the test, the actual ingredient parser is called, and the specific objects in the recipe are tested against the expected results of the parser. In the RSpec version, you do not call the ingredient parser because you are not testing it. Instead, the first line of the test sets up the `Ingredient` class as a partial mock object, returning dummy ingredient objects, and asserting that it will be called exactly three times. The dummy ingredient objects don't match what the real parser would emit (they just have the minimum amount of data not to cause nil exception), but you actually don't care — the correctness of the parser itself is a job for the tests that you are going to write against the parser. In this test, your job is to verify that the recipe object doesn't cry if it's given blank lines, so you don't care whether the parser is correct. The key here is to be very focused on the actual method under test and build a wall around that method which only mock methods need to get through.

RSpec uses its own mock object specification, similar to FlexMock. (If you'd rather use FlexMock or one of the other Ruby mock object tools, it's easy to configure RSpec accordingly.) The should_receive mock specification is very close to the FlexMock specification for mock validations. It can be augmented with once, twice, times(n), at_least, and at_most for all of those values. In addition to and_return, you can use and_raise, which takes an exception class as an argument and validates that an exception of that class is raised under the error condition being tested, there is also and_yield, which is similar to and_return, but instead of returning the values, and_yield passes them to a block argument.

There is one dynamic part of the mock in this test. Because you passed a block argument to and_return, the actual ingredient object returned can have its recipe id and order values set from the arguments that the recipe object sends. Although it's generally better practice to have mock return objects that are static to avoid interdependencies, in this case there is a dependency that needs to be verified. The order of the ingredients is not set in the parser itself, but rather is passed as an argument by the recipe object. If the ingredient order was set statically in the mock object, it would be impossible to verify that the order was being set accurately. As written, though, the test allows the order to be set dynamically, and tags each ingredient with the expected order so that the recipe order can be fully validated.

The preceding test is a good example of how RSpec allows you mix behavior testing with the state testing. RSpec also encourages playing with method names and the like to get the examples to read as clearly as possible. So, when I started writing the tests for the ingredient parser, I decided to take full advantage and put the following in spec/model/ingredient_spec.rb:

```
require File.dirname(__FILE__) + '/../spec_helper'

class String
  def parsing_to?(hash)
    expected = Ingredient.new(hash)
    actual = Ingredient.parse(self, Recipe.find(1), 1)
    actual == expected
  end
end

describe Ingredient, "basic parsing suite" do
  fixtures :ingredients, :recipes

  it "should parse a basic string" do
    "2 cups carrots, diced".should be_parsing_to(:recipe_id => 1,
        :order_of => 1, :amount => 2, :unit => "cups",
        :ingredient => "carrots", :instruction => "diced")
  end
end
```

Clearly the weird thing about this one is the additional method I added to String, which is exactly the sort of thing that your stricter software engineers warn about in hushed tones when they learn that Ruby lets you add arbitrary methods to existing classes.

In any case, because the method will only be around during testing, I think I'm probably okay from a program stability point of view, and there's no denying that with the RSpec magic naming deal, "2 cups carrots, diced".should be_parsing_to is a rather expressive and clear way of phrasing the test condition. Actually, I think it begs the question of whether the program itself should have a String#parse_to_ingredient method, but I'll restrain myself for the moment.

Writing Controller Specifications

RSpec has a clear advantage over the standard Rails test tools in that it allows for controller, view, and helper tests that are all separated from each other. Controller tests are placed in the directory spec/ controllers. Here is a start toward the specification for the RecipesController — I've translated the tests for verifying that the index method works, and that calling HTML GET for the new method returns a CAPTCHA, as set up in Chapter 3. The first part is the before(:each) method that sets up a mock object for recipes. To completely encapsulate the controller test and prevent it from interacting with the models and database, you should use RSpec stubs to intercept calls to ActiveRecord class methods like new or find to return mocked models rather than real ActiveRecord objects. To that end, you would put the following in spec/controllers/recipes_controller_spec.rb:

```
require File.dirname(__FILE__) + '/../spec_helper'

describe RecipesController do

  before(:each) do
    @recipe = mock("person")
    @recipe.stub!(:new_record?).and_return(false)
    Recipe.stub!(:new).and_return(@recipe)
    Recipe.stub!(:find).and_return(@recipe)
  end
```

The stub specification for RSpec is slightly different than the FlexMock method. This setup stubs Recipe#new and Recipe#find and causes them to return the stubbed recipe instance that was set up in the first two lines of the method.

The first specification delineates the following expectations when the user requests the index method:

```
it "should get an index when requested" do
  get "index"
  response.should be_success
  assigns[:recipes].should_not be_nil
end
```

This specification exposes some of the special methods RSpec has to test the response from a controller. The spec should be_success returns true if the response status is 200, and the related response. should be_redirect spec tests for a redirection status. Note that if you aren't rendering views in these tests, should be_success will never fail.

For controllers that render a template normally, the spec should render_template takes the path to the template and validates that the expected template would be loaded. If the controller returns text without a template, you can validate that test with should have_text, which takes a string or regular expression and validates that there is a match in the returned text. If the controller does a redirect to, you can use should redirect_to, which takes a full URL, a local path to the URL, or a hash of options that you would send to url_for.

The last line of the method uses the assigns hash, which is similar to the assigns method for standard functional tests and represents the instance variables created by the controller. You also have access to flash and session hashes, which allow you to assign to those controller variables.

The second controller test checks the `new` method like this:

```
it "should respond to GET new with a captcha" do
  @token = mock_model(Token)
  captcha = mock(MathCaptcha)
  MathCaptcha.should_receive(:create).with(3).and_return(captcha)
  get "new"
  assigns[:captcha].should == captcha
end
```

If you compare this method to the analogous traditional unit test that was written in Chapter 1, and augmented with the CAPTCHA in Chapter 3, you'll see that this one is a good deal different. In particular, the original unit test had a lot of `assert_select` calls to verify the output of the view associated with that method. In RSpec, that verification is handled in the view test, and what's tested in the controller is simply that it creates the variables or makes the database calls that you would expect.

In the original version, this test also validated that the CAPTCHA object created a token. Again, from an RSpec perspective, that's considered either redundant or mislocated, and should be placed in the test for the CAPTCHA object itself. From this spec's perspective, it's enough to know that the controller asks the `MathCaptcha` class to create a new instance, and puts that same instance into an instance variable for later usage. The creation is validated by the mock `should_receive` in line three of the example, and the assignment is validated by the last line.

The following test of an HTTP `PUT` update shows another example of how RSpec specifications differ from unit tests:

```
it "should respond to a PUT with an update" do
  @recipe.should_receive(:update_attributes).with(
      {"title" => "Grandma's Chicken Soup"}).and_return(@recipe)
  put "update", :id => 1, :recipe => {:title => "Grandma's Chicken Soup"}
  response.should redirect_to("http://test.host/recipes/#{@recipe.id}")
end
```

This example is pretty simple. The first line sets up the expectation that the one-and-only recipe mock will get an `update_attributes` call. The second line actually performs a call that should trigger the update, and the third line validates that the redirection goes to the intended URL (notice the test host placed in that URL). Again, it's important what this specification isn't testing — it's not testing that the `Recipe` class does the right thing with the attributes when `update_attributes` is called; it's just specifying the behavior of the controller.

Specifying View Behavior

If there's one point I've been trying to make about RSpec, it's how an RSpec example tries very hard to encapsulate the method under test from the rest of the system. So it shouldn't be much of a surprise that the view tests are intended to be separated from both their associated controller and from the database. As an example of RSpec view testing, I want to show you the `new.html.erb` view that renders the form. In actuality, this view does most of its work inside the partial `_form` view, so arguably the specifications should be written against the partial. However, I decided to assume that if I had written the specifications while coding, I wouldn't yet have refactored to the partial view, so I wrote the specification against the publicly facing view.

The form has one piece of logical behavior: if a `MathCaptcha` object is specified, it displays that object; otherwise it does not. In either case, a mock recipe and a mock user need to be created for the test to begin.

The specification file goes in `specs/views/recipes/new_spec.rb`, and creates the mocks as follows:

```ruby
require File.dirname(__FILE__) + '/../../spec_helper'

describe 'recipe/new' do

  before(:each) do
    @recipe = mock_model(Recipe)
    @recipe.should_receive(:title).and_return("Grandma's Soup")
    @recipe.should_receive(:servings).and_return("2")
    @recipe.should_receive(:ingredient_string).and_return("carrots")
    @recipe.should_receive(:description).and_return("description")
    @recipe.should_receive(:directions).and_return("directions")
    @recipe.should_receive(:tag_list).and_return("yummy")
    @user = mock_model(User)
    assigns[:recipe] = @recipe
    assigns[:user] = @user
  end
```

This should be a familiar pattern to you by now. First, you create a mock instance object and specify its parameters. Then you place that mock object directly in the `assigns` hash. Unlike the controller tests, view tests generally do not need to take the step of mocking the ActiveRecord class to turn it into a mock factory. In general, the views don't create objects like the controllers do, so it's enough to preset the objects into the view. The view test has access to the same `assigns`, `flash`, and `session` hashes as a controller test, plus you can set the `params` hash.

The following example specifies the behavior of the form with no CAPTCHA object:

```ruby
it "should display an entire form" do
  render "/recipes/new"
  response.should have_tag("form") do
    with_tag "input[name *= title]"
    with_tag "input[name *= servings]"
    with_tag "textarea[name *= ingredient_string]"
    with_tag "textarea[name *= description]"
    with_tag "textarea[name *= directions]"
    with_tag "input[name *= tag_list]"
  end
end
```

As you might expect from reading the code, the `render` method performs the fake rendering of the specified view for the test. The phrases `should have_tag` and `with_tag` are just synonyms for your old friend `assert_select`, so the same syntax works to validate the existence of various HTML structures in the output.

In addition to the response object that gets the `should have_tag`, there is a template object, which you can use to mock or stub calls to helper methods. Because you are supposed to be testing helper methods separately, this is probably a good idea. The syntax is the normal RSync mocking framework, and goes like this:

```
template.stub!(:helper_method).and_return("flintstone")
template.should_receive(:helper_method).once.and_return("rubble")
```

This is particularly helpful for stubbing out login/logout behavior, which in this application is governed by code in the application helper.

Of course, any further objects used in other tests should also be mocked. You can validate the behavior of this view when a CAPTCHA object exists by creating a mock object like this:

```
it "should display captcha" do
  @token = mock_model(Token)
  @token.should_receive(:token).and_return("a_token")
  captcha = mock(MathCaptcha)
  captcha.should_receive(:display_string).and_return("display string")
  captcha.should_receive(:token).and_return(@token)
  assigns[:captcha] = captcha
  render "/recipes/new"
  response.should have_tag("form") do
    with_tag "input[name *= captcha_value]"
    with_tag "input[name *= token]"
  end
end
```

This example creates a mock that is quite similar to the test in the controller, except that in this case there are additional mock validations placed on the CAPTCHA — namely that the view will ask for its display string and its token. The CAPTCHA is placed in the `assigns` hash, and then the template can be rendered. (Important safety tip: assign all the variables before you start with the render — otherwise the test won't see them.) In this case, I'm checking only for the new features in the form, mostly for brevity's sake. In a real test, you'd likely want to verify that the existing features were still there.

Testing Helpers

RSpec allows for the testing of helper methods separate from the views that invoke them. Helper test files are placed in `spec/helpers`, and both the name of the file and the description object should match the helper being tested. For example, all the Soups OnLine helper methods as I type this are in `application_helper.rb`. Here's a sample method:

```
def inflect(singular, count, plural = nil)
  plural ||= singular.pluralize
  if count == 1 then singular else plural end
end
```

The test, in `spec/helpers/application_helper_spec.rb`, would start off something like this:

```
require File.dirname(__FILE__) + '/../spec_helper'

describe ApplicationHelper do

  it "should inflect a word" do
    inflect("banana", 3).should == "bananas"
    inflect("banana", 1).should == "banana"
    inflect("is", 2, "are").should == "are"
  end
end
```

Placing the name of the helper class as the argument to `describe` puts all the methods that are in the helper into the namespace of the behavior. That means that you can call them without any scoping, just as `inflect` is called in this test.

There isn't a way to get to the template or controller objects from within the helper test, which may cause problems when you're trying to test a helper method that uses `concat` to place text directly in the template binding. I recommend that you separate the text-generating methods from the text-inserting methods for ease of testing or, alternatively, test those helpers from their calling view test, almost as though they were partial views.

Some of the remaining Test::Unit plugins will interact poorly with RSpec, and you may need to remove your spec directory before continuing.

How to Get RSpec-Like Features

RSpec has many very useful features when compared to standard Test::Unit testing. However, converting to RSpec is not trivial, and using both RSpec and Test::Unit in a program is not recommended (although the newest version of RSpec does allow you to run Test::Unit tests inside RSpec). It's awkward to get tools like `rcov`, `rake`, and `autotest` to run both sets of tests (again, this improved in RSpec 1.1). More importantly, it's very hard for team members to remember when to use RSpec and when to use Test::Unit in a system that attempts to use both.

For some RSpec features, though, there are additional plugins or tools that allow the same or similar functionality to be added to the standard Rails tests. This section briefly discusses a few of those options.

Testing Views

There are at least two separate packages that expand Rails automated test features to include separate tests for controllers and views. The good news is that if you've been playing along so far, you've already downloaded one of them: the ZenTest package that was used in Chapter 4 for its autotest functionality. ZenTest has another facet called Test::Rails. The primary purpose of Test::Rails is to augment the existing Rails tests with controller-only and view-only tests. Sounds like it might be a good match.

Test::Rails

As I mentioned, you've already downloaded ZenTest but if you haven't been following along, you can quickly catch up with a `gem install ZenTest`.

You don't need to install anything else to use Test::Rails, but you do need to make a few changes to your existing files, starting with `test_helper.rb`. The opening few lines of `test_helper.rb` need to be changed to the following:

```
ENV["RAILS_ENV"] = "test"
require File.expand_path(File.dirname(__FILE__) + "/../config/environment")
require 'test/rails'
require 'test_help'
class Test::Rails::TestCase
```

What you're doing here is adding `require 'test/rails'` as a brand new line, and changing the name of the class from `Test::Unit::TestCase` to `Test::Rails::TestCase`. You also need to go into each and every one of your existing test classes, and change the module of their parent class from `Test::Unit` to `Test::Rails` (the class name itself does not change).

After that, put the following line at the end of the `Rakefile` application:

```
require 'test/rails/rake_tasks'
```

That will customize the rake tasks to run the new kinds of tests created by Test::Rails. These tests are named `rake test:controllers` and `rake test:views`.

You can now write controller-only tests. You should place them in `test/controllers`, and normal naming conventions apply. The `RecipesController` test class is called `RecipesControllerTest` and placed in the file `recipes_controller_test.rb`. Here's a sample test:

```
require 'test/test_helper'

class RecipesControllerTest < Test::Rails::ControllerTestCase

  def test_should_get_an_index
    get :index
    assert_response :success
    assert_not_nil assigns(:recipes)
  end

end
```

In general, the only difference between a controller test and a standard functional test is that the controller test does not try to render a view.

RSpec view tests are managed a little differently. All view tests for a single controller go in one file. The file is placed in `test/views` and the name is based on the controller name. The views for `RecipesController` go in `test/views/recipes_view_test.rb` like this:

```
require 'test/test_helper'

class RecipesViewTest < Test::Rails::ViewTestCase
  fixtures :recipes, :users

  def test_new
    assigns[:recipe] = Recipe.find(1)
    assigns[:user] = User.find(1)
    render
    assert_form("/recipes/1") do
      assert_input(:text, "recipe[title]")
      assert_input(:text, "recipe[servings]")
      assert_text_area("recipe[ingredient_string]")
      #etc...
    end
  end
end
```

This looks very similar to the existing standard Rails tests. The `render` method triggers the running of the view attempts to infer the view name from the name of the test. (It will even correctly process something like `test_new_with_captcha` back to the `new` template.) Within the view test, Test::Rails defines a number of different assertions that are essentially specific shortcuts to common uses of `assert_select` — primarily searching for specific form elements, as shown in the preceding example.

view_test

Another mechanism for testing views is provided by a plugin called view_test, which can be installed with the following command:

```
$ ruby script/plugin install http://continuous.rubyforge.org/svn/tags/view_test-0.10.0
```

Keep an eye on the actual tag, though — 0.10 is the current version as of this writing, but I'd expect newer versions to come out rather rapidly. To run view_test, you also need to have two gems installed: mocha, which is another mock framework; and metaid, which has some metaprogramming shortcuts.

One nice feature of view_test is that it enables you to gradually convert your functional tests one at a time. Any functional test can have the method `stub_render` placed within it before the controller is invoked, and the view will be prevented from running. Using the method `expect_render` instead adds a mock-like expectation — `expect_render` takes a `url_for` style hash and validates that the template requested matches the expectation.

View tests live in `test/views` and have a slightly different naming convention, with one test file per template. So the tests for the recipes controller's new template would go into `test/views/recipes/new.html.erb_test.rb`. Within a view test, you can mock helper methods using a method called `expect_helper`, which takes mock-style decorators similar to what you've already seen. For example:

```
expect_helper(:my_helper).with("fred").returns(100)
```

One feature of view_test is that any partial view called from the view must be stubbed or mocked. Partials cannot be directly accessed from a parent view, but must be tested in their own test class.

The view_test plugin is still quite new and under active development. If you want to incorporate this plugin into your system, you can find out what the latest version is at www.continuousthinking.com.

More Natural Test Syntax

If like the clever, natural-language–inspired naming conventions used in RSpec, there are two small RubyGems and one plugin that will give you some improved naming within Test::Unit.

The first gem is called Behaviors and can be acquired with a quick `gem install behaviors`. It allows you to do one thing and one thing only — change a test like this:

```
test should_do_something
  # run your test
end
```

to this:

```
should "do something" do
  #run your test
end
```

To use this in your test cases, add the following line above all your test class definitions:

```
require 'behaviors'
```

Then add the following line inside your test classes:

```
extend Behaviors
```

The Behaviors gem also gives you the RSpec pending functionality — if you don't include a block with your `should` call, the test will appear as an unimplemented test when run.

The other gem is called Dust (`gem install dust`). Dust enables you to write your tests like this:

```
unit_tests do
  test "should do something" do
    #run your test
  end
end
```

You can have multiple tests in a single block, and functional tests would be surrounded by a `functional_tests` block rather than a `unit_tests` block.

Other than the naming convention, both Behaviors and Dust leave the functionality of Test::Unit unchanged.

There's also an ambitious testing plugin called Shoulda, which you can add with this call:

```
$ svn export https://svn.thoughtbot.com/plugins/shoulda/tags/rel-3.0.4 ↵
vendor/plugins/shoulda
```

Shoulda enables you to separate tests into contexts and then into individual tests. A context is analogous to an RSpec behavior, and allows each test within the context to share a common startup block. The nice thing about Shoulda is that its tests can exist alongside your existing tests and they all work together. For example, you could include the following in `test/unit/recipe_test.rb`:

```
context "a recipe" do
  setup do
    @recipe = Recipe.find(:first)
  end

  should "have an ingredient string"
    assert_not_nil @recipe.ingredient_string
  end
end
```

The actual tests are defined using the `should` method. In this example, it will show up in the test task output as `test: with a recipe should have an ingredient string`. All tests within the same context have the same `setup` block called in addition to the normal `setup` method defined by Test::Unit.

The Shoulda plugin defines a number of useful shortcuts, including a very elaborate method called `should_be_restful`, which runs as many as 40 separate individual tests validating standard RESTful behavior. The plugin also defines a number of macro tests for ActiveRecord validations, and a couple of nice assert addons for testing lists.

Improving Fixtures

As you saw previously, RSpec enables you to specify a different mock setup for each behavior and use the mock syntax to specify the data. However, both of these can be somewhat painful in standard testing because of limitations in how Rails handles fixtures. The fixture syntax can be awkward to deal with, and the global nature of fixtures makes it difficult to have separate data populations for different tests.

One way of working around this problem is by using two plugins: FixtureScenario and FixtureScenarioBuilder. You can install these plugins as follows:

```
script/plugin install http://fixture-scenarios.googlecode.com/svn/trunk/fixture_
scenarios
script/plugin install svn://errtheblog.com/svn/plugins/fixture_scenarios_builder
```

FixtureScenario lets you set up arbitrary subdirectories under `test/fixtures`. Each of these subdirectories can contain one or more YAML files in Rails fixture syntax. Then you can load all the YAML files in the directory at once in any test class by using the following command:

```
scenario :<directory_name>
```

FixtureScenarioBuilder enables you to bypass the YAML file, and write the fixture data in Ruby using the actual ActiveRecord models. You need to create a file called `test/fixtures/scenarios.rb`. Within that file, you can generate the data for your scenarios, and the plugin will convert them to YAML for you. For example:

```
scenario :my_favorite_recipe do
  Recipe.create! :title => "chicken soup", :ingredient_string => "2 cups carrots"
end
```

When you run your tests and load a scenario, a scenario directory for `my_favorite_recipe` will be created with the appropriate YAML files.

Testing Helpers

Helpers tend to be the messy attic of Rails programs, filled with the things that are too awkward or ugly to be part of the real program. Because there's no direct support for testing them, they tend to fill up with brittle and hard-to-maintain code.

Actually, it's not all that hard to test helpers. You just need to set up an environment that includes all the standard variables and methods that the helper expects. Following is an abstract class that you can place in `test/helper_test_class.rb` and use as a parent for your helper tests:

```
require File.dirname(__FILE__) + '/test_helper'

class HelperTestClass < Test::Unit::TestCase

  include ActionView::Helpers::CaptureHelper
  include ActionView::Helpers::DateHelper
  include ActionView::Helpers::FormHelper
  include ActionView::Helpers::NumberHelper
  include ActionView::Helpers::RecordIdentificationHelper
  include ActionView::Helpers::RecordTagHelper
  include ActionView::Helpers::TagHelper
  include ActionView::Helpers::TextHelper
  include ActionView::Helpers::UrlHelper
  include ApplicationHelper

  attr_accesor :text
```

This part of the class definition includes all the helper methods that you are likely to need on a regular basis. It's not a complete set of helper classes, though, so you might need to add more classes if you are testing a helper that touches another part of the system.

Continuing within the same `HelperTestClass` definition, add the following:

```
class_inheritable_accessor :controller_class

def self.set_controller_class(controller_class)
  self.controller_class = controller_class
end
```

This mechanism allows the concrete helper class you will define to set its controller class as a class-level declaration rather than requiring it to override the `setup` method or something awkward like that. Again, within the `HelperTestClass`, add this:

```
def setup
  @text = []
  return unless controller_class
  @controller = controller_class.new
  request = ActionController::TestRequest.new
  @controller.send(:params=, {})
  @controller.send(:request=, request)
  @controller.send(:initialize_current_url)
end

def teardown
  @text = []
end
```

The setup method declares a controller object of the previously declared controller class, and then creates a test request and sends it to the controller. This puts all the elements your helper will need in scope. The @text variable and related attribute are there to allow testing of helper methods that take block inputs, or any helper that calls the concat helper method. For that to work, you need to add the following to the TestHelperClass definition:

```
def _erbout
  @text
end

def test_text
  assert_equal([], @text)
end

end
```

Normally, block inputs call the hidden attribute _erbout as part of the process of converting the ERB in the block passed to the helper into HTML. The helper test isn't taking place in any kind of ERB process, so you fake it by offering a local array to put that text in, which helpfully allows the tests you write to use that array to validate the ERB output from the method. Note that when you test a block method, you need to explicitly add text to _erbout in the block because the actual ERB engine is not being invoked.

Following is an example of using this framework to test the inflect and span_for methods in the application helper (you'll see another example of testing helpers in the next chapter). This file goes into test/units/application_helper_test.rb:

```
require File.dirname(__FILE__) + '/../test_helper'
require File.dirname(__FILE__) + '/../helper_test_class'

class ApplicationHelperTest < HelperTestClass
  fixtures :recipes

  set_controller_class RecipesController

  def test_inflect
    assert_equal("apples", inflect("apple", 2))
    assert_equal("apple", inflect("apple", 1))
  end
```

The setup for the test class has to include the `helper_test_class` file you just created, and the class has to inherit from `HelperTestClass` itself. The setup somewhat arbitrarily declares `RecipeController` to be the controller in question. After that, the test for `inflect` is just a basic unit test. In the same file, add the following:

```
def test_span_for
  span_for(Recipe.find(1)) do
    text << "banana"
  end
  assert_equal("<span class=\"recipe\" id=\"recipe_1\">banana</span>", text[-1])
end

end
```

The `span_for` test shows what you need to do to test `concat` and block helpers. Any text within the block that you want to show up in the output needs to be explicitly pushed onto the text array. After the helper call is over, you can check for the expected output in the test array, which contains both the text added to the stream in the helper via `concat`, as well as anything added within the block.

References

One of the best early descriptions of automated test development is Kent Beck's description of JUnit coding, "Test Infected: Programmers Love Writing Tests," available at `http://junit.sourceforge .net/doc/testinfected/testing.htm`. Beck's early books on Extreme Programming (XP) also describe the process well.

The rcov home page is `http://eigenclass.org/hiki.rb?rcov`, where you'll find additional options and documentation. FlexMock lives at `http://onestepback.org/software/flexmock`. The other major Rails framework is called Mocha, and its home page is `http://mocha.rubyforge.org`. (By the time you read this, Mocha may have been integrated fully into RSpec.)

The RSpec home page is `http://rspec.rubyforge.org`, which also contains a lot of great documentation on how to use BDD. The classic Martin Fowler piece on mock object testing is available at `http://martinfowler.com/articles/mocksArentStubs.html`.

Find out more about Shoulda at `http://thoughtbot.com/projects/shoulda`. I learned more about this plugin at the end of the book writing cycle, and came to like it very much.

There are a couple of other testing tools created by a consulting group that calls itself the Ruby Sadists. A tool called flog (`http://ruby.sadi.st/Flog.html`) is a complexity metric that identifies the most complex methods in your system as prime candidates for cleanup. Another tool, called heckle (`http://ruby.sadi.st/Heckle.html`), provides mutation testing for your code, randomly changing part of your code and ensuring that there is a failed test to match.

A blog maintained by Jay Fields (`http://blog.jayfields.com`) often contains interesting tips and tricks for Rails testing. And Chad Fowler's *Rails Recipes* was a source for some of the ideas about testing helper methods in this chapter.

Summary

Test-driven development is a critical part of the software building process, and has an amazing amount of support within Rails. This support can be augmented with a number of other tools. You can use rcov to measure the amount of your code that is covered by your tests — a necessary but not sufficient condition for good tests.

Mock objects are a standard mechanism for simulating object behavior that would otherwise be hard to specify in a unit test. FlexMock is a Ruby mock object toolkit that enables you to extend the reach of your tests.

RSpec has some definite advantages over standard Rails unit and functional testing. Using RSpec to test controllers, views, and helpers separately greatly enhances your ability to use automatic testing to verify your program's behavior. The naming conventions and structure of an RSpec test can make the tests more readable and easier to describe both within and outside a programming team.

If you like some of the features of RSpec, but don't feel the need to jump all the way into it, other tools can cover much of RSpec's functionality. Both Test::Rails and view_test allow improved testing of views. Other plugins, such as Dust and Shoulda, allow you to mimic RSpec's syntax. The FixtureScenario plugin enables you to specify more-granular sets of fixture data. You can roll your own tests for helper methods.

8

Rails-Driven JavaScript

As it happens, I spent a significant part of the years 1999 and 2000 arguing against putting large amounts of JavaScript in the client sites I was developing. My arguments were that the tool support was weak, so a lot of developer effort was involved, it was hard to debug, and almost anything complex was guaranteed to break on one or the other of the two major browsers. Furthermore, the range of things people were doing with JavaScript at the time wasn't so compelling that it seemed to require throwing it into our sites.

That was a long time ago — the iPod didn't even exist yet — and times have changed. JavaScript is now a critical part of many of the Web's most popular sites. Much of this has been driven by a simple functionality enhancement that did not exist in 1999: the capability to call a server asynchronously from within JavaScript. That simple capability, from the `XmlHttpRequest` object that is now a standard part of JavaScript, has enabled a much richer and more interactive Web experience, ranging from special effects, to Ta-Da Lists, to scrolling Google Maps, to rich online document editing. Eventually, the new interaction structure was isolated and named Ajax, which is a pseudo-acronym for Asynchronous JavaScript And XML, and the name has stuck.

Rails was one of the first toolkits to make dealing with Ajax easy to do without having to know a great deal of JavaScript. Since the initial release of Rails, the addition of RJS scripts has made it even easier to add dynamic content to a Rails application without touching JavaScript very much. In this chapter, I focus on the features within Rails that deal with JavaScript. JavaScript is a very interesting object-oriented language in its own right, and the Prototype and script.aculo.us libraries that Rails uses have a lot of functionality to support cool Ajax effects. In this chapter, I'll be discussing them through the lens of their Rails interactions.

Revisiting the Past

In the Soups OnLine application as implemented so far, there are two separate uses of Ajax. It was used to edit ingredients in Chapter 1, and then to edit tags in Chapter 4. I'd like to revisit those implementations to talk about some ways in which they could be improved.

To refresh your memory, the ingredient editing is located in `app/views/recipes/show.html.rb`, and consists of this link:

```
<div class="ingredient">
   <span id="ingredient_<%= ingredient.id %>">
     <%= h ingredient.display_string %>
   </span>
   <% if_is_current_user @recipe.user_id do %>
     <span class="subtle" id="edit_<%= ingredient.id %>">
       <%= link_to_remote "Edit",
              :url => remote_edit_recipe_ingredient_path(@recipe, ingredient),
              :method => :get,
              :update => "ingredient_#{ingredient.id}"%>
     </span>
   <% end %>
</div>
```

On the server side, the controller is in `app/controllers/ingredient_controller.rb`, and just gets the appropriate ingredient:

```
def edit
  @ingredient = Ingredient.find(params[:id])
end

def remote_edit
  edit
end
```

This displays a partial with the form to be entered:

```
<% remote_form_for(@ingredient,
      :url => remote_update_recipe_ingredient_path(@recipe, @ingredient),
      :update => "ingredient_#{@ingredient.id}") do |f| %>
  <table>
    <tr>
      <th class="subtle">Amount</th>
      <th class="subtle">Unit</th>
      <th class="subtle">Ingredient</th>
      <th class="subtle">Directions</th>
    </tr>
    <tr>
      <td><%= f.text_field :amount, :size => "5" %></td>
      <td><%= f.text_field :unit, :size => "10" %></td>
      <td><%= f.text_field :ingredient, :size => "25" %></td>
      <td><%= f.text_field :instruction, :size => "15" %></td>
      <td><%= f.submit "Update" %></td>
    </tr>
  </table>
<% end %>
```

That form goes back to the ingredient controller, which updates the ingredient in the database:

```
def remote_update
  @ingredient = Ingredient.find(params[:id])
  if @ingredient.update_attributes(params[:ingredient])
    render(:layout => false)
  else
    render :text => "Error updating ingredient"
  end
end
```

Finally, the ingredient display string is re-rendered back into the slot:

```
<%= h @ingredient.display_string %>
<%= link_to_remote "Edit", :url => remote_tag_edit_recipe_path(@recipe),
    :method => :get, :update => "tags" %>
```

This is a fairly standard Ajax data flow for an in-place edit with a complex form — at least it is for me. There's an initial link that makes a server call to retrieve the form, and the form makes an Ajax call to perform the update and retrieve the actual text to redisplay. Looking at this code with a more critical eye, I see the following potential problems:

❑ There's a DRY (Don't Repeat Yourself) violation in the view code — the code in the initial view is almost identical to the view in the partial that displays the code after the form update.

❑ There's a probable DRY violation in the controller code — the `remote_edit` and `remote_update` methods are nearly identical to their non-Ajax counterparts. Furthermore, a strict REST analysis of the code would probably argue that the remote code should be folded into the standard REST methods if possible.

❑ There's a usability violation — users who don't have JavaScript enabled get a dead link. The application needs to degrade gracefully if the user does not have JavaScript enabled.

Let's fix the DRY violations first, because fixing the no-JavaScript issue will be easier after the code is cleaned up.

Fixing JavaScript DRY Violations

The first thing to do is consolidate the display of the ingredient string from both the normal and remote forms into a partial (I really should have done this the first time around). The new file is `app/views/ingredients/_display_in_recipe.erb` (I'll explain the slightly different extension in a moment):

```
<div class="ingredient">
  <% span_for ingredient do %>
    <%= h ingredient.display_string %>
  <% end %>
  <% if_is_current_user recipe.user_id do %>
    <span class="subtle" id="<%= dom_id ingredient, :edit %>">
      <%= link_to_remote "Edit",
          :url => edit_recipe_ingredient_path(@recipe, ingredient),
          :method => :get,
```

(continued)

(continued)

```
            :update => dom_id(ingredient) %>
        </span>
    <% end %>
</div>
```

This code has a couple of features that you haven't seen in the book yet. One is the method `span_for`, which is a helper method I wrote by analogy to the standard Rails `div_for`:

```
def span_for(record, *args, &block)
    content_tag_for(:span, record, *args, &block)
end
```

It places whatever ERB is within the block inside a `span` tag, and automatically gives that `span` tag a useful DOM ID of the form `<class>_<id>`. Later in the view, I use the similar Rails helper `dom_id`, which is part of the `simply_helpful` plugin in Rails 1.2, and is core in Rails 2.0. It creates a DOM ID of the same form, but takes an optional argument that is used as a prefix, so the inner span will have IDs that look like `edit_ingredient_1`.

This partial can be used in the recipe `show.html.erb` view, where the local variables are explicitly set for the partial as follows:

```
<% for ingredient in @recipe.ingredients %>
    <%= render :partial => "/ingredients/display_in_recipe",
        :locals => { :ingredient => ingredient, :recipe => @recipe } %>
<% end %>
```

To get the controllers to work most easily, the view that is currently `app/view/ingredients/remote_edit.html.erb` needs to be changed to a partial named `_remote_edit.erb`. The contents of the file change only slightly — the ingredient path URL changes to this:

```
:url => recipe_ingredient_path(@recipe, @ingredient),
```

The remote versions of the controller methods are going away and being consolidated into the existing CRUD actions for `edit` and `update`. You can also remove the entries for `remote_edit` and `remote_update` from the `routes.rb file`, so that the entry for recipes ingredients in the `routes.rb` file reverts to this:

```
map.resources :recipes do |recipes|
    recipes.resources :ingredients
end
```

The new controller `edit` method, in `app/controllers/ingredients_controller.rb`, is pretty simple:

```
def edit
    @ingredient = Ingredient.find(params[:id])
    if request.xhr?
        render :partial => "remote_edit", :layout => false
    end
end
```

The change is that if `request.xhr?` is `true`, meaning that it's an Ajax `XmlHttpRequest`, then the `remoteedit` form is rendered; otherwise, it shows the default .The Ajax code in the `link_to` that calls this method will take care of inserting the HTML in the correct DOM element.

The `update` method just grows a new entry in the `respond_to` blocks:

```ruby
def update
  @ingredient = Ingredient.find(params[:id])
  respond_to do |format|
    if @ingredient.update_attributes(params[:ingredient])
      flash[:notice] = 'Ingredient was successfully updated.'
      format.html { redirect_to([@recipe, @ingredient]) }
      format.xml  { head :ok }
      format.js   { render :layout => false,
          :partial => "display_in_recipe",
          :locals => { :ingredient => @ingredient, :recipe => @recipe }}
    else
      format.html { render :action => "edit" }
      format.xml  { render :xml => @ingredient.errors,
          :status => :unprocessable_entity }
      format.js   { render :text => "Error updating ingredient" }
    end
  end
end
```

The successful `update` redirects to the common display partial you just saw, and the unsuccessful one returns a text message.

By now, you're probably wondering two things: why the `.erb` files are not `.html.erb` files, and why the `edit` method uses `xhr?` to branch the logic but the `update` method uses `respond_to`. Both issues have the same root cause — namely that `respond_to format.js` has developed two separate and distinct meanings. As expected by the `respond_to` method, it means "the user has made a request and expects to get JavaScript (usually an RJS template) in return." However, the more colloquial meaning has been "the user has made an `XmlHttpRequest`," often signifying that straight HTML is being returned, because the JavaScript portion already exists client-side via `link_to_remote` or some similar feature.

The problem is that when `respond_to` is in a JavaScript block, it specifies the response as JavaScript in at least two ways. It looks for `.js.erb` RJS templates, so it doesn't find a `.html.erb` template. This problem is fixed by leaving the format type off of the partial file, so that Rails will find it. The second problem is that it sets the MIME type of the response to `text/javascript`. This probably has a number of implications, but the one I'm concerned with right now is that `assert_select` tests don't even bother trying to parse the response if the method thinks that the response is JavaScript, so all `assert_select` tests will fail (you can use `assert_select_rjs` if the response returns JavaScript). Because I was using one of those to test the Ajax edit form, I switched that method to use the `xhr?` test, which does not change the MIME type, and allows the test to pass. The Rails community at large seems to be of two minds as to the best course of action here. As I write this, I'm perusing two bug report threads on the Rails bug tracker from within the last several months that say directly opposite things about what the expected behavior actually is — but hopefully it will have been resolved by the time you read this.

As implied in the last paragraph, the three tests in `ingredients_controller_test` that depended on the remote calls will all fail at the moment. To fix them, two things need to be done:

1. The paths need to be changed from the old `remote_` routes to the standard CRUD ones.

2. Instead of using `get` and `put` as the methods to trigger the controller call, you need to use `xhr` to simulate the `XmlHttpRequest` call.

The first argument to `xhr` is `:get`, `:put`, `:post`, or whatever HTTP verb is being used. The rest of the arguments are just the same as in the other methods. The updated tests look like this:

```ruby
def test_should_get_remote_edit
  xhr :get, :edit, :id => 1, :recipe_id => 1
  assert_response :success
  assert_select("form[action *= /recipes/1/ingredients/1]") do
    assert_select "input[name *= amount]"
    assert_select "input[name *= unit]"
    assert_select "input[name *= ingredient]"
    assert_select "input[name *= instruction]"
  end
end

def test_should_remote_update_ingredient
  xhr :put, :update, :id => 1, :ingredient => { :amount => 2 }, :recipe_id => 1
  assert_match /2 cups First Ingredient, Chopped/, @response.body
end

def test_should_fail_remote_update
  xhr :put, :update, :id => 1,
    :ingredient => { :amount => 2, :order_of => 0 }, :recipe_id => 1
  assert_match "Error updating ingredient", @response.body
end
```

The tests will now pass. Similar changes to the recipe controller — consolidating the `remote_tag_edit` and `remote_tag_update` actions with `edit` and `update` — will allow those routes to be removed as well. The recipe controller `edit` and `update` methods in `app/controllers/recipes_controller.rb` should look like this:

```ruby
def edit
  @recipe = Recipe.find(params[:id])
  if request.xhr?
    render :layout => false, :partial => "remote_tag_edit",
        :locals => {:recipe => @recipe}
  end
end
```

```
# PUT /recipes/1
# PUT /recipes/1.xml
def update
  @recipe = Recipe.find(params[:id])
  respond_to do |format|
    if @recipe.update_attributes(params[:recipe])
      flash[:notice] = 'Recipe was successfully updated.'
      format.html { redirect_to(@recipe) }
      format.xml  { head :ok }
      format.js   { render :partial => "show_tags" }
    else
      format.html { render :action => "edit" }
      format.xml  { render :xml => @recipe.errors,
          :status => :unprocessable_entity }
      format.js   { render :text => "Error updating tags "}
    end
  end
end
```

Being Graceful

Here's the actual HTML emitted by the `link_to_remote` call in the `show` recipe partial view for editing tags:

```
<a href="*"
   onclick="new Ajax.Updater('tags', '/recipes/1/edit',
   {asynchronous:true, evalScripts:true, method:'get'});
   return false;">Edit</a>
```

This is a perfectly normal Ajax call via the Prototype library, but for users without JavaScript enabled, the target of the link is just #, which doesn't enable them to do much. Luckily, Rails makes it easy for you to have the link degrade gracefully so that JavaScript-averse users can still use your site.

So you need to put an actual URL as the target of the link, which leads to the question of exactly what that link should do. The idea is to allow the non-JavaScript user to get as close as possible to the full experience. The easiest thing to do would be to just display a page with the tag editing form, but in the interest of keeping the experience a little closer to what has already been defined, I'm going to show the user the same recipe page, but with the tag form embedded inside it. In other words, exactly the same page the JavaScript user would have seen, only as the result of a full call back to the server instead of an Ajax update of the single page section.

The first step in this process is to put the alternative URL into the `link_to_remote` call. This is accomplished by using the optional second hash argument to `link_to_remote` that contains the html_ options — which means that the remote options already specified need to be bundled into an explicit hash. This change goes into `app/views/recipes/show_tags.erb`:

```
<%= link_to_remote "Edit", {:url => edit_recipe_path(@recipe),
  :method => :get, :update => "tags"},
  :href => url_for(:controller => "recipes", :id => @recipe,
       :action => "show", :edit_tags => true) %>
```

This code provides `recipes/1?edit_tags=true` as an alternative URL if JavaScript is not enabled.

Now would be a good time to add a controller test or two to specify the expected behavior. The first test verifies that the tag form is displayed if the `edit_tags` URL flag exists and the user is logged in. Place the following in `test/functional/recipes_controller_test.rb`:

```
def test_should_show_with_edit_tags
  setup_recipe_tags
  get :show, :id => 1
  session[:user_id] = 1
  get :show, :id => 1, :edit_tags => true
  assert_response :success
  assert_select("form[action=?]", recipe_path(1)) do
    assert_select "input[name *= tag_list]"
  end
end
```

The first line is needed because the Rails test facility exposes a session object only after a request has been made. Then, by setting the `user_id` in the session to simulate a login, the test validates the existence of the form.

The second test validates that if there is no logged in user, the tag list is shown inside a `span`. Here's the code to be added for that test:

```
def test_should_not_show_with_edit_tags_if_not_logged_in
  setup_recipe_tags
  get :show, :id => 1, :edit_tags => true
  assert_response :success
  assert_select("span[id=tags]", "yummy, vegetarian")
end
```

The first step in making this work is for the controller to add the parameter to the mix:

```
def show
  flash[:login_message] = "Logged out"
  @recipe = Recipe.find(params[:id])
  @edit_tags = params[:edit_tags]
  respond_to do |format|
    format.html # show.html.erb
    format.xml  { render :xml => @recipe }
  end
end
```

When the controller passes the parameter to the view, the view needs to decide what partial to display based on that flag and the status of the user login. Here's the relevant part of the `show.html.erb` file:

```
<p>
  Tags:
  <% if is_logged_in? and @edit_tags %>
    <%= render :partial => "remote_tag_edit", :locals => {:recipe => @recipe} %>
  <% else %>
    <%= render :partial => "show_tags" %>
  <% end %>
</p>
```

This enables any logged-in user to edit the tag list. So if a user is logged in, and the flag has been set, this call renders the `remote_tag_edit` partial, exactly as the Ajax call would have. If not, the tag string is shown normally.

Amazingly, that's enough to make tag editing work without JavaScript. (You can verify this by turning off JavaScript in your browser.) When the form comes up, it will do the right thing in this case, even though it is declared as a remote Ajax form. The behavior of remote forms without JavaScript is already set by Rails — they attempt to make a normal form call to the same controller action. Because you already unified the `update` actions in the last section, the remote form then makes a normal HTML request to `update`, which triggers the normal response — redirecting to the `show` action. As it happens, the `show` action is precisely what you want here, so that part is done. If you had not consolidated the `update` and `remote_update` actions, there would have been more work to do because the old `remote_update` action would not have caused the `show` action to be displayed.

The ingredient in-line edit is a little bit more complicated in the absence of JavaScript. For one thing, the `update` method happens in the ingredients controller, so it's not going to automatically degrade and redirect to the recipe `show` action. Also, the logic is just a tiny bit more complex. Start by changing the `link_to_remote` call in `app/views/ingredients/_display_in_recipe.erb` to take a backup URL, as follows:

```
<%= link_to_remote "Edit",
    { :url => edit_recipe_ingredient_path(recipe, ingredient),
        :method => :get,
        :update => dom_id(ingredient) },
      :href => url_for(:controller => "recipes", :id => recipe,
          :action => "show", :ingredient_to_edit => ingredient.id) %>
```

The extra argument in this case will be a flag that represents which ingredient should have the edit form displayed.

The controller tests that cover this behavior are similar to the previous tests. The first one says that if the right user is logged in, and the `edit` URL has the ingredient flag, then an ingredient form should be displayed. These tests go in `test/functional/ingredients_controller_test.rb`:

```
def test_should_show_with_edit_ingredient
  get :show, :id => 1
  session[:user_id] = 1
  get :show, :id => 1, :ingredient_to_edit => "1"
  assert_response :success
  assert_select("form") do
    assert_select "input[name *= amount]"
    assert_select "input[name *= unit]"
    assert_select "input[name *= ingredient]"
    assert_select "input[name *= instruction]"
  end
end
```

If the correct user is not logged in, then the user should not get the edit form, even if he or she passes in the URL flag:

```ruby
def test_should_not_show_with_edit_ingredient_for_wrong_user
  get :show, :id => 1
  session[:user_id] = 2
  get :show, :id => 1, :ingredient_to_edit => "1"
  assert_response :success
  assert_select "span[id *= ingredient]", "1 1/2 cups First Ingredient, Chopped"
end
```

Instead, the test validates that the user gets the complete display string of the ingredient.

To make this work, the URL flag has to be handled by the recipes controller as follows:

```ruby
def show
  flash[:login_message] = "Logged out"
  @recipe = Recipe.find(params[:id])
  @ingredient_to_edit = params[:ingredient_to_edit].to_i ||= 0
  @edit_tags = params[:edit_tags]
  respond_to do |format|
    format.html # show.html.erb
    format.xml  { render :xml => @recipe }
  end
end
```

Using 0 as a default is a convenient way of avoiding nil errors and spurious matches.

The relevant section of the show.html.erb has to branch on the logic of whether the flag exists:

```erb
<div class="ingredients">
  <h2>Ingredients</h2>
  <% for ingredient in @recipe.ingredients %>
    <% if can_edit_ingredient @ingredient_to_edit, ingredient %>
      <%= render :partial => "/ingredients/remote_edit",
          :locals => { :ingredient => ingredient, :recipe => @recipe,
              :redirect_to_recipe => true } %>
    <% else %>
      <%= render :partial => "/ingredients/display_in_recipe",
          :locals => { :ingredient => ingredient, :recipe => @recipe } %>
    <% end %>
  <% end %>
</div>
```

The can_edit_ingredient method is a small helper I wrote and placed in app/helpers/application_helper.rb to move some complexity out of the view template. It does essentially what you'd expect — the ingredient is editable if the ID of the ingredient matches the requested ID, and the user of the ID is logged in. Also note that I added an `ingredient.user` method that just proxies `ingredient.recipe.user`. Here are those methods:

```
def can_edit_ingredient(requested_ingredient_id, actual_ingredient)
  id_match = requested_ingredient_id == actual_ingredient.id
  user_match = is_current_user?(actual_ingredient.user.id)
  id_match and user_match
end

def is_current_user?(user_id)
  is_logged_in? and user_id == @user.id
end
```

The controller switches to one partial or the other based on whether the ingredient is expected to be editable. If so, it displays the same `remote_edit` partial that would have been inserted by the Ajax request.

That solves the first half of the non-JavaScript–user issue. The next half is to have the form submission do the right thing. As mentioned earlier, Ajax form remote calls that are made when JavaScript is disabled degrade to a regular form call to the same URL. From our perspective for this call, that's functionally okay — it will call the ingredient controller's `update` method and change the values. However, it would also replace the recipe display with just the ingredient string, which is not exactly the desired behavior. The desired behavior is to have the `show` recipe page displayed with no edit forms and the new value — exactly what you'd see if you submitted the form via Ajax.

What you want to do is have the ingredient update redirect back to the `recipe_show` if the form submission has been triggered from the no-JavaScript version of the page. Here's the functional test to place in `ingredients_controller_test` that will isolate the situation:

```
def test_should_redirect_to_recipe_show_on_update_when_requested
  put :update, :id => 1, :ingredient => { }, :recipe_id => 1,
      :redirect_to_recipe => true
  assert_redirected_to recipe_path(assigns(:recipe))
end
```

The test sets up the `update` request with an additional `redirect_to_recipe` parameter, and then validates that the redirected URL is as expected.

The first part of making this redirection was actually in the previous show view code, where `redirect_to_recipe` is one of the variables placed in the `locals` hash and sent to the form partial. This is the updated edit method of the ingredients controller:

```
def edit
  @ingredient = Ingredient.find(params[:id])
  if request.xhr?
    render :partial => "remote_edit", :layout => false,
        :locals => {:ingredient => @ingredient,
            :recipe => @ingredient.recipe, :redirect_to_recipe => false }
  end
end
```

The form then includes the value as a hidden value passed back to the controller on form submit:

```
<% remote_form_for(ingredient,
     :url => recipe_ingredient_path(recipe, ingredient),
     :update => "ingredient_#{ingredient.id}") do |f| %>
   <% if redirect_to_recipe %>
     <input type="hidden" name="redirect_to_recipe" value="<%= true %>">
   <% end %>
   # rest of form
<% end %>
```

The controller method then uses that value to determine where to redirect to after a successful update. Here is just the HTML branch of the `respond_to` block:

```
format.html do
  if (params[:redirect_to_recipe])
    redirect_to(@recipe)
  else
    redirect_to([@recipe, @ingredient])
  end
end
```

In this case, the RESTful routes are used. If the `redirect_to_recipe` flag is set, the controller redirects to the display for just `@recipe`; otherwise, it redirects to the display for the ingredient whose route is nested inside the recipe.

Easy JavaScript Integration

Inserting JavaScript into your application need not be a major hassle. Many developers have worked hard to create packages in JavaScript and Rails to allow you to insert significant behavior with very little fuss. This section describes three easy ways to insert some very helpful JavaScript.

Tooltips

Users have come to expect tooltips (or "those things that float on the screen" as some users call them). Although many browsers will automatically overlay the alternate (alt) text from an image or link over those elements, you may want to include a more elaborate floating-text behavior. Once you have an easy way to display tooltips, having a layer of content on your application that is invisible except during mouseover (when the mouse hovers over a screen element) becomes an irresistible way of increasing the amount of content on your pages.

What I'd like to do, by way of example, is build an extremely thin Ruby layer around a JavaScript package called Prototip. Prototip is a tooltip library written by Nick Stakenburg on top of the Prototype JavaScript library. As I write this, Prototip is at version 1.1, and can be picked up at www .nickstakenburg.com/projects/prototip/. The zip file will contain a .js file, which you should put in your public/javascripts folder, and a .css (Cascading Style Sheets) file, which goes in `public/stylesheets`. To make these files available, you need to load them in the layout header. In `app/views/layouts/recipes.html.erb`, edit the header thusly:

```
<head>
  <meta http-equiv="content-type" content="text/html;charset=UTF-8" />
  <title>Recipes: <%= controller.action_name %></title>
  <meta name="keywords" content="" />
  <meta name="description" content="" />
  <%= stylesheet_link_tag 'scaffold' %>
  <%= stylesheet_link_tag 'prototip' %>
  <%= javascript_include_tag :defaults %>
  <%= javascript_include_tag 'prototip' %>
</head>
```

The `stylesheets` can be in any order, but the JavaScript `include` for Prototip must come after the `:defaults` JavaScript load. (You also need at least version 1.6 of Prototype. If it's been awhile since you updated everything, you might need to run the rake `rails:update:javascripts` task.)

The basic JavaScript syntax of a Prototip declaration is really simple:

```
new Tip(dom_id, text);
```

There's an optional third argument which takes a hash of options which affect the tooltip display. The `Tip` declaration can take place either before or after the `dom_id` it's attached to, but it cannot be declared within the tag with that `dom_id`. The text of the tip can contain some HTML, and the optional arguments govern things like placement and script.aculo.us special effects. You can also change the visual look of the tips by modifying the `.css` file.

Even with this minimal amount of JavaScript, you're going to get cleaner view code if you wrap it inside a helper. The best bet is probably a block helper that takes an arbitrary block of ERB and wraps it in a span tag, and then declares a tip to go along with that tab. A couple of tests written using the helper test mechanism from Chapter 7 should show this nicely:

```
require File.dirname(__FILE__) + '/../test_helper'
require File.dirname(__FILE__) + '/../helper_test_class'

class RecipeLinkHelperTest < HelperTestClass

  include CategoriesHelper

  def test_tooltip_for
    tooltip_for("dom", "content") { _erbout << "x" }
    assert_equal "<span id='dom'>", @text[0]
    assert_equal "x", @text[1]
    assert_equal "</span>", @text[2]
    assert_match "<script", @text[3]
    assert_equal "new Tip('dom', 'content', {})", @text[4]
    assert_equal "</script>", @text[5]
  end
```

The first test shows the `span` around the block (using the mocked `_erbout` function to simulate block output), and then a `script` tag containing the `Tip` declaration:

```
def test_tooltip_with_title
  tooltip_for("dom", "content", :title => "title") { @text << "x" }
  assert_equal "new Tip('dom', 'content', {title: 'title'})", @text[-2]
end
end
```

The second test adds the `title` syntax. `Tip` takes more complex options, as you'll see from the implementation, but those aren't handled yet because my helper implementation is not fully robust. This is a great piece of functionality to write via unit tests, because the need for the output to be strict JavaScript means that there are all kinds of ways this code can fail without actually throwing an exception.

The implementation of this goes in `application_helper.rb` and uses `concat` extensively:

```
def tooltip_for(dom_id, content, options = {}, &block)
  concat("<span id='#{dom_id}'>", block.binding)
  yield
  concat("</span>", block.binding)
  concat("<script type='text/javascript' language='javascript'>", block.binding)
  op_strings = options.collect do |key, value|
    "#{key}: '#{escape_javascript(value)}'"
  end
  op_string = "{#{op_strings.join(", ")}}"
  concat("new Tip('#{dom_id}', '#{escape_javascript(content)}', #{op_string})",
      block.binding)
  concat("</script>", block.binding)
end
```

The method starts by surrounding the incoming block with the `span` tag, and then puts together the options in JavaScript format before it constructs the `script` tag with `Tip` declaration. The code to convert the options to JavaScript is perhaps incomplete — it's a little messy and doesn't handle the case where the value of the option is itself a hash — but it will serve for the moment.

To see this code in action, you can add a tooltip around each of the categories in the tag cloud display that shows the name and count of recipes attached to each tip. That makes the index view for the category controller exactly three lines more complex:

```
<% @title = "Recipe Tag Cloud" %>

<div class="tag_cloud_whole">
  <% @tags.each do |tag| %>
    <% tooltip_for "tag_#{tag}", "#{tooltip_string(tag)}",
        :title => "#{tooltip_title(tag, @tag_counts)}" do %>
      <%= link_to tag, category_path(tag),
          :class => "tag_cloud_bucket_#{@tag_cloud[tag]}"%>
    <% end %>
  <% end %>
</div>
```

Notice how the tooltip functionality just wraps itself around the code being tipped.

There are, however, a couple of helpers and controller changes behind that code. Rather than recalculate the tag counts from the database each time, you can add a class method to `TagCloud` to return them all at once from the taggable class. This goes in `app/models/tag_cloud.rb`:

```
def self.tag_counts(taggable_class)
  TagCloud.new(taggable_class).tag_count_hash
end
```

This also needs to be added to the `app/controolers/categories_controller.rb` controller, like this:

```
def index
  @tag_cloud = TagCloud.calculate(Recipe)
  @tag_counts = TagCloud.tag_counts(Recipe)
  @tags = @tag_cloud.keys.sort
end
```

The title and body text of the tooltip are written as helpers in the `category_helper.rb` file. Just this once, I'll spare you the unit tests because they are pretty straightforward text manipulation. The title takes in the category name and the tag counts hash and returns a simple string:

```
def tooltip_title(category, tag_counts)
  count = tag_counts[category]
  "#{count} #{inflect('recipe', count)}:"
end
```

For the tooltip, go back to the database to get all the recipes with the given tag:

```
def tooltip_string(category)
  recipes = Recipe.find_tagged_with(category, :order => "title ASC")
  recipes.collect(&:title).join(", ")
end
```

Because this method is potentially making an expensive database call, it's a prime candidate for some kind of performance enhancement, such as indexing the tag columns in the database, denormalizing the list of recipes, or simple object- or page-caching. It's not necessary to mess with it now though — for all you know, somebody will take the feature out of the code before you even need to think about performance optimization.

Figure 8-1 shows a finished tooltip. (If you don't like the colors, you can easily change them in the Prototip `.css` file.)

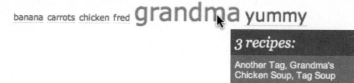

Figure 8-1

In-Place Editing

In-place editing is one of my favorite ways to add usability to a site with some quick JavaScript. In fact, it was the first whizzy Ajax thing I added to my first serious Rails application, and one of the features that really made Rails pop for me. At the time, the helper method for adding in-place editing for text fields didn't exist (well, maybe it did, but I just didn't know about it). With this method, adding quick editing is a snap.

In-place editing has moved out of Rails core and into a plugin, so first you need to install the plugin:

```
$ ruby script/plugin install ↵
http://dev.rubyonrails.org/svn/rails/plugins/in_place_editing
```

With the plugin installed, the API is unchanged from older versions of Rails. However, now systems that don't use the in-place editing feature don't need to have it in their deployment.

Let's add some in-place editing to the recipe display page. In `app/views/recipes/show.html.erb`, change the beginning of the file as follows:

```
<h1><%= in_place_editor_field :recipe, :title %></h1>

<%# some stuff I don't need to show here %>

<p class="servings">
  Servings: <%= in_place_editor_field :recipe, :servings %>
</p>

<p class="description">
  <%= in_place_editor_field :recipe, :description, {}, :rows => 5 %>
</p>
```

The `in_place_editor_field` is a Rails helper method that wraps around the script.aculo.us `Ajax.InPlaceEditor` object. Like a form helper, the first argument is a symbol that matches the instance variable containing the attribute being edited. This is a limitation on what you can do via this helper — the object being edited must be declared as an instance variable, not a local variable. The third argument is a standard Rails HTML options hash, with the values placed in the span tag that surrounds the text. There are several options you can pass to the last argument, in_place_editor_field, to adjust the display of the field. The most important options are :rows and :cols, which specify the size of the eventual edit field — if :rows is greater than 1, then a textarea field is used.

Here's what the generated HTML and JavaScript code looks like for the title field:

```
<span class="in_place_editor_field" id="recipe_title_1_in_place_editor">
  Grandma's Chicken Soup
</span>
<script type="text/javascript">
  //<![CDATA[
  new Ajax.InPlaceEditor('recipe_title_1_in_place_editor',
      '/recipes/set_recipe_title/1')
  //]]>
</script>
```

In the browser, the text gets a background-highlight effect on mouseover, and clicking in the text switches to the edit field with an OK button and Cancel link.

This change, by the way, will break the controller test for showing the recipe page because all the tags are now span tags. The test needs to change to this:

```
def test_should_show_recipe
  get :show, :id => 1
  assert_response :success
  assert_select("span[id *= title]", "Soup One")
  assert_select("span[id *= servings]", "1")
  assert_select("span[id *= description]", "A Scrumptious Soup")
  assert_select("p.direction", "Eat, drink, and be merry.")
  assert_select("span[id *= ingredient]")
end
```

To get this to work on the server side, you need to add some class-level method calls that will create the set_recipe_title action shown in the preceding JavaScript. Each call is of the following form:

```
in_place_edit_for :recipe, :title
```

The first argument is the model type, and the second argument is the attribute. However, listing a whole bunch of these one after the other is hardly Rails-like, so add the following helper method to application.rb:

```
def self.in_place_edit_for_all(model, *attrs)
  attrs.each do |attr|
    self.in_place_edit_for model, attr
  end
end
```

Then you can put the following line in the recipes controller:

```
in_place_edit_for_all :recipe, :title, :servings, :description
```

I want to show you the definition of in_place_edit_for from the Rails core, because it's such a nice example of how brief and powerful Ruby metaprogramming can be. I think this example is particularly easy to read:

```
def in_place_edit_for(object, attribute, options = {})
  define_method("set_#{object}_#{attribute}") do
    @item = object.to_s.camelize.constantize.find(params[:id])
    @item.update_attribute(attribute, params[:value])
    render :text => @item.send(attribute)
  end
end
```

This implementation of in-place editing has a couple of nice advantages, one of which is how little coding you need to do to make it work. Another advantage is that the JavaScript editor is actually part of the view template, which means that the browser does not need to contact the server to display the edit form. This results in less load on the server and a faster response for the user.

On the down side, it can be a little awkward to go outside the base functionality to display and edit a derived field rather than a base field, for example, or to change the style of the display. It's doable, but at that point, it might be easier to use a regular Ajax call via link_to_remote, the way the tag edit field was handled.

As I write this, there is no out-of-the-box solution for a fully client-side, in-place selection list edit, although a solution that goes through the server can be easily written via link_to_remote. Again, watch the plugin skies for changes here.

Autocomplete

Another easy-to-add JavaScript feature is an autocomplete text field, which produces a pull-down menu of options that match the text as a user types it into the text field. This is also a set of methods that was pulled from Rails core into a plugin:

```
$ ruby script/plugin install ↲
http://dev.rubyonrails.org/svn/rails/plugins/autocomplete
```

Adding the autocomplete feature to a field is almost ridiculously easy. In your view, add the following helper call (which ordinarily would be within a form):

```
<%= text_field_with_auto_complete :recipe, :name %>
```

The two arguments are the object and attribute name, just as they would be used in an ordinary form tag helper method. This gives you a text field with some attached JavaScript that automatically makes an Ajax call back to the server when the user types, and fills a pull-down list with any entries that match what the user has typed. The eventual SQL call uses LIKE as the operator, so the typed text does not have to match the beginning of the actual text — a match anywhere in the string will work. (Also, on MySQL, the search is not case-sensitive.)

For this to work, you need to catch the request in the controller. Add the following declaration to your controller:

```
auto_complete_for :recipe, :name
```

And that makes it all work nicely. The `auto_complete_for` method takes additional key/value arguments that are passed directly to the `find` method, which you can use to customize results. For example, the default behavior is to return no more than 10 results, but you can change that behavior by adding a value such as `:limit => 20` as a key/value argument. Any `find` argument can be used.

Sometimes you'll want to use an autocomplete field outside a regular form, and you'll want it to automatically trigger a server-side call when the user makes a selection. You can do that with the following helper method, which you'd add to your `application_helper.rb` file:

```
def text_field_with_auto_complete_and_submit(obj, attr, controller, action,
    update_id)
  remote = remote_function(
      :url => {:action => action, :controller => controller, :id => nil},
      :with => "'name=' + escape(element.value)",
      :update => update_id)
  text_field_with_auto_complete obj, attr, {},
      :after_update_element => "function(element,value) { #{remote} }"
end
```

This helper takes additional arguments for a controller, an action, and a DOM ID to be updated. It augments the call to `text_field_with_auto_complete` with a JavaScript function call that invokes that controller and action specified, and updates the given DOM ID with the result of the call. The `remote_function` method used here is a Rails API method that is effectively the JavaScript equivalent of `link_to_remote`, and attaching it to `:after_update_element` causes the call to be invoked automatically after the user selects an option in the pull-down menu.

If you want to do something a little more idiosyncratic with your data, you can write your own controller method. The naming convention is `auto_complete_for_<object>_<attribute>`. You can do whatever you want within this method, but your return value needs to be a valid HTML unordered list (`ul` tag). Here's an example:

```
def auto_complete_for_recipe_name
  @items = #### SOME KIND OF FANCY FIND METHOD HERE..
    render :inline => "<%= auto_complete_result_symbol @items, :name %>"
end
```

The following helper method takes a list of objects and a method name symbol, and returns the unordered HTML list:

```
def auto_complete_result_symbol(entries, method_name)
  return unless entries
  items = entries.map do |entry|
    content_tag("li", h(entry.send(method_name)))
  end
  content_tag("ul", items.uniq)
end
```

Writing JavaScript in Ruby

The remote tag helper methods are easy to use and well suited to the basic task of updating the HTML inside a particular element on the page. That's a rather limited subset of what you can do with JavaScript, however. You'll often want to update more than one spot on the page, or do JavaScript manipulation on an element based on changing its style rather than its text. Although you could do all of that using the one of the various callback features to embed JavaScript into various nooks and crannies of the `link_to_remote`, that can be awkward. The Rails facility for writing more complex JavaScript effcts is an RJS template, which allows you to write Ruby code that is converted to JavaScript commands.

It's important to start the discussion of RJS with the disclaimer that although RJS is a nifty way to get a lot of JavaScript functionality into your application, it's in no way a substitute for actually writing JavaScript — especially if you want to try something really new and unique. Also, this book isn't about JavaScript per se, so let's focus on what you can accomplish with Ruby and Rails.

RJS code can be injected into your Rails page in one of two ways. The originally intended behavior was that the code would be placed in a view similar to an `html.erb` view, with the extension `.rjs`. However, over time, because many RJS invocations are pretty short and because they don't really behave like the HTML templates, it's more and more common to see them in the controller or in a helper method called from the controller.

Unlike the `html.erb` files, which convert to HTML and are designed to be displayed directly in the browser as a result of the request, RJS templates convert to JavaScript code and are designed to be executed in the browser. Executing RJS templates causes a display change in the browser. RJS is best thought of as a kind of domain-specific language shortcut for injecting JavaScript rather than a template tool.

An RJS Example

I have a modest example to show you.

Perhaps you recall the category tag cloud created back in Chapter 4 (which you modified with rollover tool tips in this chapter). As you may remember, the tag cloud took up only a small area at the top of the page. Wouldn't it be nice if clicking a tag in the cloud showed the recipes containing that tag on the same page? Sure it would. And wouldn't it be even cooler if there was some kind of fade in/fade out effect as a transition between two tags? Maybe. But this is Rails, and it's only going to take us about 25 lines of code or so to find out.

The first step is to change the category `index.html.erb` again to make the links trigger Ajax calls, and add a couple of empty tags to place the content that will be returned from them:

```
<% @title = "Recipe Tag Cloud" %>

<div id="tag_cloud_whole">
  <% @tags.each do |tag| %>
    <% tooltip_for "tag_#{tag}", "#{tooltip_string(tag)}",
       :title => "#{tooltip_title(tag, @tag_counts)}" do %>
      <%= link_to_remote tag, {:url => category_url(tag), :method => :get},
          :class => "tag_cloud_bucket_#{@tag_cloud[tag]}"%>
    <% end %>
```

```
      <% end %>
    </div>

    <br /> <br />
```

```
    <h2 id="category_being_shown"></h2>
    <div id="recipes_to_show"></div>
```

Notice that, unlike the other `link_to_remote` calls you've seen so far, this one does not specify a DOM ID to be updated by the result of the call. Instead, that information will be transmitted in the JavaScript generated by the RJS template. Also notice that, once again, you need to explicitly specify that the method call is an HTTP GET to enable the RESTful routes to understand it correctly.

The two empty tags at the bottom of the view will be retrieved by the RJS template and then used to insert the content implied by their names.

The index method in `category_controller.rb` needs to grow an RJS response block as follows:

```
    def show
      @category = params[:id] ||= ""
      @recipes = Recipe.find_tagged_with(@category)
      respond_to do |format|
        format.html #default
        format.xml { render :xml => @recipes}
        format.js  #default
      end
    end
```

Because there isn't any behavior specified for the block, Rails will invoke the default behavior — searching for a `show.rjs` template and evaluating it. The decision of whether to place the RJS code in a separate template or in a `render :update do |page| #stuff end` call is largely a matter of personal taste. This RJS code got a little longer than I was comfortable with inside a main controller method, although I could have easily moved it to a private method inside the controller. In the end, even though I think the RJS templates are structurally a little weird because they aren't really templates at all, that still seems like the expected location for the code. So, place the following code in `app/views/categories/show.rjs`:

```
    page.visual_effect(:fade, 'recipes_to_show',   :duration => 0.5)
    page.visual_effect(:fade, 'category_being_shown', :duration => 0.5)
    page.delay 0.5 do
      page.replace_html("category_being_shown",
          "<span>Recipies For: #{@category.capitalize}</span>")
      page.replace_html("recipes_to_show", :partial => "recipes")
      page.visual_effect(:appear, 'recipes_to_show', :duration => 0.5)
      page.visual_effect(:appear, 'category_being_shown', :duration => 0.5)
    end
```

All RJS templates have the special variable `page`, which is of the type `ActionView::Helpers::PrototypeHelper::JavaScriptGenerator`. It responds to about 20 different methods that produce JavaScript. Three of those methods are used in this template. The `visual_effect` method is a front-end to the script.aculo.us library, the first argument is the name of the effect, the second argument is the DOM ID of the element being affected, and the exact contents of the options hash depends on the effect being used. The list of effects can change, and the call will always dynamically match the list of effects offered by the version of script.aculo.us in use by your application.

The `replace_html` method mimics what an ordinary `link_to_remote` `:update` call would do — it changes the inside contents of an HTML element (the innerHTML, in JavaScript parlance) without affecting the external tag. The argument to this method is either a string used as-is or a hash of items that is then sent to the normal `ActionController#render` method for processing. In this case, the [div] tag with the DOM ID [recipes_to_show]. takes the contents of a partial view called `recipes`.

The `delay` method takes a block and executes the contents of this block after sleeping the Javascript for the amount of time specified in the argument (in seconds).

This template, therefore, fades out the existing contents of the `recipes_to_show` and `category_being_shown` elements, waits for a half-second for the fade to complete, and then swaps the text in both of those elements and fades them back in. The result, which I can't quite show in a static screenshot, is actually a kind of nice fade effect that calls attention to the changing content without being dramatic about it. (Although I have to admit that a real application wouldn't need to have both this Ajax call and the tooltip.)

To tie up the remaining loose end, the `recipes` partial is just extracted from the categories show view as follows:

```
<ul>
  <% for recipe in @recipes %>
    <li><%= link_to(h(recipe.title), recipe) %></li>
  <% end %>
</ul>
```

The `crossfade` feature is easily generalized to the following helper method, which you can use in other applications:

```
def crossfade(page, *dom_ids)
  dom_ids.each do |dom_id|
    page.visual_effect(:fade, dom_id, :duration => 0.5)
  end
  page.delay 0.5 do
    yield
    dom_ids.each do |dom_id|
      page.visual_effect(:appear, dom_id, :duration => 0.5)
    end
  end
end
```

The arguments to this method are the RJS `page` variable and the list of DOM IDs to update. The method expects a block, which is the action to take between fade down and fade up. To use this method, place it in `applications_helper.rb`, and change the RJS view to this:

```
crossfade(page, 'recipes_to_show', 'category_being_shown') do
  page.replace_html("category_being_shown",
      "<span>Recipies For: #{@category.capitalize}</span>")
  page.replace_html("recipes_to_show", :partial => "recipes")
end
```

Other RJS Methods

I mentioned before that an RJS page can take several different methods. The `delay`, `replace_html`, and `visual_effect` methods have already been covered, and this section examines some of the other methods. This is a list of the generator methods that Rails defines. There are further methods that are essentially converted directly to Prototype functions — check out the Prototype documentation for more information.

There are a couple of ways to select a DOM element. The preceding `replace_html` call took the DOM ID as the first argument of the method. However, you can also use array syntax to get at the DOM ID, and then call most of the RJS methods on the result:

```
page['category_to_show'].replace_html "#{category}"
```

The object resulting from the array reference works with most (but not all) of the RJS methods (for one thing, it doesn't work with `visual_effect`, which takes the name of the effect, not the DOM ID, as the first argument).

You can similarly get a collection of DOM elements by using the `select` method. The argument to the method is a CSS selector pattern, or essentially the same thing you might pass to an `assert_select` test. For example, you can get a list of all the category tags in the tag cloud. You can even use an `each` method and a block, which is converted to the following Prototype enumeration:

```
page.select(span[id*=tag_]) do |element|
   element.insert_html("gotcha")
end
```

There are a few methods that change the visibility of a set of DOM IDs. The methods `show` and `hide` take a list of DOM IDs and either show all the invisible ones or hide all the visible ones. There's also the `toggle` method, which just swaps the visibility state of all the DOM IDs that are passed to it. If you want to completely remove the DOM element, the conveniently named `remove` method will do that for you.

There are two methods that are related to `replace_html` (which you've already seen in action). The `replace` method changes the HTML for the entire element, including the outer tag itself. It takes the same argument options as `replace_html`. The `insert_html` method is similar, but it takes an initial argument that, specifies where you want the new text placed relative to the existing text: `:before` or `:after` to place it outside the element in question, or `:top` or `:bottom` to place the new text inside the existing text.

The `visual_effect` method is a wrapper around a script.aculo.us object. Similarly, the `draggable` and `drop_receiving` methods are wrappers that make the element ID passed to the method work within the script.aculo.us drag-and-drop framework, and the `sortable` method makes the element work as part of the script.aculo.us sortable list framework.

There are a few methods that let you drop arbitrary JavaScript into the page with various amounts of structure. The `assign` method takes a variable name as a string or symbol and a value, and produces JavaScript to set a variable with that name to that value. The `call` method takes a JavaScript function name that would be in scope for the page in question and the series of arguments to that function, and inserts a JavaScript call to that function. The `<<` method is used to inject an arbitrary string into the page to be evaluated as JavaScript. Finally, the `alert` method takes a string argument and puts up a JavaScript alert box with that message.

Using RJS for Lightboxing

This section shows you a quick example of using RJS to manage a different external JavaScript library, specifically the Control.Modal library, which is built on top of Prototype and adds modal windows and lightboxes. The lightbox effect is becoming common in web applications, especially photo sites. With this effect, a modal-like window appears in the browser, and the rest of the browser window fades out behind it. In JavaScript terms, the effect is managed by placing a dark-gray overlay on top of the entire screen, and then placing the new `div` tag on top.

Download the Control.Modal library from `http://livepipe.net/projects/control_modal/`, place it in your `public/javascripts` directory, and add the following line to the headers of your layout file (the exact name of the file to include will depend on the version of Control.Modal):

```
<%= javascript_include_tag "control.modal.2.2.4.js" %>
```

Control.Modal has many options that I won't go into here (see the resources section for more information), but I do want to pass along a couple of RJS helper methods that you can use to incorporate the lightbox effect into your application:

```ruby
def control_modal(div_id, options = {})
  to_open = if options.key?(:open) then options[:open] else true end
  options.delete(:open)
  option_strings = []
  options.each do |key, value|
    value = "'#{escape_javascript value}'" if value.is_a? String
    option_strings << "#{key}: #{value}"
  end
  options_string = "{#{option_strings.join(', ')}}"
  result_string = "new Control.Modal('#{div_id}', #{options_string})";
  result_string = "m = #{result_string}; m.open();" if to_open
end

def close_control_modal
      "Control.Modal.close();"
end
```

The first method takes a DOM ID (which is somewhat arbitrary) and a hash of Control.Modal options, and builds up the JavaScript string for creating the modal window. The most important options are `:contents`, which contains the contents of the window being created, `:position`, which can either be relative to the location of the link or absolute, and `:fade`, which, if `true`, causes a nice fade in and fade out effect for the lightbox.

You can control the look of the windows by adding the following entries to your CSS page:

```css
#modal_container {
  padding:5px;
  background-color: #FFFFCC;
  border:1px solid #666;
  overflow:auto;
  font-family:"Lucida Grande",Verdana;
  font-size:12px;
  color:#333;
```

```
    text-align:left;
  }

#modal_overlay {
  background-color:#000;
}
```

The `modal_overlay` is the layer between the modal `div` and the background — what you are setting here is the color that the background fades to. The `modal_container` is the actual modal `div` created by Control.Modal.

You can use this by injecting the code into your RJS `page` variable using <<. You can build the contents string by rendering a partial, as in this example:

```
contents = render :partial => "recipes/form"
page << control_modal('new_recipe_link', :contents => contents,
    :position => "relative", :offsetLeft => -350, :fade => true)
### later
page << close_control_modal
```

Testing RJS

If you are like me, then you are wondering at this point how you go about writing automated tests for RJS templates. Perhaps you noticed that the last section was not presented with testing code first, and you thought that there may not be a good way to test RJS. However, there are a couple of useful ways to do this. First is the Rails core method `assert_select_rjs`.

Using assert_select_rjs

The `assert_select_rjs` method takes zero, one, or two arguments and a block. The block can take any arbitrary assertions, specifically including further `assert_select_rjs` calls and further `assert_select` calls. An `assert_select` call inside the `assert_select_rjs` block will validate against the HTML code being sent inside the RJS calls, which is very handy.

If there are no elements, the method only asserts that there is RJS output and then performs whatever validations are inside the block. The arguments narrow down the search. A single argument is a DOM ID, which verifies that there is RJS activity for that DOM ID and then performs validations inside the block. If there are two arguments, the first is a symbol for an RJS call, and the second is a DOM ID. The method validates that the specific call was made against the specific DOM ID, and then checks the block. For example:

```
def test_should_make_xhr_call_on_category
    setup_recipe_tags
    xhr :get, :show, :id => "yummy"
    assert_select_rjs replace_html, "category_being_shown" do
      assert_select "span", "Recipies For: Yummy"
    end
    assert_select_rjs :replace_html, "recipes_to_show" do
      assert_select "li", /Soup One/
    end
  end
end
```

There's also a plugin that helps validate the JavaScript output of an RJS script: ARTS.

Using the ARTS Plugin

The ARTS plugin (ARTS stands for Another RJS Testing System) was written by Kevin Clark. The recommended installation procedure is this:

```
$ ruby script/plugin discover
$ ruby script/plugin install arts
```

To show you how this plugin works, I wrote a functional test against the preceding RJS template. More or less as a matter of principle, I chose to test for only the actual HTML changes, rather than the visual effects, on the theory that the visual effects will have to be validated manually and are more likely to change and break tests. This test is in category_controller_test.rb:

```
def test_should_make_xhr_call_on_category
  setup_recipe_tags
  xhr :get, :show, :id => "yummy"
  assert_rjs :replace_html, "category_being_shown", "Recipies For: Yummy"
  assert_rjs :replace_html, "recipes_to_show", /Soup One/
end
```

The test makes the xhr GET call to the show method. Then the testing is done using the assert_rjs method, which makes up the bulk of the functionality of ARTS. The assert_rjs method validates that somewhere in the JavaScript output, there's a line of code that matches the parameters of the assertion — it doesn't test that the method calls are in any order. For negative testing, the assert_no_rjs method is also provided — it passes in any case where assert_rjs would fail.

The first argument to assert_rjs is a method name that corresponds to one of the methods that the page object in an RJS template can accept. Subsequent arguments to assert_rjs are expected to match exactly the arguments to the RJS method. The only exception is an argument that is expected to match the HTML output for an insert or replacement call — in that case, the argument can be a string that matches the JavaScript output exactly, or a regular expression that passes a regular expression match against the JavaScript output. The regular expression version is shown in the last line, where the actual output is an HTML anchor tag with an href attribute, and a lot of odd JavaScript escape characters. It's much cleaner to just match against the regular expression of the content you actually care about.

ARTS is pretty nifty, but it does have some limitations. If you use the square-bracket syntax to get a DOM ID, then plain assert_rjs won't work — you need to use the method assert_rjs_page, and then you can make the DOM ID the first argument to the assertion, just as in the preceding examples. Also, ARTS doesn't seem to handle the RJS select call, although it would presumably match any JavaScript calls inside the block.

One nice feature of ARTS is that failure messages include the entire text of the JavaScript output from the RJS template, which makes it much easier to see what's going on.

Cross-Site Scripting Security

Most of this chapter has been spent discussing how to generate JavaScript from Rails. This section is about *preventing* JavaScript from being generated — or more specifically, how to prevent a malicious user from injecting JavaScript into a client page pointed at your system and carrying out a cross-site scripting (XSS) attack.

The basic idea behind an XSS exploit is that unintended JavaScript injected on to a browser page in your system can cause sensitive information to be retrieved from the server and displayed in the client's browser. For example, an XSS exploit might occur if JavaScript is inserted into a recipe description or tag list on the Soups OnLine site, or is inserted in a forum comment of some kind on other sites.

Although many of these exploits are only fully dangerous when combined with some kind of phishing scam (where an unsuspecting user is tricked into injecting the malicious code), you should try to avoid any openings by which cross-site code can be sent to your server.

The basic mechanism for preventing XSS attacks is to aggressively verify and scrub any data that comes in from a user and will eventually be displayed on the screen (or sent to the database — user-generated SQL can also wreak havoc on your system). Information with a known format should be validated against that format. This is relatively easy for numerical data, and a lot of text data (such as names) can be scrubbed to include only alphabetical or alphanumeric content. Filenames for uploaded files also need to be scrubbed.

The larger problem comes when you allow users to type open text, as in a comment or description field. In general, these fields need to be stripped of any potentially malicious code. However, it's not just a simple matter of removing `script` tags. There are a number of ways in which JavaScript could potentially be executed — the `src` attribute of the `img` tag is just one such vector, as in:

```
<IMG SRC="javascript:alert('XSS');">
```

In Rails 2.0, the `sanitize` method no longer tests against a black list of forbidden elements; instead, it does a much more secure check against a white list of allowed elements. It has incorporated the functionality that used to be provided by a plugin called WhiteList.

Use `sanitize` instead of `h` wherever you are displaying user-generated text, as follows:

```
<%= sanitize text_to_clean %>
```

By default, `sanitize` removes all HTML tags, and does its best to get rid of anything with an `src` attribute, or which might be carrying JavaScript. You can limit the tags and attributes allowed on a case-by-case basis by adding attributes to the helper call, like this:

```
<%= sanitize @comment.text, :tags => %w(b em), :attributes => %w(id class style)
```

Only the tags and attributes specifically mentioned in the helper call will be allowed.

If there are certain tags that you want to allow, such as <em>, you can add tags to the allowed tag list on a global basis in your config.rb file. Add this within the Initializer.run block:

```
config.after_initialize do
  ActionView::Base.sanitize_allowed_tags.add "em"
end
```

You can similarly use the delete method to remove tags from the allowed list. The sanitized_allowed_attributes list governs what attributes are allowed.

For more information on what sanitize checks for and how it checks for it, look at the test suite in vendor/rails/actionpack/test/template/sanitize_helper_test.rb, which is one of my favorite unit test classes of all time. It does a very thorough job of walking sanitize through a set of known potential XSS exploits.

Resources

Prototype and script.aculo.us are JavaScript libraries distributed with Rails. Prototype's home page (which includes API documentation) is www.prototypejs.org. The home page for script.aculo.us is (conveniently) http://script.aculo.us. Both of these libraries are sometimes updated on a different schedule than Rails releases, so it's worth keeping an eye on them.

You can find documentation and other information about the Prototip library at www.nickstakenburg .com/projects/prototip. Control.Model lives at http://livepipe.net/projects/control_ modal, with a complete list of options and parameters.

The ARTS plugin was introduced by its author, Kevin Clark, at http://glu.ttono.us/ articles/2006/05/29/guide-test-driven-rjs-with-arts. There seems to be very little online discussion of assert_select_rjs, however.

The Ruby on Rails Security Project has a blog at www.rorsecurity.info, which frequently discusses JavaScript bases security issues. A good description of various types of XSS attacks is available at http://ha.ckers.org/blog/category/webappsec/xss/.

Summary

Web 2.0 is largely powered by JavaScript via the asynchronous server call structure often called Ajax. Rails provides a number of different features that you can use to enable Ajax in your applications. The most basic structure is link_to_remote and remote_form_for helpers that enable an ordinary link or form to trigger an Ajax call and update an arbitrary part of the page. You can test these calls with the xhr functional test helper. You can also easily augment them to give users who don't have JavaScript some functionality.

You can add tooltips to your Rails applications with the Prototip library and a couple of simple helpers. Two former pieces of the Rails core, in-line editing and autocomplete text fields, are available as plugins and are still quite easy to use. You can also combine the Control.Modal library with some simple helpers to give a modal dialog, lightbox effect.

RJS allows you to write Ruby code that is converted to JavaScript, which enables you to use more complex effects than what you get with the base behavior of the remote helpers. RJS templates have a wide array of operators to manipulate the DOM of the client browser, including full access to the script. aculo.us effects library. You can use the Rails `assert_select_rjs` helper method or the ARTS plugin to test the result of an RJS call.

JavaScript applications can be vulnerable to cross-site scripting attacks. By using the `sanitize` helper, you can minimize the risk of such attacks dramatically.

Talking to the Web

Increasingly, the content produced by web applications and distributed over web servers is aimed not directly at the user, but at other computer programs that use the data in different ways. Applications can take web data and present it to the user in a different user interface (UI) — such as the Twitteriffic application, which gives Twitter a Mac OS X front-end. Or a site can aggregate data from multiple sites — such as Bloglines or Google Reader.

All it really means to be a web service is to output data from HTTP requests in a machine-readable format. At the moment, XML is the most common format (especially because the RSS format for blog syndication is just a specification within XML). In fact, the formal definition of web services seems to sort of absurdly say that a web service can only be in XML. However, you'll frequently see JavaScript Object Notation (JSON) used (especially for data specifically earmarked for Ajax and JavaScript), and most web pages still render HTML, so it's useful to have a tool that can extract useful data from those pages as well.

There have been a few attempts to standardize web services. These days, the most prominent standards are SOAP (which is currently an ex-acronym because the original acronym was officially declared misleading) and REST (REpresentational State Transfer), which has already cropped up numerous times in this book. Without getting into the detailed arguments over which standard is better, the Rails core team has chosen REST as a preferred mechanism for managing web services from Rails. As a result, this chapter focuses on REST and similar lightweight web communication systems such as RSS and Atom. It also tackles producing web service data and consuming web services.

ActiveResource

In the beginning there was ActiveWebService, part of the Rails core that allowed Rails to act as a SOAP or XML-RPC client and server. And it was . . . okay. Then David Heinemeier Hansson (the creator of Ruby on Rails) announced in his keynote address at the 2006 RailsConf that Rails was going to be supporting REST as a web services architecture in a big way. ActiveWebService would be removed from the Rails 2.0 core, although it would still be available as a plugin.

In the Rails 2.0 world, Rails applications act as web service servers through the support of REST in the design of the controllers, and as web service clients through a new Rails library called ActiveResource. The ActiveResource library is specifically designed to work with external sites that follow the REST standard.

Why the change? It seems as though Hansson and the Rails team saw the opportunity to improve the design of Rails applications in multiple directions at once. By encouraging the limitation of controller classes to the CRUD (Create, Read, Update, Delete) set of actions, it moves Rails even further in the "convention, not configuration" direction. Simultaneously, the more that Rails controllers have a consistent, predictable set of actions, the easier it is to write and maintain client applications that rely on those servers to acquire their data. At that point, it becomes possible to have a smart web services client that can infer the structure of their objects in much the same way that ActiveRecord is a smart consumer of database information that can infer the structure of its objects.

As I write this, ActiveResource is available only in Rails 2.0. If you are using an older version of Rails, and go to Edge Rails via a subversion external, you'll pick it up just fine — but if you get there via the `rake rails:edge:freeze` command, you will have to repeat the command a second time for ActiveResource to get picked up (because ActiveResource is added to the list of directories to download only after the first run). The ActiveResource API and feature set is very much a work in progress, and existing documentation or examples of production experience are pretty thin. So this is going to be kind of a high-level overview. Please check in with the latest Rails documentation to see how things have changed since this book went to press.

The Client Side of REST

In Chapter 1, you saw how REST works as a structure for designing Rails controllers in terms of a standard set of actions. Now let's take a look at REST as an architecture for web services.

REST is a set of principles or a way of structuring the interaction between multiple elements in a network. Unlike SOAP or XML-RPC, there isn't any formal specification of what a REST system is, and the REST police aren't going to come after you and say you're not really doing a web service if your implementation is a little idiosyncratic. That said, the Rails style of RESTfulness does depend on a certain consistency in the interface.

A RESTful system is made up of resources, each of which has a unique identifier and a limited set of operations that can be performed on it. In contrast, a SOAP system is conceptually made up of a set of commands that are used to access some set of data — the overall functionality is similar, but the structures are orthogonal. When you access a REST resource via its identifier, you are supposed to get a straightforward representation of the resource itself — Rails uses XML (the conventional choice for web services), but again, there's no technical reason why you couldn't use some other data representation. The response to a REST system should not contain other information about the state of the server. A REST connection is stateless.

If that bare-bones description of resources, unique identifiers, simple data structures, and stateless interactions sounds familiar, that's because it also describes the Web as a whole. That's not a coincidence — Roy Fielding, who coined the term REST, was one of the people who defined the Web's HTTP protocol in the first place (among other things, he was a cofounder of the Apache web server project).

In theory, at least, a RESTful client-server interaction can be developed with much less overhead, both on the part of the client and of the server. In Chapter 1, you saw that a RESTful resource can be created in just a few lines of server-side Ruby.

Now let's look at the client side.

Activating Your Resources

An ActiveResource object is essentially a front-end to the REST web server. It obtains and modifies its data by making HTTP calls back to the server and parsing the XML results back into a Ruby object. You call basic CRUD actions such as find, save, delete, and create on the ActiveResource object, and those changes are sent to the server. Assuming that the server has a typical relationship with its database, those changes are reflected in the database and are seen by the rest of the server-side application.

Finding Resources

The following code snippet shows what a minimal ActiveResource client script looks like. For this to work, the Soups OnLine application has to be running at the URL in the example. You can put this example anywhere, but the first line must point to the `active_resource` file in your Rails distribution.

```
require '<RAILS_APP_ROOT>/vendor/rails/activeresource/lib/active_resource'
ActiveResource::Base.site = "http://localhost:3000"

class Recipe < ActiveResource::Base
end

recipes = Recipe.find(:all)
p recipes.collect(&:title)
```

Here's the line-by-line-breakdown:

1. The first line loads in the ActiveResource library. Because this client script is normally outside the Rails application, either in a separate Rails application or in a standalone script or desktop application, you can't assume that ActiveResource will already be loaded.

2. The `site` attribute tells ActiveResource what the base URL of the server containing the resource is. In this case, all the resources you want in this application are coming from the same site, so you set that attribute once at the superclass level for all the resources that might be added.

3. `Recipe` is declared as a subclass of `ActiveResource::Base`. By default, the assumption is that the newly declared class will have the same name as the `ActiveRecord` model being targeted on the server. (In the case where there's a REST resource on the server that doesn't have an explicit model, this resource class has the singular name that you'd expect based on the controller name.) To set the base site for this class to be different from the parent default, use the method call `self.site = "http://`*whatever*`"`. Despite the name similarity, the ActiveResource `Recipe` is a completely different class than the server-side ActiveRecord `Recipe` (as you'll soon see).

4. The next line runs the `Recipe.find(:all)` command. Watch your server logs when this script runs, and you'll see an HTTP request be sent to `http://localhost:3000/recipes.xml`. The result of this is an XML list that contains, by default, each recipe in the database, and each database attribute of each recipe (see the next section for a discussion of how to customize the XML output). The ActiveResource library parses the XML and converts it into an ActiveResource recipe object for each element in the XML list.

5. The final line just proves that the actual `Recipe` data has been gathered by printing out the names of the recipes that have been gathered.

This is all extremely cool, but it's worth keeping in mind that the ActiveResource API is currently much less extensive than the ActiveRecord API.

The ActiveResource `find` functionality is extremely limited — in general, you are relying on the server to do any kind of fancy filtering by exposing different actions or attributes that perform server-side filtering. Basically, you have four modifiers: `find(id)`, `find(:all)`, `find(:first)`, and `find(:one)`. The `:first` modifier tells ActiveResource to request all the data but only return the first element — I suggest doing that sparingly. The `:one` modifier is generally for when you are using a nonstandard URL — it serves as a message to ActiveResource that you are only expecting one result.

To use a nonstandard URL, you need to specify it with a `:from` argument, as in the following example:

```
recipe = Recipe.find(:one, :from =>
'localhost:3000/recipes/most_recent_recipe.xml')
```

This assumes that `most_recent_recipe` has been added as a route to the server-side controller. Any other option you include in the key/value part of the `find` call is added to the query string for the URL sent back to the server, so that mechanism can be used to provide more sophisticated search capability (again assuming that the functionality exists on the server side).

The ActiveResource object is not the same class as the server-side ActiveRecord (and I really wish DHH had come up with two names that sounded less alike). Specifically for this example's purpose, any derived object or calculated attribute present in the model will not be present on the client. If there are a number of such things, I highly recommend creating a mixin that can be included into both the ActiveRecord object and the ActiveResource object, taking advantage of Ruby's duck typing to use the same names for the methods in both classes.

The active resource does not, by default, include information about related classes. In the preceding code, the ingredient data is not included with the returned recipes. There are a couple of ways around this. On the server side, you can have the related objects included as nested objects in the XML, in which case ActiveResource converts the subordinate elements to their own classes.

To access a resource that is defined on the server as being nested, you need to define the collection that contains the resource on the client side, like this:

```
require '../../vendor/rails/activeresource/lib/active_resource'
ActiveResource::Base.site = "http://localhost:3000"
```

```
class Ingredient < ActiveResource::Base
  self.set_collection_name :recipes
end
class Recipe < ActiveResource::Base
end
ingredients = Ingredient.find(:all, :recipe_id => 1)
p ingredients
```

The `set_collection_name` call tells ActiveRecord how to construct the URL needed to get `Ingredient` resources from the server side.

Copying, Updating, and Deleting with ActiveResource

ActiveResource can also be used for the C, U, and D actions, with essentially the same interface as ActiveRecord objects.

Changes to an object can be saved back to the server using `save`. For example:

```
r = Recipe.find(:first)
r.title = "Changed Soup"
r.save

#verify the result
recipes = Recipe.find(:all)
p recipes.collect(&:title)
```

This can even be managed with newly created objects, as follows:

```
r = Recipe.new(:title => "A New Soup")
r.save
```

which has the expected shortcut:

```
r.create(:title => "A New Soup")
```

ActiveResource cannot, at the moment, be relied on to do validation before sending the data to the server, although any server-side validation you have set up on the model class will be run on the server-side when the object is saved.

For the big D of deletion, you can use the following class method:

```
Recipe.delete(1)
```

and an instance method:

```
Recipe.find(1).destroy
```

which both have the same outcome.

Producing Web Service Data

If you've set up your application using RESTful controllers, then you're already halfway toward acting as a web service. Your application is set up with a standard API that other applications will be able to hit. The second half involves producing machine-readable code in the expected formats.

Producing XML

You've already seen the first part of the Rails XML response mechanism — it's part of the RESTful controller scaffold. As a reminder, here it is again:

```
def index
  @recipes = Recipe.find(:all)
  respond_to do |format|
    format.html # index.html.erb
    format.xml  { render :xml => @recipes }
  end
end
```

The `render :xml` method call immediately turns around and calls the `to_xml` method on the argument. Rails defines `to_xml` for most classes, including `ActiveRecord::Base`, `Array`, and `Hash`. For example, the default XML result for a `Recipe` object would look something like this:

```
<?xml version=\"1.0\" encoding=\"UTF-8\"?>
<recipe>
  <cached-ingredient-string></cached-ingredient-string>
  <cached-tag-list>grandma, chicken, fred</cached-tag-list>
  <created-at type=\"datetime\">2007-08-05T20:03:33-05:00</created-at>
  <description>Yummy!</description>
  <directions>Things</directions>
  <id type=\"integer\">1</id>
  <servings>3</servings>
  <title>Grandma's Chicken Soup</title>
  <updated-at type=\"datetime\">2007-09-04T23:04:45-05:00</updated-at>
  <user-id type=\"integer\">2</user-id>
</recipe>
```

The default XML for an array of recipes is similar, but it wraps the whole thing in a `<recipes type="array"></recipes>` tag pair.

Although the default is rather useful all by itself, in this case, there are some attributes that you would not necessarily want passed on to your web service consumer. For instance, you might not want to pass both the cached ingredient string and the ingredient objects themselves. On the other hand, passing the cached strings could potentially minimize the amount of data retrieved from the database and sent over the network, so it's not necessarily a cut-and-dried choice.

The `to_xml` method for ActiveRecord takes several options to adjust the output XML. You could include these options in the `render :xml` call, and they will be passed along. However, if you are doing anything at all complex that will affect the model class every time it's used, you probably want to actually override `to_xml` in your model class to call the `super` method with your custom options. Along with avoiding duplication by specifying the options once, this also ensures that the options will be picked up if the object is included in an array or hash XML output.

The option to remove attributes from the output is `:except`, which takes either a single symbol argument or a list of symbol arguments (attributes passed will not be included in the XML output). For example:

```
Recipe.find(1).to_xml :except => [:cached_ingredient_string, ↵
:cached_tag_list]
```

The flip side of `:except` is `:only`, which allows you to specify a whitelist of only the attributes that should be included in the output. (By the way, if you specify both elements, `:only` wins.) These attributes apply only to the ActiveRecord version of `to_xml`, not to the ActiveResource version.

There are a couple of options that allow you to include elements in the XML that are not simple attributes of the object. The `:include` option takes a single symbol or a list of symbols. The arguments must be symbols that represent ActiveRecord associations on the model. So for a `Recipe`, the argument could be `:ingredients`, `:user`, or `:rating`. The selected associations are then included as subobjects on the XML (in an array, if necessary). For example:

```
Recipe.find(1).to_xml :include => :ingredients
```

You aren't limited to just raw attributes in the XML output — you can also include arbitrary calculated attributes by using the `:methods` argument. This is helpful if you have a derived value that is also of importance to a potential web services client.

Some options affect the specific details of the XML output. You might have noticed in the XML output shown earlier that underscores in attribute names such as `user_id` were converted to dashes, as in `user-id`. That's in keeping with more conventional XML naming patterns, and is governed by the option `:dasherize`, which is `true` by default. The XML output contains an XML processing instruction as a header. This is important if the output is meant to be a stand-alone document, but is an error if the object is actually a subordinate element in a larger document. You can turn off the processing instruction with the option `:skip_instruct => true`. The default output also explicitly includes the type as an XML attribute for all values that are not strings. You can turn that feature off with `:skip_types => true`.

With all those options, you have a fairly wide range of ways to generate XML from your object. If you need something fancier, you can bounce up to the `Builder::XmlMarkup` class, which lets you define pretty much any XML you want as a series of Ruby method calls.

For example, say you wanted something odd, like the number of ingredients in the XML output. You could implement it like this:

```
def to_xml(options = {})
  builder = Builder::XmlMarkup.new
  builder.instruct! unless options[:skip_instruct]
  builder.recipe do |element|
    element.name = title
    element.ingredient_count = ingredients.count
    element.ingredients = ingredient_string
  end
  builder
end
```

`Builder::XmlMarkup` is an interesting implementation, in that almost everything you throw at it is processed via the `method_missing` method so that it becomes an XML tag. The few methods that are actually defined all have a `!` suffix. In this code, that means the `recipe` becomes a top-level tag, and the block structure is used here to define the element/subelement structure of the XML file. The tags `name`, `ingredient_count`, and `ingredients` are defined in the output.

Sample output from that method is shown in the following code snippet from an interaction with the Rails console (some spacing and indentation was inserted manually):

```
r = Recipe.find(1)
=> ### the description
>> r.to_xml
=> <?xml version="1.0" encoding="UTF-8"?>
<recipe>
  <name=>Grandma's Chicken Soup</name=>
  <ingredient_count=>2</ingredient_count=>
  <ingredients=>2 cups stock 1/2 oz. carrot</ingredients=>
</recipe><inspect/>
```

Note the weird little `<inspect/>` tag at the end. That's actually an artifact of being in the console — specifically, it's an artifact of the fact that the console calls `inspect` on the builder to display the output. The `inspect` call gets duly processed by `method_missing` and converted to an XML tag — which is both cool and a little disconcerting.

Builder Templates

Another way to produce XML is by using a *builder template*. Builder templates are view files with the extension `.builder` (or in older Rails versions, `.rxml`). Rendering the builder template is the default action for XML requests in exactly the way that RJS templates are for JavaScript requests and `.html.erb` files are for HTML requests.

Within the `.builder` template, you have access to a local variable named `xml`, which is an instance of `Builder::XmlMarkup`. Inside the template, you can make arbitrary method calls to build up the XML, and the output sent to the browser is the final state of the builder object.

If you wanted the odd `to_xml` file that ended the last section to be expressed as a builder file, the syntax would change only slightly. For one thing, you would need to include the variable name of the builder and recipe. For another, you know for sure this is a full XML page, so you don't need an `if` clause on the `instruct!` call. Here's the syntax:

```
xml.instruct!
xml.recipe do |element|
   element.name = @recipe.title
   element.ingredient_count = @recipe.ingredients.count
   element.ingredients = @recipe.ingredient_string
end
```

By inserting this into a file named `app/view/index.builder` and removing the `render :xml` call from the index controller, you can ensure that your custom builder is the source of the XML sent in the response. The full constructor block looks like this:

```
def index
    @recipes = Recipe.find(:all)
    respond_to do |format|
      format.html # index.html.erb
      format.xml
    end
end
```

Builder templates aren't limited to just XML. Imagine rewriting that builder like this:

```
xml.h1 = title
xml.div = ingredients.count
xml.div do |div|
   ingredients.each do |ingredient|
     div.div = ingreient.string
   end
end
```

There are developers who find writing output views in this style to be easier and more intuitive than ERB. As you'll see in Chapter 16, there are multiple alternatives to ERB that you can install in your Rails application to allow a more code-like structure for your output.

Producing Feeds

Web site syndication via RSS (which once stood for Rich Site Syndication, but now stands for Really Simple Syndication) has become the standard mechanism used to convert web data into a time-based stream, primarily for use by feed-reading programs that take RSS feeds from multiple sources and aggregate them.

RSS is typically associated with blogs and blog readers, but it's readily adaptable to any website where you want to push notification of a data change to interested users. It's the mechanism behind podcasting. It's also used by CruiseControl and other continuous integration tools to push build information. You can get an RSS feed of the status of your UPS deliveries, and so on.

As you may be aware, there are actually two competing standards for syndication formats: RSS and Atom. (RSS claims to be the more commonly used generic term for syndication.) There is also a long and sometimes contentious debate over the relative merits of the two. I have no particular side in that fight at all. At the moment, the dynamic of the situation is such that pretty much any serious feed-reading tool will handle either format, and Rails lets you output in either format. I focus on Atom here because there's a Rails plugin that supports it, although supporting RSS itself is extremely similar.

Both RSS and Atom can be used as the format in a `respond_to` block. The exact mechanism for producing RSS and Atom is in a state of flux as I write this (a plugin that supported both was deprecated because it was "too restrictive"). The current state of play is a helper called Atom Feed Helper, which true to its word, is a helper for creating Atom feeds. This helper is installed as part of Rails 2.0, and earlier versions can access it as a plugin.

Generating Atom

Let's use the Atom Feed helper to create an Atom feed for newly created recipes. The proper place to call this from is the `index` method of the recipe controller — from a REST standpoint, generating the recipes for an index page and generating for an Atom feed is essentially the same action. You need to add the following new `respond_to` block (notice that I've taken the custom XML builder out of the index):

```ruby
def index
  @recipes = Recipe.find_for_index(params[:format])
  respond_to do |format|
    format.html # index.html.erb
    format.xml  { render :xml => @recipes }
    format.atom { render :layout => false }
  end
end
```

There are two changes to the `index` method. The addition of the new `respond_to` block sets up Atom as the response format for the URL `/recipes.atom`. Rails then looks for `app/views/recipes/index.builder` as the location of the file to render from.

The second change moves the actual `find` call into the model, so that the Atom feed has a different number of elements than the index displayed in the main page. Putting any logic at all around the `find` method is a strong hint that all the logic should get moved to the model, here's the new method:

```ruby
def self.find_for_index(format)
  limit = if format == :atom then 25 else 100 end
  find(:all, :limit => limit, :order => "created_at DESC")
end
```

This also ensures that the recipes are always returned in reverse chronological order.

The next step is to create the builder. In the builder, you start by calling the `atom_feed` helper provided by the Atom Feed Helper plugin. To do this, you replace the code in `app/views/recipe/index.builder` with the following (alternately, you could place this in `app/views/recipe/index.atom.builder`):

```
atom_feed(:url => formatted_recipe_url(:atom)) do |feed|
  feed.title("Soups OnLine Recipe Feed")
  feed.updated(if @recipes then @recipes[0].created_at else Time.now.utc end)
  @recipes.each do |item|
    feed.entry(item) do |entry|
      entry.title(item.title)
      entry.content(item.content)
      entry.author do |author|
        author.name(item.user.full_name)
        author.email(item.user.email)
      end
    end
  end
end
```

The `atom_feed` helper provides a wrapper around the normal XML builder, which takes care of some of the paperwork associated with creating an Atom feed. Specifically, it manages the following:

❏ The XML header, including the language and namespace attributes

❏ Creating a unique ID for the feed and a link back to the `feed` URL inside the feed itself

❏ Creating a custom ID and a link back to the `show` URL for each entry

❏ Putting timestamps into the feed

❏ Providing an interface for adding entries to the feed

The feature that isn't directly supported is populating the data for each entry. At a minimum, you need to fill the `title` field and the `content` field. In this case, the `title` is just the title of the recipe, and the `content` was defined within the recipe especially for this builder and is a reasonable aggregation of the fields that define the recipe:

```
def content
  "#{title}\n\n#{description}\n\n#{ingredient_string}\n\n#{directions}"
end
```

Within the builder, the `atom_field` helper takes the URL for the feed and a block. The argument to the block is actually an XML Builder object — in this case, it's an alias to the one that would normally be provided to a builder template, but that's not always so. Within the block, you set the title and update time for the feed as a whole. After that, you loop over the recipes, giving each one an entry in the feed. (`entry` is actually a method that the feed helper intercepts before sending to the XML builder so that the timestamp and link can be added into the XML element.) Inside each entry are the title and content, as well as the author's name and e-mail address.

Exactly what you get when you try to hit this page depends on your browser. Firefox usually tries to add to your default RSS reader. In Safari, the URL `feed://127.0.0.1:3000/recipes.atom` loads the feed in Safari's RSS reader. It will look something like Figure 9-1. (Strangely you get an error in Safari if you try to do this using `localhost` because of the way Safari tries to redirect the page; however, using the numerical URL works, and other browsers don't seem to have this problem.)

Figure 9-1

The code works as-is, but I'm not completely satisfied with it — builder knows more about the inner workings of the Recipe model than I think it should, and the double block to get an entry for each recipe looks weird to me. To clean this up, you first need to move the recipe code into the Recipe model by changing the builder template as follows:

```
atom_feed(:url => formatted_recipe_url(:atom)) do |feed|
  feed.title("Soups OnLine Recipe Feed")
  feed.updated(if @recipes then @recipes[0].created_at else Time.now.utc end)
  @recipes.each do |recipe|
    recipe.to_atom_feed_entry(feed)
  end
end
```

That changes the recipe method to this:

```
def to_atom_feed_entry(feed)
  feed.entry(self) do |entry|
    entry.title = title
    entry.content = content
    entry.author do |author|
      author.name = user.full_name
      author.email = user.email
    end
  end
  feed
end
```

I like this a lot better. For one thing, it simplifies the builder template, which is a worthy goal all by itself. For another, it keeps the details of the recipe encapsulated inside the `Recipe` class, so changes to the recipe data structure do not need to be propagated outside the class.

You can actually pull the loop out of the builder template, although that requires a little bit of monkey patching in the `Array` class:

```
atom_feed(:url => formatted_recipe_url(:atom)) do |feed|
  feed.title("Soups OnLine Recipe Feed")
  feed.updated(if @recipes then @recipes[0].created_at else Time.now.utc end)
  @recipes.to_atom_feed_entries(feed)
end
```

If you've been following along, you should have an extensions.rb file that already opens up Array to add a method. Now you need to add another one:

```
def to_atom_feed_entries(feedbuilder)
  self.each do |item|
    item.to_atom_feed_entry(feedbuilder)
  end
end
```

Remember, because the extensions.rb file is not a model, you need to restart the server for changes in that file to be loaded.

This puts the looping logic in Array, which makes for a pretty clean builder object, but it also makes a strong assumption about the model class — namely that it implements a to_atom_feed_entry method. However, as far as you or I know, there's only one class in the entire world that has such a method, so it might seem a little presumptive to assume such a thing.

One other thought about generating RSS feeds: you are going to need to cache the results of the feed in a file somewhere so that most accesses to the feed are served statically. If the RSS bots get hold of your site, they are capable of producing a large amount of hits, so you want to make sure that's done with a minimum of effort. See Chapter 13 for more details on caching.

Generating RSS

If you want to work with the regular RSS output, you don't (at this writing) have a semi-official core plugin to help, but you do have a Ruby standard library. The basic idea is pretty similar, though — it's an object that converts method calls into XML elements. To use this library, all the files involved need to import it using the following statement:

```
require 'rss/2.0'
```

The files in question are extensions.rb and recipe.rb. First, you need to add RSS to the respond_to block in the index method, as follows:

```
def index
  @recipes = Recipe.find_for_index(params[:format])
  respond_to do |format|
    format.html # index.html.erb
    format.xml  { render :xml => @recipes }
    format.atom { render :layout => false }
    format.rss  { render :xml => @recipes.to_rss_feed("Soups OnLine",
      formatted_recipes_url(:rss), "New Recipes from Soups OnLine")}
  end
end
```

In this case, the RSS block doesn't go to a builder. (You could use a builder — RSS is just XML — but since you've been there and done that, this is showing you a different way.) In this case, render :xml tells Rails to return the text as MIME-type XML, and the to_rss_feed method returns a string that is just passed on to the client.

The arguments being passed represent the title of the RSS feed, its link, and a brief description. I'm using the same trick here of adding a method to Array and doing the specific work in Recipe. The Array method is similar to the Atom version — but without the helper method, there's some additional tag work that needs to be done:

```
def to_rss_feed(title, link, description="")
  rss = RSS::Rss.new("2.0")
  channel = RSS::Rss::Channel.new
  rss.channel = channel
  channel.title = title
  channel.link = link
  channel.description = description
  self.each do |item|
    channel.items << item.to_rss_item
  end
  rss.to_s
end
```

Using the RSS library, an RSS item is created. The outer element of an RSS document is called the *channel*, and title, link, and description are the three required attributes of a channel. The individual elements of the feed are called *items*, and I'll delegate that behavior to the model object. I'm assuming that the model object in question will have a to_rss_feed method. Each item is added to the channel. At the end, the RSS object is converted to a string, which is retuned.

The Recipe method is also similar to the Atom version, but some of the names have changed:

```
def to_rss_item
  returning RSS::Rss::Channel::Item.new do |item|
    item.title = title
    item.link = "http://localhost:3000/recipes/#{id}"
    item.description = content
    item.author = user.email
    item.pubDate = created_at
    item.guid = RSS::Rss::Channel::Item::Guid.new
  end
end
```

Have I mentioned the returning method yet? It's a Rails-defined utility method that takes one argument. All it does is pass the argument to the block, and return the same argument at the end of the block. It's a replacement for all the times where you have to have a single variable at the end of the method to ensure the return value. The normal way of writing that would look like this:

```
def to_rss_item ### the version without the returning method
  item = RSS::Rss::Channell::Item.new
  item.title = title
  ### and so on
  item
end
```

So `returning` is a little bit of syntactic sugar if that single variable in the last line has always struck you as just a little odd-looking.

In any case, the method rather straightforwardly goes through the relevant item attributes. According to the RSS specification, the only required element is either the title or the description, but the attribute set shown here is pretty common for, say, blogs.

And that is that, for RSS. If you hit `http://<host>/recipes/index.rss` in Camino, it will look something like Figure 9-2.

```
- <rss version="2.0">
  - <channel>
      <title>Soups OnLine</title>
      <link>http://localhost:3000/recipes.rss</link>
      <description>New Recipes from Soups OnLine</description>
    - <item>
        <title>Another Tag</title>
        <link>http://localhost/recipe/3</link>
      - <description>
          Another Tag Something taggy 2 cups carrots Do something
        </description>
        <author>noelrappin@gmail.com</author>
        <pubDate>Mon, 13 Aug 2007 22:14:38 -0500</pubDate>
      </item>
    - <item>
        <title>Tag Soup</title>
        <link>http://localhost/recipe/2</link>
      - <description>
          Tag Soup A soup of tags 2 cups parrots 1 cup stock heat and eat
        </description>
        <author>noelrappin@gmail.com</author>
        <pubDate>Mon, 13 Aug 2007 21:54:39 -0500</pubDate>
      </item>
    - <item>
        <title>Grandma's Chicken Soup</title>
        <link>http://localhost/recipe/1</link>
      - <description>
          Grandma's Chicken Soup Yummy! 2 cups stock 1/2 oz. carrot Things
        </description>
        <author>noelrappin@gmail.com</author>
        <pubDate>Sun, 05 Aug 2007 20:03:33 -0500</pubDate>
      </item>
  </channel>
</rss>
```
Figure 9-2

Producing JSON and YAML

After all that, producing standard JSON and YAML is straightforward. Rails has included the following helpers for the basic case, analogous to the `to_xml` case:

```ruby
def index
  @recipes = Recipe.find_for_index(params[:format])
  respond_to do |format|
    format.html # index.html.erb
    format.xml  { render :xml => @recipes }
    format.atom { render :layout => false }
    format.rss  { render :xml => @recipes.to_rss_feed("Soups OnLine",
        formatted_recipes_url(:rss), "New Recipes from Soups OnLine")}
    format.json { render :json => @recipes.to_json }
    format.yaml { render :text => @recipes.to_yaml, :layout => false}
  end
end
```

JSON has its own type in the `render` method, which sets the output MIME type to `text/javascript`, but YAML doesn't, so you can just set the type to `text`. Because the render type is `text`, you also need to explicitly suppress the layout from the output.

Here's what the JSON output looks like:

```
[{attributes_cache: {}, attributes: {cached_tag_list: "carrots, yummy, banana,
grandma", updated_at: "2007-08-15 13:39:52", title: "Another Tag", directions: "Do
something", id: "3", description: "Something taggy", cached_ingredient_string:
null, servings: "2", user_id: "2", created_at: "2007-08-13 22:14:38"}},
{attributes_cache: {}, attributes: {cached_tag_list: "yummy, grandma", updated_at:
"2007-08-15 13:39:42", title: "Tag Soup", directions: "heat and eat", id: "2",
description: "A soup of tags", cached_ingredient_string: null, servings: "10",
user_id: "2", created_at: "2007-08-13 21:54:39"}}, {attributes_cache: {},
attributes: {cached_tag_list: "grandma, chicken, fred", updated_at: "2007-09-04
23:04:45", title: "Grandma's Chicken Soup", directions: "Things", id: "1",
description: "Yummy!", cached_ingredient_string: null, servings: "3", user_id: "2",
created_at: "2007-08-05 20:03:33"}}]
```

The YAML output looks like the following (only part of the output is shown here, and some browsers may not display it properly):

```
---
- !ruby/object:Recipe
  attributes:
    cached_tag_list: carrots, yummy, banana, grandma
    updated_at: 2007-08-15 13:39:52
    title: Another Tag
    directions: Do something
```

```
        id: "3"
        description: Something taggy
        cached_ingredient_string:
        servings: "2"
        user_id: "2"
        created_at: 2007-08-13 22:14:38
attributes_cache: {}
```

Both of these include the cached tag lists and other features that you might not want in the output, but you can customize them as you see fit.

Consuming Web Services

Although ActiveResource is a convenient and useful way of consuming RESTful web services, you still need a way to use services that are not RESTful. You'll often need to hit something that is stored at a particular URL and that is delivered via XML. Hitting an RSS or Atom feed is a particular example of that kind of interaction.

Although there are modules that allow you to specifically parse RSS and Atom files as things in their own right, it's significantly easier to just treat them the same as any other XML file and use the Ruby Standard Library's REXML toolkit. REXML can also be used to generate XML documents, although I'm not going to be focusing on that functionality here.

Starting with an XML document is straightforward:

```
require 'rexml/document'
document = REXML::Document.new(source)
```

The source can be one of three things: another REXML::Document instance, a string that is itself a valid XML document to be parsed, or a file containing a valid XML document (of course, the file is duck typed, so any object that responds to the same messages as a file will work just fine). For our purposes, the input is most likely to be a URL, which you can access via the Ruby Net::HTTP library. The Net::HTTP library doesn't let you treat the remote URL as a file, but it does let you programmatically execute an HTTP request as follows and receive the result as a string:

```
Net::HTTP.get(URI.parse(url))
```

The arguments to the get method are either a single argument that is a Ruby URI object, which can be created from the string URL using the parse method as shown, or a three-argument — host, path, port — combination.

Once you have the document in hand, you can get at the root element by using the root attribute. Every element has an attribute that is actually called attributes, which is a hash of any value defined in the XML as an attribute. If you want the free text inside the element, use the attribute text.

Given this XML:

```
<content content_type="todo list">
  <header>Things To Do</header>
  <item>Finish Chapter</item>
  <item>Get Milk</item>
</content>
```

you can do the following:

```
document.root
document.root.attributes["content_type"]   #### "todo list"
```

Each element also has an attribute called `elements`. The `elements` object is basically a filter for extracting child elements from the parent element using XPath. For our purposes, there are two interesting methods of the `Elements` class. The `[]` operator and `each` both take an XPath expression. The bracket operator returns the first element that matches that expression, while `each` takes a block and iterates over each matching expression:

```
document.root.elements["header"].text #### Things To Do
document.root.elements.each "//item" {|x| print x.text}   #### Finish Chapter
                                                          #### Get Milk
```

The following snippet converts the Atom feed into Atom objects (it assumes that you've predefined an `AtomEntry` class somewhere). Some of the Atom elements are left off here for readability purposes, but I hope you'll get the general idea.

```
result = []
document.elements.each '//entry do |xml_entry|
  atom_entry = AtomEntry.new
  [:title, :link, :id, :updated, :summary, :content].each do |symbol|
    element = xml_entry.elements(symbol)
    if element
      atom_entry.send("#{symbol}=", element.text)
    end
  end
  result << atom_entry
end
```

For each entry in the XML, the code is searching for a list of expected Atom elements. If the element is there, a setter message is sent to the newly created Ruby object. After all the elements are checked, the Ruby object is added to the result list. It's a bit simplified, but the basic idea will work for Atom or RSS feeds, or any other XML object you have.

An even simpler Rails-based mechanism is the Rails ActiveSupport method `Hash#from_xml`, which takes an XML document as a string and returns a nested `Hash` based on the structure of the XML document. For example:

```
Hash.from_xml(document)
{"content" => {"header" => "Things To Do", "item" => ["Finish Chapter", ◄
"Get Milk"]}}
```

There are several nice features of this conversion. Rails does some basic data-type conversion for you. Also, the resulting `Hash` (or subhash) is suitable for passing to `ActiveRecord#new` or `#create` if the XML represents one of your ActiveRecord objects. A downside is that anything in an XML attribute is ignored. Also, the `Hash` structure may not always preserve the relative order of different elements at the same level, although it does seem to preserve the order of different instantiations of the same element.

Resources

There's still relatively little online documentation about ActiveResource. One of my primary guides was a presentation by Chad Fowler at one of Pragmatic Studio's Rails Edge conferences; however, that does not appear to be available online. Try `http://ryandaigle.com/articles/2006/06/30/whats-new-in-edge-rails-activeresource-is-here` or `http://wiki.rubyonrails.org/rails/pages/ActiveResource` for more information.

The complete RSS 2.0 specification can be found at `http://cyber.law.harvard.edu/rss/rss.html`. The current Atom specification (at the time of this writing) is at `www.ietf.org/rfc/rfc4287.txt`. You can learn more about XPath at `www.w3.org/TR/xpath`.

The RSS parser example in this chapter was initially based on the snippet presented at `http://snippets.dzone.com/posts/show/68` and `www.superwick.com/archives/2007/06/09/rss-feed-parsing-in-ruby-on-rails`. Also see `http://simple-rss.rubyforge.org` for another RSS parser object.

Summary

ActiveResource is the Rails 2.0 solution to acting as a web service and consuming other web services. If you have created a RESTful interface to your application, then you have a web service API more or less for free.

ActiveResource is the web-client equivalent of ActiveRecord, allowing you to find, update, create, and delete resources on a remote server, given the base URL and a REST interface. Although it's not as fully functional as ActiveRecord, ActiveResource remains a useful way to deal with remote objects that you can access via HTTP.

Rails provides `to_xml` methods for most classes, such as `ActiveRecord::Base`, to enable creation of web service data. Rails also provides XML builder templates for even more customization of the XML output from your controllers.

To produce feed data, you can use the Atom Feed helper to produce Atom feeds, or the Ruby RSS library to create RSS feeds. Rails also provides mechanisms to output JSON and YAML.

To parse XML data, Ruby Standard Library's REXML toolkit is recommended. It converts XML files to Ruby objects, and can be used to parse RSS and Atom feeds.

10

Internationalizing Your Application

A funny thing happens when you put your application on the World Wide Web. People start accessing it from all around the world. Even my tiny little blog (10printhello.blogspot.com), which gets a whopping 20 hits per day as I write this, has gotten visitors from 60 different countries or territories during the past month.

This is a wonderful thing, and I wouldn't change it. But it can make things complicated for you as the developer of a web application. For one thing, all of these visitors insist on living in different time zones. Most of them don't speak English, and respond to different cultural cues based on color or icon elements. They use other currencies, and are subject to different laws, the details of which might be critically important depending on what kind of site you are operating.

This chapter discusses various facets of internationalization and localization, starting with how to manage dates and times, and moving on to how to support running your site in multiple languages and locales.

Does Anybody Really Care About Time?

Working with date and time information is frankly among the most frustrating parts of nearly every software project I've done. At some point, it seems like I always need some date or time arithmetic in my program and I always confront the same problems.

❑ **Data problems**: How does the language represent a duration, as opposed to a calendar date? How is a range of dates represented?

❑ **Ambiguities and complications**: What does it really mean to add a month to a date? What happens to date calculations as you cross time zones? Or, even more fun, when you cross the daylight savings time boundary? At some point, what seems like a simple date calculation becomes a mind-bending exercise in juggling time zones.

❑ **Toolkit limitations**: Nearly every programming language library that deals with dates and times has some kind of quirk or frustration. (I'm looking at you, Java Calendar class . . . but Ruby is no exception here, so don't think I'm letting it off the hook easily.)

In this section: your guide to the jungle that is international time.

Dates and Times

The confusion starts immediately. Ruby has two separate implementations of date and time functionality, each of which has its own distinct strengths and weaknesses. In one corner is the `Time` class, which is a wrapper around the same Unix/C-language time libraries that every other scripting language has. As you'd expect from a library that has its origins in the early days of Unix, the programmer interface is somewhat on the cryptic side. Worse, it's based on the number of seconds since the beginning of the Unix epoch (0:00:00 UTC, January 1, 1970). And if you want a sense of how big a headache exact time can be, I invite you to peruse the Wikipedia article on Unix time (http://en.wikipedia.org/wiki/Unix_time). For one thing, although Unix time is based on UTC time in 1970, there was no official UTC definition in 1970. Plus, as stated in the Wikipedia article, "the UTC second was slightly longer than the SI second" — which should give you a sense of the level of detail here. Most systems limit the time value to a 32-bit integer, so Unix time is only definable for a range that is bounded somewhere in 1901 and somewhere in 2038. This limitation is passed on to Ruby time as follows:

```
>> x = Time.utc(2037)
=> Thu Jan 01 00:00:00 UTC 2037
>> x = Time.utc(2038)
=> Fri Jan 01 00:00:00 UTC 2038
>> x = Time.utc(2039)
ArgumentError: time out of range
        from (irb):10:in `utc'
        from (irb):10
```

The second implementation is the `DateTime` class, which is written in pure Ruby. The basic unit of `DateTime` is what's called the Julian day number (JDN), or days since January 1, 4713 BC. Today, as I write this, is JDN 2,454,357 (just thought you might want to know). The biggest plus side of the `DateTime` implementation is that it can represent any date you throw at it from the big bang through the heat death of the universe. It also has what I think is a cleaner API, and if you happen to be doing dates around the Middle Ages, it handles the switch from Julian to Gregorian calendars. However, `DateTime` has two significant flaws. The first is that it's not very good at dealing with time-zone or daylight-savings information, and the second is that it's significantly slower than `Time`.

The `Time` class is preferred by Rails for things like database timestamps, and has also gotten somewhat more attention from Rails programmers adding extensions to the core Ruby functionality. I recommend that you use `Time` for nearly everything within its span.

Rails defines conversion methods for both `Time` and `DateTime`, so you can always convert from one to the other with `to_time` or `to_date`. Both methods are defined for both classes, so even if you aren't sure whether you have a `Time` or `DateTime`, the conversion is still safe.

Timestamps and Time Zones

As you probably know, if you include columns in your database called `created_at` or `updated_at` (or `created_on` and `updated_on`), Rails will automatically track timestamps for each record as it is created or updated. At this point, you should be asking what time zone that timestamp is created in. By default, the timestamp is the local time zone of the server. Although this is a convenient default for a small-scale system, if you are planning on displaying any time information to clients in multiple time zones, then you almost certainly want to store all times in your database as UTC times.

You can do this by uncommenting the following line from your `environment.rb` file (any running servers will need to be restarted for the change to take effect):

```
config.active_record.default_timezone = :utc
```

If possible, you should set your server's native time to UTC as well, but that's not always feasible.

What's UTC?

UTC (Coordinated Universal Time) is the international standard zero point for time zones. All other time zones are defined in terms of their offset from UTC. The UTC standard is a historical evolution from the older user of Greenwich Mean Time (GMT) based on the Prime Meridian through Greenwich, England, and as such is 5 hours ahead of U.S. Eastern Standard Time (EST).

The differences between the GMT standard and the UTC standard have to do with how to coordinate the unchanging value of 1 second with the ever-slightly slowing down of the Earth's rotation. Unless you're doing something involving split-second coordination of atomic clocks, the main takeaway is that UTC is the default time zone to use when you are coordinating users from several time zones.

Transitioning times from the server local time to UTC is quite easy because the `Time` class defines instance methods `localtime` and `utc`, which do the translation based on the local time of the server. One thing to watch for when you use these methods is that even though they don't have the `!` character as a suffix, they do destructively change the object that receives the message.

Converting from UTC to some set of custom user time zones is dramatically more complex. For one thing, there are dozens upon dozens of different time zones. For example, you normally think of the mainland United States as having four time zones. However, when calculating local times from your server, you need to be aware of various local jurisdictions that handle daylight saving time (DST) differently. Counting all those, the standard tz database (also called the zoneinfo database) of time zones defines 20 different time zone regions for mainland United States alone.

Trust me, you do not want to keep up with the maintenance of 20 different time zone regions in the United States, let alone the 396 regions currently defined in the tz database. You want somebody to manage a lot of this for you. Luckily somebody already has. There are three different add-ons you need to install to gain full time zone mastery for your Rails application.

The first one is the `tzinfo` gem, which you can install via the following command:

```
gem install tzinfo
```

This gem defines a Ruby front-end to the tz database. The tz database is the gold standard for time zone information placed in a context that is usable by computer programs. The database defines a set of regions where local clocks have all remained identical since 1970 (the beginning of the Unix Epoch). You've likely seen the names of the time zone regions in the database if you've ever set a computer for the first time — each region is specified as part of a larger area and then a major city within that region. So the time region I'm in as I type this is America/Chicago. The goal is to try to keep the regions continuous — there are multiple places inside the U.S. Central Time Zone that do not support daylight savings time, but they are all separate regions in the tz database. The tz database provides a thorough record of local changes in timekeeping, including the exact dates of daylight savings changes and leap seconds.

As it happens, the Rails core defines a `TimeZone` class. However, the zones defined in that class are just simple offsets from UTC and do not include daylight savings information. Because of this, the implementation is too simplistic for a truly globalized application. What you really want is a `TimeZone` class that is backed by the tz database. You can get that by installing the `tzinfo_Timezone` plugin as follows:

```
script/plugin install -x
http://dev.rubyonrails.org/svn/rails/plugins/tzinfo_timezone/
```

As usual, the `-x` option makes the plugin a Subversion external.

The plugin defines the `TzinfoTimezone` class, which is a drop-in replacement for the core `TimeZone` class. For both classes, there is a class `[]` method to acquire a time zone, and `local_to_utc` and `utc_to_local` conversion methods. Typical usage goes like this:

```
>> t = Time.now
=> Sat Sep 15 00:06:07 -0500 2007
>> zone = TzinfoTimezone["Central Time (US & Canada)"]
=> #<TzinfoTimezone:0x2820274 @name="Central Time (US & Canada)", ↵
@utc_offset=-21600>
>> zone.utc_to_local(t)
=> Fri Sep 14 19:06:07 UTC 2007
>> t
=> Sat Sep 15 00:06:07 -0500 2007
>> zone.local_to_utc(t)
=> Sat Sep 15 05:06:07 UTC 2007
```

There are three things you should take away from this code snippet:

❑ The `TzinfoTimezone` class uses the same naming convention for time zones as the Rails core `Timezone` class does. This is not the same as the tz database names I described previously, and frankly the naming convention used by Rails is a little on the goofy side. There are two workarounds. You can use the `TzInfo::Timezone` class directly (as in `TZInfo::Timezone .get('America/Chicago')`), which is nice, but it has a slightly different API than the Rails `TimeZone` class (although `utc_to_local` and `local_to_utc` both work). Alternately, there is a version of the `tzinfo_Timezone` plugin that has been patched to allow tz naming conventions to be used (see the "References" section at the end of this chapter for a link to this plugin).

❏ Any time zone information associated with the `Time` object (generally the local time zone of the server) is ignored by both `utc_to_local` and `local_to_utc`. In `utc_to_local`, the incoming time object is assumed to be in UTC; and in `local_to_utc`, it is assumed to be in the time zone of the time zone object. You can see this in the example, where even though the time object was originally defined in the same local time as the time zone, the `utc_to_local` call still shifts the time the 5-hour offset between U.S. Central Time and UTC.

❏ If you are a heavy user of `local_to_utc`, you might someday be unlucky enough to try to transfer a time that actually has no UTC equivalent because it's part of the hour that is leapt over during the daylight savings transition. In this case, Rails will throw an exception. On the other side of the calendar, you may try to transfer a time that has two UTC equivalents because it's part of the hour that was leapt back and repeated. In this case, the `TimeZone` classes will default to using the daylight savings version of the time (the earlier one), although this behavior can be changed by passing `false` as the second argument to `local_to_utc`. (The `TzInfo` version of this method does not default to either side and will raise an exception if a second argument is not provided.)

Part of the problem with all this time zone stuff is that there's no real way to associate a time object with a time zone and make the association stick. In order to do that, you need a third plugin, called tztime. You can install this plugin as follows:

```
$ script/plugin install tztime
```

The tztime plugin does two very useful things. First, it creates a class called `TzTime`, which is a drop-in replacement for `Time`, but which associates each object with a time zone. Although that instance will behave like a `Time` instance for most purposes, it has a couple of extra features. The most notable of these is an extension of the `to_s` method that automatically converts the time to UTC if and only if the requested mode is `:db` or `:rfc822`.

You can set the time zone used by the `TzTime` class globally, which means that the specified zone is used for all `TzTime` instances. You can use the following `around_filter` method to set this up on any controller you want to automatically adjust to each client request:

```
around_filter :set_timezone

private

def set_timezone
  TzTime.zone = current_time_zone
  yield
  TzTime.reset!
end
```

The exact definition of `current_time_zone` is application-specific.

You can also use the tztime plugin to specify time zone–aware attributes of an ActiveRecord model. It's a class-level method called among the declaration-type things at the top of your class. For example:

```
tz_time_attributes :time_to_make_the_donuts
```

Any attribute specified in the arguments to this method is automatically converted to UTC before being saved in the database, and is converted back to a local `TzTime` when it's retrieved (based on the `TzTime.zone` value if specified).

Inputting Dates

Rails core comes with a default set of view helpers for entering date and time data. The helpers come in two different sets. If you are inside a `form_for` block, then you use `date_select` or `datetime_select`, with the first argument being the attribute of the model being targeted (as in other form helpers). In a form that does not have an ActiveRecord model attached, you use the methods `select_date` and `select_datetime` (this breaks with the naming convention that other non-model form helpers end with `_tag`). In either case, you wind up with a set of `select` pull-down fields that look something like those shown in Figure 10-1.

Figure 10-1

Although most of the options for the two types of date selectors are similar (both versions take a `:default`, which is either a `Time` object or a hash of values), there are a few differences between the two:

❑ The mechanism for only including some of the fields is different between the two types. In the `form_for` version, you pass `:discard_year`, `:discard_month`, or `:discard_day`. The appropriate `select` method and all `select` methods that are of shorter time durations are not included (they default to a value of 1). This option does not exist in the non-model version — instead, there are separate `select_year`, `select_month`, `select_day`, `select_hour`, and `select_minute` functions that you can call to build up your desired form.

❑ Both versions allow you to change the order of the fields by passing a list of symbols to an `:order` option (`:order => [:month, :day, :year]`). In the ActiveRecord version, any symbols left off the list are not displayed. In the other version, any symbols not included are appended at the end of the list in default order.

❑ The ActiveRecord version stores its values in a format suitable to be read into the ActiveRecord model when the form is submitted. The standalone version stores its values in a hash at `params[:date]`. The default uses `:date`, but this can be changed with the `:prefix` option.

Inputting Time Zones

When you need a user to tell you explicitly what time zone he or she is in, you can use the helper method `time_zone_select`, which is a non-form-builder helper. The first two arguments are the typical object and attribute symbols, which are used to give the resulting `select` tag the correct DOM ID and name. If you just use the default values, you get a nice little pull-down menu that contains the names of all the Rails-core defined time zones (see Figure 10-2).

(GMT−06:00) Central Time (US & Canada)

Figure 10-2

The value for each time zone is just the string name of the time zone — the GMT offset is only in the display.

There are a couple of useful options. If you want to have the most likely set of time zones appear first in the list, you can pass the list of preferred time zones as the third option of the list. The Rails time zone class provides a `TimeZone.us_zones` class method (this method is also duplicated by `TzTimeZone`), which returns a list of all the U.S. zones suitable for usage as a preferred list. Those of you dealing with users from the rest of the world will need to roll your own list, but it's not that hard.

If you'd rather use the tz database names directly, the options part of `time_zone_select` takes a `:model` argument that specifies the class to use to acquire the list of time zones. The class you choose needs to be able to respond to the method `all` with a list of time zone objects. To use the tz naming conventions, enter this:

```
<%= time_zone_select(:recipe, :zone, :model => TZInfo::Timezone) %>
```

You can get all the American time zones in the preferred list with this:

```
<%= time_zone_select(:recipe, :zone,N
  TZInfo::Timezone.all.select {|tz| tz.to_s.starts_with?("America")}, :model =>
TZInfo::Timezone) %>
```

The preferred list is made up of all the time zones whose string name starts with `"America"`, which is probably more time zones than you want to present to a U.S. user.

When you get this information on the server side, it's just a string, and you'll have to convert it to whichever version of the time zone classes you are using.

It would obviously be useful to convert the user's address directly into a time zone without requiring the user to navigate the swamp of a time zone pull-down list. On an international level, you can use the information in the `TZInfo` gem to convert a country to a time zone, given that country's two-character country code. For example:

```
>> TZInfo::Country.get('NZ').zone_names
=> ["Pacific/Auckland", "Pacific/Chatham"]

>> TZInfo::Country.get('RU').zone_names
=> ["Europe/Kaliningrad", "Europe/Moscow", "Europe/Volgograd", "Europe/Samara",
"Asia/Yekaterinburg", "Asia/Omsk", "Asia/Novosibirsk", "Asia/Krasnoyarsk",
"Asia/Irkutsk", "Asia/Yakutsk", "Asia/Vladivostok", "Asia/Sakhalin",
"Asia/Magadan", "Asia/Kamchatka", "Asia/Anadyr"]

>> TZInfo::Country.get('PL').zone_info
=> [#<TZInfo::CountryTimezone: Europe/Warsaw>]
```

The method `zone_names` returns a list of strings (the the tz identifier names attached to that country), and `zone_info` returns actual `TZInfo::CountryTimezone` objects. You can get a list of countries using `TZInfo::Country.all`, and a list of just the identifiers as follows:

```
TZInfo::Country.all.collect { |c| c.code }
```

In many cases, knowing the country will limit the time zone options to just one or two choices. Unfortunately, the United States and Canada are both exceptions to the general rule — each has well over a dozen tz choices. At the time of this writing, I'm having trouble finding a free and stable database on the Web that matches U.S. ZIP codes to time zones. If you are willing and able to part with a small amount of money, it looks like there are some demographic databases that break down the United States by ZIP codes and include time zone information — which could well be worth it for the right kind of website.

Text Input

The list of `select` methods is serviceable (if a bit dull), but they are potentially unwieldy for a user, particularly if setting a time requires the user to set five pull-down lists. One other option is to use a text box that enables users to enter the time directly in a text field, and then parsing it.

Ruby core has two separate methods for parsing strings into times and dates. If you are comfortable requiring the user to format the date in a particular format, then you can use the class method `DateTime.strptime(string, format)`, converting to a `Time` object if needed. The `string` is the string to be parsed, and the `format` is the expected format string using the same set of escapes that you would use in outputting the date or time via `strftime`. This method will throw an exception if the string cannot be matched to the format.

If you're willing to try a best guess in the absence of requiring a specific format, the method `DateTime` `.parse` or `Time.parse` will attempt to parse any date/time string you throw at it. The `DateTime` and `Time` versions are actually slightly different in terms of the arguments they take. The `Time` version is a bit more useful. The first argument is the string to be parsed. By default, any missing parts of the date potion of the string are filled in with the current date information. So if you try this:

```
Time.parse("11:17")
```

you'll get a `Time` object back with the current day, and the time 11:17.

Similarly, if you just pass in a date, the time values are filled in with the minimal values. If you want to specify a specific date other than the current one as the default, it goes in the second argument — you can't change the default time behavior away from the minimums. There's also an optional block that tells the method how to manage two-digit year numbers. The default is that any value of 70 or more is considered to be in the 1900s, and any value of 30 or less is considered to be in the 2000s (which matches the Unix Epoch date). The `DateTime` version just takes a second argument that is `true` if you want the default parsing of two-digit years, and `false` if you want them to raise an exception.

This method is very handy, although it's still going to be a problem if part of your user base uses the American day/month/year convention and the other part uses the European month/day/year one, although you may be able overcome that with proper localization. It's still a little limited, however, in that you can't specify things like "tomorrow at 3:00." To specify things like that, you need a RubyGem called Chronic.

Enter the following command to install the Chronic gem:

```
gem install chronic
```

Once that's done, you have an API consisting largely of the following method (based on a current date of September 15, which is when I'm writing this):

```
>> require 'chronic'
=> []
>> Chronic.parse("thursday at 3:00")
=> Thu Sep 20 15:00:00 -0500 2007
```

The method, Chronic.parse, takes the string to be parsed as its one argument, and a handful of options. Chronic attempts to convert a wide range of date and time strings to Ruby Time objects. In doing so, it makes a few assumptions. The options allow you to tweak these assumptions.

For instance, in the previous example, Chronic interpreted 3:00 to mean 3:00 P.M., not 3:00 A.M. That behavior is governed by an option called :ambiguous_time_range, which defaults to 6. Ambiguous times are assumed, therefore, to be in the 12-hour range starting at whatever the argument is, A.M. — which in this case is the range 6 A.M.–6 P.M. If you changed the range to include 3 A.M., you'd get a different response, as shown here:

```
>> Chronic.parse("thursday at 3:00", :ambiguous_time_range => 2)
=> Thu Sep 20 03:00:00 -0500 2007
```

The time is now 3:00 A.M.

Chronic has also assumed that I mean the next Thursday, as opposed to the last Thursday. You can change this as follows:

```
>> Chronic.parse("thursday", :context => :past)
=> Thu Sep 13 12:00:00 -0500 2007
```

The default behavior shown in the first code snippet is :context => :future. For some reason, Chronic appears to use the past context only if the time is not specified, so you also get this:

```
>> Chronic.parse("thursday 3:00", :context => :past)
=> Thu Sep 20 15:00:00 -0500 2007
```

I'm not sure whether that's a bug or a principled choice.

In the previous example, when I passed in just "Thursday", Chronic converted that to 12 noon on Thursday. Chronic guesses the specific time if there is a range of times that match the input string. But you can get it to give you the entire range, like this:

```
>> Chronic.parse("thursday", :guess => false)
=> Thu Sep 20 00:00:00 -0500 2007..Fri Sep 21 00:00:00 -0500 2007
```

You can also use the :now option to specify a base date other than the current one, as follows:

```
>> Chronic.parse("thursday", :now => 2.months.ago)
=> Thu Jul 19 12:00:00 -0500 2007
>> Chronic.parse("thursday 3:00", :now => 2.months.ago)
=> Thu Jul 19 15:00:00 -0500 2007
```

JavaScript Calendars

Chronic manages a wide range of different text formats for dates and times. Sometimes, though, the user wants to see an actual graphical calendar for their data entering pleasure. There are several Rails plugins and snippets that provide a wrapper around a JavaScript calendar. I'll be discussing one of them here, ActiveCalendar, written by Christopher Peterson. ActiveCalendar is a wrapper of Dynarch.com's DHTML JavaScript calendar. I chose this one because it's pretty simple to install and run. It does have a slight limitation — it's a complete replacement for the ActiveRecord date helpers, date_select and datetime_select. If you install ActiveCalendar, then the row of pull-down lists will no longer display at all. However, the non-ActiveRecord version of the date helpers is not affected, so you can still build up a date pull-down list where needed.

Install the plugin at:

```
./script/plugin install
http://activecalendar.googlecode.com/svn/trunk/activecalendar
```

As usual, include the -x under Subversion. This installs a fair number of JavaScript files.

At this point, the only thing standing between you and dynamic calendar goodness is the following four lines of code:

```
<%= stylesheet_link_tag "/javascripts/jscalendar-1.0/calendar-win2k-cold-1.css" %>
<%= javascript_include_tag "jscalendar-1.0/calendar.js" %>
<%= javascript_include_tag "jscalendar-1.0/lang/calendar-en.js" %>
<%= javascript_include_tag "jscalendar-1.0/calendar-setup.js" %>
```

You need to place this code in the header of the appropriate layout file.

A server restart later, and all your ActiveRecord forms will look like the one shown in Figure 10-3. (There's a button hidden by the calendar that is used to display the calendar itself.)

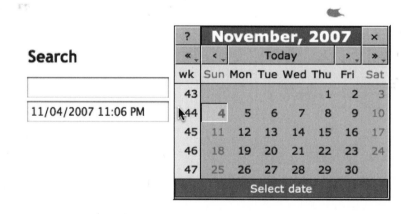

Figure 10-3

If you don't like the layout, feel free to go into the CSS file and tweak away — the file is in the `vendor/plugins/activecalendar/public/javascripts/jscalendar-1.0` directory.

There is one change here on the server side: the value of the form is now the string in the text field, which is also user-editable (and there's nothing stopping you from giving the user free entry, and using Chronic to parse the dates on the server side — that could give you the best of both worlds). On the client side, additional key/value pairs passed to the `date_select` or `datetime_select` function are passed directly to the JavaScript calendar, giving you the full flexibility of that code as well.

Date Arithmetic and Outputting Dates

On its own, Ruby does not have a dedicated class for date and time durations (although Rails adds some support); instead it uses integers to represent the difference between two `Time` or `DateTime` objects. For `Time` objects, the integer indicates the number of seconds between two times. For `DateTime`, the integer indicates the number of days between two dates.

Duration Helpers

Rails provides two helper methods that you can use in view code to convert time differences to words. The method `distance_of_time_in_words` takes two `Time` or `DateTime` objects as arguments, and returns a reasonable English phrase describing the amount of time between them, such as "about 5 days" or "over a year." If the optional third argument is `true`, then seconds are included in the sentence, which is generally only useful if the distance is under 1 minute.

The method `time_ago_in_words` is similar, but it takes only one argument and compares it to the current time. This is the method you want to use for things like archived lists of blog posts or comments — when you want each entry to have a description of when it was posted.

Rails has also added a number of methods to core Ruby classes to convert integers into useful times. Witness the following console session:

```
>> Time.now
=> Sun Sep 16 23:16:28 -0500 2007
>> 3.seconds
=> 3 seconds
>> 3.seconds.class
=> Fixnum
>> 3.days
=> 3 days
>> 3.days.to_i
=> 259200
>> 3.days.from_now
=> Wed Sep 19 23:16:59 -0500 2007
>> 3.days.ago
=> Thu Sep 13 23:17:04 -0500 2007
```

All numeric types respond to the methods `seconds`, `minutes`, `hours`, `days`, `weeks`, `fortnights`, `months`, and `years` (as well as the singular versions of all of those words), converting the number to a new number — the amount of seconds in the time period. So, 3 days is 259200 seconds. A month is considered to be 30 days, and a year is 365.25 days.

All numeric types respond to the methods `from_now` and `ago`, which adjust the current date and time by the amount given — `from_now` moves into the future, and `ago` moves into the past. This is done using a Rails extension time-duration object. So even though the preceding raw months resolve to 30 days, when you use `from_now` or `ago`, month arithmetic behaves as expected. For example:

```
>> 1.month.from_now
=> Tue Oct 16 23:19:41 -0500 2007
>> 2.months.from_now
=> Fri Nov 16 23:19:47 -0600 2007
>> 30.days.from_now
=> Tue Oct 16 23:22:32 -0500 2007
>> 60.days.from_now
=> Thu Nov 15 23:22:38 -0600 2007
```

Although both `from_now` and `ago` take arguments to specify a different base time other than the current moment, they both have aliases that are designed to read better when combined with an argument. For example:

```
>> base = 7.months.ago
=> Fri Feb 16 23:29:36 -0600 2007
>> 1.month.since(base)
=> Fri Mar 16 23:29:36 -0500 2007
>> 1.month.until(base)
=> Tue Jan 16 23:29:36 -0600 2007
```

These methods represent some of the best of Ruby's DSL-like behavior in allowing extremely clear and readable code. Use them whenever you can.

String Formats

You should never use the `strftime` method in Rails to convert a time to a string. Instead, use the Rails extension method for both `Time` and `DateTime` `to_s(:format)`, where *format* is one of a series of formats predefined by Rails or that you add manually. Here are the predefined formats:

```
>> base.to_s(:db)
=> "2007-02-16 23:29:36"

>> base.to_s(:long)
=> "February 16, 2007 23:29"

>> base.to_s(:long_ordinal)
=> "February 16th, 2007 23:29"

>> base.to_s(:rfc822)
=> "Fri, 16 Feb 2007 23:29:36 -0600"

>> base.to_s(:short)
=> "16 Feb 23:29"

>> base.to_s(:time)
=> "23:29"
```

The :db format uses the SQL standard, although some databases may differ. You can specify your own custom formats by adding to the hash in your environment.rb file, outside the initializer block, like so:

```
Time::DATE_FORMATS[:usa_short] = "%b %d %H:%M"
```

Then you can use it like any other format:

```
>> base.to_s(:usa_short)
=> "Feb 16 23:29"
```

There's a super-special format method for a range of dates:

```
>> (1.week.ago..1.week.from_now).to_s(:db)
=> "BETWEEN '2007-09-09 23:39:13' AND '2007-09-23 23:39:139'"
```

I personally witnessed an entire room full of Ruby developers, myself included, "ooh and ahh" audibly when this feature was demonstrated.

Internationalization with Globalize

Time zones are not the only kind of content that needs to change from country to country. There are also changes in the default style used to display numbers and dates, differences between imperial and metric units, and currency changes — all of which are dwarfed by the challenge of dealing with multiple languages. The generic terms for all this are *internationalization* and *localization*. Strictly speaking, internationalization is the creation of a structure by which content can be created in multiple countries, and localization is the act of actually populating the structure with content for individual locales. In practice, the terms are used more-or-less interchangeably or in pairs to mean "we need this site to work in places where people talk differently." You'll also often see the terms *i18n* and *l10n* with the numbers cleverly indicating the number of missing letters in each word.

Internationalization brings with it many challenges. You need some mechanism to either assign or allow users to choose the location they are in. Even if you aren't translating language, date and number display formats and units differ throughout the English-speaking world, as do the spellings and meanings of multiple words. If you are translating into multiple languages, you've just multiplied the amount of content you need to create. And your development team and primary content creators are unlikely to be fluent in all languages, making double-checking that content even more difficult. The varying lengths of words in different languages can play havoc with a tightly arraigned website, even before you start worrying about the languages that go right-to-left or up-and-down. After all that, you still need to worry about images, color, and cultural cues.

I can't solve all those problems here, but I can show you how to use Globalize, a Rails plugin that manages locale-based text displays. It can help you manage translated text, as well as the format of numbers, dates and currency.

Using The Globalize Plugin

Globalize is a Rails plugin. Install it via the following command:

```
script/plugin install http://svn.globalize-rails.org/svn/globalize/trunk
```

The version in `trunk` is the Edge Rails version of Globalize. If Rails 2.0 has been released by the time you read this, then there is likely a `/svn/globalize/branches/for-2.0` directory; if you are using Rails 1.1 or 1.2, then there is a similarly named branch for those Rails versions. Also, unlike many plugins, Globalize distributes a `.tar.gz` version for people who might be behind a firewall or have other issues hitting the Subversion server.

The Globalize plugin installs a number of different files. In order to fully enable Globalize, you need to run a `setup` command. Before you do this, you should ensure that your database is using UTF-8 as its character set. If you have been using MySQL and following along in this book, that should have happened by default — it should be the default encoding for MySQL tables as created by the Rails commands used here. You can also add an `encoding: utf8` key/value pair to the entries in your `database.yml` file, which will work for other databases as well.

The Globalize `setup` command is as follows:

```
rake globalize:setup
```

There's no actual output to this command, but behind the scenes, Globalize is adding three tables to your development database. Unfortunately, it just adds the tables directly, rather than generating a migration, so you'll need to run this command again whenever you reset your database (or, alternately, create your own migration that runs this command).

Ruby, Unicode, and You

Unicode is the international standard for encoding strings in multiple languages — an ambitious attempt to allow all characters in all human languages to be represented in 32 bytes (as opposed to the 8 bytes traditionally used in the English-only character set). Fully representing each Unicode character in its full 32 bits would require four times the storage for strings that use just the regular set of English characters, so there are various encodings of Unicode that are more compressed if only English or Western European characters are used. The most common of these is UTF-8, which uses the same amount of space as a regular string for the 128 characters in the basic ASCII set, and only requires more space for characters outside that set.

Although you can set up the database and web browser to used UTF-8 encoding, Ruby does not support Unicode or UTF strings internally (this is expected to change in Ruby 1.9 and 2.0). Perhaps surprisingly, this is only a problem when you are actually performing character-based manipulation on a string that contains multibyte characters. As long as you are just dealing with ASCII characters, or are just passing text between the database and the browser, you won't notice a problem.

If you are in the problem zone, Rails 1.2 and higher has a workaround, in the form of a `chars` string method, which returns a proxy object that contains UTF-8–aware versions of all the problem methods. Otherwise, the proxy object behaves exactly like a normal string.

Globalize creates three database tables in your development database. The first is `globalize_languages`, which contains language data including the English name, native name, various ISO and RFC codes, the direction the language is written in, and any odd pluralization rules. The `globalize_countries` database contains country information including the English name, two-character code, and numerical, date, and currency formatting. Both of these tables are effectively read-only for the purposes of your application. The `globalize_translations` table contains the translated data for all your multilingual content. Each entry contains the translated text, the type information needed to associate it with the base language text, and the language of translation. This table is pre-populated with date and month names in several languages. All the data that Globalize uses, which you might use to populate your production or test databases, is stored in CSV files in `vendor/plugins/globalize/data`. Fixtures suitable for using in your own unit tests are stored in `vendor/plugins/globalize/test/fixtures`.

To complete your Globalize setup, head over to the `environment.rb` file and place the following two lines at the end of the file:

```
include Globalize
Locale.set_base_language('en-US') # or whatever your base locale is
```

The first line includes the Globalize plugin everywhere in your Rails application. The second line sets up the base locale for the application. If you've done internationalization in other programming languages, you're probably familiar with the concept of a locale as the combination of a language and a country — which in this case is English as spoken and written in the United States.

Setting the base language in Globalize has two related effects. It is the default locale used by Globalize to determine formatting for numbers, dates, and currency if another locale is not specified. The language portion of the base locale setting tells Globalize which text to look up in the actual model table. The text for all other languages will be stored in the `globalize_translations` table.

You can change the locale for a particular page interaction by calling `Locale.set`. For example:

```
Locale.set("fr-FR")
```

Local Formatting

Globalize adds the method `localize` (also aliased to `loc`) to the classes `Integer`, `Float`, `Date`, and `Time`. You would use these methods instead of `to_s`, to ensure that the correct formatting is used for the current place. For numbers, this is primarily a case of using the decimal points and commas properly. For example:

```
>> 123456789.localize
=> "123,456,789"
>> 1.23.localize
=> "1.23"

>> Locale.set("de-DE")
=> #<Globalize::Locale:0x3703fe8 @currency_decimal_sep=",", @currency_format=
"%nâ,¬", @code="de-DE", @decimal_sep=",", @date_format=nil, @thousands_sep=".",
@language=German, @number_grouping_scheme=:western, @currency_code="EUR",
@country=#<Globalize::Country id: 55, code: "DE", english_name: "Germany",
```

(continued)

(continued)

```
date_format: nil, currency_format: "%nâ,¬", currency_code: "EUR", thousands_sep:
".", decimal_sep: ",", currency_decimal_sep: ",",
number_grouping_scheme: "western">>
>> 123456789.localize
=> "123.456.789"
>> 1.23.localize
=> "1,23"
```

The `localize` method works a little differently for times and dates. It does not force you to a preferred ordering of date elements. Instead it acts just like the ordinary `strftime` method except that day names, month names, and a.m./p.m. are translated into the language of the current locale. Here's an example (I'd show a more exotic example, but the terminal doesn't like Unicode characters by default):

```
>> Time.now.localize("%A %B %d %Y")
=> "Tuesday September 18 2007"

>> Locale.set("de-DE")
=> #<Globalize::Locale:0x3703fe8 @currency_decimal_sep=",", @currency_format=
"%nâ,¬", @code="de-DE", @decimal_sep=",", @date_format=nil, @thousands_sep=".",
@language=German, @number_grouping_scheme=:western, @currency_code="EUR",
@country=#<Globalize::Country id: 55, code: "DE", english_name: "Germany",
date_format: nil, currency_format: "%nâ,¬", currency_code: "EUR",
thousands_sep: ".", decimal_sep: ",", currency_decimal_sep: ",",
number_grouping_scheme: "western">>
>> Time.now.localize("%A %B %d %Y")
=> "Dienstag September 18 2007"
```

As I write this, about 90 separate languages have their date and time words preset in the Globalize database. If the language you are trying to translate to is not there, Globalize will default to the base locale.

Notice, though, that Globalize happily printed `September 18` as the date, when it's extremely likely that the local preferred form is `18 September`. Also, the `localize` method is not directly compatible with the handy `to_s(:format)` method discussed earlier in this section. (Although that seems a simple enough patch that it might have been taken care of by the time you read this.)

Translations

Globalize has a number of different ways to manage translated text. The most direct is simply to tell Globalize that you have a translation, like this:

```
>> spanish = Language.pick("es-MX")
=> Spanish
>> Locale.set_translation("recipe", spanish, "receta")
=> [nil, "receta"]
>> Locale.set_translation("soup", spanish, "sopa", "sopas")
=> [nil, "sopa", "sopas"]
>> Locale.set_translation("Soups OnLine", spanish, "Sopas en Linea")
=> [nil, "Sopas en Linea"]
>>
```

```
>> Locale.set_translation("%d bunches of carrots", spanish, "%d manojo de
zanahoria", "%d manojos de zanahorias")
=> [nil, "%d manojo de zanahoria", "%d manojos de zanahorias"]>>
Locale.set_translation("Eat Up, It's Good For You", spanish, "El Es Bueno Para
Usted")
=> [nil, "El Es Bueno Para Usted"]
```

This console session starts by setting a variable to the Globalize language object for Spanish. Then it uses the `set_translation` method to define a few translations. The method assumes that the first argument is some text in the base language, and the second argument is the language being translated to.

The first example is a straightforward translation of the English word "recipe" to its Spanish equivalent. In the next line, "soup" is being translated to both its singular Spanish equivalent "sopa" and its plural Spanish equivalent "sopas". (Languages that have more complex pluralization rules generally allow you to place all the variants in increasing order of the size of the set they represent.) The third example shows that you can translate an entire phrase, and the last example shows that the phrase can include a wildcard to be filled in later — the wildcard can either be %d for a number or %s for a string.

If the second argument to `set_translation` is not a language, then the assumption is that the current locale is not the base language and the word or phrase is being translated to the main language. Because translation is language-based and not locale-based, it seems that Globalize cannot be used to mediate between dialects of the same language such as American and British English unless you add the various regional versions to the languages database as separate languages. (A separate plugin called Globalite has this capability out of the box.)

Each one of these items sets up multiple rows in the `globalize_translations` database, with each row containing the base-language key, the language being translated to, the translated text, and the pluralization number. (The `nil` at the front of all the return values indicates that Spanish does not use a separate form for the case of zero elements.) The relevant portion of the database table is shown in Figure 10-4.

tr_key	table_name	language_id	pluralization_index	text	*id
recipe	NULL	5889	0	NULL	7078
recipe	NULL	5889	1	receta	7079
soup	NULL	5889	0	NULL	7080
soup	NULL	5889	1	sopa	7081
soup	NULL	5889	2	sopas	7082
Soups OnLine	NULL	5889	0	NULL	7083
Soups OnLine	NULL	5889	1	Sopas en Linea	7084
%d bunches of carrots	NULL	5889	0	NULL	7085
%d bunches of carrots	NULL	5889	1	%d manojo de zanahoria	7086
%d bunches of carrots	NULL	5889	2	%d manojos de zanahorias	7087

Figure 10-4

Once this information has been placed in the database, you can start using it via an entirely different console session — or, of course, in the live application. This makes it easy for to seed your translation database via a batch script or separate content management system.

To use translated text, call the method t on the base text as follows:

```
>> Locale.set("es-MX")
=> #<Globalize::Locale:0x377dcbc @currency_decimal_sep=".", @currency_format=nil,
@code="es-MX", @decimal_sep=".", @date_format=nil, @thousands_sep=",",
@language=Spanish, @number_grouping_scheme=:western, @currency_code="MXN",
@country=#<Globalize::Country id: 150, code: "MX", english_name: "Mexico",
date_format: nil, currency_format: nil, currency_code: "MXN", thousands_sep: ",",
decimal_sep: ".", currency_decimal_sep: ".", number_grouping_scheme: "western">>
>> "soup".t
=> "sopa"
>> "soup".t(nil, 2)
=> "sopas"
>> "%d bunches of carrots".t(nil, 2)
=> "2 manojos de zanahorias"
```

If there is no translated text available, the original text is returned instead. You can override that behavior by passing a desired default to the first argument of the t method. The second argument is used as the substitute for the %d or %s in the phrase. If the argument is a number, it is also used to resolve the plural state of the entire phrase. Therefore, using 2 in the last example triggered the plural form of the phrase "bunches of carrots."

If you find the t method too wordy, Globalize also overrides the / operator as an alias for t(nil, arg). Again, the argument can either merely indicate plural status or be a wild card in the string being translated. For example:

```
>> "soup" / 2
=> "sopas"
>> "soup" / 1
=> "sopa"
>> "%d bunches of carrots" / 1
=> "1 manojo de zanahoria"
>> "%d bunches of carrots" / 2
=> "2 manojos de zanahorias"
```

For my part, although this syntax is perhaps a bit shorter, it's right at the edge of the amount of cryptic functionality I'm willing to accept in operator overloading.

Displaying Your Translation

Displaying the translated text is a matter of putting translation operators in your views and setting the locale on each user hit.

As an example, you're going to translate the header of the Soups OnLine site, because you've already placed the two components in the database. In the app/views/layouts/recipes.html.erb layout file, change the display of that text to this:

```
<div id="header">
  <h1><a href="#"><%= "Soups OnLine".t %></a></h1>
  <p><a href="#"><%= "Eat Up, It's Good For You".t %></a></p>
</div>
```

The only difference is that the strings are now passed through a Globalize translation.

Then, in the controller, you need to set the locale. Right now, you're doing the simplest thing possible: checking for a `locale` parameter in the URL that might be `es` for Spanish. In a page or so, I'll show you how to manage the locale in a more complex way. But the basic idea of setting the locale via a `before` filter is generally going to be part of the program. Put the following `before` filter in each controller, and the `set_locale` method in `application.rb`:

```
before_filter :set_locale

def set_locale
  if params[:locale] == 'es'
    Locale.set ('es-MX')
  else
    base = if Locale.base_language
           then Locale.base_language.code
           else 'en-US'
           end
    Locale.set base
    params.merge( 'locale' => base )
  end
end
```

With that code in place, pointing the browser at the URL `http://localhost:3000/recipes?locale=es` displays the header shown in Figure 10-5.

Figure 10-5

I'm hoping I got the translation correct — my Spanish skills are pretty close to nonexistent. I do know that I had to cut off part of the tag line "Eat Up, It's Good For You" (the text shown translates as "It's Good For You"), because the longer Spanish phrases did not fit together in the browser.

ActiveRecord Translations

Whether you are using the `t` method or the `/` operator, peppering your Globalized Rails application with a gazillion of them is bound to get tedious. Globalize offers a couple of ways to specify the need to translate content at a higher level of abstraction.

For content that is being accessed via ActiveRecord, you can specify the text attributes that you want to have covered by the translations. This is done via a class-level declaration called `translates`:

```
class Recipe < ActiveRecord::Base
```

```
translates :title, :description, :directions
```

This declaration informs Globalize that the listed attributes will have translated versions in the `global_translations` table. When these values are accessed, Globalize will automatically look for the version that matches the current locale. If that version doesn't exist, Globalize will default back to the base version in the original ActiveRecord table. This translation happens automatically on attribute retrieval, and does not require a call to the `t` method to display the localized content.

Saving the translated data is relatively straightforward. All you need to do is change the locale, and then reset the translated attributes in the new language. Saving the ActiveRecord back to the database in the new Locale will automatically create the `global_translations` entry.

Here's an example from the console:

```
>> Locale.set('es-MX')
=> ### Globalize stuff here
>> recipe = Recipe.find(1)
=> ###
>> recipe.title
=> "Grandma's Chicken Soup"

>> recipe.title = ("Sopa de Pollo de me Abuela")
=> "Sopa de Pollo de me Abuela"

>> recipe.title
=> "Sopa de Pollo de me Abuela"
>> recipe.save
=> true

>> Locale.set('en-US')
=> ####
>> recipe = Recipe.find(1)
=> ###
>> recipe.title
=> "Grandma's Chicken Soup"

>> Locale.set('es-MX')
=> ###
>> recipe.title
=> "Sopa de Pollo de mi Abuela"
```

If you change the locale after loading the object, you need to call `reload` on the object in the new locale. When the record is saved in the Spanish locale, Globalize creates the record in the `globalize_translations` table, associating the new data with the original table using something very much like the polymorphic association feature you saw in Chapter 7. In addition, Globalize also creates records for the translatable fields you did not change (`description` and `directions`) and populates them with the existing English versions of the data because no new information was added for those fields.

This is a handy mechanism. However, the way in which it interacts with ActiveRecord precludes certain kinds of ActiveRecord actions — in particular, it precludes using the `:include` and `:select` options to `ActiveRecord#find`, and it interacts poorly with `has_many :through`. It also requires a second data table to access all the localizations.

There is another way. Include the following line in your ActiveRecord model:

```
class Recipe < ActiveRecord::Base
  self.keep_translations_in_model = true
  translates :title, :description, :directions
```

The localized data will now be stored in columns in the model table. You need to add the columns via migration, with the naming convention `<attribute>_<lang>`. To support Spanish in the Soups Online application, the recipe table would have to have `title_es`, `description_es`, and `directions_es` columns. This can get a bit unwieldy if you are supporting a lot of attributes or a lot of languages, and you need to know in advance what languages you are supporting. There's a Rails generator called `script/generate globalize internal` that will create migrations to generate the new columns for all languages passed as arguments, so `script/generate globalize internal es` would work for the previous examples.

Which method you choose depends on the particulars of your application. For an application in which you are targeting a small number of defined languages, I think the internal method is clearly superior. It will probably have better performance, and it plays better with the rest of Rails. However, if you need to support many languages that you might not be able to specify in advance — especially if that's combined with multiple columns — most databases aren't really optimized to deal with tables that have hundreds of columns. In that case, the flexibility of the external method would probably be superior.

Tracking Routes

As shown in the previous examples, you need to be able to set the locale based on the specifics of the user request. The place to actually set the locale for the connection is usually in a `before` filter on the controller. However, there are a few different mechanisms for managing the locale.

One option that you see on a lot of international corporate sites requires the user to explicitly select a region before entering the main site. That information can then be stored in the session or in the database as part of the user table, depending on which makes sense for your user model. The `before` filter can then take the information from the session or database to set the locale. In this case, it's generally considered good UI practice to both display the current locale somewhere in the page and allow the user to change locations.

Another option is to make the locale part of the URL. In the previous example, the locale was specified as part of the query string. Although that works, it's often considered ugly, and even worse, all the `link_to` and `link_to_remote` methods in the application need to know to pass the locale around as a parameter. One possible plus-side of this mechanism is that it allows URLs in the base domain to be displayed without locale information.

Some applications (such as Wikipedia) make the locale part of the actual domain name (as in `en.wikipedia.com`). That's doable, but within Rails it's somewhat easier to use the route mechanism and allow Rails to parse the locale out of the URL for you.

There are a few different ways to manage locales in routes. The one that seems to work best in a RESTful routing system is to do something like this:

```
map.resouces :recipes, :path_prefix => ":locale"
```

This will correctly map URLs of the form:

```
http://hostname/en/recipes/1
http://hostname/es/recipes/1
```

There is only one change that needs to be made to your application in order to support this change. Because the locale now appears before the object ID in the URL, the following single-argument, named route call:

```
recipe_url(@recipe)
```

will now slot the recipe ID into the locale part of the URL, which is not what you want. For this to work, you need to either explicitly specify the locale or explicitly specify that the recipe is being used as the ID parameter of the URL, like this:

```
recipe_url(locale, @recipe)
recipe_url(:id => @recipe)
```

The locale will automatically get picked up from the previous request parameter unless it's otherwise specified during the processing of the request.

References

There is a nice post on time zones in Rails at `http://cho.hapgoods.com/wordpress/?p=140`. The tztime plugin is introduced by its creator, Rails core developer Jamis Buck, at `http://weblog.jamisbuck.org/2007/2/2/introducing-tztime`. ActiveCalendar's home page is at `http://developer.assaydepot.com/?p=5`.

As this book was in review, a new time zone plugin called Timezone_fu was released. It automates conversions between UTC and the user's localtime, and can be found at `http://hackd.wordpress.com/2007/11/23/sexy-time-zones-in-ruby-on-rails-with-timezone_fu/`

The Globalize home page at `www.globalize-rails.org/globalize` has a lot of documentation. I also used Sven Fuchs Globalize tutorial at `www.artweb-design.de/2006/11/10/get-on-rails-with-globalize-comprehensive-writeup`, which is a very detailed explanation of how to use Globalize.

The Globalite plugin referenced in the chapter is available online at `http://code.google.com/p/globalite`. The best source I know of for Unicode and Rails is `http://wiki.rubyonrails.com/rails/pages/HowToUseUnicodeStrings`.

Summary

If your application is on the World Wide Web, you may need to acknowledge the "world wide" part. Time and time zones are some of the first obstacles you'll face. Ruby has both `Time` and a `DateTime` classes, each with different strengths and weaknesses. In addition, there are a few Rails plugins that add more complex support for time zones.

Inputting time zones can be managed via the `time_zone_select` helper. The Ruby gem called Chronic, and the Rails plugin ActiveCalendar can both provide a richer experience for a user who is entering date information.

Globalize is the most feature-rich Rails plugin to manage internationalization of an application. It provides mechanisms to localize date and time references, and to translate content into different languages and display that content in the correct language given the user's locale. Translation can also be integrated directly into ActiveRecord, and local information can be embedded into Rails routing.

11

The Graphic Arts

The biggest innovation in the original NCSA Mosaic web browser — the one that that changed the Web from just a way to hyperlink physics papers into a multimedia content platform — was the img tag, supporting inline image display. Since then, the capability to manipulate graphics has remained an important part of working on the Web.

This chapter examines several ways to integrate dynamic graphics into your web system. You'll see how to acquire images from the user via file upload. You'll explore the various libraries available for manipulating images from within Ruby, and take a look at some packages for creating charts from those images.

Getting Started

I'm going to focus on three different Ruby gems that manage basic graphics transformations — resizing, basic effects, thumbnails, and that kind of thing. The three Ruby gems are wrappers to three different native C libraries, but like a logic puzzle gone slightly awry, there isn't an exact one-to-one correspondence between the gems and the libraries. Two of the gems — RMagick and MiniMagick — can wrap around either ImageMagick or GraphicsMagick, which are two forked versions of the same basic functionality. The third gem, ImageScience, requires a separate graphics library called FreeImage.

> As this book was in production, RMagick 2 was released. RMagick 2 does not support GraphicsMagick. Other than that, there are few substantial API differences in the new release. See http://rmagick.rubyforge.org/rmagick2.html for more information.

Installing these gems is somewhat more complex than the typical Ruby gem because the external graphics libraries are so large, have a number of external dependencies, and tend to expect their users to be comfortable with compiling from source (to be fair, it's probably advantageous for performance reasons to compile from source). Unfortunately, this isn't a case where you can just type **gem install** and be done with it. Don't worry, it's not that hard, and in most cases, there's a helpful installer of one form or another to get you home.

Graphics Packages

RMagick is the oldest and still most commonly used graphics package for Ruby. It will act as a wrapper around either the ImageMagick library or the GraphicsMagick library, whichever one it finds. ImageMagick and GraphicsMagick are command-line tools for image manipulation, both offering a wide variety of features including image transformation, animation support, special effects, and adding various kinds of decorations. GraphicsMagick is a fork from ImageMagick version 5.5.2, claiming to be more concerned with API stability and performance than the addition of new features. RMagick will wrap either one, and for the examples in this chapter it shouldn't matter what the underlying library is. RMagick attempts to give Ruby access to all the functionality of the ImageMagick libraries, and calls the libraries directly from within your Ruby program.

In contrast, MiniMagick offers a stripped-down library that invokes an external shell process that calls the underlying library via its command line interface. You perhaps lose some API expressiveness, but there can be a significant gain in memory and speed performance because the image processing takes place in a separate process — any memory leaked by ImageMagick is recovered immediately when the shell command ends.

ImageScience is a focused Ruby module that does one thing — resize images. It's very efficient at that task.

Installing for Windows

Somewhat unusually, the Windows installation is the most straightforward of the bunch. For RMagick, head over to the RubyForge RMagick download page at `http://rubyforge.org/projects/rmagick` and grab the `rmagick-win32` executable. This is a binary installer that installs ImageMagick, all the needed prerequisites, and the RMagick RubyGem. Nice and neat. You should be aware, though, that the compilation of RMagick depends on the specific version of ImageMagick bundled in the installer. You can't change the version of ImageMagick (or swap it out for GraphicsMagick) without updating the entire installation.

With ImageMagick installed, you can then install MiniMagick as a regular gem, like this:

```
gem install mini_magick
```

MiniMagick will find the already installed ImageMagick and run against it.

FreeImage, the library used by ImageScience, also has a Windows installer, which you can grab at `http://freeimage.sourceforge.net/download.html`. After that is installed, ImageScience can be installed as a regular gem, like this:

```
gem install image_science
```

There are some reports of problems getting FreeImage set up on Windows platforms. Please check out the mailing lists at `http://freeimage.sourceforge.net` if you are having difficulties. In a pinch, the image resize functions of RMagick duplicate all the functionality of ImageScience.

Installing for Mac OS X

If you are a Mac user, there are a couple of different options for getting image libraries onto your system. If you are using the Locomotive environment to run Rails, you can get RMagick as a binary bundle within that system. However, that installation may not work for Rails systems that you do not run through Locomotive.

The next level on the complexity scale is to run a Mac OS X installation script provided as part of the RMagick distribution. From the RubyForge RMagick page (`http://rubyforge.org/projects/rmagick`), download `rmagick-osx-installer`, and unpack it somewhere convenient. This installation has the following prerequisites:

❑ You need to have the Max OS X Xcode tools installed (and if you've already installed Ruby and Subversion as suggested, you do).

❑ You need to have the aforementioned Ruby installation from source — the built-in Mac OS X Ruby won't work in OS 10.4.x (Although the built-in Ruby in OS 10.5 may be a different story).

❑ You need the X11 SDK and the X11 application. The SDK is on the installation disk as a package in Xcode tools, and X11 itself is in the optional items installer.

❑ You need to have the installer package in a valid folder. When I tried it, the package actually unzipped itself into an invalid folder — the complete path name to the installation script cannot contain spaces.

From a command line, type **ruby rm_install.rb**, and wait. The installation will take some time, and you'll be periodically prompted for an administrator password. The official installation instructions suggest backing up your entire `/usr/local` directory before starting; alternately, you can install with an option `--prefix` *some other directory* and install RMagick there. This script will install ImageMagick and all prerequisites. The main command line may not update for a while, but you can always monitor the `install.log` file to see what's going on.

The next level of complexity is to attempt to do all the steps of the installation script yourself. Full instructions for this are provided on the RMagick website.

After ImageMagick is installed, MiniMagick is just the same gem install on the Mac as it is for Windows.

The easiest way to install FreeImage is to install MacPorts from `www.macports.org`. MacPorts is an ambitious attempt to provide Linux-style package installers for many open source packages so that they will run on Mac OS X. MacPorts itself uses a standard Mac installer. Once that is in place, the following terminal command will install FreeImage:

```
sudo port install freeimage
```

From that point, ImageScience is just a gem install, as shown previously.

You can also install ImageMagick separately as a MacPort (`port install ImageMagick`) or a binary download from `www.imagemagick.org`. You can then attempt to install RMagick as an ordinary gem.

The MacPort installation of ImageMagick will work in Mac OS 10.5.x with a slight tweak. See `http://nullstyle.com/2007/10/27/how-to-build-imagemagick-and-install-rmagick-with-macports-on-mac-os-x-leopard` *for details.*

Installing for Linux

Your best bet on Linux, as it is on Mac OS X, is to try and find a binary installation package. Your Linux distribution may contain an RMagick package; however, none of those packages are officially maintained. Both ImageMagick and GraphicsMagick maintain `.rpm` packages for several Linux distributions — check those sites for a current list. Failing that, the manual instructions for compiling from source are available from the RMagick website. Again, once ImageMagick or GraphicsMagick is in place, both RMagick and MiniMagick can be installed as gems.

FreeImage provides a make file, and the following standard commands should work on most Linux distributions:

```
make
sudo make install
```

After that, ImageScience can be downloaded as a gem.

Uploading Files to Rails

To demonstrate some graphics features, I'm going to show you how to give a user the ability to upload a picture of their soup recipe, and then show you how to manipulate those images for some simple effects. Although you could roll this up yourself, I'm going to recommend the use of the attachment_fu plugin, which offers nice features for managing image metadata, automatic thumbnail generation, and validation of image parameters.

The plugin is available via the usual mechanism:

```
script/plugin install http://svn.techno-weenie.net/projects/plugins/attachment_fu/
```

To upload via attachment_fu, you need to align a data model, a controller, and a view. Once the file is uploaded, you'll need to change other views to display the image within the page. The attachment-fu plugin has specific expectations for the way the data is saved in your Rails application. In the Soups OnLine project, you can either include the image data columns within the recipe table or create a separate model and table to manage the metadata. On the theory that different things should be stored in different places, I'm opting for the separate table, which means you need the following model and migration:

```
$ script/generate model soup_image --svn
```

For what it's worth, I chose the name `soup_image` rather than just `image` on the vague theory that `image` is the sort of generic model name that is highly likely to have a nasty name collision somewhere down the road. It's unlikely that there's another class named `SoupImage` running around in the wild.

Setting Up attachment_fu Data

The attachment_fu plugin allows you to name your image-metadata model arbitrarily, but the columns within the table need a specific set of names. Unfortunately, there isn't a generator to create the migration. It needs to look something like this:

```
class CreateSoupImages < ActiveRecord::Migration
  def self.up
    create_table :soup_images do |t|
      t.string :filename
      t.string :content_type
      t.integer :size
      t.integer :height
      t.integer :width
      t.integer :parent_id
      t.integer :thumbnail
      t.timestamps
    end

    add_column :recipes, :soup_image_id, :integer
  end

  def self.down
    drop_table :soup_images
    remove_column :recipes, :soup_image_id
  end
end
```

Not all the columns are required for every usage of attachment_fu. You always need :filename, :content_type, and :size. The columns :height, and :width must be added if you are uploading images. If you are going to use attachment_fu's automatic thumbnail feature, then you also need the :parent_id and :thumbnail columns. The add_column command in the migration is specific to the Soups OnLine application, setting up a one-to-one relationship between recipes and images.

This migration is suitable for using attachment_fu to store files in the server filesystem. If you want to store files in the database itself, you need some more elements in the migration. This is not part of the Soups OnLine application, but the additional migration would look like this:

```
def self.up
  create_table :db_files do |t|
    t.data :binary
  end

  add_column :soup_images, :db_file_id, :integer
end
```

The db_files table will store the binary data for your upload — this table name is required by attachment_fu. The additional column being added to the soup_images metadata table sets up the one-to-one relationship between metadata and binary data.

Run rake db:migrate to make the changes in the database.

Creating an attachment_fu Model

It's time to create the model. (In case it's not clear, these steps aren't necessarily dependent on each other. If you're more comfortable doing the view code first, go right ahead.) Connect the SoupImage file to the attachment_fu plugin using the plugin's has_attachment method:

```
class SoupImage < ActiveRecord::Base

  has_attachment :content_type => :image,
                 :max_size => 1.megabyte,
                 :thumbnails => {:tag => "100x100>" },
                 :storage => :file_system

  validates_as_attachment

  has_one :recipe
end
```

The has_attachment method defines parameters of the attachment data. It takes about a dozen optional arguments, which fall into the following categories:

❑ **What to accept** — The :content_type argument takes either a string representing a single MIME type, an array of such strings, or the special symbol :image, which matches all image types. The :image symbol can be used within an array of options. The :min_size and :max_size arguments give a range of file sizes that are acceptable for the upload — use this to prevent files that are too big from clogging up your storage. Note the use of Rails number helpers to define the size in the example. You can set both values by using the :size option, which takes a Ruby range (50.kilobytes..500.kilobytes).

❑ **Where to put it** — The :storage option can be :db_file (the default), :file_system, or :s3. Using :db_file causes the binary upload to be stored in the database table set up in the second migration that included the binary database field -- you must have that table set up to use this option. Using :file_system stores the file in the server file system, and :s3 uses the Amazon S3 online storage repository. The default storage location is public/<table_name> for the local file system and just <table_name> for S3. This can be changed by using the :path_prefix option, which takes a string representing the location. Using :path_prefix changes the default storage location for :file_system, but you would still need to explicitly specify the use of S3.

❑ **What to do with it** — The :processor option specifies which of the graphics plugins should be used for resizing, and the value can be ImageScience, MiniMagick, or RMagick (symbol or string). If you don't specify one of these, attachment_fu will pick from among the installed graphics packages. The :resize_to option causes attachment_fu to automatically resize the incoming image, and the argument is either an array [width, height] or an RMagick geometry string. The :thumbnails option allows you to specify an arbitrary number of thumbnails to be automatically generated on upload. The hash keys are identifiers for the generated images, and the values are either [width, height] arrays or geometry strings. The :thumbnail_class argument takes a Ruby class as a value, and allows you to specify a different class model for the thumbnail images if you want them to be subject to different validation rules or be stored in a different location.

> ### RMagick Geometry Strings
>
> Size specifications for resizing or creating thumbnail images can be specified in RMagick geometry strings, which are generally of the form wxh, as in 100x75. The basic meaning of this is that your image will be proportionally resized until one of those boundaries is reached. You can affect the default behavior in a few ways. You can specify only a width (100), or only a height (x75), in which case the resize will adjust the specified dimensions to that value and the other dimension proportionally. Using a percent sign (%) causes the number to be interpreted as a percentage of the existing height. Appending a greater than sign (>) causes the image to be resized only if one of its dimensions is outside the specified dimension, and using a less than sign (<)resizes the image only if both dimensions are inside the specification. Appending an exclamation point (!) to the string forces the image to be resized to both dimensions regardless of aspect ratio.

The validates_as_attachment method ensures that the file-type and file-size limitations set up in has_attachment are honored. If an uploaded file fails the validation, it is not saved to storage; however, it will be loaded temporarily into memory while it is checked. Finally, because the image is currently set up to have a recipe, that relationship must be specified. Don't forget to add the following to the Recipe class in the app/models/recipe.rb file to catch the other end of the relationship:

```
belongs_to :soup_image
```

Testing attachment_fu

If you are anything like me, then the first question you're asking as you approach dealing with attachments is, "How do you test a file upload?" As it happens, it's not actually that hard. Add the following test to the recipes_controller_test.rb file:

```
def test_should_create_recipe_with_image
    create_mock_captcha_token("fred", "3")
    assert_difference('Recipe.count') do
      post :create, :recipe => recipe_hash, :token => "fred",
          :captcha_value => "3",
          :soup_image => {:uploaded_data => fixture_file_upload(
              "../data/soup.jpg", "image/jpeg")
          }
    end
    newbie = Recipe.find(:all, :order => "id DESC", :limit => 1)[0]
    assert_not_nil(newbie.soup_image)
    assert_equal("soup.jpg", newbie.soup_image.filename)
    assert_equal("image/jpeg", newbie.soup_image.content_type)
    dir = "/soup_images/0000/000#{newbie.soup_image.id}"
    assert_equal("#{dir}/soup.jpg",
        newbie.soup_image.public_filename)
    assert_equal("#{dir}/soup_tag.jpg",
```

(continued)

(continued)

```
            newbie.soup_image.public_filename(:tag))
      assert(File.exists?("public/#{dir}/soup.jpg"))
      assert(File.exists?("public/#{dir}/soup_tag.jpg"))
      newbie.soup_image.destroy
   end
```

Structurally, this is very similar to the existing creation test for recipes. The `recipe_hash` value called in the `post` method was created by refactoring out the hash already used in the existing test.

The data for the actual upload is created by calling the Rails test helper method `fixture_file_upload`. This method fakes the data from a multipart form submission. The two arguments are the file location of the file being mock-uploaded and its MIME type, which in this case are `../data/soup.jpg` and `image/jpeg`. You need to actually put an image file in the expected location for the test to work. The name of the form attribute for an attachment-fu upload must be `:uploaded_data` — attachment-fu expects to look there for data.

After the pretend upload, the test validates that the soup image metadata is correctly added to the database, and then checks that the controller has placed the image and the thumbnail image in the expected location underneath the `public/soup_image` directory. The `destroy` method at the end is supposed to keep the file system clean. Destroying the soup image item deletes the entire `000#{id}` directory. You might need to be a little careful, though, if your development and test database are sharing the same file system. Often, you'll see this kind of `destroy` method placed in the `ensure` clause of a rescue exception block so that it will always be cleaned up. In a test, I often choose not to clean the data up if there's a problem, so that I have more information available for diagnosis.

Getting the controller working from here is just a single line because attachment_fu does most of the work. All you need to do is add the following highlighted line to the `RecipeController#create` method:

```
def create
    @recipe = Recipe.new(params[:recipe])
    @recipe.soup_image = SoupImage.new(params[:soup_image])
    ## Rest of method is unchanged
```

attachment_fu will take the upload data, looking in the `params` hash for the `:uploaded_data` attribute, and save the file to your chosen storage method, create the metadata object, and do any resizing or thumbnail creation as specified in the `has_attachment` call for `SoupImage`. The metadata object is saved to the database when the recipe is saved. A validation failure will prevent the metadata object and the recipe from being saved.

You also need to change the `update` method as follows:

```
def update
    @recipe = Recipe.find(params[:id])
    @recipe.soup_image = SoupImage.new(params[:soup_image]) if params[:soup_image]
```

Note that the existing create test is now also serving as proof that everything works just fine if the image is not uploaded. To enhance that check, add the following line to the end of the existing create test:

```
assert_equal(0, SoupImage.count)
```

Also, if you're debugging attachment_fu behavior, you should know that the metadata for an attachment, such as height or size, is not actually added to the object until it's needed. If you just attempt to look at the state of the object right after it's created from the `params` hash, the object will have a lot of `nil` values. These will be filled in when the object is saved or otherwise used.

Adding an attachment_fu Form

The controller is only the receiver of the upload. You also need to add the form that will generate the real upload data for the image. There are two changes that you need to make to the `app/views/recipe/_form.html.erb` view page. First, you need to change the declaration of the form to have an encoding type of `multipart/form_data`. This tells the browser that there will be an attached file as part of the form. Here's the new declaration:

```
<% form_for(@recipe, :html => { :multipart => true }) do |f| %>
```

This will include the proper multipart declaration in the form.

Next, you need to add the actual form uploader widget. Somewhere in the form itself, add the following:

```
<% fields_for :soup_image do |img| %>
  <p>
    <b>Image</b>
    <%= img.file_field :uploaded_data %>
  </p>
<% end %>
```

There are a couple of helpful Rails features in that snippet. First is the `fields_for` block, which is used when you want to have a single form manage data for multiple ActiveRecord objects. In this case, the upload data will belong to `SoupImage`, not the recipe. Logistically, this means that the field for the uploaded data must comply with the naming convention that will tell the controller that the upload field is not part of the recipe. Specifically, this means that the HTML name of the field has to be `soup_image[uploaded_data]` and not `recipe[uploaded_data]`. Ordinarily the name of the field is generated from the object specified as the target in the initial `form_for` block. The `fields_for` block, however, allows you to have an interlude nested inside the larger form that is targeted at a different object or class.

The resulting form has an upload field as shown in Figure 11-1.

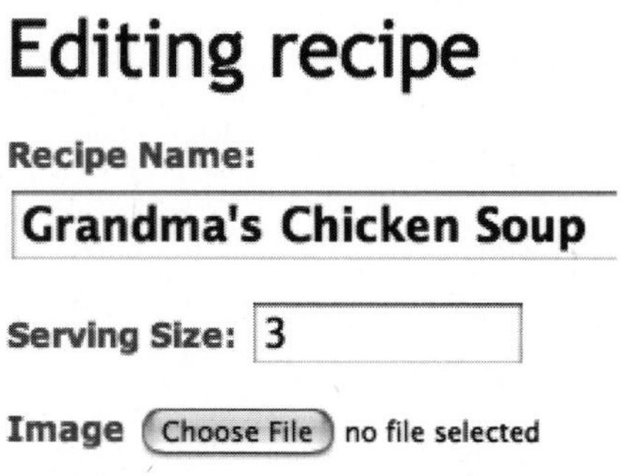

Editing recipe

Recipe Name:

Grandma's Chicken Soup

Serving Size: 3

Image (Choose File) no file selected

Figure 11-1

After you select a file, the display shows the file as shown in Figure 11-2.

Editing recipe

Recipe Name:

Grandma's Chicken Soup

Serving Size: 3

Image (Choose File) 📄 soup.jpg

Figure 11-2

With these changes, submitting the form will upload the file, place the file in the correct /public directory, generate the thumbnail, and save the metadata.

As I write this, there appears to be an incompatibility between attachment_fu and Rails 2.0. It seems as though the issue can be worked around by explicitly saving SoupImage *before saving the recipe in the* create *and* update *methods. Please be on the lookout for a new release of attachment_fu to address Rails 2.0 issues.*

Displaying attachment_fu Images

Displaying images is straightforward, and you've already seen most of the pieces. First, it will be a little cleaner if you give Recipe this little predicate method:

```
def has_image?
  not soup_image.nil?
end
```

To show the main image in the recipe detail page, add the following highlighted code just above the servings field in the display:

```
<% if @recipe.has_image? %>
  <%= image_tag(@recipe.soup_image.public_filename, :align => :right) %>
<% else %>
   
<% end %>

<p class="servings">
  Servings: <%= in_place_editor_field :recipe, :servings %>
</p>
```

You are using the Rails `image_tag` helper to create an `img` tag whose source is the public filename of the image for this soup. If there's no image, just display a blank space. Then the image will display as shown in Figure 11-3.

Grandma's Chicken Soup

Tags: grandma, chicken, fred Edit

Servings: 3

Yummy!

Ingredients

2 cups stock Edit
2 cups stock Edit
2 cups stock Edit
1/2 oz. carrot Edit
1/2 oz. carrot Edit
2 cups stock Edit
1/2 oz. carrot Edit
1/2 oz. carrot Edit

Directions

Things

Edit Back

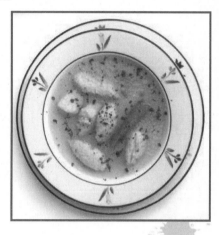

Figure 11-3

You can place the thumbnail image in the index display of the recipes with a similar piece of code in the recipe `index.html.erb` file:

```
<tr>
  <td>
    <% if recipe.has_image? %>
      <%= image_tag(recipe.soup_image.public_filename(:tag)) %>
    <% else %>
       
    <% end %>
  </td>
  <td><%= link_to(h(recipe.title), recipe) %></td>
  <% if_is_current_user recipe.user_id do %>
    <td><%= link_to 'Edit', edit_recipe_path(recipe) %></td>
    <td>
      <%= link_to 'Destroy', recipe, :confirm => 'Are you sure?',
          :method => :delete %>
    </td>
  <% end %>
</tr>
```

Figure 11-4 shows the result.

Recipes

Title

Changed Soup   Edit Destroy

Tag Soup   Edit Destroy

Grandma's Chicken Soup   Edit Destroy

New recipe

Figure 11-4

Allowing the user-uploaded image to be placed directly in the public web server path is a potential secu-
rity risk, just as directly displaying text from user input can be. Although attachment_fu does some val-
idating on the type and size of your file, you might want to place image files outside the web server root,
and then mediate access to them either manually or via the server.

Using Your Graphics Library

Now that you've got some images in your system to manipulate, it's time to discuss how to use the
libraries to do fancy graphical stuff (to use the technical term). A lot of these examples are going to be in
the console because you generally don't want to have long-running graphics manipulation running in
your web server process (although MiniMagick spins off a separate command-line process on its own, so
including it is much less of a performance problem).

ImageScience

ImageScience has a very simple API, as you might expect from its focus on just resizing images. All the
manipulation is done via the method `ImageScience.with_image(filename)`. The method takes
the following block, in which you do whatever manipulation you need:

```
ImageScience.with_image("data/soup.jpg") do |image|
  image.thumbnail(150) do |thumbnail|
    thumbnail.save("data/soup_thumbnail.jpg")
  end
end
```

The `with_image` method opens the file and converts it to an ImageScience instance. Within the
block, the call to `thumbnail` takes a single size dimension. The image is scaled proportionally until its
longest side is the given length. The method returns another ImageScience instance, which should be
used inside another block. The `save` method saves the new file to the given file location. If you change
the extension on the file, then ImageScience will perform the image type conversion for you.

The only attribute information you can get out of an ImageScience instance is the width and height of the image (although I suppose you could infer the image format from the file extension). In addition to the thumbnail method, you can try cropped_thumbnail, which forces a square thumbnail by cropping the image to a square and then resizing the image. You can also use resize, which takes a width and a height as arguments and resizes the image to fit. There's also with_crop, which takes x, y offsets and a rectangle width and height, and crops the image accordingly. The only other thing you can do with the image is save it, as shown in the previous code listing.

All in all, this is a tidy little API for a commonly used task.

RMagick

Here's a nifty little method to place in your application.rb file. For this to work, you must have require 'RMagick' (note the capitalization) at the top of the file and include Magick in the class definition. Long term, you probably want the require statement in the environment.rb file, to prevent RMagick from loading twice (loading twice can cause problems).

```
def create_animated_gif(recipes, tag)
  with_image = recipes.select { |r| r.has_image? }
  image_names = with_image.collect do |r|
    "public/#{r.soup_image.public_filename(:tag)}"
  end
  image_list = ImageList.new(*image_names)
  image_list.delay = 100
  filename = "#{tag}.gif"
  image_list.write(filename)
  filename
end
```

This uses basic RMagick read-and-write functionality to create an animated GIF file from the uploaded images associated with recipes. The first four lines convert the list of recipes to a list of image file names, for those recipes which have images. The filenames assume that the naming convention from the upload example earlier in this chapter has been followed.

The fifth line creates an instance of one of the core RMagick classes, ImageList. An ImageList is created from a list of filenames, each representing an existing image file on the system (if the file contains more than one image, then all images are loaded into the list). The images are loaded into memory. The next step sets the delay for the eventual animation at one second per frame (you can also set the number of iterations that the animations will run using the iterations= method). In the last lines, a filename is generated and the image list writes to that file. When you attempt to write an ImageList to a file format that supports animation, each element in the list is becomes a frame in the animation. The result is a quick few lines of code to create an animated GIF. (If you attempt to write to a file format that doesn't support animation, then each element is sent to its own file with the image name given and the further suffixes .0, .1, .2 and so on. Note that this means that the output image name will not end with the file type extension.) The method returns the filename.

To use this RMagick method, you need to include it in the category controller `show` method as follows:

```
def show
  @category = params[:id] ||= ""
  @recipes = Recipe.find_tagged_with(@category)
  @gif_name = create_animated_gif(@recipes, @category)
```

The `@gif_name` attribute can then be slotted into the output view via an `image_tag` call, and you've got yourself a snazzy — and possibly annoying — animated GIF for each category tag.

ImageList

An RMagick `ImageList` is a subclass of a Ruby array that will only hold RMagick `Image` objects (more about this in a moment). Most `Array` and `Enumerable` methods will work directly on an `ImageList`. `ImageList` also defines a number of methods that work on the entire list. You've already seen a few of them. A few others combine the images into a single image. The `average` method averages all the images together into a single `Image`, and the `montage` method tiles all the images. You can also use the `to_blob` and `from_blob` methods to convert from an `ImageList` to binary database storage.

In addition to the normal array features, an `ImageList` also maintains a *current scene*, which is basically a pointer to a specific index in the array. The current scene attribute can be changed with the attribute accessor `scene=`. When a new `ImageList` is created, the current scene is initially set to the last image in the list.

The current scene mechanism allows `ImageList` to respond to nearly all instance methods of plain, ordinary RMagick `Image` objects — the method is applied to the image in the current scene. Whether this is a better mechanism than explicitly referencing the image via its array index is debatable, but the feature does have the interesting consequence of making `Image` and `ImageList` duck-type identical for many purposes. This means that many of the methods you write using the RMagick API don't have to test whether they are being applied to an `Image` or an `ImageList`.

Image

The `Image` class has the bulk of the fancy processing features. I'm going to demonstrate a few of them by writing them as methods on the `SoupImage` class already created, and then processing them in the Rails console. This is by no means a complete list of RMagick's image transformations, but it will serve to give you the most commonly used features and a general guide toward the rest. Check out the RMagick documentation for a complete list.

To start, add the `require` and `include` commands listed previously to the `environment.rb` or `soup_image.rb` file. Then add the following two methods:

```
def local_filename
  "public/#{public_filename}"
end

def to_rmagick_image
  Image.read(local_filename)[0]
end
```

These methods will enable the easy transformation of the uploaded data to an RMagick `Image`. As you can see, the `Image#read` method is used to convert a filename to an RMagick `Image`, and the file type is inferred from the filename. The `read` method returns an array of all the images in the file — for example, an animated GIF would return an array with each image. For some reason, this result is an actual array and not an `ImageList`. Other class methods of `Image` include `from_blob`, which takes in a database BLOB object, and `new(width, height)`, which creates a blank image.

To start with the functionality that you've already seen elsewhere, RMagick has no less than four separate methods for changing the size of an image. The flagship method is `resize`, which takes either a width and height or a single scaling factor. In the Soups OnLine world, that could be called as follows:

```
def resize_me(width, height)
  File.new(local_filename).copy("#{local_filename}.old")
  to_rmagick_image.resize(width, height).write(local_filename)
end
```

This version rewrites the new sized image over the original image, copying the old image first. The `resize` method also takes optional arguments to specify a filter and a blur factor on the changed image. If the new image is going to be less than 10 percent of the size of the original, then it's faster to use the `thumbnail` method, which also takes either a width and a height or a scale factor (but not a filter or blur). The `scale` and `sample` methods also take the same kind of arguments, although the `sample` method is different in that it does not do any color manipulation on the resulting image — the color set of the new image is a strict subset of the original. All four of these methods return a new `Image` object, and all four have a related method ending in an exclamation point (`!`), which changes the `Image` object in place.

The `write` method saves the image to the given filename, transferring the format if needed.

Cropping is managed via the `crop` method, which takes in the size of the new bounding rectangle you'd expect, as well as an optional `x, y` offset as the first two arguments, and another optional first argument called `gravity` that tells where to place the bounding rectangle relative to the image. The `gravity` argument anchors the bounding rectangle to a side or corner of the image. Generally you'd use either a `gravity` argument or an `x, y` offset, but not both. Here's an example, with a helper method being used to save the image with a new filename based on the old one:

```
def adjusted_filename(suffix)
  filename, ext = local_filename.split(".")
  "#{filename}_#{suffix}.png"
end

def crop_me(width, height)
  r_image = to_rmagick_image.crop(CenterGravity, width, height)
  r_image.write(adjusted_filename("cropped"))
end
```

And then:

```
>> Recipe.find(1).soup_image.crop_me(150, 150)
```

This results in the 150-pixel-square center of the image, as shown in Figure 11-5.

Figure 11-5

Now for some effects. How about this nice old-time sepia tone (assuming that reads on the page at all):

```
def sepia
  to_rmagick_image.sepiatone(MaxRGB * 0.8).write(adjusted_filename("sepia"))
end
```

The argument to `sepiatone` is a threshold value — the argument passed is the one recommended by the RMagick documentation. Figure 11-6 shows the result of this example code.

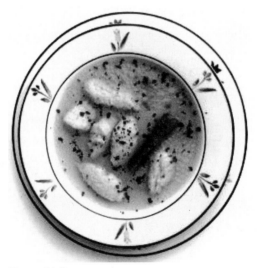

Figure 11-6

Here's one that I think is really cool: the Polaroid effect (see Figure 11-7). Under the right circumstances, I'd probably have to be forcibly restrained from having every image on my site look like this.

```
def polaroid
  img = to_rmagick_image
  img[:caption] = recipe.title
  img.polaroid(-15).write(adjusted_filename("polaroid"))
end
```

Figure 11-7

The argument to `polaroid` is the angle to tilt the image in degrees. The line with the caption indicates a general feature of images, namely that you can use the bracket syntax to set arbitrary properties on them that some methods might look for. In this case, `polaroid` looks for a `caption` property.

This brief sample should give you a feel for the vast amount of image transformations that RMagick makes available.

Draw

You can also use more typical graphics commands to draw on a blank image or an existing image. Let's draw a big, fat X on an image:

```
def x_me_out
  img = to_rmagick_image
  draw = Draw.new
  draw.stroke('red')
  draw.stroke_width(5)
  draw.line(0, 0, img.columns, img.rows)
  draw.line(img.columns, 0, 0, img.rows)
  draw.draw(img)
  img.write(adjusted_filename("x"))
end
```

This should look broadly familiar if you've ever done any programming in a graphics library with drawing primitives. If you know the Scalable Vector Graphics (SVG) specification, you'll find the RMagick API very similar. The basic idea here is that the `Draw` class stores the list of primitive drawing operations that are called on it. The primitive commands are not drawn as they are called (if you look at the code, you'll see there's no association between the `Draw` object and the image when the primitives are called). The result is something like a metafile — a set of instructions for drawing. The `draw` method associates the `Draw` object with the images. and the commands are drawn on the image one by one. The same `Draw` object can be used to draw the same pattern on multiple images.

The coordinate system matches normal graphic conventions, the 0, 0 coordinate is in the top left, and positive rotation is clockwise. So the first line draw goes from top-left to bottom-right and the other one crosses it from top-right to bottom-left. Figure 11-8 shows the result.

Figure 11-8

There are more than 55 primitives in `Draw`, so I'm not going to cover all of them here. Besides, having all these subtly different pictures of soup is making me feel a bit like Andy Warhol. I do want to cover one other feature — placing text on the image like this:

```
def with_caption
  img = to_rmagick_image
  draw = Draw.new
  draw.annotate(img, 0, 0, 0, 30, recipe.title) do
    self.fill = 'blue'
    self.gravity = NorthGravity
    self.font_family = 'Helvetica'
    self.pointsize = 24
  end
  img.write(adjusted_filename("caption"))
end
```

The key method here is annotate, which takes as arguments the image being written on, the width, height, x offset, and y offset of the bounding rectangle for the text (a width and height of 0 means resize to fit); and the text itself. Inside the optional block, you can call any attribute accessor of Draw and have it applied to the text draw. Notice that because annotate is not a graphics primitive, it's automatically associated with the image and a separate call to draw is not needed. Figure 11-9 shows an annotated image.

Figure 11-9

MiniMagick

MiniMagick offers an alternative mechanism for accessing most of the ImageMagick functionality. Where RMagick has an elaborate Ruby API with several classes and methods that individually wrap much of the underlying functionality, the bulk of MiniMagick is a single class with fewer than 10 methods. Where RMagick manipulates images in memory, MiniMagick invokes the ImageMagick command line and writes to temporary files. The main negative feature of MiniMagick is that it does not allow you to create new images, nor does it support the image composition features that RMagick supports in the ImageList class.

MiniMagick is basically a four-trick pony. Trick one is acquiring an image. The MiniMagick::Image class has three ways to create an image. The new and from_file methods take a file location, which must point to an existing image. The difference between the two is that from_file will create a temporary file for MiniMagick to write to, and new will continually overwrite the existing file. There is also a from_blob method, which takes serialized binary data, writing it to a temporary file for use by other methods.

Trick two is saving the image, which is accomplished with the write method. This method takes a file location as an argument. (I trust this needs no further elaboration.)

Trick three is the use of the Ruby [] method to wrap calls to the ImageMagick identify -format command by making them look like hash lookups. In general, the symbol inside the brackets when the [] is used is passed directly as an argument to the ImageMagick command line; however, :width and :height are special cases.

To run this example, add `require 'mini_magick'` to the top of `soup_image.rb`, and define the following methods:

```
def to_mini_magick_image
  MiniMagick::Image.from_file(local_filename)
end

def mini_size
  mini = to_mini_magick_image
  [mini[:width], mini[:height]]
end
```

The sample usage goes like this:

```
>> Recipe.find(1).soup_image.mini_size
=> [296, 300]
```

Beyond width and height, there are a number of options that can be arguments to this method. For example, you can use the following ImageMagick format string (see the references section for a link to a complete reference):

```
def some_mini_info
  mini = to_mini_magick_image
  "Image Depth #{mini['%z']}, File Size #{mini['%b']}"
end

>> Recipe.find(1).soup_image.some_mini_info
=> "Image Depth 8, File Size 20520"
```

If the image contains Exchangeable image file format (Exif) metadata, then a format string of the style `EXIF:ImageHeight` can be used to extract the data. The special string `EXIF:*` will print all metadata in a `key=value` format.

MiniMagick's fourth trick is probably the most interesting. It's a `method_missing` hack. Any other method calls that are made to a MiniMagick image are passed as arguments to ImageMagick's `mogrify` command-line utility, which can do just about any image transformation defined by ImageMagick. (Again, see the references for a complete list). So the following:

```
image.method(args)
```

is transformed to this command-line call:

```
mogrify -method args
```

By way of example, here's the MiniMagick version of the earlier method that cropped the middle of the image:

```
def mini_crop(width, height)
  mini = to_mini_magick_image
  mini.crop("#{width}x#{height}+0+0\" -gravity \"Center")
  mini.write(adjusted_filename("cropped"))
end
```

The first line and the third line should look normal — it's the second line that looks a little weird. It's getting mapped to the following ImageMagick command-line call (assuming it was called with `150, 150` as arguments):

```
mogrify -crop "150x150+0+0" -gravity "Center"
```

The `mogrify` call needs to have a flag for both the cropping of the image and the information that the crop should be centered. Unfortunately, the way MiniMagick handles multiple arguments if you format them as multiple arguments is to put them all in a single string. This would mess up the quote marks in the resulting `mogrify` call (it would eliminate the two marks that are explicitly placed in the second line of the example), which would cause the call to fail. And doing the `gravity` call separately from the `crop` call doesn't work either. The general rule is that you are best off formatting all options to one call as a single string when it goes to MiniMagick (this cries out for a helper method or perhaps a slight patch to MiniMagick).

To see another way to work around some naming weirdness, here's a sepia toner again:

```
def mini_sepia
  mini = to_mini_magick_image.send("sepia-tone", MaxRGB * 0.8)
  mini.write(adjusted_filename("sepia"))
end
```

The actual command-line flag for sepia toning is `sepia-tone`, and the dash plays havoc with attempts to create a method named `sepia-tone`. Therefore, I resorted to the `send` method to allow me to create the oddly-named method call.

The other examples all fall out similarly. The basic functionality is there, but you get to it differently. Here's the `polaroid` method:

```
def mini_polaroid
  mini = to_mini_magick_image
  mini.polaroid("15\" -caption \"#{recipe.title}")
  mini.write(adjusted_filename("polaroid"))
end
```

It uses the same trick for managing quotation marks. Weirdly, if you have a negative number as the degree argument to `polaroid`, MiniMagick wants to treat it as a command-line flag because of the dash character, making it pretty much impossible to get the formatting right if there's a second argument.

The "draw an X" method shows how composing these command-line strings can get tangled:

```
def mini_x
  mini = to_mini_magick_image
  stroke_info = "-stroke \"red\" -strokewidth \"5"
  mini.draw("line 0,0 #{mini[:width]},#{mini[:height]}\" #{stroke_info}")
  mini.draw("line #{mini[:width]},0 0,#{mini[:height]}\" #{stroke_info}")
  mini.write(adjusted_filename("x"))
end
```

In this case, the `draw` command needs the line data and the stroke color and width for each call, so I factored out the common stroke information into a separate string that is added into each command call.

And, to wrap up the comparison, here's the text annotation method:

```
def mini_with_caption
  mini = to_mini_magick_image
  mini.annotate("+0+30\" \"#{recipe.title}\" -pointsize \"24\" -gravity \"North\"
-fill \"blue" )
  mini.write(adjusted_filename("caption"))
end
```

The conclusion here is that MiniMagick is probably faster than RMagick on a production system but with a more awkward API (at least at the time of this writing, although I suspect that a cleaner way of dealing with image options could be devised).

Charts

There are several different charting tools available for Rails — some use Flash, and others use just CSS and HTML. This section focuses on two graph packages that build on top of RMagick.

Gruff

The more traditional chart package is called Gruff, written by Geoffrey Grosenbach. It is Ruby built on top of RMagick, and it offers the typical variety of bar, line, area, and pie charts. Gruff is available as a Ruby gem or as a Rails plugin. The plugin option adds a generator to create a controller for your chart. You can install the Gruff plugin as follows:

```
$ script/plugin install -x http://topfunky.net/svn/plugins/gruff
```

After the plugin is installed, you should create a controller for the chart. RESTful thinking would imply one controller for each chart (with the controller in the show method); however, that one show method could take various arguments to serve the data in different forms, or to serve different slices of the data. You can generate a Gruff chart controller just by giving it a name.

Getting Started

To get Gruff to work, you're best off creating a separate controller for the graph data. Gruff provides the following migration to do so:

```
$ script/generate gruff CategoryGraphs
```

In a comment in the generated controller, Gruff recommends adding the following line to the routes.rb file:

```
map.graph "graph/:action/image.png", :controller => "category_graphs"
```

This line will match routes of the form graph/show/image.png. You could also try a RESTful route, but given the single method and the image file suffix, a traditional route is probably easier. If you do want to have different graphs based on an ID, change the route to graph/:action/:id/image.png.

As a first-look at the Gruff API, here's what the Gruff controller produces by default, with a couple of comments excised and some respacing:

```ruby
class CategoryGraphsController < ApplicationController

  def show
    g = Gruff::Line.new
#      g.theme = {
#        :colors => ['#663366', '#cccc99', '#cc6633', '#cc9966', '#99cc99'],
#        :marker_color => 'white',
#        :background_colors => ['black', '#333333']
#      }
#    g.font = File.expand_path('artwork/fonts/VeraBd.ttf', RAILS_ROOT)
    g.title = "Gruff-o-Rama"
    g.data("Apples", [1, 2, 3, 4, 4, 3])
    g.data("Oranges", [4, 8, 7, 9, 8, 9])
    g.data("Watermelon", [2, 3, 1, 5, 6, 8])
    g.data("Peaches", [9, 9, 10, 8, 7, 9])
    g.labels = {0 => '2004', 2 => '2005', 4 => '2006'}
    send_data(g.to_blob, :disposition => 'inline', :type => 'image/png',
      :filename => "gruff.png")
  end
end
```

This code produces the graph shown in Figure 11-10.

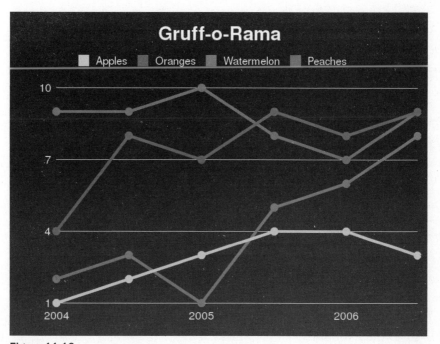

Figure 11-10

There are four basic steps to generating a Gruff graph (try saying that 10 times fast). First, you choose the class of graph you are shooting for. All graphs are subclasses of `Gruff::Base` — in most cases, they differ only in how they are drawn, so the basic API doesn't change. This graph uses `Gruff::Line`, but other options include `Gruff::Area`, `Gruff::Bar`, `Gruff::SideBar`, `Gruff::Pie`, `Gruff::Spider`, `Gruff::StackedBar`, and `Gruff::StackedSideBar`. There are also `Gruff::Mini` versions of the basic set.

Step two is specifying the theme and font, which are commented out in the preceding code. The theme takes a hash, which in this case consists of a `:colors` option that lists the colors used for the data sets, in the order they are added, a `:marker_color` option that sets the color of the grid lines, and a `:background_colors` option that takes two colors and sets up a top-to-bottom gradient between them. If you'd rather have an image than a gradient, you can set `:background_image` instead. There are also a handful of predefined themes that you can call, such as `theme_37signals` and `theme_keynote`. If you want to add a font, the argument is a path to the font file.

Step three is adding the data and labels. This is generally the same for each graph type. Each data series is brought in separately. The first argument to the `data` method is a name for the dataset, the second argument is the actual data series, and the third argument is an optional color. If the color is not specified, then the next color is used from whatever theme is in effect. *The theme must be specified before you add data*. The specific meaning of the data is dependent on the graph. For a line graph, each series is a line. In a bar graph, each series is a set of bars, and multiple series are represented as bars next to each other for each data point (in a stacked graph, they are on top of each other). A pie chart uses only the first element in each data series. The labels represent the x-axis labels, and are specified as a hash, where the key is the placement in the data series and the value is the string label.

Finally, use the Rails `send_data` method to send the graph as a binary blob. In this case, the `send_data` method is telling the browser to render the image inline, allowing it to be used in an HTML image tag (the alternative is `:attachement`, which triggers a file download). The filename argument is for the browser to use when the user attempts to save the image from within the browser.

A Custom Example

Now let's do something with our own data. In this example, you're going to build a pie chart of the counts for each of the tags that can be displayed on the tag page. Change the graph controller to this:

```ruby
class CategoryGraphsController < ApplicationController

  def show
    graph = Gruff::Pie.new(400)
    graph.theme_37signals
    add_data(graph)
    send_data(graph.to_blob, :disposition => 'inline', :type => 'image/png',
        :filename => "categories.png")
  end

  private

  def add_data(graph)
    counts = TagCloud.tag_counts(Recipe)
    counts.keys.sort.each do |key|
      graph.data(key.capitalize, counts[key])
    end
  end

end
```

This should all seem familiar. The graph type is set to `Pie`, and the argument is the width of the graph (the graph maintains a 4::3 ratio unless you pass in a string like `200x200`). A predefined theme is set, and every tag adds a one-element data set. Then the graph can be sent.

To place that on the category index page, put the following line in the view:

```
<%= image_tag '/graph/show/image.png' %>
```

And voilà! Figure 11-11 shows the result.

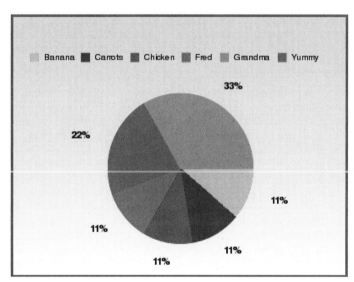

Figure 11-11

Sparklines

In his book *Beautiful Evidence*, famed information-graphics designer Edward Tufte introduced the concept of *sparklines*: small, data-rich graphics embedded inline with text or a table. Although sparklines are perhaps best suited to the higher resolution of print, several implementations of the basic concept have been done for the Web, including a Ruby on Rails plugin. As it happens, the Ruby sparklines implementation is by Geoffrey Grosenbach, who is responsible for Gruff.

You can get sparklines by installing the plugin as follows:

```
$ ruby ./script/plugin install http://topfunky.net/svn/plugins/sparklines
```

And you can use the following generator to create a single sparkline controller:

```
$ ruby ./script/generate sparklines
```

With the controller up, sparklines can be created inline via a helper method. Here's an example that generates some random data and displays it in several different sparkline formats:

```
<% data = (1..100).collect { rand (100) }  %>

<%= sparkline_tag data, :type => :area, :upper => 50, :has_max => true %>
<br/>
<%= sparkline_tag data, :type => :bar %>
<br/>
<%= sparkline_tag data, :type => :discrete, :upper => 50 %>
<br/>
<%= sparkline_tag data, :type => :smooth, :upper => 50, :has_max => true,
    :line_color => 'blue' %>
<br/>
<%= sparkline_tag [25], :type => :pie %>
<br/>
<%= sparkline_tag data.collect {|i| (i / 20 ) - 2}, :type => :whisker %>
```

Figure 11-12 shows the on-screen result.

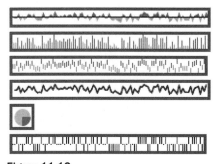

Figure 11-12

The top sparkline is an area plot, with values above a baseline in one color, and values below it in another color. The second sparkline is a bar graph. The third sparkline is a discrete graph, which is similar to a bar graph but the lines are a constant height. Then there's a simple line graph, and then a pie chart that only draws a single value. The last sparkline is a whisker plot, which is often used to plot win-loss data for sports teams.

The sparkline helper tag takes a number of general options, including `:height` for the height of the image, with a default of 14 pixels. The CSS class defaults to `sparkline`, but this can be changed with the `:class` option. You can set the `:background_color`, `:line_color`. You can also specify `:above_color` and `:below_color` for graph types that make a distinction, although the actual value to switch on is covered by the `:upper` option. And as you can tell from the preceding code, the `:type` option specifies which kind of sparkline to draw.

The line and area graphs can highlight the maximum, minimum, or final value by setting `:has_max`, `:has_min`, or `:has_last` to `true`. You can specify colors with `:min_color`, `:max_color`, or `:last_color`. For a whisker plot, the data values are -2, -1, 0, 1, and 2. Negative values indicated a down line, positive values are up, 0 means no data. 2 and -2 are considered "exceptional values." Colors can be modified with the options `:whisker_color` and `:exception_color`.

Resources

The image of chicken soup used in this chapter was taken by Sanja Gjenero, who apparently lives in Croatia (have I mentioned that I love the Internet sometimes?). I found it on a stock photo site at `www.sxc.hu/photo/519735`, and created the examples in this chapter following the usage options presented on that site.

ImageMagick lives at `www.imagemagick.org`. This site contains an extensive list of the ImageMagick command-line interface, which can be invaluable if you are using MiniMagick. GraphicsMagick is housed at `www.graphicsmagick.org`. RMagick's home page is `http://rmagick.rubyforge.com`. The site has a detailed look at the RMagick API as well as some installation troubleshooting information. ImageScience has its home page at `http://seattlerb.rubyforge.org/ImageScience.html`. MiniMagick doesn't seem to really have a home page, but it can be downloaded from `http://rubyforge.org/projects/mini-magick`. Gruff and sparklines are both hosted on the same server, Gruff is introduced at `http://nubyonrails.com/pages/gruff`, and you can get the sparklines plugin at `http://nubyonrails.com/pages/sparklines`.

Here are some other links of note. Mike Clark has an excellent introduction to uploading files at `www.clarkware.com/cgi/blosxom/2007/02/24`. A useful presentation on the differences between RMagick and MiniMagick is online at `http://marsorange.com/files/rmagick_vs_minimagick.pdf` — the author goes by the name Mars. The same author has a cautionary note about using RMagick with the Rails `tempfile` naming scheme: `http://marsorange.com/archives/of-mogrify-ruby-tempfile-dynamic-class-definitions`.

I regret not having more of a chance to include Flash- and Flex-based solutions here. There are a number of Flash-based graph libraries that can use Rails as a data source, but there doesn't seem to be much Rails-specific tool support, and many of the libraries are commercial. The definitive source for Rails interaction with Flex is Peter Armstrong's blog (`www.flexonrails.net`) and the associated book, which should be out by the time you read this.

Summary

Graphics have been an important part of the Web since the beginning. There are a number of different tools for supporting graphic manipulation in Rails. The most important library is RMagick, but MiniMagick and ImageScience are also useful. Installing any of the three projects can be complex.

The attachment_fu plugin offers great support for accepting uploaded files such as images from users, validating them, and storing the metadata in the database. attachment_fu supports storing the file in the file system, the database, or Amazon's S3 online storage.

ImageScience is used only for resizing images. RMagick allows for a wide variety of different image-manipulation functions, including piecing together animated GIFs, various kinds of color filtering, and low-level primitive drawing. MiniMagick offers most of the same functionality as RMagick, but it relies on command-line calls to the underlying graphics library, rather than on an ongoing process.

Gruff is a simple library for creating charts. You can easily set chart types and data in your code, and there's a flexible API to tune the output display. Sparklines are small, inline graphs that can be created using a sparkline plugin.

12

Deploying Your Application

It's inevitable. At some point your Rails application has to leave the comforting home of your development setting and make its own way in the cold, cruel world of production environments. Deploying Rails applications has been an area of extremely rapid change and development — even by Rails standards — with the definition of deployment best-practice tools changing completely every few months. As I write this, though, the field appears to have settled on a consistent set of tools. This toolset is designed to take you from your development environment to low-traffic, high-traffic, and very-high–traffic production sites using the same basic technologies.

Every deployment is different, of course, and the requirements for deploying high-traffic Rails sites like Basecamp or Twitter are different than you might need for an internal sales tool, or for a soup-recipe trading site. This chapter focuses on two of the most generally valuable tools in the Rails deployment kit: Capistrano, which is used to automate deployment activities, and Mongrel, which has emerged as the Rails application server of choice.

Deployment can be complex, and one of the best ways to mitigate that complexity is to start practicing the deployment early and often. Even during the earliest part of development, you should try to set up a staging server and start deploying to it, to test out all the various connections between the web server, source control, the database, and so on. That also gives you a platform to try out various server configurations and do some baseline performance measurements. This chapter gives you the basic tools to manage your deployment. The next chapter tackles managing performance and security on a production Rails application.

Capistrano

Deployment has always been a uniquely stressful period in the web development cycle. On most projects, it requires an elaborate protocol of copying files, restarting web servers, shutting down databases, possibly migrating data, restarting databases, and possibly rebooting machines. (Crossing your fingers is optional.) Often the process is mediated by a checklist, or by the memory of the developer who has been with the project the longest. It's time-consuming and error prone at exactly the time you most want to move quickly and accurately. If you are in a cycle where you are deploying frequently, then the time and effort quickly becomes a drag on the development process in general.

Capistrano aims to change all that by automating deployment tasks in much the same way that Rake automates build tasks. Capistrano assumes a particular structure for your development and deployment environments, but within that structure it's amazingly helpful at managing the copy and restart dance. It's especially helpful as your deployment moves to multiple servers — Capistrano enables you to make the same changes on all your servers with a single command.

Starting with Capistrano

Capistrano is distributed as a Rubygem, so naturally, you install it as follows:

```
$ sudo gem install capistrano
```

As of this writing, the current version is 2.1.0.

Capistrano requires you to have done some design and preparation of your deployment environment before you can use it. In particular, you need to know what your web server or servers are going to be and what commands need to be run remotely on those servers for them to start, stop, and restart. Although it's quite easy to extend your Capistrano deployment to multiple servers, it's preferable to start with just one server, especially while you're making sure the script works. Your database instance must already be available, although it does not have to have any tables or data in it — Capistrano performs Rails migrations as needed.

Capistrano communicates between the development machine and the deployment target using Secure Shell (SSH) protocol. This means that the target server must be capable of receiving SSH commands in a POSIX (Portable Operating System Interface) shell. Linux is preferred, although Mac OS X would probably work, and some people have been able to make Capistrano work with a Windows server and a Unix command-line emulator such as Cygwin. Capistrano assumes that you'll be able to connect to the remote machines via a public key rather than a password, although connection via password is posible.

You must have an active source control system to use Capistrano effectively. To perform a deployment, Capistrano checks out a clean version of your application from source control. In fact, Capistrano holds on to recently deployed versions of your application unless explicitly told to clean up. This makes it extremely easy to roll back a deployment to a previously known state (at least for the code — rolling back database data is more challenging). This means that you need to be using a source control system that is known to Capistrano. Not surprisingly, Subversion is the preferred choice here, although the source code also claims it supports Bazaar, CVS, Darcs, Mercurial, and Perforce. For a default deployment, the deployment target server must be capable of accessing the source control server.

With all that in place, you can go to your Rails root and run the following from the command line:

```
capify .
```

That adds two Capistrano files to your application. The first is called `Capfile`, and just loads the second file, which is in `config/deploy.rb` (much the same way that Rake creates a rakefile that just loads other task files). Capistrano files are often referred to as *recipe* files, but I'll try to avoid that usage here because it's a little confusing with the actual details of the Soups OnLine application. The actual configuration script is basically a place for you to give Capistrano the information it needs to get started. The important thing about this file is that it's just a plain Ruby file — although, like Rake, some custom methods are defined to make it read cleanly as a build file.

The first line of the deployment file asks you to specify a name of your application. Change the lines to the following:

```
set :application, "soupsonline"
set :repository, "svn://desktop.local./soupsonline/trunk"
```

This application name is used as part of the default deployment directory, so it needs to be a valid Unix directory name. However, it doesn't have to be the same name of the root application directory as given in the code or the source control. The second variable set here is the URL of your source repository, from the perspective of the target machine.

Next up, the default file gives you the following two variables, which are commented out but you might want to set:

```
# set :deploy_to, "/var/www/#{application}"
# set :scm, :subversion
```

The :deploy_to variable is the directory on the target machine where Capistrano is going to set up shop. As you'll see in a moment, Capistrano sets up a series of directories there so it can manage releases. The default target directory is /u/apps/#{application}, where the application is whatever you just set it to on the first line.

In addition to setting the source control type, there are a couple of variables not shown here that are helpful if you are using Subversion. By default, Capistrano will try to log into the source control system using the same username and password that the Capistrano script itself runs under. If you need to specify a different name you can add the following:

```
set :svn_user, '<user_name>'
set :svn_password, '<password>'
```

If you don't want to put the password in clear text in the deployment file, you can work around that as follows:

```
set :svn_password, Proc.new do
  Capistrano::CLI.password_prompt('Subversion password: ')
end
```

This causes Capistrano to prompt the user at the command line when it needs Subversion access.

Capistrano assumes that the account running the script needs to use the Unix sudo command to gain root access. If that's not true (which generally means that the user can gain the necessary access without using sudo), set the following variable to keep your scripts running properly:

```
set :use_sudo false
```

If your Subversion is in some unusual location outside the command path, you can specify the exact command to trigger it. For example:

```
set :svn_command, '/some/weird/path/to/svn'
```

Finally, you can set the addresses of the server or servers that you will be deploying to. Initially, you'll need to set only one of these (by convention, set :app), and the others can be commented out or deleted. For example:

```
role :app, "your app-server here"
role :web, "your web-server here"
role :db, "your db-server here", :primary => true
```

One of Capistrano's big selling points is the capability to manage multiple servers from the same command line. When you want multiple servers in your deployment, just add them in their roles as additional arguments to each list. For example:

```
role :app, "server1.serverfarm.com", "server2.serverfarm.com"
```

Capistrano's default behavior is to run all executed tasks on all defined servers. As your deployment adds servers and servers take on more specific roles, you aren't going to want to do all the tasks on all the servers (it makes no sense to restart a web server on your database box). That's where roles come into play. A Capistrano task can be defined to run only on a specific role or roles, in which case Capistrano will run the task only on the servers that are part of that task.

If your server setup is such that the servers are accessible only via a gateway server, Capistrano can handle that with no difficulty. Just add the following line to your deployment file:

```
set :gateway, "www.thegatewayserver.com"
```

Capistrano will then route requests to the machines through the gateway server via an SSH tunnel.

Basic Capistrano Tasks

You can run Capistrano tasks from the command line by using the following command:

```
cap <your capistrano command here>
```

Basic Deployment

To prepare the target server for Capistrano deployment, the first command you need to run is this:

```
cap deploy:setup
```

This command just sets up the Capistrano directory structure for your application:

```
<app root>
      |-------releases
      |-------shared
                  |----------system
                  |----------log
                  |----------pids
```

Capistrano places each new deployment of your code into a fresh new subdirectory and places a symbolic link called current in the app root, which is the public face presented to the web server. The shared directories are used for information common to all releases, such as log files.

You need to run the `setup` command each time you add a new server to the deployment. Although there's no particular harm in running the command on a server that has already been set up, you can limit the command to just the new server with a command like this:

```
cap deploy:setup HOST=mynewhost.com
```

After the server has been set up, you can do the initial, or *cold*, deployment as follows:

```
cap deploy:cold
```

The initial deployment is different from most of your other deployments in that your web server is not actually running. A cold deployment will run three subtasks.

First is the update subtask. This task performs a fresh download from your source control system into a new release directory. It then does some file manipulation, including redirecting the system, log, and PIDS (protocol-based intrusion detection system) directories to the shared directory and pointing the current symbolic link to the new directory.

The second subtask is a standard Rails migration, to update the production database to the current data schema. Given the structure of the Subversion repository for Soups Online as created in Chapter 1, and the current state of this deployment file, this step will not complete. That's because you did not actually put a `database.yml` file under Subversion control, opting instead to create a `database.yml.template` file to be managed locally, so the migration task cannot find the production database. This problem is easily solved by adding custom tasks to the `deploy.rb` file, which is the topic of the next section.

The third task is to start the web server. This calls a shell script in your Rails application called `script/spin`, which is expected to have the specific commands needed get the server or servers going. If you are running a Rails application, and using a basic Mongrel or FCGI (FastCGI) server setup, a good place to start is to just defer to the standard Rails `script/process/spawner` script, which will set up multiple server instances (the default is three) on consecutive ports. Otherwise, you'll want to populate the script with whatever matches your installation. If you do not have a `spin` script, Capistrano will perform the update and migration, but will report an error when it attempts to start the server. At that point, you can start the server manually either by making a separate connection to the server, or by using Capistrano to send commands.

When the time comes to perform a second deployment, the command is just this:

```
cap deploy
```

This is a *hot* deployment. It does an update and a server restart, but it does not perform a data migration. The update is the same code update performed for a cold deployment — it checks a fresh copy out of source control, creates a new directory, and performs symbolic link manipulation.

The `restart` command is different from the command performed in the cold deployment. All it does is call the standard Rails `script/process/reaper`. The `reaper` script is meant to run under Unix. It searches for running applications using known process names (basically, anything that can be started by the `spawner` script), and restarts all the processes. If your startup process is nonstandard, you'll likely have to write a custom version of this task as well.

If you need your deployment to perform a data migration, you need to instead run the `migrations` task; run the `update`, `migrate`, and `restart` tasks by hand; or write your own custom task.

Standard Capistrano Tasks

Capistrano comes with about two dozen predefined public tasks, although there are a few other ones defined that are just used internally by other Capistrano tasks. This section gives you a quick look at them all. Many of these tasks expect certain variables to be set, and there's a full discussion of setting Capistrano variables in the next section.

The following table describes the tasks that upload or manipulate the server environment in some way.

Task	Description
deploy	Deploys your project to an already running server, and performs the `update` and `restore` tasks in order.
deploy:cold	Deploys your project to a server that is not currently running, and performs `update`, `migrate`, and `start` in that order.
deploy:migrate	Runs the Rake `migrate` task. By default, this task runs the most recent version of the code in the deployment. If, due to a rollback, the most recent version is not the currently active one, target this task at the currently active version by setting `:migrate_target` to `:current`. You can also specify the path to the Rake in use by setting the `:rake` variable. Specify any environment variables that need to pass to Rake in `:migrate_env`.
deploy:migrations	Similar to `deploy`, but performs the Rake `migrate` task before updating the symbolic link and performing the restart.
deploy:restart	Invoked by `deploy` to restart the servers, but can be invoked separately. This task is typically invoked in a `sudo` shell. If that is not available in your server environment, set the `:use_sudo` variable to `false`.
deploy:rollback	Performs a rollback of the most recent deployment. It deletes the most recent deployment code, repoints the symbolic link at the next most current deployment, and calls the `restart` task.
deploy:rollback_code	Does just the code rollback, without restarting the server.
deploy:simlink	Does just the symbolic link manipulation. Although this is a public-facing task, normally it would only be called via `update` or `rollback`.
deploy:update	The actual update from the source control system with the symbolic link update, but without a server restart. This is transactional — if the update fails, the target system will not be changed.
deploy:update_code	The update from the source control system without the symbolic link manipulation. The default here is to use `checkout` for the `update` command — if you need to change that for some reason, set the `:deploy_via` variable.

The tasks described in the following table enable you to validate or perform maintenance on the server target.

Task	Description
`deploy:check`	Checks for a variety of dependencies, including that the directory structure is in place. You can add your own items to be checked by using the `depend` method in your deployment script. The first argument to `depend` is either `:remote` or `:local`, which specifies on which side of the deployment the requirement is checked. The second argument is `:gem`, `:command`, or `:directory`. For a gem, the third argument is the string name of the gem, and the fourth argument is a string denoting the minimum version (for example, `">=1.0"`). For a command, the third argument is a command name that needs to be executable in the selected context. For a directory, the third command is the path to a directory that must exist.
`deploy:cleanup`	Removes non-current deployment directories from the server. By default, five old deployments are kept. Set the `:keep_releases` variable to a different number to change this behavior. This task also looks at the value of `:use_sudo` to determine whether to use `sudo` in the cleanup.
`deploy:pending`	Returns a list of all commits since the current deployment if your source control system supports this. In other words, this task returns the code changes that have not been deployed to the production environment.
`deploy:pending:diff`	Like `pending`, but returns the actual `diff` instead of just the list of files.
`deploy:setup`	Creates the Capistrano directory structure on any new servers in the deployment.
`deploy:start`	Starts a non-running web server by calling `script/spin` in the Rails deployment directory.
`deploy:stop`	Stops a running web server without restarting it, by calling `script/reaper` in the Rails deployment directory.
`deploy:web:disable`	Places a maintenance `.html` page on all your web servers. If your web server is configured to do so, this page will then be displayed on all requests, allowing for a message such as "This site under construction, be back soon" to be displayed during long shutdowns. Again, for this to work, your web server must be configured (a sample Apache configuration is shown after this table). The template for the page is in `shared/system/maintenance.html`, although you can change it if you want. The default maintenance page looks to environment variables named `REASON` and `UNTIL` to fill slots in the page.
`deploy:web:enable`	Removes the `maintenance.html` page.

From the Mongrel website, here are the commands to enable the maintenance task for an Apache server (these go in your Apache web configuration):

```
RewriteCond %{DOCUMENT_ROOT}/system/maintenance.html -f
RewriteCond %{SCRIPT_FILENAME} !maintenance.html
RewriteRule ^.*$ /system/maintenance.html [L]
```

Finally, there are a few tasks that let you do arbitrary one-off changes to your server (the "Break Glass In Case Of Emergency" commands). These tasks are described in the following table.

Task	Description
`deploy:upload`	Uploads arbitrary files within your Rails distribution to the server. To specify the file list, set the `FILES` environment variable with a comma-delimited list of files and/or directories. If a directory is specified, all files and directories inside it are transferred. System hidden files that start with . are not transferred.
`invoke`	Allows you to run an arbitrary command on specified hosts. The command to execute is placed in the `COMMAND` environment variable. If the command needs to run as root, set the environment variable `SUDO` to any true value.
`shell`	Runs an interactive shell that lets you send commands to all your servers. Essentially, this is like running `invoke` repeatedly within the same session without dropping and reconnecting to each server. Current documentation says this feature is still experimental.

Customizing Capistrano

Although Capistrano is quite powerful out of the box (or should that be out of the gem?), to get it working properly with your installation, you're going to need to customize it. Customization can take the form of changing Capistrano variables, writing your own tasks, and attaching your tasks as dependencies to other tasks.

Setting Variables

Capistrano looks for two different kinds of variables: environment variables and variables local to Capistrano. As far as I can tell, there's no principled way to predict whether a value is expected to be stored in the environment or in Capistrano's own storage, but the two are set differently.

Within your Capistrano file, you configure environment variables by setting elements of the ENV pseudo-hash as follows:

```
ENV["REASON"] = "Server upgrade"
```

However, to set Capistrano variables, you use the Capistrano `set` method. For example:

```
set :svn_user, "kermit_the_frog"
```

The first argument is the symbol name of the variable to be set, and the second argument is the new value. These variables are global to your Capistrano file. Several of the commands listed in the previous section expect specific variables to be set, but you are free to set any arbitrary symbol name you like.

Instead of a value as the second argument, you can pass a block. This is often done in conjunction with the `Capistrano::CLI` module to prompt the user for a value during deployment. Earlier in the chapter, you saw this used to obtain a password. It's worth pointing out that you can use `Capistrano::CLI` `.ui.ask` to give the user a prompt for a non-password masked response.

You can set both kinds of variables from the command line using slightly different syntax. You specify environment variables with a simple `name=value` syntax, like this:

```
cap deploy HOST="server1.soupsonline.com"
```

You can apply the `HOST` environment variable to any Capistrano command to limit the set of servers which will receive the command. If multiple servers are specified, the names are separated by commas.

You set Capistrano local variables using either a `-s` option switch or a `-S` option switch followed by an arbitrary number of `name=value` pairs. The only difference between the two is when the variable value is applied. The lowercase `s` switch sets the value after the Capistrano files have been loaded, which means that any default value set in the script will be overridden by the command-line call — which is the desired behavior most of the time. The preceding tables describe many cases where the command expects a Capistrano value that can be reset at the command line, as in this example:

```
cap deploy -s keep_releases=3 deploy:cleanup
```

The capitol `S` switch sets the variable values before the deployment files are loaded. You would do this only in the case where the loading itself changes based on the variable value. For example, you might have a logging variable where the actual method created depends on the preexisting value for the log level. This feature is used less often than the lowercase `s` option.

Subversion Extraction Strategies

By default, Capistrano retrieves code from the Subversion server using the `checkout` command, just as in a development environment. Although that's fine in a development or staging environment, it does create a whole slew of hidden `.svn` directories and the associated files underneath them. This is something of a security risk because under many web server configurations, the `.svn` files would be publicly readable. That could be annoying, or embarrassing, or catastrophic, and in any case should probably be avoided.

To prevent this on your deployments to production, tell Capistrano to do a Subversion `export` instead of a `checkout` by using the `:checkout` variable, like this:

```
set :checkout, :export
```

This tells Capistrano to do a Subversion export rather than a checkout, giving you the files without the metadata. One downside to this choice is that you will no longer be able to manually update your deployment with a Subversion update (which you might do if you had only updated one or two files). Instead, you'll need to export the entire project again. If you want both the update behavior and the protected `.svn` files, your best bet is to configure your web server to deny requests to filenames containing `.svn`.

Writing New Tasks

Remember when I mentioned that the deployment would fail out of the box because of the `database` `.yml` file? Well, now it's time to write your own Capistrano task to fix the problem. The basic syntax of a Capistrano task is very similar to a Rake task. The main difference is that Capistrano does not define dependencies in the task definition. Here's a first pass at the task — in the simplest case, the template has already been set to the proper values for production, so all you need to do is copy the file to `config/deploy.rb`:

```
require 'FileUtils'

desc "Copy the template to the database.yml"
task :create_database_yml, :roles => :app do
  filename = "#{release_path}/config/database.yml"
  FileUtils.copy "#{filename}.template", filename
  File.chmod 664, filename
end
```

Because I'm deploying to a Unix system, and I don't want to spend hours tracking down mysterious little permission issues, I explicitly set the file mode of the `database.yml` file to world-readable.

This should all look really familiar. The `desc` and `task` methods are similar to Rake in that they set the documentation for a task and then define the task. Capistrano also has a `namespace` method that behaves just like Rake. For a Capistrano task, you can specify the `:roles` for which the task applies. The default available roles are `:app`, `:web`, and `:db`, each of which corresponds to a set of servers dedicated to that particular task. At this point, there's only one server in development, so specifying the role is kind of redundant, but it's a useful habit to have.

As the deployment gets more complex, there may be more than one `database.yml` file in production — for example, there may be multiple database servers to point to. In that case, you may need to generate the file from scratch, like so:

```
desc "generate a new database.yml"
task :generate_database_yml, :roles => :app do
  servers = find_servers :roles => :db
  buffer = {:production => {
    :adapter => 'mysql',
    :database => 'soupsonline_production',
    :host => servers.rand,  ### DON'T DO THIS IN PRODUCTION
    :username => 'user'
    :password => 'pass'
  }
  put YAML::dump(buffer), "#{release_path}/config/database.yml", :mode => 0664
end
```

The YAML module is required for this to work, and on a real system, you'd do something more sensible to map servers to hosts rather than just pick one at random. (In a related note, the special variable `$HOSTNAME` will contain the name of the host being deployed to each time the task is run.)

Another task you're probably going to want to do on your production environment is remove test code. Here's a sample task:

```
desc "remove tests"
task :remove_test_code, :roles => :app do
  run "rm -Rf #{release_path}/test"
  run "rm -Rf #{release_path}/vendor/plugins/arts"
  run "rm -Rf #{release_path}/vendor/plugins/footnotes"
  run "rm -Rf #{release_path}/vendor/plugins/rails_rcov"
  run "rm -Rf #{release_path}/vendor/plugins/rspec"
  run "rm -Rf #{release_path}/vendor/plugins/rspec_on_rails"
end
```

This removes all code in the test directory as well as all test-related plugins. As far as I know, the one that's most necessary to remove is rails_rcov, which reacts badly if rcov is not installed on the server (this is fine, you wouldn't need rcov on a production server,). If you find that you want the tests back because something weird is happening and you want to run diagnostics, it's easy enough to check them back out from Subversion.

This task also shows the Capistrano run method, which runs a shell command on all participating servers. A related method is sudo, which runs the shell command inside a sudo shell on all servers.

Within your task, you can place the following code inside a transaction block:

```
task :scary_task do
  transaction do
    on_rollback { undo_scary_task}
    scary_subtask
  end
end

task :scary_subtask do
  on_rollback {undo_scary_subtask}
end
```

The transaction mechanism is pretty simple. If you are inside a transaction block and the main task or a subtask fails, Capistrano checks for an on_rollback call in the main task and in any subtask that has already run (including the one that failed). The on_rollback blocks are invoked. What you do in the on_rollback block is completely up to you — Capistrano does no checking to ensure that your rollback hook actually returns you to a stable state. However, if things get messed up, you can always call the global deploy:rollback task and return to a known stable state.

Unlike Rake, creating a new task with the same name as an existing task will override the existing task completely. This is particularly useful for tasks like restart, start, and stop, where the defaults may be too simplistic for a full-scale production deployment.

Sadly, though, the Soups OnLine deployment still won't quite work — at least not with the default commands. To get those to work, you need to set dependencies.

Creating Dependencies

Capistrano handles dependencies between tasks differently than Rake. In Capistrano, you explicitly specify that a task needs to be run before or after another specified task using methods that are helpfully called `before` and `after`. In the case of Soups OnLine, there are two tasks: one to remove the tests and another to create the `database.yml` file. These tasks should be run after every update. That means they will be run on both cold and hot deployments. Include the following in your `deploy.rb` file.

```
after 'deploy:update', 'create_database_yml', 'remove_test_code'
```

The first argument to either `before` or `after` is the fully qualified task name of the task being hooked. The name can be a symbol or a string, but remember that a name inside a namespace with a colon is not a valid symbol. The remaining arguments are one or more fully qualified task names that will be tied to the first task, running before it if the `before` method is used and — you guessed it — after the task if the `after` method is used. You can have both `before` and `after` methods on the same task, and they can be specified in more than one command (in other words, this command could have been split into two `after` calls with no problem).

Instead of a list of tasks, the methods can also take a block such as the following:

```
before 'reload' do
  # something
end
```

In this case, the block is invoked in the same place that a defined task would have been.

Both `before` and `after` are general cases of a method called `on`. Here's a sample:

```
on :after, 'deploy:update', 'create_database_yml', 'remove_test_code'
```

The `on` method has a couple of hooks that `before` and `after` don't. It has four additional event descriptions beyond `before` and `after`. There's a pair for `:load` and `:exit`, with `:load` executing before any Capistrano files are loaded, and `:exit` executing after all tasks have completed. There's another pair for `:start` and `:finish`, executing at the beginning and end of a top-level task invoked via a command line. And there's the `:before` and `:after` events mimicking the `before` and `after` methods you've already seen, which fire at the beginning or end of any Capistrano task.

So far, you haven't specified any existing events to be the base for the dependency. By default, `on` `:before` and `on` `:after` work when any task starts or ends (the other events are not based on individual tasks). To specify a task or set of tasks, set the last argument of `on` to either `:only =>` `{"task1", "task2"}` or `:except => {"task1", "task2"}`. As with other places in Rails, the `:only` argument specifies an exclusive list of fully-qualified tasks to hook the dependency on, whereas the `:except` specifies the opposite — a list of tasks not to hook the dependency on, while all other tasks are connected to the dependency.

So, the `after` method you started with translates to this:

```
on :after 'create_database_yml', 'remove_test_code', :only => {'deploy:update'}
```

Multistage Deployment

A common deployment pattern is to have a staging server that mimics the production environment, although usually on a smaller scale. For a while, this was only possible to manage in Capistrano if you manually tracked the roles of the staging server. However, with Capistrano 2.0 and the Capistrano-ext gem, you can manage an arbitrarily multistaged deployment.

First, download the gem as follows:

```
$sudo gem install capistrano-ext
```

Then make sure that the file `capistrano/ext/multistage` is visible to your Capistrano deployment file.

There is some information that will be specific to each stage. Most likely this is just the identity of the various servers in that stage, but there may be some custom task definitions and whatnot (although if there's much difference between staging and production, the staging server is probably not that helpful).

The idea here is that stage-specific settings are stored in separate files. By default, those files are called `config/deploy/staging.rb` and `config/deploy/production.rb`. The deployment file can be as simple as just the server-name section of the original Capistrano file. For example:

```
role :app, "staging.soupsonline.com"
role :web, "staging.soupsonline.com"
role :db,  "staging.soupsonline.com", :primary => true
```

In a multistaged deployment, the main Capistrano file in `deploy.rb` doesn't have any of this server information — all of it is in the stage-specific file.

When invoking a Capistrano task in a multistaged environment, you need to include the name of the stage before the name of the task, as in this example:

```
cap staging deploy:cold
```

Capistrano complains if you don't specify a stage name. If that strikes you as too much of a pain, you can specify a default stage in the main deployment file by setting the `:default_stage` variable like this:

```
set :default_sage, production
```

If a default stage is set, that will be the stage used if no stage name is included in the command.

You can also specify your own stage name by setting the `:stages` variable. For example:

```
set :stages, %w(soup_staging soup_production soup_testing)
```

The custom stage names are used for the names of the files in the `config/deploy` directory, and as the stage names when invoking a Capistrano task.

Mongrel

Mongrel was developed to fill a need. It's a small, Ruby-based web server (with C extensions for speed) that integrates nicely with Rails and other Ruby web frameworks. It's easy to set up for a small site, and you can cluster and scale it to manage high-traffic loads as well. In this section, you'll see how to set up and install a simple Mongrel installation, and how to create a clustered Mongrel setup and integrate it with Capistrano.

Please note that as web deployments need to manage more and more traffic, they become somewhat specialized to the needs of that particular web application. They also increasingly rely on server components that are external to Rails and this book. See the "Resources" section at the end of this chapter for suggestions on managing high-traffic Rails web applications.

Getting Started

Mongrel is distributed as a Ruby gem. Install it as follows:

```
$ sudo gem install mongrel
```

As of this writing, the current version is 1.1.2, and you will be prompted to select a specific version based on whether you are on Windows or something else.

If Mongrel is installed, the script/server command you run during development will auto-detect it and run Mongrel instead of the default WEBrick. However, the preferred way of starting Mongrel as a Rails server, even during development, is by running the following command from your Rails root:

```
mongrel_rails start
```

When the mongrel command has no arguments, it will run in the foreground and can be stopped with a normal Ctrl+C. However, the -d option at the end of the command causes Mongrel to run as a background application (a daemon, hence the -d argument), in which case, you stop it with the following (conveniently named) command:

```
mongrel_rails stop
```

The -d option does not work in Windows systems. You need to also install the Windows service gem win32-service (described shortly) to get background behavior on Windows.

Mongrel takes a few other command-line options, in addition to the standard -h to retrieve a help message and --version to get the running version. These options are described in the following table.

Option	Description
-a --address	The IP address to run under. The default is localhost.
-B --debug	Runs in debug mode.
-C --config	Filename of a configuration file containing further options. If this option is used, Mongrel will load the file and ignore any other command-line options.
-c --chdir	A directory name to change to before starting.
-e --environment	Rails environment: debug, test, or production.
-G --generate	Generates a configuration file based on all the command-line options instead of starting the server. This file can then be loaded via the -C option.
--group	The name of the group to run as.
-l --log	A filename to write log files to. This option does not work in Windows. The default is log/mongrel.log.
-m --mime	The name of a YAML file with additional MIME types to serve beyond the default list. The default set of detected file extensions is .css, .gif, .htm, .html, .jpeg, .jpg, .png, .swf, and .txt, all of which go to the expected MIME type.
-n --num-procs	An integer, which is the number of simultaneous requests that can be queued before users see an access-denied message.
-P --pid	A file to write PID information to. This option does not work under Windows. It defaults to log/mongrel.pid.
-p --port	The port number to bind to. The default is 3000.
--prefix	A URL prefix that would need to be stripped before the URL is processed by Rails.
-r --root	The path to the public document root. It defaults to public.
-S --script	The pathname to a Ruby script that sets options.
-t --timeout	The amount of time to wait before sending a time-out message. The integer value is in hundredths of a second.
--user	The name of the user to run as.

If you are on Windows, you should be aware that a dependent gem called win32-service might not have been loaded by your system when you installed Mongrel. Please install it (choose the mswin32 version when prompted). You'll also want to get the mongrel_service gem, which enables you to run Mongrel as a Windows service.

Creating a Windows service is actually dirt-simple. Run the `mongrel_rails` command, but instead of `mongrel_rails start`, use `mongrel_rails service::install`. You'll need the full complement of command-line options, including the `-c` option to set the starting directory and the `-N` option to set the name of the service:

```
C:\mongrel_rails service::install -N soups_online_production -c d:\apps\
soupsonline -e production
```

To start the service, use this:

```
C:\mongrel_rails service::start -N soups_online_production
```

Newer versions of Mongrel may require the command to look like this:

```
c:\mongrel_rails service::start -e production
```

And stop it with this:

```
C:\mongrel_rails service::stop -N soups_online_production
```

Newer versions might also work with this:

```
C:\mongrel_rails stop
```

Of course, after the service is installed, you can manage it via the Windows Server control panel rather than the command line. You can have multiple services pointing to the same application, which is useful if you want to keep both development and production versions of the service available to run.

The only weird thing that I've seen in this is that stopping a Mongrel service takes a while and, when stopped from the control panel, it kicks up a dialog box claiming that Windows couldn't shut down the service. Windows is incorrect, though, and the service has actually shut down. This may have been fixed in recent versions of Mongrel.

Basic Deployment

Start your deployment with a single Mongrel instance. Then you need to get your Capistrano script playing nicely with Mongrel. You can do this by rewriting the Capistrano deployment `start`, `stop`, and `restart` tasks to invoke Mongrel. The following example assumes that you've created a Mongrel configuration file using the `-G` option described earlier, and placed it in `config/deploy/mongrel.yml`:

```
mongrel_file = "#{release_path}/config/deploy/mongrel.yml"

namespace :deploy do
  task :start, :roles => :app do
    invoke_command "mongrel_rails start -C #{mongrel_file}",
        :via => run_method
  end

  task :stop, :roles => :app do
    invoke_command "mongrel_rails stop -C #{mongrel_file}",
```

```
        :via => run_method
    end

    task :restart, :roles => :app do
      invoke_command "mongrel_rails restart -C #{mongrel_file}",
          :via => run_method
    end
  end
```

Capistrano's `invoke_command` method runs a command in either a regular shell or a `sudo` shell, depending on the value passed to the `:via` key. In this example, the `:via` key is set to `run_method`, which is an internal Capistrano variable that looks for the `:use_sudo` value you set from the command line. If `:use_sudo` is `true`, `run_method` is `sudo`, and the command is run in a `sudo` shell. Otherwise the command is run in a regular shell.

By redefining these tasks, the default Capistrano behavior is overridden, which means that the `script/spin`, `script/spawner`, and `script/reaper` scripts will not be used (although you'll read about `spawner` and `reaper` again in a moment). Alternatively, instead of putting a `:start` command in the deploy file, you could just put the `mongrel_rails` start command in `script/spin`. However, I think I prefer the preceding solution because it keeps all the commands in a single location for easier maintenance.

The problem with a single Mongrel instance is that Mongrel is not multithreaded. This is a deliberate design choice. Rails is not thread-safe, and rather than mess around with the complexity of trying to manage multiple Rails threads, Mongrel chooses to remain simple and quick. The obvious downside of this approach is that a single Mongrel instance can respond to only one request at a time. That would seem like a big problem, but who said that you're limited to a single Mongrel instance?

Clustered Deployment

Currently, best practice for Mongrel deployment is to deploy multiple Mongrel instances, each listening on a different port, and have a separate piece of software balance the loads between the various instances. Although you could set this up by creating different Mongrel configuration files for each instance and starting and stopping them, that is both a pain in the neck and prone to error.

You've already seen one mechanism for creating a cluster of Mongrel items — the `script/spawner` and `script/reaper` standard Rails scripts. Another commonly used mechanism is the Mongrel extension `mongrel-cluster`, which can be downloaded as a Ruby gem like this:

```
gem install mongrel-cluster
```

Basically, `mongrel-cluster` is significantly more configurable than `spawner`, which allows you to set only the port, Rails environment, and number of mongrel instances.

After `mongrel-cluster` is installed, you need to set up the cluster. The general idea is that instead of a single Mongrel instance listening to the web server port, a series of Mongrel instances listen on a set of different ports, while a server capable of load balancing and reverse-proxying listens at the actual web server port and directs requests to the clustered Mongrels in a balanced way.

To configure the cluster, you still use the `mongrel_rails` command, but with a new subcommand called `cluster::configure`. There are other subcommands for `cluster::start`, `cluster::stop`, `cluster::status`, and `cluster::restart`. The configuration options are the same as for a single instance of Mongrel, with one new option: `-N --num_servers`. It provides the number of Mongrel instances to start.

The `-p` option specifies the port number of the first instance, and subsequent instances are given consecutive port numbers. A typical starting value is `8000`.

So, to set up five servers in a typical environment, you might do this:

```
$ mongrel_rails cluster::configure -e production -N 5 -p 8000
```

On a Unix system, it's good practice to set up a separate user account just to run the Mongrels. That is easier in the clustered environment because the Mongrels are no longer on port 80, and therefore no longer need special access to grab their ports.

This command places a configuration file in `config/mongrel_cluster.yml` under your Rails root. You can then go in and edit the YAML file to make configuration changes.

With the configuration file set up, you can start and stop the cluster. The `mongrel-cluster` gem will find the configuration file in the default location, or you can use the `-C` option to specify a different location. While the cluster is running, you can verify it by hitting any of the ports specified in the configuration — in this case, 8000, 8001, 8002, 8003, and 8004.

Capistrano and Clusters

The `mongrel_cluster` gem comes with its own set of Capistrano tasks to simplify deployment of a Mongrel cluster. To make them available to your deployment, you need the following line in `deploy.rb`:

```
require 'mongrel_cluster/recipes'
```

As I write this, the Mongrel cluster tasks have not yet been updated to Capistrano 2.0. However, I expect that to be completed by the time you read this, so I'm writing this as though the cluster tasks are compatible.

After you load this file, the `deploy:start`, `deploy:stop`, and `deploy:restart` default tasks will have been overridden to call the appropriate Mongrel cluster commands. These tasks redirect to tasks called `deploy:start_mongrel_cluster`, `deploy:stop_mongrel_cluster`, and `deploy:restart_mongrel_cluster`. There is also a `deploy:status_mongrel_cluster` task that runs the `status` command, and a `deploy:configure_mongrel_cluster` task that creates a `mongrel_cluster.yml` file based on a set of Capistrano variables, which are also loaded as part of the cluster recipe.

The defined variables match the Mongrel command-line options mostly one-for-one, but you can set them from within your own Capistrano script or from your Capistrano command line. The variables are listed in the following table, with some comments where it's not completely clear what the variable does.

Variable	Comment
:mongrel_address	The IP address to listen at.
:mongrel_clean	If true, Mongrel runs with the --clean option.
:mongrel_conf	Location of the cluster YAML file.
:mongrel_config_script	Location of the script to set values.
:mongrel_environment	
:mongrel_group	
:mongrel_log_file	
:mongrel_pid_file	
:mongrel_port	
:mongrel_prefix	
:mongrel_rails	The command to start Mongrel. The default is mongrel_rails.
:mongrel_servers	The number of Mongrel instances to start.
:mongrel_user	

This should enable you to manage a cluster of Mongrel installations flexibly through Capistrano.

Load Balancing

At this point, you have a number of Mongrel instances running on nonstandard ports. Unfortunately, it's not practical to politely request that the Internet as a whole hit your website at a random port between 8000 and 8004. What you need is some kind of tool that sits on port 80 and redirects requests to the Mongrel instances, balancing traffic between them.

There are a few different solutions to this problem, which can be divided into two categories. On the one hand, there are some tools that are simply load-balancing proxies, such as Pen and Pound. These tools are relatively small and simple to configure. However, they don't bring a whole lot to the table beyond simply balancing load. On the other hand, you have full-fledged web servers that also happen to be load-balancing proxies. The leading contenders in the Rails world are Apache (version 2.2 and up) and Nginx. Nginx has been getting some attention recently as a static server, but there isn't a whole lot of web-wide production experience to fall back on with that server yet. These tools are much larger and much more complex to set up (especially Apache), but they are far more powerful and flexible. In particular, the web server can be configured to serve static content such as images, JavaScript files, and static HTML. This will further lower the load on the Mongrel servers and speed the overall throughput of the system.

How Many Mongrels?

The obvious question about Mongrel clustering is how many Mongrel instances should you run? Perhaps unsurprisingly, the short answer is "it depends." The medium-size answer is: roughly 8–12 per CPU, depending on available RAM, program usage, the phase of the moon, and sunspot activity — in other words, it's a bit more art than science at this point.

The "References" section of this chapter has a link to a detailed description of how Zed Shaw, developer of Mongrel, arrived at the 8–12 range. It's the web analog of driving heavier and heavier trucks over a bridge to determine its maximum load. The steps are as follows:

1. Use the `httperf` command, or another benchmarking tool to get a baseline speed for a typical static page in your system under no-load, best-case conditions and also for a typical Rails page under best conditions.

2. Verify the reported response rate, by running `httperf` at that rate.

3. Add another Mongrel instance.

4. Check the new rate.

Eventually, adding another instance will not improve the response time.

Which load-balancing tool should you use? I'm personally a big fan of keeping it simple where possible, and I'm not so much a fan of messing around with Apache configuration files, so I'd be inclined to try the Pen solution, particularly if I had a good idea what the upper boundary of my traffic was likely to be. Pen's support for SSL is described as "experimental," so that could be a deal-breaker. (Pound does handle SSL.)

Still, there's no denying the power of Apache, and using it to serve static content can be a big performance boost. If you or somebody on your team is an Apache expert or is willing to pretend to be one, this is the way to go for large-traffic sites.

Pen can be downloaded from `http://siag.nu/pen`, although if you're on Linux, it might be available through your system's package manager. If you download it from source, it has a pretty typical `configure–make–make install` build sequence.

After Pen is compiled, you run it with the following command:

```
pen 3000 localhost:8000 localhost:8001 localhost:8002 localhost:8003 localhost:8004
```

That puts your five-instance Mongrel cluster back on port 3000, where it would have been originally. You can use an `-H` command option before the initial port to add the `X-Forwarded-For` header and store the original client IP there — however, you should not do this if Pen is itself behind an Apache server of some kind.

Now, hitting the server at port 3000 should work, with Pen passing the request off to a Mongrel. Pen attempts to have clients that hit the server multiple times in a short period go to the same client again, or you can set it to use a straight round-robin mechanism with the -r switch.

To make this work as part of your regular deployment, you'll need to augment your Mongrel-cluster Capistrano start tasks to also start Pen using the preceding command.

Mongrel, Apache, and You

Apache is the 8,000-pound gorilla of web servers. As of Apache 2.2, it includes a module for load balancing called mod_proxy_balancer. When you feel like you are at the point where you need Apache to serve your static content, then you'll also want it to handle the Mongrel load balancing. Much of this discussion is based on the best practice for Apache information at the Mongrel website (http://mongrel.rubyforge.org/docs/apache.html) — check there for any recent updates.

Apache can be downloaded from www.apache.org, and there are installers for all platforms.

Here are some sample pieces of Apache configuration that manage various features that are desirable in a Rails configuration. All of these pieces should be placed inside a virtual host configuration in your .conf file:

```
<VirtualHost *:80>
  # put stuff here
</VirtualHost>
```

The following configuration option causes Apache to serve all the content in the /public directory:

```
<Directory "/u/apps/soupsonline/current/public">
  Options FollowSymLinks
  AllowOverride None
  Order allow,deny
  Allow from all
</Directory>
```

Remember, Capistrano always maintains a symbolic link between /current and the most recent deployment.

The following lines cause Apache to serve cached files, and redirect other requests to the Mongrel cluster:

```
RewriteRule ^/$ /index.html [QSA]
RewriteRule ^([^.]+)$ $1.html [QSA]
RewriteCond %{DOCUMENT_ROOT}/%{REQUEST_FILENAME} !-f
RewriteRule ^/(.*)$ balancer://mongrel_cluster%{REQUEST_URI} [P,QSA,L]
```

Caching is discussed in more detail in the next chapter.

The balancer referenced in the last line of the preceding code needs to be defined in a separate part of the configuration, outside the virtual host, as follows:

```
<Proxy balancer://mongrel_cluster>
  BalancerMember http://localhost:8000
  BalancerMember http://localhost:8001
  BalancerMember http://localhost:8002
  BalancerMember http://localhost:8003
  BalancerMember http://localhost:8004
</Proxy>
```

Each member is the IP address and port of one of the Mongrel instances that needs to be balanced. If and when you change the server count or port numbers, you need to update this part of the configuration file and restart Apache. (The "References" section has a link to some sample Capistrano tasks to manage an Apache server.)

This only scratches the surface of Apache configuration options. The Mongrel website has some complete sample configurations under different circumstances that you should probably take a look at.

References

Capistrano's home page is www.capify.org. The official documentation is a little light at the moment, but there's a push on to fix that. A wiki with Capistrano information is available at http://capify .stikipad.com/wiki. Jamis Buck, main developer of Capistrano, introduces the multistage features at http://weblog.jamisbuck.org/2007/7/23/capistrano-multistage.

A good presentation on Rails deployment and performance issues is "Scaling a Rails Application from the Bottom Up," by Jason Hoffman, founder of Joyent. Slides are available at http://jxh.bingodisk .com/bingo/public/presentations/JHoffmanRailsConf-Berlin-Sept2007.pdf.

If Mongrel and Capistrano 2.0 haven't worked out their issues by the time you read this, try http://thinedgeofthewedge.blogspot.com/2007/08/mongrel-and-capistrano-20.html for details on reconciling them. Zed Shaw's post mentioned in the "How Many Mongrels?" sidebar in this chapter is available at http://mongrel.rubyforge.org/docs/how_many_mongrels.html.

For more information about load balancers, see http://blog.codahale.com/2006/11/07/pound-vs-pen-because-you-need-a-load-balancing-proxy and http://httpd.apache.org/docs/2.2/mod/mod_proxy_balancer.html.

The book *Deploying Rails Applications: A Step-By-Step Guide* by Ezra Zygmuntowicz and Bruce Tate, from Pragmatic Books, is not out as I write this, but it promises to be a thorough look at the subject.

Summary

Deployment can be the scariest time in the lifecycle of your Rails application. Too often you are forced to be manual when you most need to be automatic. Capistrano is the predominant Rails tool for supporting automated and repeatable deployment.

Capistrano assumes certain features of your deployment. It expects to be able to communicate with the server via SSH, specifically using public keys. To get the most use out of Capistrano, use source control, preferably Subversion.

Capistrano enables you to split your servers into different roles and allows different tasks to be applied to all servers in the specified roles. There are several different tasks predefined by Capistrano to support the most common deployment and rollback tasks. In most cases, you'll need to customize somewhat to make sure that the scripts match your web server setup.

If those tasks are not enough, you can write your own tasks using a Ruby syntax that is very similar to Rake, although dependencies among tasks are managed differently. Capistrano can also handle the common case where there is a staging server that mimics the production environment.

Mongrel is the current best-of-breed Ruby web server for serving Rails applications. It can easily be integrated with Capistrano. However, Mongrel is single-threaded, so in production environments it is run in a cluster. Load balancing is handled by a proxy, of which Pen is a simple example and Apache is a more complex example. Apache can also be configured to serve the static content while passing dynamic content to the Mongrel cluster.

13

Performance

If you are lucky, when your web application goes out into the world, it will be used. Users are lovely people in general, but they tend to have some specific expectations about the responsiveness of a web application — expectations that have been honed from years of using Google. Of course, Google has spent millions of dollars on server farms the size of football fields while you have two Linux boxes on a rack in a back room somewhere.

This chapter tackles strategies for keeping your web application's performance up to speed. You'll look at some mechanisms for identifying under-performing code, and then examine common bottlenecks and performance issues in Rails applications.

Measurement

People have been writing software for over a half century now, and the following three facts about performance have proven true in nearly every circumstance:

❑　It's almost always possible to buy speed at the expense of storage space.

❑　People are actually quite bad at predicting which parts of a computer program are the biggest performance problems.

❑　Optimizing software too aggressively or too early is usually bad for the quality of your software.

Luckily there are ways to work around these issues. The basic approach is to start gathering data about the performance of your application very early in the process, to gain some background data for guidance when the time comes to fix the issues. This section discusses some tools for gathering that data; the next section covers how and when to mitigate some of the problems you discover.

Railsbench

In general, there are two steps to identifying bottlenecks in your Rails application:

1. Determine which page hits are slow.

2. Determine what part of the calculation of the page is causing the problem.

Railsbench is a solution to the first problem. I should clarify here that the performance issue I'm referring to at this point is the server-side time spent turning the HTTP request into an HTML response, not the bandwidth time spent getting the HTML and images down to the browser. This doesn't mean that the bandwidth issues are unimportant (the user doesn't care where the slowdown is), but they are somewhat easier to diagnose and fix.

> *The Firebug extension for Firefox, which you should be using for many diagnostic purposes, includes a nice graphical representation of the time it takes to load your page, broken down by component.*

Railsbench's main purpose in life is to generate traffic to your application and time how long it takes to respond. Although it started its life as a simple Ruby script, Railsbench has gotten more and more powerful over its lifetime, and it's now distributed as a Ruby gem. Install the `railsbench` gem as follows:

```
sudo gem install railsbench
```

Using Railsbench, you can set up multiple test sequences that are run multiple times to determine a meaningful average time for each page in the sequence. The data is stored in a text format, and multiple data runs can easily be aggregated into a graph. Let's see how it's done.

Setting Up Railsbench

Getting Railsbench to work is (or at least can be) somewhat on the nontrivial side, although it's possible that some of these quirks will get ironed out by the time you read this.

To start getting Railsbench up and running with your application, run the following command from the root directory of your Rails application:

```
railsbench install
```

The `railsbench` command is installed by the gem, and is the front-end to almost all of the subcommands offered by the Railsbench gem. (It's possible to maneuver things so that you can access the internal scripts directly, but there's not really much reason to unless you have existing scripts that reference the other names.)

The `install` command does four things. First, it creates a file `config/benchmarks.rb`. This is a setup file for the benchmark object. It contains one active line and some commented-out suggestions as shown in the following code (I took the text comments out of the file for clarity):

```
RAILS_BENCHMARKER = RailsBenchmark.new

# RAILS_BENCHMARKER = RailsBenchmarkWithActiveRecordStore.new
```

```
# RAILS_BENCHMARKER.relative_url_root = '/blog'

# require 'user'
# RAILS_BENCHMARKER.session_data = {'account' => User.find_first("name='stefan'")}
```

The actual active line here creates a `RailsBenchmark` object, which is what drives the benchmarking test. The first commented-out line should be used if you're storing sessions using ActiveRecordStore and you want those sessions to be automatically deleted from the database at the end of the testing. The comment in the actual file notes that you really don't want to do this on your actual production data — you'll lose all your sessions.

The second commented line is used if the URLs, as entered by the user, require a prefix that is not part of your Rails routing (in other words, the Rails application is not the top level of the server). This is actually optional, but recommended — particularly if your application is page caching. Just adjust the right side of the variable assignment to match the application root in your system.

The last commented lines allow you to set arbitrary data in the session for all requests generated by Railsbench. As you'll see in a moment, you can also set session data specifically for individual server requests.

The second file created by the installation is `config/benchmarks.yml`. This file contains the list of requests the benchmarking test is supposed to hit. The default is just to target the application's main index, as shown here:

```
default:
    uri: /
```

The data format here is somewhat similar to that for fixtures. Each target has an abritrary name and a series of key/value pairs below it, starting with a URI, which is relative to your application root. The URI attribute is required, and there are also optional attributes, described in the following table.

Attribute	Description
method	The HTTP method. The default is get, but post is also supported.
new_session	The default Railsbench session behavior is to create a single session and continually pass it to each request for each target. If new_session is true, then that test session is not passed to any requests in that target, causing a new session to be created each time.
post_data	A string of the form key=value used to store data for a post. The format of this string is identical to a get query string, but Railsbench looks to this value for post requests.
query_string	The query string section of the request for this target. This information can also be placed in the URI attribute. It is only applicable for get requests.
session_data	Data that should be stored in the session for all requests to this target.

session_data expects a hash, formatted as a subelement in the YAML file like this:

```
with_session:
  url: restaurants/new
  session_data:
    user_id: 1
    last_viewed_recipe: 3
```

You can also create targets that are aggregations of other targets, like so:

```
full_test:
  default, with_session, recipe_test, ingredient_test
```

Also, when this file is loaded by Railsbench, it's interpreted as an ERB file. Therefore, you can use the ERB syntax to change values in the file dynamically.

The third creation of the installer script is to add an entry to the database.yml file (remember to copy it over to the template file if that file is stored in source control). The new entry is called benchmarking, and by default it mimics your development database as follows:

```
benchmarking:
  encoding: utf8
  socket: /tmp/mysql.sock
  username: root
  adapter: mysql
  password:
  database: soupsonline_development
```

In practice, I suspect that pointing at production is just as common, so adjust the file as needed.

The fourth element created by Railsbench is a new environment, config/environments/benchmarking.rb. This environment file is run when you set up a benchmarking test. By default, Railsbench copies your existing production environment file. You'll need to adjust it to suit your needs.

> As I write this, Railsbench does not support the cookie method of storing session data, which is the new default mechanism in Rails 2.0. You'll need to change the session storage method to something else. See the "Managing Sessions" section later in this chapter for options. If you have been playing along so far, you probably have cookie storage, and Railsbench will not work until you change the storage method.

Using Railsbench

You can add a whole bunch of benchmark targets to your application by running the following command:

```
railsbench generate_benchmarks
```

This will generate a new target for each method in each controller, as well as an aggregate method for each controller containing all the methods. Needless to say, this is probably overkill, although it's likely to be easier to prune the larger file than to add up the smaller files.

What should you use in your benchmark suite? A good representative sample of the application is fine. Definitely include the main index page. Include some of the detail pages, possibly under slightly different data patterns. Include a form submission. Include any controller that you think is doing particularly tricky things, or any page that feels particularly slow during development. Don't forget to include Ajax calls if you can. Railsbench doesn't support XHR (XMLHttpRequest) directly, but `link_to_remote` and `form_for_remote` calls that have controller methods that can be mimicked with a GET request should be included.

Here's the starting point for Soups OnLine benchmarking:

```
recipes:
  uri: /recipes

one_recipe:
  uri: /recipes/1

categories:
  uri: /category

one_categeory:
  uri: /category/grandma

search:
  uri: /category/search
  method: post
  post_data: search=chicken

default:
  recipes, one_recipe, categories, one_categeory, search
```

That's the index page for recipes, a detail page for a single recipe, the index page for category tags, a single page category display (which is accessed via `link_to_remote` in the application), and a sample search. That's a good cross-section of the system as it currently stands, including some of the graphics as well as a couple of page hits that do some processing and might strain the database.

You probably don't want to do this benchmarking on your production server, at least not while it's live, but you do want to do it on a staging server that's as close to the production hardware setup as you can get. This isn't a load test, so you don't have to worry about clustering or anything like that for the benchmark tests — a new request won't be spawned until the old one has completed. You also want the size and makeup of the benchmarking database to be similar to the production server. If the production server is already running, then a duplicate of that data would be helpful. Otherwise, you might want to create enough fake data to strain the database a little bit.

If you are planning to compare multiple benchmarks over a span of time, you'll get more meaningful comparisons if the database is constant. Obviously, this isn't going to be completely possible during development because the database schema is likely to change over time, but the more similar the data store can stay, the more useful your benchmarks will be.

The simplest way to run Railsbench is with the `perf_run` command, as shown in this example:

```
$ railsbench perf_run 100
```

This command will run the `default` benchmark target in the `benchmarks.yml` file. It will hit that target 100 times in a run, and it will make three separate runs. If the target in the YAML file is a compound target, then each individual target will get its own 100 hits per run.

Results are reported in a couple of ways. The raw data from each run is placed in a file, which by default is `~/perf_run<benchmark>.txt`. That file contains system and user time for each separate benchmark target. Here's an example of what that file looks like:

```
ruby /usr/local/lib/ruby/gems/1.8/gems/railsbench-0.9.2/script/perf_bench 100
                          user      system      total        real
loading environment     1.580000   0.610000   2.190000 (  5.379068)
recipes                 0.730000   0.130000   0.860000 (  1.018847)
one_recipe              0.740000   0.130000   0.870000 (  1.024061)
categories              0.720000   0.130000   0.850000 (  1.008967)
one_categeory           0.740000   0.130000   0.870000 (  1.014466)
search                  0.680000   0.070000   0.750000 (  0.888731)
                          user      system      total        real
loading environment     1.150000   0.390000   1.540000 (  1.650157)
recipes                 0.740000   0.140000   0.880000 (  1.059861)
one_recipe              0.740000   0.140000   0.880000 (  1.068661)
categories              0.720000   0.130000   0.850000 (  1.053160)
one_categeory           0.690000   0.130000   0.820000 (  0.988471)
search                  0.680000   0.060000   0.740000 (  0.908554)
                          user      system      total        real
loading environment     1.200000   0.410000   1.610000 (  1.760356)
recipes                 0.730000   0.130000   0.860000 (  1.081788)
one_recipe              0.730000   0.140000   0.870000 (  1.056404)
categories              0.720000   0.130000   0.850000 (  1.028765)
one_categeory           0.730000   0.140000   0.870000 (  1.488667)
search                  0.690000   0.060000   0.750000 (  0.916095)
```

The categories here are as follows:

❑ `user`: The amount of chip clock time devoted to Rails activity.

❑ `system`: The amount of chip clock time taken by operating system activities.

❑ `total`: Adds the `user` and `system` values. The totals are the sum of all 100 requests.

❑ `real`: The actual amount of calendar time spent serving the request, regardless of whether the server was actually processing the request or doing some other simultaneous task.

If you find this raw data a little opaque, Railsbench also prints out a slightly processed version of the data when a run is complete. This information can always be regenerated with the following command:

```
railsbench perf_times <filename>
```

The output aggregates the raw data somewhat, as shown here:

```
perf data file: /Users/noel/perf_run.default.txt
    requests=100, options=

loading environment                 2.92986

page request                  total   stddev%      r/s   ms/r
recipes                     1.05350    3.0327    94.92  10.53
one_recipe                  1.04971    2.1950    95.26  10.50
categories                  1.03030    2.1485    97.06  10.30
one_categeory               1.16387   24.1938    85.92  11.64
search                      0.90446    1.5627   110.56   9.04

all requests                5.20183    6.2717    96.12  10.40
```

Each benchmark target gets its own row of data. The `total` in this report is somewhat misleading — it's the average from all runs of the column listed in the raw data as `real`. The `stddev%` is the standard deviation of the three runs expressed as a percentage of the average. You'll notice that the `categories` target seems to be extremely variable for some reason, which is possibly just a server hiccup. The third column, `r/s`, is the number of requests of that target the system would be able to process in one second based on the raw data. The `ms/r` column is the inverse — the average number of milliseconds needed to process a single request.

Want to do something a little bit different? Railsbench has options aplenty. A few of them are specified as environment variables, which means you might want to write a little wrapper script that sets them via the Ruby `ENV` variable. The variable `RAILS_PERF_DATA` sets the directory in which to save the performance files — the default is the user home directory. If you want to have more or less than three runs per test, change the environment variable `RAILS_PERF_RUNS`.

The command line for `railsbench perf_runs` takes an optional second argument, which is a string. The string can contain anything you want, but if it contains a substring of the form `-bm=target`, then the specified target is run from the `benchmarks.yml` file. The entire string is kept as the Ruby variable `ARGV[1]`, and you can access it in your benchmark environment file, where you would adjust the properties of the environment based on the string. For instance, you could turn logging on or off based on the existence of a `-loglevel` option. This is especially useful when you're trying to determine the performance implications of a particular feature or setting (different session stores, perhaps).

In fact, it's so useful, that Railsbench offers the following shortcut for it:

```
$railsbench perf_diff 100 "-bm=recipes" "-loglevel=0" "-loglevel=1"
```

This will trigger two `perf_run` calls: one with the option string `-bm=recipes -logloglevel=0`, and one with the string `-bm=recipes -loglevel=1`. The output is sent to files named `perf_run1` and `perf_run2`.

There seems to be a name crash if you use an option named `log` *in* `perf_diff` — *Railsbench appears to treat that as a special case.*

An optional third argument after the string is a tag that will be appended to the output filename before the extension. For perf_diff, you can include two tags: the first tag goes with the first run, and the second tag goes with the second run.

Railsbench also allows you to create graphs that aggregate the results of a number of raw files. For this to work, you need to install Gruff as a gem with gem install gruff (in Chapter 11, you installed Gruff as a plugin instead). Then run this command:

```
$ railsbench perf_plot ~/perf_run.default.txt ~/perf_run.default_old.txt
```

The results are saved to graph.png. Figure 13-1 shows a sample graph produced with the gruff gem.

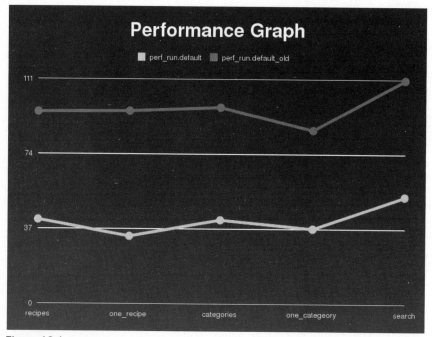

Figure 13-1

For this to work best, each file needs to have run against the same benchmark targets. The graph is the amount of requests per second, with each file getting its own series. The perf_plot script takes a number of command-line options that let you modify the format. I'll just mention that -bar makes the graph into a bar graph, which you might consider to be a better representation of the noncontinuous data. Similar commands called perf_html and perf_table give other reader-friendly interpretations of the benchmark data.

Railsbench has several other handy commands, such as perf_run_gc and perf_times_gc, which produce information about garbage collection. (You need to run a patch against Ruby to enable the data tracking for these.)

Performance Profiling

Railsbench is a great tool for letting you know what pages are slow from top to bottom. However, it doesn't tell you what part of the page is causing the slowdown. In this section, I'll show you three ways of getting some of that partial information out of Rails.

Logs — The Quick Way

The simplest way to get information on partial performance of your Rails application is simply by scanning your log files. The default log status for Mongrel under development prints the time spent processing each request, broken down into rendering and SQL time, and further broken down into the time and SQL request text for each SQL request. Figure 13-2 shows an example from my terminal for the recipe index page of Soups OnLine.

```
Processing RecipesController#index (for 127.0.0.1 at 2007-10-07 21:28:18) [GET]
  Session ID: e95eacd6959587cee7eed4cf276f3522
  Parameters: {"action"=>"index", "controller"=>"recipes"}
  User Columns (0.002614)   SHOW FIELDS FROM users
  User Load (0.001683)    SELECT * FROM users WHERE (users.`id` IS NULL) LIMIT 1
Cookie set: token=; path=/; expires=Thu, 01 Jan 1970 00:00:00 GMT
Asked for a remote server ? nil, ENV["FERRET_USE_LOCAL_INDEX"] is nil, looks like we are not the server
Will use local index.
using index in /Users/noel/Documents/rails_book/soupsonline/index/development/recipe
default field list: [:directions, :ingredient_string, :description, :title, :tag_list]
  Recipe Load (0.000313)   SELECT * FROM recipes ORDER BY created_at DESC LIMIT 100
Rendering template within layouts/recipes
Rendering recipes/index
  Recipe Columns (0.003260)    SHOW FIELDS FROM recipes
  SoupImage Columns (0.003127)   SHOW FIELDS FROM soup_images
  SoupImage Load (0.000508)    SELECT * FROM soup_images WHERE (soup_images.`id` = 5)
  SoupImage Load (0.000292)    SELECT * FROM soup_images WHERE (soup_images.`id` = 3)
  SoupImage Load (0.000225)    SELECT * FROM soup_images WHERE (soup_images.`id` = 1)
Rendered /users/_login (0.01328)
Rendered /shared/_navigation_sidebar (0.01006)
Completed in 0.16587 (6 reqs/sec) | Rendering: 0.04009 (24%) | DB: 0.01202 (7%) | 200 OK [http://localhost/re
cipes]
```

Figure 13-2

There's a lot of information here. In order:

- ❑ The controller method being used, and the host, date, time, and HTTP verb
- ❑ The session ID
- ❑ The `params` hash
- ❑ The two database calls that are used to determine the current user ID, and the amount of time the calls take
- ❑ The fact that a cookie was set, and that Ferret is using a local index

❑ The database request to get the actual recipes to display, and then the individual database requests to get the image data

❑ The name of all the views and partial views rendered

❑ The time it took to serve the request, and the percentage of that time spent rendering output, and spent in the database

❑ The final response code with the request URL

That's a boatload of information. I can't stress enough that you should be checking this log regularly to get a sense of what Rails is actually doing. On this page, the performance is acceptable at this point, but it's worth noting that the three SQL requests to `soup_images` is a potential bottleneck because the three calls could possibly be made either at one time or as a join when the recipes are loaded. The next section discusses ways to mitigate the problem when it becomes a performance issue.

This information is so easily accessible and so useful that you should be monitoring it from day one for the location of potential issues even if you have no intention of doing anything about performance issues yet. You should be noting some potential problem areas, though, so you won't forget where to look when the time comes to start worrying about speed.

If you want even more information in your logs, try the query_trace plugin by Nathanial Talbot. You can access this plugin as follows:

```
$ ruby script/plugin install http://terralien.com/svn/projects/plugins/query_trace/
```

This plugin does one thing, and one thing only. It adds a stack trace to your log for every SQL statement, identifying exactly where in your code the statement was triggered. Depending on the desperation of your performance testing, this will fall somewhere between quite helpful and indispensable. Although its initial purpose is to track down long-running SQL queries, it's also quite useful for just about any SQL-related debugging. (Also see `http://pivots.pivotallabs.com/users/alex/blog/articles/300-rake-query-trace` for a handy Rake task to turn query_trace on and off.)

Profiling Method Timings with ruby-prof

The log file information is extremely helpful, and very detailed when it comes to tracking down slow SQL queries. However, even though database issues are frequently the source of Rails performance issues, a slow query is far from the only way Rails can slow down. A helper method might be taking a long time to build up an output string, or a model might be doing something weird in verifying or creating data. The log files, verbose though they may be, are simply not helpful in that particular case.

The next two methods use a profiler to break down a Rails request or command into its component method calls, yielding a breakdown of which method in the call tree is using up the lion's share of the time and resources. Ruby ships with a default profiler module; however, the examples in this section will use a separate gem called `ruby-prof`. Install this gem as follows:

```
$ gem install ruby-prof
```

I chose `ruby-prof` over the standard profiler because it has a slightly larger feature set, has multiple output formats, places a somewhat smaller performance overhead on the running code than the standard controller, and has a nice Rails integration plugin.

Using the Rails Profile Script

The quickest way to get some Rails code profiled is to run `script/profiler`. A sample call looks something like this:

```
$ script/performance/profiler "Recipe.new().ingredient_string = ↵
'2 cups carrots, chopped'" 100
```

The arguments to the script are a string of code to execute, and the number of times to execute it. Rails will then run the line of code via `ruby-prof` (the default profiler will be used if `ruby-prof` is not available). Since the output tends to be pretty long, you may want to redirect it to a file. The normal output goes to STDERR, so if you are on a Unix or Unix-like system, you'll need to do this via the STDERR redirect symbol 2>, as follows:

```
$ script/performance/profiler "code to run" 100 2> profile_output.txt
```

As I write this, Rails 2.0 has not quite caught up to the current version of `rails-prof`. *For this script to work, the line of code in* `/vendor/rails/railties/lib/commands/performance/` `profiler.rb` *that reads* `RubyProf.clock_mode = RubyProf::WALL_TIME` *needs to be changed to* `RubyProf.measure_mode = RubyProf::WALL_TIME`. *A patch is available for this, and it will hopefully have been incorporated by the time you read this.*

The output looks like this:

```
Using the ruby-prof extension.
Thread ID: 202500
Total: 3.835309

 %self     total     self      wait     child     calls  name
 41.46      1.59      1.59      0.00      0.00       200
Ferret::Index::IndexWriter#commit (ruby_runtime:0}
 10.04      0.39      0.38      0.00      0.00       807  Mysql#query (ruby_runtime:0}
  5.13      0.20      0.20      0.00      0.00       100
Ferret::Index::IndexWriter#delete (ruby_runtime:0}
  1.90      0.07      0.07      0.00      0.00       306  <Class::Dir>#[]
(ruby_runtime:0}
  1.64      0.28      0.06      0.00      0.21         3  Kernel#gem_original_require
(ruby_runtime:0}
  1.61      0.51      0.06      0.00      0.45       807  <Module::Benchmark>#realtime
(/usr/local/lib/ruby/1.8/benchmark.rb:306}
  1.49      0.06      0.06      0.00      0.00       100
Ferret::Index::IndexWriter#add_document (ruby_runtime:0}
  1.30      0.05      0.05      0.00      0.00       205  Module#module_eval
(ruby_runtime:0}
  1.01      0.07      0.04      0.00      0.04      4200
ActiveRecord::ConnectionAdapters::Quoting#quote
(/Users/noel/Documents/rails_book/soupsonline/vendor/rails/activerecord/lib/active_
record/connection_adapters/abstract/quoting.rb:6}
  0.93      0.67      0.04      0.00      0.64       800  Kernel#eval (ruby_runtime:0}
  0.88      0.04      0.03      0.00      0.01     45915  Hash#[] (ruby_runtime:0}
  0.69      0.03      0.03      0.00      0.00      1800  Kernel#clone (ruby_runtime:0}
  0.68      0.04      0.03      0.00      0.02      8301
```

(continued)

(continued)

```
ActiveRecord::Base#column_for_attribute
(/Users/noel/Documents/rails_book/soupsonline/vendor/rails/activerecord/lib/active_
record/base.rb:1907}
    0.66      3.21      0.03      0.00      3.18      1426  Array#each (ruby_runtime:0}
    0.63      0.18      0.02      0.00      0.15       843  Hash#each (ruby_runtime:0}
    0.56      0.07      0.02      0.00      0.05      4200
ActiveRecord::AttributeMethods#read_attribute
(/Users/noel/Documents/rails_book/soupsonline/vendor/rails/activerecord/lib/active_
record/attribute_methods.rb:190}
    0.55      0.03      0.02      0.00      0.01        13  Kernel#gem_original_require-4
(ruby_runtime:0}
    0.54      0.02      0.02      0.00      0.00      1612  IO#write (ruby_runtime:0}
    0.52      0.79      0.02      0.00      0.77      1628  Array#each-1 (ruby_runtime:0}
    0.51      0.45      0.02      0.00      0.43       807  <Module::Benchmark>#measure
(/usr/local/lib/ruby/1.8/benchmark.rb:291}
```

What the profiler does, in general, is note every single method call made by Ruby, and track how long it takes. When the call is done, the profiler rolls all that information up into the simple, easy-to-interpret chart shown here. Okay, that's at least mild sarcasm. One of the problems with using profilers is that, even with all the timing data, it's still not always clear how best to interpret the data. (There's a great little story, probably apocryphal, about a software team that noticed that half of the program's time was in one particular loop, so they put all their efforts into optimizing the heck out of it. But that effort was of very little practical benefit because it was the program's idle loop, and therefore the user saw no actual change.)

The chart you see has six columns of data for each method call. The first column (% self) is the percentage of time actually spent in that method. I reproduced here all 20 method calls that have over 0.05 percent of the call time. There are something like 1,000 methods in the profile overall. Column two, total, is the total amount of clock time spent in that method and all of the methods called by that method. Column three, self, is the amount of time actually spent in the method. The column marked wait is any time spent not doing anything during the method call, and the column marked child is the time actually spent in child methods. So self, wait, and child should add up to total. The final numeric column, call, is the number of times that method is called. Remember, the totals are for the aggregate number of runs, which are 100 in this case. The final column is the method name itself.

You are looking for outliers in the data, and one presents itself immediately: Ferret. Between the indexing and deleting, nearly half of the time this code spent running was spent doing Ferret things. I would not have predicted that in advance, which I suppose is why we actually run these tests. It also seems like this code spends a lot of time running MySQL queries, and then a full 45 percent of the code time is spent on other items, none of which seem like they are using enough resources to be good candidates for optimization at this point (although it does seem like the code spends a lot of time running through arrays).

The fact that 10.04 percent of the time is spent on MySQL queries is potentially interesting, although from this presentation of the data you can't get any sense of what is calling the MySQL queries or what those queries actually call. For that, you need a call graph. You can see a call-graph representation of the data to get some kind of handle on where each method fits in the call trace (it also can help if you are overwhelmed by the amount of data in the regular profile). All you need to do is add the following `graph_html` switch to your command (and you really do want to redirect this one to a file):

```
script/performance/profiler "Recipe.new().ingredient_string = ↵
'2 cups carrots, chopped'" 100 graph_html 2> out.html
```

Figure 13-3 shows the appropriate part of the output, where `MySQL#query` is located.

		0.00	0.00	0.00	0.00	100/11169	String#==
		0.00	0.00	0.00	0.00	2056/17068	Hash#[]=
		0.00	0.00	0.00	0.00	300/21973	Kernel#==
		0.00	0.00	0.00	0.00	700/27756	Module#===
		0.01	0.01	0.00	0.00	300/300	Kernel#eval-1
		0.00	0.00	0.00	0.00	456/2278	Module#const_get
		0.50	0.50	0.00	0.00	807/807	<Module::Benchmark>#measure
11.40%	**11.39%**	**0.50**	**0.50**	**0.00**	**0.00**	**807**	**Mysql#query**
		0.00	0.00	0.00	0.00	205/1088	Object#initialize
		0.04	0.00	0.00	0.04	1600/4102	ActiveRecord::Base#clone_attribute_value
		0.36	0.00	0.00	0.36	300/4102	Array#each-2
		0.01	0.00	0.00	0.01	600/4102	Array#each-3
		0.00	0.00	0.00	0.00	1/4102	ActiveRecord::AttributeMethods#method_missing
		0.00	0.00	0.00	0.00	400/4102	ActiveRecord::Callbacks#callback
		0.00	0.00	0.00	0.00	1/4102	<Class::ActiveRecord::Base>#define_attr_method
		0.00	0.00	0.00	0.00	800/4102	ActiveRecord::Callbacks#callback-1

Figure 13-3

There's also a non-HTML version of the graph, which you can get by using plain old `graph` in place of `graph_html`. Personally, I recommend that version only to people who find performance testing insufficiently complicated as it is.

So, what do the numbers mean this time? Each marked section is the call stack surrounding a single method, which is the method displayed in bold. Methods above that line are all methods that called the bolded method, and methods below are methods that are called by the bolded method.

Columns are similar to the original report. The first column is reported only for the bolded method, and is the `total%`, or percentage of time spent in the bolded method and any of its children. The second column, `%self`, is also reported only for the bolded method and is the percentage of time actually spent in the method. The next four columns are `total`, `self`, `wait`, and `child`. For the bolded method, these columns are the same as in the original report — however, notice that there is a slight discrepancy between the two reports in that they represent two separate runs and each run is slightly different. For the other methods in each section, the timing columns represent the share of the bolded methods time performed on behalf of or via that method. The `Mysql#query` case is actually not that clear here because it has only one caller and one callee. Figure 13-4 shows a better example.

		0.03	0.00	0.00	0.03	100/300	Recipe(id: integer, title: string, servings: string, description: string, directions: string, created_at: datetime, updated_at: datetime, user_id: integer, cached_tag_list: string, cached_ingredient_string: string, soup_image_id: integer)#validate_associated_records_for_ingredients
		0.02	0.00	0.00	0.02	100/300	Recipe(id: integer, title: string, servings: string, description: string, directions: string, created_at: datetime, updated_at: datetime, user_id: integer, cached_tag_list: string, cached_ingredient_string: string, soup_image_id: integer)#cache_ingredient_string
		0.71	0.00	0.00	0.71	100/300	Kernel#eval
17.54%	**0.08%**	**0.77**	**0.00**	**0.00**	**0.76**	**300**	**ActiveRecord::Associations::AssociationCollection#method_missing**
		0.76	0.00	0.00	0.76	300/600	ActiveRecord::Associations::AssociationProxy#method_missing
		0.00	0.00	0.00	0.00	300/10450	Kernel#respond_to?

Figure 13-4

The method in focus here is `method_missing` for `AssociationCollection`, which is sort of in the weeds as far as stuff you're actually going to be able to fix, but is a nicely constrained call graph for the purposes of explaining the chart. This `method_missing` is called 300 times, for 0.77 seconds spent in this method or its children, and 0.00 seconds spent in the method itself. That method is called by `validate_associated_records_for_ingredients` 100 of the 300 times, and calls from that method represent 0.03 of the 0.77 seconds spent in `method_missing`. The third line shows that `Kernel#eval` calls `method_missing` 100 times, but those calls represent 0.71 of the 0.77 seconds. (To see how much total time was spent in `Kernel#eval`, you would click on it to access its focus section in the file.) In other words, the four timing columns for all the caller methods should sum up to the totals in the bolded method.

The children work analogously. The `method_missing` under focus calls a different `method_missing` 300 times out of the 600 total times that method is called, and that represents 0.76 of the 0.77 seconds spent in children of the bolded method. It also calls `respond_to?` 300 times of the 10,450 times that method is called, but to an amount of time less than one-hundredth of a second.

Profiling Rails

The Rails profiler script works nicely for Rails model scripts, but it is a little awkward for profiling controller methods. The `ruby-prof` profiler provides a mechanism for profiling controller calls from a browser. The mechanism is a touch on the awkward side, but it works.

Here's the mechanism. The `ruby-prof` gem distribution contains a Rails plugin that you can find in the gem directory, as follows (note that the version number of `ruby-prof` may have changed by the time you read this):

```
<Ruby Root>/gems/1.8/gems/ruby-prof-0.5.2/rails_plugin
```

Copy the `ruby-prof` directory to your `vendor/plugins` directory — and that's it. While the plugin is in place, any server request has a profile table appended to the log file for that request. Actually, you get one for each separate thread, but only one of them is likely to be interesting. Here's a bit for the controller index page:

```
%self    total    self    wait    child    calls   name
25.71    0.22     0.18    0.01    0.03      76     Array#select
18.57    0.13     0.13    0.00    0.00      12     Magick::Draw#annotate
 8.57    0.06     0.06    0.00    0.00      10     Magick::Draw#get_type_metrics
 5.71    0.04     0.04    0.00    0.00       1     Magick::Image#to_blob
 4.29    0.03     0.03    0.00    0.00    18647    Hash#key?
 2.86    0.02     0.02    0.00    0.00     518     Module#constants
```

```
2.86     0.21     0.02     0.00     0.19       17   Kernel#gem_original_require
2.86     0.02     0.02     0.00     0.00        2
Magick::GradientFill#initialize
2.86     0.03     0.02     0.00     0.01      396   Array#each-2
2.86     0.02     0.02     0.00     0.00        1   Magick::Draw#draw
```

The format should seem familiar. You will likely want to run the plugin only occasionally since profiling does have some overhead and can get tedious. However, running the plugin occasionally is awkward because there's no way to turn the profiling on or off short of removing the plugin from your source tree and putting it back. However, you can control the task via Rake. Add the following to a Rake file in your lib/tasks directory:

```
namespace :profiler do

  task :start do
    from_dir = "/usr/local/lib/ruby/gems/1.8/gems/ruby-prof-0.5.2/⏎
rails_plugin/ruby-prof"
    to_dir = "vendor/plugins/ruby-prof"
    FileUtils.mkdir(to_dir)
    FileUtils.mkdir("#{to_dir}/lib")
    ["init.rb", "lib/profiling.rb"].each do |each|
      File.copy("#{from_dir}/#{each}", "#{to_dir}/#{each}")
    end
  end

  task :end do
    FileUtils.rm_rf("vendor/plugins/ruby-prof")
  end

end
```

Just update the from_dir to match your local system. You'll need to restart your local server for this to take effect. If you want to do this on a staging server via Capistrano, the following variant should work:

```
namespace :deploy do

  task :start do
    from_dir = "/usr/local/lib/ruby/gems/1.8/gems/ruby-prof-0.5.2/⏎
rails_plugin/ruby-prof"
    to_dir = "vendor/plugins/ruby-prof"
    run "mkdir #{to_dir}"
    run "mkdir #{to_dir}/lib"
    ["init.rb", "lib/profiling.rb"].each do |each|
      run "cp #{from_dir}/#{each} #{to_dir}/#{each}"
    end
    restart
  end

  task :end do
    run "rm -Rf vendor/plugins/ruby-prof"
    restart
  end

end
```

This moves the files and restarts the server for you. I'd only do this on a staging server, not a production server.

The default output of the plugin is the flat table. However, there is a way for you to get a call graph HTML table. Within the plugin `profiling.rb` file, you'll see some commented lines that look like this:

```
## Example for Graph html printer
#printer = RubyProf::GraphHtmlPrinter.new(result)
#path = File.join(LOG_PATH, 'call_graph.html')
#File.open(path, 'w') do |file|
    #printer.print(file, {:min_percent => 1,
                          #:print_file => true})
#end
```

Uncomment them, and you'll get an HTML file for each call. If you are on Linux, there's another block there that will give you a graph that can be read by a program called KCachegrind to produce an actual graphical graph of the call tree.

Fixing Performance Problems

Hopefully, I've established that, as a Rails developer, you have access to lots and lots of data about performance issues in your application. The question then becomes what to do with that information. When is it time to try and remedy a potential or an actual performance problem, and what sort of intervention is feasible? We all know that premature optimization is bad, but who gets to define when it's premature? The pressure from clients and managers to speed up code, even early in development, can be hard to resist, and people unfamiliar with Rails or Agile development styles may be unwilling to trust that speed improvements will come.

As a somewhat simplified guide for when to optimize, I find that performance enhancements tend to fall into one of the following three groups:

❑ **Good practice techniques that happen to also have good performance characteristics.** An example might include limiting the amount of data you create in a controller method. It's good practice because thin controllers are easy to test, and has a good performance profile because there's some overhead involved in passing the controller instance variables around. Similarly, splitting views into separate partials is both easier to read and easier to cache. These aren't enhancements as much as things that you should just be doing as part of your regular practice.

❑ **Legitimately suboptimal implementations in your code that can be fixed by bringing the code in line with standard Ruby and Rails conventions, or by relatively straightforward algorithm improvement.** An example might be a controller method that calls the same model `find` method multiple times, or a parent model that should use the `:include` flag to automatically grab its child objects. In general, it's reasonable to make these changes as they are identified. For me, the key here is that the objective quality and maintainability of the code is being enhanced, rather than compromised.

❑ **Performance optimizations that move the code away from Rails conventions or readability in the name of pure performance.** This can be relatively benign, such as replacing `link_to` calls with wrapper functions that use string interpolation. Or it can be slightly more awkward, such as replacing an ActiveRecord `find` with a raw SQL query. Or it can be extreme refactoring, such as replacing a metaprogramming construct with something less dynamic. I tend to put caching in this category as well, because caching doesn't necessarily reduce the readability of the code but it does introduce a behavior difference between development and production that can make a system harder to debug and maintain.

It's dealing with the third category where the art and the headaches come in. For my part, I'm extremely reluctant (perhaps to a fault) to significantly reduce the long-term viability of the code in the name of a short-term performance boost. A lot of the maintainability issues can be managed by continuing to use good programming techniques. Replacing `link_to` with custom wrapper methods doesn't bother me much, for example (although making sure the custom method is actually used can be a problem). However, if it turned out that, say, the metaprogramming in a table form builder was a little slow, I'd be loathe to replace all that code with raw HTML if I could improve performance another way — via caching or server settings. I'd have to see a really serious performance problem to take the short-term and long-term hit of adding all that duplication to a series of forms.

I don't mean to minimize the importance of good performance. Clearly, poor performance will make your application significantly less valuable to your users. Every improvement comes with a cost, short-term in making the change, and long-term in making future changes more difficult. In this discussion of performance enhancements, it's important to keep the costs in mind, so that you can effectively manage the tradeoffs and make the choices that are appropriate for your application.

Managing Sessions

Most applications store at least some persistent data in the session object, and Rails has to put that session data somewhere. Between the core and commonly used extensions, Rails offers several ways to store session data, of which there are about five that are reasonable choices. Prior to Rails 2.0, the default behavior was to store the data in a series of flat files. This had a certain admirable simplicity to it, but it had extremely poor performance characteristics under heavy load, because operating systems tend to have an upper limit on the number of files that can be in a directory before they go blooey.

Cookie-Based Sessions

The Rails 2.0 default is different, and a little unusual. By default, Rails stores session content as a user cookie. There are a number of potential issues involved in keeping this from being a massive security problem, and the implementation deals with them the best it can. The Rails cookie store takes the session data, encrypts it with a hashing algorithm — the default is SHA1, but any system available in Ruby's SSH implementation can be used. If the values in the session change, the old cookie automatically expires. If the uploaded cookie doesn't decrypt, the cookie is discarded. Plus there's nothing stopping you from putting your own secret value in the session and validating that as well.

If you use cookie-based storage, you need the following line in your `environment.rb`:

```
config.action_controller.session = { :session_key => "_soupsonline",
    :secret => "this phrase is a really, big secret. W0)oT!" }
```

This sets some parameters for the cookie store. The session key is used as the name of the session, and disambiguates it from other session cookies that you might be storing from other applications. The secret is used as the passphrase for the encryption of the data, so long and random is indicated here. Another option, `:digest`, allows you to set the encryption mechanism used. Alternately, you can arbitrarily specify the encryption mechanism by monkey patching the class `CGI::Session::CookieStore` and the method `generate_digest(data)`. This would, for example, let you arbitrarily change the secret passkey on a per-user basis.

There are two very strong positives to using the cookie session store: speed and scaling. Although I don't think there's a whole lot of production-level evidence as I write this, there's every reason to believe that recovering session data from the cookie is much faster than recovering it from a database. Even better, because the session data is actually stored on the client, issues of scaling the session storage just vanish. The time to get session data from a cookie should not materially change from storing one session to storing jillions of them.

Cookie storage is definitely not the perfect solution for all needs, though. First off, cookies have a very tight limit on the amount of data they can store — usually 4 kilobytes. The idea here is that most Rails applications don't store a lot of data in the session — typically just a user ID, an authentication token, some preferences, and maybe a string that's about to be displayed. If you are storing a lot more data than that, you should think about whether the information really needs to be stored in the session at all. In particular, if you are storing entire ActiveRecord objects in the session, then you have one of those cases where you are violating good practice and should stop immediately. You might think that you are saving time by avoiding the lookup from the ID, but in fact, the marshalling and unmarshalling of the object to a string is far slower.

The second issue is the security issue. The data is being stored on the client, and even though it's being encrypted, the mere fact that the information leaves the server is going to give security-minded IT managers fits, especially if the cookie is the key to highly private information. Although I might not have a problem with storing the user ID to a recipe-swapping site on the client side, I'd probably think twice before storing an ATM PIN number, even if it's encrypted. And I'd definitely pause before I'd store anything where there might be legal privacy issues, such as an ID to a medical site.

Finally, there are some logistical issues common to cookies. Some people just shut them off, and the cookie store doesn't seem to have a graceful default — those people just don't get session values. Also, the sessions need to be uploaded with the request, which adds a slight overhead that's probably too small to make a meaningful difference.

Sessions in the Database: ActiveRecord Store

If you don't like the cookie session store — either for security reasons or because you are storing too much data in the session — there are a couple of options for storing session data in some kind of database. If you go to your `environment.rb` file, you'll see the following line (which is commented out by default):

```
config.action_controller.session_store = :active_record_store
```

You need to uncomment it.

The ActiveRecord store stores your session in your ActiveRecord database, just as though it was any other model in your application. For this to work, you need to also create the database table. Here's a convenient Rake task for doing that:

```
rake db:sessions:create
```

This creates the following migration:

```
class CreateSessions < ActiveRecord::Migration
  def self.up
    create_table :sessions do |t|
      t.string :session_id, :null => false
      t.text :data
      t.timestamps
    end

    add_index :sessions, :session_id
    add_index :sessions, :updated_at
  end

  def self.down
    drop_table :sessions
  end
end
```

After you migrate the database and restart your server, sessions will work as before, but behind the scenes, the data will be stored in the new `sessions` table. Using ActiveRecord as your storage medium has a couple of nice features. The data stays on your server, and you're using core Rails mechanisms to access it. The timestamp allows you to sweep the session data to expire old sessions using an external process. The ActiveRecord store also stays reasonably consistent under load, at least when compared to file-based cookie storage.

Sessions in the Database: SQLSessionStore

The ActiveRecord store can be slow. And if this is starting to cause you pain, you can try a faster option, called SQLSessionStore, created by Stefan Kaes, who is also responsible for Railsbench. It's available as a plugin, which you install as follows:

```
script/plugin install -x http://railsexpress.de/svn/plugins/sql_session_store/trunk
```

SQLSessionStore is faster largely because it avoids ActiveRecord overhead and uses SQL queries directly. It also is nontransactional. Currently, the plugin is designed for MySQL, PostgreSQL, and Oracle.

SQLSessionStore uses the same migration and database table as the ActiveRecord store. To use it, you need to add some code to the `environment.rb` file. Toward the bottom of the file, after the initializer block, add the following:

```
ActionController::CgiRequest::DEFAULT_SESSION_OPTIONS.
    update(:database_manager => SqlSessionStore)
```

And then add whichever one of the following three lines is appropriate:

```
SqlSessionStore.session_class = MysqlSession
SqlSessionStore.session_class = PostgresqlSession
SqlSessionStore.session_class = OracleSession
```

That should do it. Kaes's data suggests you can get an increase of about 150–200 percent in requests per second from SQLSessionStore as compared to ActiveRecordStore. Your mileage may vary somewhat, but there seems to be little doubt that SQLSessionStore is faster at saving session data in a database.

Other Storage Methods

There are two other widely used methods for storing Rails sessions. One method uses memcached, which is a separate program which maintains a global, memory-based, object-caching program. Another method uses Distributed Ruby (DRb), which is a common mechanism for doing remote method invocation or data transfer between Ruby programs. In this case, the DRb server would store the data for you. Both of these methods are extremely fast, and both require much more complex setup than the methods you've seen so far. If you are already using DRb or memcached to manage other data in the system, then it's probably worth it to add session data as well — but unless sessions are becoming a really significant bottleneck, I wouldn't recommend installing one of those systems just to manage session data.

ActiveRecord and Database Issues

It's highly likely that your first point of performance pain in a new Rails application will involve your database. The clever use of your database via ActiveRecord is one of Rails' great strengths, although the database independence and general assumptions made by ActiveRecord will cause it to perform suboptimally at some point in your program. Often, though, the problem isn't ActiveRecord itself, but the usage pattern of your program that can be improved. It's easy to forget that ActiveRecord objects are more expensive to create and save than regular Ruby objects, but keeping in mind the database layer and actual SQL requirements as you work with your models will take you a long way.

Database issues often fall cleanly into the three-way split of "dumb things you should stop doing right now," "smart things you should do more of," and "tricky things you should try when all else fails."

Render Unto MySQL

There are some things that databases don't do particularly well. They generally aren't optimized for complex math, multi-table relationships can be hard to model, and they make lousy cheese omelets. There are two very important things, though, that your database is going to do faster than anything else in your program stack: sort things and find things.

You should almost never call the Ruby sort on a list of ActiveRecord objects that just came from the database. Instead, use the :order option when you do your ActiveRecord find, and let the database do all that work. If you are sorting on a derived attribute, you should consider deriving the column using the :select option of an ActiveRecord find (alternatively, depending on your database, you could create a view with that column, or if it's a value you're sorting or searching on frequently, cache the value in the table).

> While I'm on the subject, here's a quick coding tip. Do you remember whether the default sort order in your database is ascending or descending? Me neither. So always specify the direction of the sort in your order by clause (name DESC, rather than just name). Your future self will thank you.

Similarly, when you do a `find`, use the `:conditions` option to limit the number of records sent from the database, rather than running a Ruby `select` on the resulting list. If the condition gets a bit more complex, try the `find_by_sql` method to pass in your own lovingly handcrafted SQL query.

The database is also pretty fast for counts, sums, averages, and the like. Try to use the Rails ActiveRecord counting features rather than the Ruby standard Enumerable functions where you can because the ActiveRecord features use the faster database aggregators.

Don't Repeat Yourself (Have I Said That Before?)

Here's an example of a duplication that I've certainly done in my own code:

```
if Recipe.find_by_serving("2").name == "Chicken"
  return Recipe.find_by_serving("2")
else
  return nil
end
```

This is kind of a simple example, but the issue here is the duplicate ActiveRecord `find` call. It's easy to forget how expensive an ActiveRecord `find` can be relative to a normal Ruby method call. However, it's one of the quickest ways to overload your database by requesting duplicate information unnecessarily.

This one is usually pretty easy to mitigate, once you have identified the problem. The easiest way to fix the preceding example is to use a local variable like this:

```
recipe = Recipe.find_by_serving("2")
if recipe.name == "Chicken" then recipe else nil end
```

Just to point out how tricky performance tuning can be, if your database is set to do object caching or if you are using memcached, then this example probably won't have much of a performance hit — the second database call will just go to the cache and return the cached data. (In Rails 2.0, there is a new ActiveRecord caching mechanism that might also catch issues like this.)

Using a local variable works only if the data object is used locally in a single method. Data that is used globally can be stored in model class variables. This is especially useful for data that is in the database but is rarely changed. Most applications will end up storing data that is rarely, if ever, changed in a database because it's easy to manage the data there. An example of this type of data might be a list of U.S. states, or a standard list of occupation types that you might place in a pull-down list from which users can choose.

Let's say you have a list of job types in the database, but this data is essentially static. You can preload the data with something like this:

```
@@all_types = JobTypes.find(:all, :order => "name ASC")

def all_types
  @@all_types
end
```

This can also be done with a lazy load rather than a load at start up as follows:

```
@@all_types = nil

def all_types
  @@all_types ||= JobTypes.find(:all, :order => "name ASC")
end
```

Congratulations — you've achieved your own mini-cache. This is even compatible with updating the information, provided you clear the cache as follows:

```
after_save :clear_cache
after_create :clear_cache

def clear_cache
  @@all_types = nil
end
```

N + 1

A common performance problem is caused by inefficient use of child objects. Look at the following code:

```
@recipes = Recipe.find(:all, :limit => 25, :order => "created_at DESC")
@result = []
@recipes.each do |recipe|
  @result << recipe.user.name
end
```

The problem here is that the initial `Recipe.find` triggers one database query, and then each request within the loop to get a user name from the subordinate user object triggers a separate database query to get that one user object — which means that the call to get 25 recipes triggers 26 separate database calls. This is often referred to as the "N+1" problem. It's a pretty fast way to overwhelm your database.

This example is composed deliberately to show the problem — normally, I'd do something like this using `collect`, but the same issue would still apply. The most common manifestation of this problem in Rails is probably an index page, where the collection is generated in the controller, and the loop making the calls across the relationship is in the view code. Again, the same issue would still hold, perhaps even more insidiously because the list generation and list walkthrough are separated in the code.

There are a couple of workarounds for this, increasingly elaborate. The recommended mechanism within ActiveRecord is to use the eager loading feature by passing an `:include` parameter to the `find` method.

```
@recipes = Recipe.find(:all, :limit => 25, :order => "created_at DESC",
    :include => :users)
```

This tells Rails to generate a SQL statement using a `JOIN` that will load the user information in the initial query, such as:

```
SELECT * from recipes, users LEFT OUTER JOIN users ON users.id = recipes.user_id
```

That's for those of you with the SQL skills to correctly tell the difference between an outer join and an inner join. The upshot for the rest of us is that the user data comes in with the same query as the recipe, and is converted to ActiveRecord objects that are associated correctly. Now, when the code goes walking through the loop, it doesn't need to perform another query to get the user name because the data has already been loaded.

The :include parameter can also be a list if there are multiple relationship objects — which in Soups Online would be users and ingredients. And the parameters can be nested like this to include the users and user addresses:

```
:include => [{:users => :addresses}]
```

If you find yourself in a position where nesting your :include parameters seems like the thing to do, please consider reconsidering. An :include with a very complex set of joins can easily slow down the database so much that it defeats the purpose of using the :include in the first place.

The typical use of :include is a pretty straightforward technique, cleanly implemented in Rails, and is recommended in just about any case where you know that there's a subordinate object that is going be needed for each entry in the list.

There are a couple of down sides. You're not actually going to get the 2500-percent increase in speed that going from 26 database queries to one database query might imply. Because you're actually gathering the same overall amount of information from the database either way, the savings is largely in the setup and overhead of the queries. Exactly how much that savings is going to be is dependent on how much data you're talking about. There will probably be a noticeable speedup, but it's not going to solve your problems all by itself.

Also, because the generated query needs to custom-write the SELECT portion of the SQL statement, any use of the :select option in the find command to limit the data transfer will be ignored. For similar reasons, this technique is not recommended for :has_many :through relationships.

If you know that there's only going to be one or two attributes of the child object that you need, then you have some other options that might cause a more dramatic speedup by reducing the amount of data transfer. One option is denormalizing, as discussed in Chapter 6, which would in this case mean adding another column or two to the parent object with the needed child data. This works best in a one-to-one relationship.

If you're more comfortable with SQL joins, you can customize the join in the find code to take only the child attribute that you need, a technique that's sometimes called *piggybacking*. Here's an example (which is similar to the example in Stefan Kaes's discussion of piggybacking, where he coincidentally uses recipes and users):

```
Recipe.find(:all, :limit => 25
    :conditions => "recipes.user_id = users.id",
    :joins => "recipes, users",
    :select => "recipes.*, users.name as username")
```

Personally, I'd only recommend this kind of manual join if it was clear that the call was a huge bottleneck. I'd try some other things first, like manually getting just the name from the user table with the :select option, like this:

```
@recipes = Recipe.find(:all, :limit => 25, :order => "created_at DESC")
@result = []
@recipes.each do |recipe|
    @result << recipe.user.find(recipe.user_id, :select => :name)
end
```

This still has the overhead of the multiple queries, but the amount of data being transferred is much lower. In some circumstances, that's a tradeoff worth exploring.

Indexing

Database indexing is one of the simplest ways to improve your database performance. Adding indexing is as simple as putting a line like this in a migration:

```
add_index :recipe, :servings
```

This is simple, easy, and without fuss. If the index is on multiple columns in tandem, then just add all the columns to the method call. If you'd like the database to enforce unique values in the column (rather than having ActiveRecord do it), throw in :unique => true.

Indexing helps only if you are searching on or sorting by the column being indexed. And there is a downside to indexing on too many columns. Not only does it increase the size of your database instance on the hard drive, but too many indexes can actually slow down performance by causing the database to spend time trying to decide which index to use.

My recommendation is to not worry about indexing during early development, but once you have a good sense of which columns are frequently searched and sorted, add indexes later on for those columns. If the search is on two columns at the same time, adding a combined index will be much faster than adding two single indexes.

Dynamism

Here's a final tip to shave a little bit of time off of a potential bottleneck. The find_by and find_all_by dynamic methods are really cool — but they are also kind of slow because each one needs to run through method_missing and parse the filename against the list of columns in the database table. If you've identified a hotspot that includes a dynamic method, you'll get some performance improvement by converting it to a regular find with conditions.

Caching

Databases aren't the only places where your Rails application might need a speed boost. Your view code can slow to a crawl as well. This section discusses a way to speed up views, and provides a look at what can slow them down.

Caching is the purest way to speed up your Rails application. By that, I mean that caching has a sort of strict adherence to the Don't Repeat Yourself (DRY) principle — don't redo page generation that you've already done. The basic idea of caching is that your Rails application automatically stores generated HTML for a page or some segment of a page. When the next user requests that part of the application, the cached file is sent to the browser, saving you from regenerating the data. The performance improvement here can be substantial, not just because you are saving the render time, but also because you are saving the bandwidth to and from the database. Where applicable, caching can give you a multiple order-of-magnitude speedup.

Caching is applicable for any page or portion of a page that will be identical for multiple users. Even if the underlying data changes rapidly, you can still get a performance speedup for a cache that is expired frequently. If you're getting 10 hits a second, then even with a cache that lives for 30 seconds, well over 99 percent of your page hits will be served from the cache.

Rails can cache at three different scales: an entire page, an entire controller action, or an arbitrary fragment of a view. Each scale has the same basic issues — you need to tell Rails what to cache, you need a place to store the cached information, and you need a way to expire old caches.

To test caching on your development machine, turn it on in the `environment.rb` file as follows:

```
config.action_controller.perform_caching = true
```

Caching is turned on in production mode by default. You need to be careful if you are going to keep caching in development mode — it can make debugging kind of a pain because you need to clear the cache to see any changes.

Page Caching

Page caching is far and away the fastest way to cache in Rails. An entire URL request is cached, and when the request is made again, Rails is completely bypassed. Unfortunately, page caching is also far and away the least flexible of all the Rails caching structures. Because a page cache stores the entire page, this means that the entire page must display identically to all users (at least for a certain period of time). Among other things, this means that any page that has a different face for a user who has logged in is disqualified, as is any page that displays any user-customized content at all.

You inform Rails of your desire to cache a page in the controller, by including the following method call in the controller:

```
caches_page :index, :show
```

The arguments to the `caches_page` method are publicly accessible actions within the controller, and you can use as many of them as you want. When a user request goes to one of those actions, Rails will take all the HTML for that page and store it in the Rails public directory based on the request URL.

In other words, the index page for recipes would be stored in `public/recipes.html`, and the show page would be stored in something like `public/recipes/1.html` (the default directory root can be changed in the `environment.rb` file as well — it is `config.action_controller.page_cache_ directory`). This method of storing the cached data explains how Rails can be completely bypassed when the same URL is requested again. Because an HTML page that matches the URL exists in the public directory, your Rails server knows to serve that page up without passing the request along to the Rails application proper. If you are using a web server such as Apache for static serving, you can configure Apache to look for cached pages before sending the request on to Mongrel (see the "References" section in this chapter for more information on this).

There's one thing to watch out for in page caching. As a result of how the page cache filename is generated, any information in the URL query string is completely ignored. This means that a URL that differs from the cached URL only in the query string will still receive the same cached file. This can be a big problem that affects pagination queries as well as any dynamic request to the page. The workaround is to adjust the Rails route for the page to include any parameters in the main part of the URL, and not in the query string. If you can't do that for your page, then look into action or fragment caching.

Action Caching

Action caching is like page caching, only different. Rather than caching an entire page, you instead cache the results of an entire action. Now you may ask, "But isn't the action the entire page?" Well . . . yes, but in action caching, Rails is actually invoked before the cache file is sent out. In particular, any `before_filter` actions defined for your controller action are invoked, and then the cache file is sent out in lieu of actually invoking the action. The primary practical advantage this has over page caching is in the case where you have a `before` filter that authenticates that the user has the rights to access the page, and redirects away if access is denied. In the action caching world, that redirect will be performed if needed, and if the user qualifies, then the cached action can be sent. So, although action caching is not quite as fast as page caching, it's a good deal more flexible — although it still assumes that the entire page can be cached together.

Action caching is also determined at the controller level with this very similar command:

```
caches_action :index, :show
```

The only issue with the placement is that any `before` filters you want triggered for those actions need to be defined before the `caches_action` call.

The default storage location for action cached files is in the `tmp/cache` directory. The file naming is broadly similar to page caching, except the filenames end in `.cache`. Because Rails is no longer worried about having the page name actually match a request URL, you also don't have to worry about query strings in the cached request.

Fragment Caching

The most flexible way to cache in Rails is fragment caching, which works on any arbitrary part of your view. A fragment cache is set up in your view code by wrapping the desired fragment in a `cache` block, like this:

```
<% cache do %>
  <% for recipe in @recipes %>
    <%# expensive code %>
  <% end %>
<% end %>
```

The fragment is also stored in `tmp/cache`, and the default name is based on the controller and action being partially cached. You can give the cache a different name by passing an argument to the `cache` method. This can be a string, like this:

```
<% cache "recipe_cache" do %>
```

Or it can be a set of hash keys that conform to the options for `url_for`. A nice thing about using this mechanism is that the resulting URL is only used to tag the cache fragment in storage, and does not have to correspond to any actually existing controller and action. Here's an example:

```
<% cache :controller => :recipe_cache, :action => :cached_list %>
```

Why would you want to name a cached fragment? So you can identify it in the controller. Where page caching bypasses Rails entirely, and action caching bypasses the controller action in question, fragment caching calls the action in question, and it's up to you to tell Rails which parts of the action can be skipped if a fragment is already cached. This is accomplished with the `read_fragment` method, returning `true` if there is a fragment there to read. For example:

```
def index
  unless read_fragment({}) do
    @recipes = Recipe.find_for_index(params[:format])
    respond_to do |format|
      format.html # index.html.erb
      format.xml  { render :xml => @recipes }
      format.atom { render :layout => false }
      format.rss  { render :xml => @recipes.to_rss_feed("Soups OnLine",
          formatted_recipes_url(:rss), "New Recipes from Soups OnLine")}
      format.json { render :json => @recipes.to_json }
      format.yaml { render :text => @recipes.to_yaml, :layout => false}
    end
  end
end
```

If the cached fragment already exists, then the database call and the other calculations are not necessary.

The argument to `read_fragment` is the name of the cache as specified in the view. If an empty hash is specified, then the default controller and action is used, but you can also use matching custom names as in this example:

```
read_fragment("recipe_cache")
read_fragment(:controller => :recipe_cache, :action => :cached_list)
```

This means that you definitely want to name your caches whenever you have more than one of them in an action. Otherwise, you'd have no way of distinguishing between them for retrieval or for blocking out database code.

Cache Expiring

Cached data exists until explicitly expired by Rails, Rake, or some other external process. One way to explicitly expire a page is with the `expire_page` method, which takes the same set of arguments as the `url_for` method:

```
expire_page(:controller => :recipes, :action => :index)
```

Action and fragment caches are removed with the analogous methods `expire_action` and `expire_fragment`.

You don't have to do all this expiring by hand, however. You can set up a special object called a *sweeper*, which will do it for you. Sweepers are sort of mutant hybrids of observers and filters. Here's an example of a sweeper:

```
class RecipeSweeper < ActionController::Caching::Sweeper
  observe Recipe

  def after_save(record)
    expire_page(:controller => :recipes, :action => :index )
  end
end
```

The `observe` method takes one or more model arguments. Those are the models that the sweeper looks at for life-cycle methods. The sweeper can define actions on the full set of filter methods, but the most commonly used ones are going to be `after_create`, `after_save`, `after_update`, and `after_destroy`. Within those methods, you can do whatever you want, but it should probably include expiring any cache that contains data that is now obsolete. The `record` argument is the actual ActiveRecord under consideration, so you can use that to determine which `show` page to expire, for example.

For a sweeper to work, it must be registered with the appropriate controller like this:

```
cache_sweeper :recipe_sweeper, :only => [:save]
```

The `:only` argument is a list of the life-cycle actions that have defined filters in the sweeper.

There is also a Rake task called `tmp:cache:clear` that expires all action and fragment caches by simply deleting the contents of the `tmp/cache` directory.

Cache Storage

Page caches have to be stored in the file, but action and fragment caches have a couple of options that are similar to session options: DRb and memcache. The storage mechanism can be changed in the `environment.rb` file as follows:

```
ActionController::Base.fragment_cache_store = :drb_store
```

As with sessions, I don't recommend starting out with one of these mechanisms, but if you are using them elsewhere, they are probably faster than the file store.

References

The most recent release of Railsbench was announced at `https://railsexpress.de/blog/articles/2007/04/01/new-railsbench-release-0-9-2`. Watch this blog for further updates. Also watch it for some interesting insights into Rails speed improvements, such as `http://railsexpress.de/blog/articles/2005/11/06/the-case-for-piggy-backed-attributes`. A tutorial on profiling Rails applications is available at `http://cfis.savagexi.com/articles/2007/07/10/how-to-profile-your-rails-application`.

Jason Hoffman's presentation on Rails performance is available at `http://jxh.bingodisk.com/bingo/public/presentations/JHoffmanRailsConf-Berlin-Sept2007.pdf`. There are a couple of different versions of this talk online, and this may have been updated by the time you read this.

You can find information on optimizing ActiveRecord from Bruce Tate at `www.ibm.com/developerworks/java/library/wa-rails3/index.html?ca=drs`. A similar look at Ajax is at `www.thinkvitamin.com/features/ajax/5-ways-to-optimize-ajax-in-ruby-on-rails`. A general look at improving Rails performance is at `www.infoq.com/articles/Rails-Performance`.

A good rundown of cookie sessions is available at `http://blog.caboo.se/articles/2007/2/21/new-controversial-default-rails-session-storage-cookies`. That blog also has other articles on Rails performance and scaling. Also, the Rails Envy team has a great overview of Rails caching at `www.railsenvy.com/2007/2/28/rails-caching-tutorial`.

Summary

Eventually you'll get to the point where you need to squeeze more speed out of Rails. Before you do that, it's very important that you have good diagnostic data. Railsbench is a tool for automatically hitting your application and measuring timings. It provides useful data for finding where slow controller actions are located. Railsbench also allows you to compare two runs made under different server settings.

The Rails log contains a lot of useful information about the timing of pages, especially the timing of individual SQL statements. The query_trace plugin augments that information with a stack trace showing the code location of each SQL query.

The `ruby-prof` gem is a profiler that runs specific calls to your Rails application and breaks down the time spent by method. It's a firehose of information, but the various reporting options allow you to find the bottlenecks of interest.

When making performance changes, never compromise the maintainability of the program unless absolutely necessary. Using benchmarks to narrow down the problem can help tremendously. Sessions are potential speed bottlenecks for high-load sites, and cookie- or SQL-based storage can speed up their behavior. ActiveRecord is often the root cause of the initial performance problems. The SQL generated by ActiveRecord can be tuned in many ways to improve database response time.

Caching is a common way to improve the performance of a web application. Rails provides support for caching at the entire page level, at the level of an individual controller action, and at the arbitrary fragment level. Fragments can be stored in a file, or by an external system such as DRb or memcache.

14

Going Meta

If you've been playing along with the book to this point, you've created a functional (albeit quirky) Ruby on Rails application, added some features, and deployed it. What's left? In the real world, you'd move the deployed code to a separate Subversion branch for bug fixes, and move on to version 2.0. In our book world, the next few chapters will be spent talking about various extensions and expansions of Ruby and Rails that are going to be useful additions to your set of tools.

First up is Ruby and metaprogramming. Ever since Rails first came out, it has been accompanied by claims that the Ruby programming language is not just a useful way to script behavior, but an integral part of the Rails architecture. There were also remarks that Rails could only have been written in Ruby, although now that most of the major features have been ported (one way or another) to other languages, you hear that somewhat less these days. Even so, all the statements about how Rails depends on Ruby are responding to something real and different about Ruby: its extraordinary support for changing the program's context and structure at runtime, or *metaprogramming*.

Throughout the book, you've seen some examples of how metaprogramming can be used to create elegant and flexible code, and you've also seen a little bit of how metaprogramming constructs are used throughout Rails. In this chapter, you'll take a full tour of Rails metaprogramming and see how it can be used effectively.

Any discussion of metaprogramming tends to bog down because the concepts are kind of mind-twisting and everybody tends to use a slightly different set of terms. For our purposes here, metaprogramming is any attempt to dynamically change not just the data that the program is running on, but the actual code structure itself. The structural change can be as simple as using an `eval` statement to dynamically generate code to execute or as complex as a Rails plugin changing the behavior of preexisting core Rails tasks.

Eval and Bindings

Many scripting languages have a facility to allow an arbitrary string to be executed at runtime. In Ruby, that feature comes from the `eval` method. Here's an example of that method:

```
>> eval("2 + 2")
=> 4
```

By default, variables in the code string are evaluated in the current context, as follows:

```
>> x = 3
=> 3
>> y = 5
=> 5
>> eval("x * y")
=> 15
```

However, you can evaluate the string in a more-or-less arbitrary environment by passing in an optional second argument, which must be a Ruby *binding*. Bindings are kind of odd entities that encapsulate the context of a block, which is basically a lookup table that stores the values of all accessible variables and constants. From the binding, the state of variable values when the block is created can be revisited.

Every block or `Proc` object defines its own binding, within which it can set local variable values. Under normal circumstances, this binding is accessed only when the block is executed, to determine the values of variables used by the block. However, you can retrieve just the binding and execute an arbitrary statement within it using the variable values as defined when the block was created.

Here's a test script that shows how bindings work:

```
def some_crazy_thing
  a = 10
  b = 20
  Proc.new {c = 10}
end

p eval("a * b", some_crazy_thing.binding)
```

The method `some_crazy_thing` sets a couple of variables and returns a `Proc` object. The last line of the script takes that block, grabs its binding, and tries to add two variables. When run, a and b are evaluated in the binding of the `Proc` object returned by `some_crazy_thing`, with this result:

```
>>> eval_binding.rb

200
```

Even though the actual block does not contain the variables a and b, both are accessible from the block because they were in scope when the block was created. The block itself is never executed.

By using a binding argument, you are re-entering the variable context as it existed when the block was created — any variable that was available to be used inside the block can also be referenced inside the eval string. On the other hand, the binding doesn't know or care what variables are actually created inside the block because the block is never run. Those values are not available to the binding and cannot be referenced inside the eval string. In other words, placing the following line at the bottom of the preceding script would result in an error:

```
p eval("a * c", some_crazy_thing.binding)
```

Because c is defined only inside the block and is not accessible at the time the block was created, it cannot be referenced in the eval string. You can, however change the values of a variable that is then used in the block, like this:

```
def another_crazy_thing
  a = 10
  Proc.new {a * a}
end

proc = another_crazy_thing
eval("a = 5", proc.binding)
p proc.call
```

This code snippet returns 25, because the eval changes the value of a in the binding, and therefore in the block execution context as well. It seems, though, that you are limited to changing the value of existing variables in the binding, you can't add a new variable to the scope.

Ruby offers a couple of other ways to choose an execution context for an eval string. Probably the most important is instance_eval, shown in the following code:

```
>> r = Recipe.find(1)
=> #<Recipe id: 1, title: "Grandma's Chicken Soup", servings: "3", ↵
description: "Yummy!", directions: "Things", created_at: ↵
"2007-08-05 20:03:33", updated_at: "2007-09-25 00:55:17", user_id: 2, ↵
cached_tag_list: "grandma, chicken, yummy", cached_ingredient_string: "2 cups stock
2 cups stock
1/2 oz. carrot
1/2 oz. ca...", soup_image_id: 1>
>> r.instance_eval("title")
=> "Grandma's Chicken Soup"
```

The instance_eval method uses the method receiver instance as the context for evaluating the string. Specifically, the code string will be evaluated as though the self object is implicitly set to the receiver of the instance_eval. In this example, the simple string title is evaluated as though it was r.title. Instead of calling instance_eval with a string, you can also call it with a block, like this:

```
>> r.instance_eval do
?> title
>> end
=> "Grandma's Chicken Soup"
```

The contents of the block are then evaluated within the receiving object's context.

Ruby also has analogous methods called `class_eval` and `method_eval`. You can use `class_eval` as one of several mechanisms to dynamically add instance methods to a class at runtime. For example:

```
class EvalTest

end

EvalTest.class_eval do
  def hello
    p "hi there"
  end
end

test = EvalTest.new
test.hello
```

In this example, the `class_eval` method evaluates its block in the context of the `EvalTest` class. Within that block, a method is defined, so when the `class_eval` is executed, that method definition is evaluated in the context of that class, adding the instance method `hello` to `EvalTest`. Note that the method is added as an instance method because the evaluation is done in the class context. If you want to use `eval` to add a method as a class method, then you need to use `instance_eval`, like so (but I'll show you a better way of adding class methods in a moment):

```
EvalTest.instance_eval do
  def good_bye
    p "so long"
  end
end
EvalTest.good_bye
```

And this is where metaprogramming can start to get a little headache-inducing. Calling `class_eval` creates an instance method, while calling `instance_eval` creates a class method (technically, an instance method of the class). This is all perfectly logical within the counterintuitive world of treating classes as instances in their own right. More on this when we discuss singleton classes in a couple of sections.

Introspection Tools

Metaprogramming and introspection are fairly tightly integrated. When you're writing metaprogramming code, you will usually need to call methods or get the value of variables whose names are only determined when the code is run. Ruby contains a rich set of methods to allow access to the internal state of its objects. Most of this functionality is in the classes `Class`, `Module`, and `Object`.

The following tables provide a quick guide to the most commonly used methods. The `eval` family of methods is not included in this section, and some methods will be explained in more detail later in this chapter. The `Module` class, in particular, has some less commonly used introspection methods involving access control levels that are not listed here.

The first table describes the introspective methods of the `Class` class.

Method	Description
inherited(subclass)	Automatically called when a subclass of the class is defined.
superclass	Returns the superclass of the class. If the class is `Object`, this returns `nil`.

The following table describes the introspective methods of the `Module` class.

Method	Description
self.constants	Returns an array of all constants currently defined. This contains not just system-level constants, but also the classes and modules available. The names are returned as strings.
self.nesting	Returns an array of all the nested modules currently in scope, innermost to outermost.
alias_method(new_name, old_name)	Defines `new_name` as a copy of the definition of `old_name`. Even if `old_name` changes, `new_name` still points to the original definition.
ancestors	Returns a list of all the modules currently included in the given module.
class_variable_defined?(symbol)	Returns `true` if the class or module has a class variable (`@@` syntax) named `symbol`. The symbol name must include the `@@` signs.
class_variable_get(symbol)	Introspectively gets the value of `symbol`, if `symbol` is a class variable. The symbol name must include the `@@` signs.
class_variable_set(symbol, value)	Introspectively sets the value of `symbol`, if `symbol` is a class variable. The symbol name must include the `@@` signs.
class_variables	Returns a list of all class variable names, as strings.
const_defined?(symbol)	Returns `true` if the `symbol` is a constant in the given module.
const_get(symbol)	Returns the value of the constant in the module.
const_set(symbol, value)	Sets the `symbol` as a constant with the given value.
constants	Returns an array of the names of all constants in the receiving module.
define_method(symbol)	Takes a block and dynamically defines a method within the module. See the "Defining Methods Dynamically" section later in this chapter for a full description of this method.

Table continued on following page

Method	Description
`include(*modules)`	Includes all the given modules, with the defined methods becoming instance methods on the containing class.
`included(other)`	Automatically called when this module is included within another class or module.
`instance_method(symbol)`	If the containing class contains an instance method named `symbol`, returns a Ruby `UnboundMethod` with that method. The method can be invoked by passing it the bind message with an instance of the class as an argument.
`instance_methods(include_super)`	Returns a list of the names of all the public instance methods in the receiving module. If `include_super` is `true` (the default), then superclass methods are also listed.
`method_defined?(symbol)`	Returns `true` if a method named `symbol` is defined in the module.
`private_class_method(*symbols)`	Makes the class method named in the symbols list into private methods.

The following table describes the introspective methods of the `Object` class.

Method	Definition
`extend(*modules)`	Extends the object by adding the methods defined in each module. Note that if `extend` is applied to a class object, then the methods are instance methods of the class, making them class modules from the perspective of instances of that class.
`instance_variable_defined?(symbol)`	Returns `true` if the symbol is currently defined as an instance variable in the instance. The symbol name needs to have the @ sign.
`instance_variable_get(symbol)`	Returns the value of the instance variable named `symbol`. The name must include the @ sign. An undefined symbol will raise an exception.
`instance_variable_set(symbol, value)`	Assigns the instance variable named `symbol` the value, "thereby frustrating the efforts of the class's author to provide proper encapsulation", the Ruby documentation observes. The symbol name must have the @ sign.
`instance_variables`	Returns an array of currently defined instance variables.
`method(symbol)`	Returns the instance method named `symbol`. The method can then be invoked by sending it the `call` message.

Method	Definition
`methods`	Returns a list of the names of all public methods in the object as strings.
`respond_to?(symbol, include_ private=false)`	Returns `true` if the object will respond to a message named `symbol`. If `include_private` is `true`, then private methods are included in the search.
`send(symbol, *args)`	If the object responds to a method named `symbol`, this calls that method with the passed arguments. This can also be referenced as `__send__` if `send` is already defined (or if you are a Python programmer feeling nostalgic for double underscores). This works even if `symbol` is a private method.
`singleton_method_added(symbol)`	Automatically called when a method is added to the object's singleton class (see the next section for an explanation).
`singleton_methods`	Returns a list of the names of all methods of the object's singleton class.

Classes, Metaclasses, and Singletons

Consider the following `irb` session.

```
irb(main):001:0> "abcd".class
=> String
irb(main):002:0> "abcd".class.class
=> Class
irb(main):003:0> "abcd".class.class.class
=> Class
irb(main):004:0> "abcd".class.class.class.class
=> Class
```

In this code, the `abcd` string is, like everything in Ruby, an object. Every object in Ruby belongs to a class. The class for `abcd` is, naturally, `String`. The class for the class `String` is the class `Class`.

It's hard to proceed from this point without sounding a little bit like a deranged Philosophy professor: "What is the meaning of *self*","What is the essence of *object*?" "What is the nature of being a *class*?" "What does it mean if a *class* is also an *object*?" "If a *class* is an *object*, where do *classes* come from?"

Classes and Objects

A Ruby object has two essential features. It has some set of attributes, which define its state, and it belongs to a class, which defines its behavior. For example, in Soups OnLine, a `Recipe` object contains several pieces of data representing its state, including a title, a list of ingredients, and a description.

It also belongs to the `Recipe` class, which defines a number of useful things that the object can do with its data, such as converting it to XML. And `Recipe` is a subclass of `ActiveRecord::Base`, which defines a whole boatload of useful things to do with data. Similarly, the characters abcd represent the state of a `String`, and all the methods of `String` define what you can do to and with a `String`.

Unlike some other programming languages, Ruby classes do not impose a set of data on their instances. Although the class may set data or expect certain attributes in defined methods, there's nothing stopping you from adding attributes to the object that no method knows about. The class can define accessors — but accessors are methods, not descriptions of data.

A Ruby class has three additional features, beyond a typical object. A class has a lookup table that maps symbols to executable methods — this provides the behavior for instances of the class. There's a special link to a parent class, which allows the class to use previously defined behavior (technically, the class `Object` is a special case because it has no parent class). Classes also have the ability to create objects that are instances of that class, which in this context means that the objects will look to the class's symbol table to respond to messages. (I'm leaving Ruby modules out of this discussion. Modules have the first two properties but cannot create instances of their own without being included inside a class.)

The graph in Figure 14-1 shows the relationships. There's the traditional `isa` link between a class and its superclass, and I've also added an `instance of` relationship. The string abcd is an instance of `String`, which is an instance of `Class`, which is also an instance of `Class`.

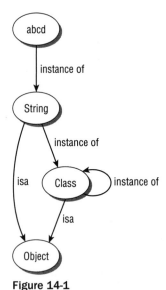

Figure 14-1

So, classes have some special powers, but they are also objects. Everything in Ruby is an object. (I know I've said that already, but I find that repeating that point a few times really does help.) This means that a class can have instance variables and belong to another class. The class that classes belong to is actually called `Class`. And the class of `Class` is itself also `Class`. If this is becoming confusing, go back to the IRB session at the beginning of this section which explores the same concept.

> ### What Is Ruby's Metaclass?
>
> If you wander through online Ruby discussions about dynamic programming and metaprogramming in Ruby, you'll probably see statements that say something like "Class is the metaclass of Ruby". What does this mean?
>
> Conceptually, just as a class is the thing that creates instances, a metaclass is the thing that creates classes. In some object-oriented programming languages, most notably Smalltalk, there is an actual class called Metaclass, which is the source of class behavior and class instances. (Actually, the Smalltalk hierarchy is a little more tangled than this, but that's the basic idea.) However, there isn't an explicit Metaclass in Ruby, and the source of class instances and class behavior is `Class` itself — hence "Class is the metaclass of Ruby."

Adding instance variables to a class makes them available to that class instance, of course, but the variables are also available to instances of that class. I find the following helps me remember the relationship:

Instance variables of the class are class variables of the instances.

This is also true if you substitute "methods" for "variables." (Plus, it has the added benefit of sounding like a lost Zen koan.)

The relationship works the other way as well. When you use the `@@` syntax to add a class attribute, you are actually adding an instance attribute to the class object. And when you define a class method using `def self.method_name`, you are actually adding an instance method to the class . . . sort of. As I mentioned only a few paragraphs earlier, Ruby instances don't have methods — only classes do. There is, however, a way to attach methods to specific instances.

Singletons

Take a closer look at the syntax for creating a class method:

```
def self.do_something
end
```

The use of `self` in this location is a recent addition to Ruby. You used to have to define a class method explicitly using the class name, like this:

```
def Recipe.do_something
end
```

What's going on here?

Well, remember when I said that instances don't have methods? Strictly speaking, that's true, but there's a way around that. Every object in Ruby can have a special attribute, often called a *singleton class*, not to be confused with the Singleton design pattern.

This special class goes by a number of different names — you'll often see it called a metaclass, which technically, it isn't.

The singleton class can have instance methods, and the methods in a singleton class have precedence over the normal instance method hierarchy of an object — a method declared in an object's singleton class will be executed instead of a normally defined method of the same name. (This is the key to mock objects in Ruby.)

When you define a method using the `def object.method_name` syntax, you are actually adding an instance method to the singleton class of the object, implicitly creating the singleton class if necessary. Later, you can call that method by normal means. Note that there's only one singleton class for each object — no matter how many different times or places you define something in the singleton context, it will always go to the same class.

So, in the preceding `def Recipe.do_something` example, the method is added to the singleton class for the class instance `Recipe`, and can then be called with the same `Recipe.do_something` syntax. Remember, Ruby will not search the class singleton object when looking for an instance method (this is different from the way other languages, such as Java, handle class methods). Therefore, the following will not work:

```
r = Recipe.new
r.do_something  ## needs to be Recipe.do_something
```

The form `def self.do_something` also works in this case only because the method is presumably being defined within the `Recipe` class definition. Inside that definition, `self` resolves to the class `Recipe`, so the method names are effectively identical.

Even though this syntax is usually used to define class methods, there's nothing privileged about classes here — any Ruby object can have singleton methods defined this way. Consider the following script:

```
x = "Are you hungry?"
y = "Are you thirsty?"

def x.add_response
  self << " Yes I am"
end

x.add_response
p x

y.add_response
```

When this code is run, the output is as follows:

```
>>> singleon.rb

"Are you hungry? Yes I am"
NoMethodError: undefined method 'add_response' for "Are you thirsty?":String
```

What happened? The method definition def x.add_response creates a singleton method for the x instance, but not for the y instance. When the method call x.add_response is made, the singleton class is the first place Ruby looks for a method definition, and it finds one there. But the singleton method has been added only to x, so y.add_response finds no definition and returns an error.

There's actually another syntax for accessing the singleton class of a method, which is much more popular for instance singleton classes and is becoming increasingly popular for class methods. The x.add_response method in the previous example could have been written as follows:

```ruby
class << x
  def add_response
    self << " Yes I am"
  end
end
```

The class << object syntax is a Ruby special form. It sets up a block, which is evaluated in the context of the singleton class belonging to object. Any methods defined in that block become singleton methods, and any instance variables defined in the block become singleton instance variables.

Having singleton instance variables in a singleton class for an ordinary Ruby object isn't usually that helpful, but having singleton instance variables for a class is very interesting. Take a look at this example:

```ruby
class SingletonParent
  @@greeting = "I am"

  def self.set_greeting(greeting)
    @@greeting = greeting
  end

  class << self
    attr_accessor :name

    def who_am_i
      p "#{@@greeting} #{name}"
    end
  end
end

class SingletonChild < SingletonParent
end

SingletonParent.name = "Ernie"
SingletonParent.who_am_i

SingletonChild.who_am_i
SingletonChild.name = "Bert"

SingletonChild.who_am_i
SingletonParent.who_am_i

SingletonParent.set_greeting("My name is")
SingletonChild.who_am_i
```

Take a second and see if you can work out what the output of this program will be.

Here's the output:

```
"I am Ernie"
"I am "
"I am Bert"
"I am Ernie"
"My name is Bert"
```

This code sample shows two different ways of defining class variables. The `@@` syntax is used for the greeting, while a conventional instance atribute accessor is used for the name.

Although the two definitions seem similar, there's an important difference. Because the `name` variable is set inside the singleton context it's reevaluated dynamically for each subclass. Practically speaking, this means that each subclass gets its own copy of the variable. This fact can be seen in the example — setting the parent's name to Ernie does not set the child's name. However, the greeting variable is common to both the parent and child classes. In the last two lines, the greeting is reset in the parent class, but the greeting has also changed in the child class.

Going through the Rails source, you'll see that the singleton mechanism is the preferred method of defining class methods. The capability to have separate instance values for subclasses is one reason, plus it's also nice to have all the class methods defined within a specific, dedicated block.

Monkey Patching and Duck Punching

One of Ruby's most distinctive features is that class definitions never close — you can always add new methods to existing classes, even classes that are in the core Ruby library. I've already shown you some examples of this functionality in action, most of which have been along the lines of adding utility methods to core classes like this:

```
require 'rss/2.0'
class Array
  def to_rss_feed(title, link, description="")
    rss = RSS::Rss.new("2.0")
    channel = RSS::Rss::Channel.new
    rss.channel = channel
    channel.title = title
    channel.link = link
    channel.description = description
    self.each do |item|
      channel.items << item.to_rss_item
    end
    rss.to_s
  end
end
```

The feature is still controversial. The most commonly used term for it — monkey patching — comes out of the Python community, and was originally a derogatory way of describing the practice of changing classes at runtime (which can be done in Python, although somewhat awkwardly). Ruby programmers adopted the phrase as their own, although there has been some searching for an alternate term with a less negative connotation. However, the phrase presented as an alternative — duck punching — doesn't sound like all that much of an improvement.

Anyway, the question at hand is "Monkey Patching: Threat or Menace?" Strict software-engineering types argue that the ability to change the definition of any method in the system at whim is a recipe for chaos — "How can you verify the correctness of a program," they argue, "when you can't even count on the definition of a string?" Even less-strict programmers feel a certain amount of queasiness at the idea of going in and potentially messing with the very guts of the system. In answer to this, Ruby programmers point out that it's often useful to add features directly to existing classes, and that it can lead to more readable code. They point to Rails as an example of a system that relies heavily on monkey patching, and yet somehow manages to not fall apart. In fact, Rails does an unusually good job of supporting extensions via plugins, and the plugin system is almost impossible to imagine without monkey patching.

At the risk of sounding wishy-washy, I do want to point out that, in one way or another, everybody in this discussion is somewhat right. It is possible to shoot yourself in the foot pretty dramatically via a monkey patch — and yet, monkey patching is an extremely useful thing to be able to do. For example, I've always wanted to be able to add functionality String in both Java and Python.

Where the people who criticize the practice tend to go a little overboard, in my opinion, is by assuming that the most damaging uses of monkey patching are the most common, or are even common at all. My experience is that radical alterations in the core classes are pretty rare, and although Rails does sort of encourage extending Rails base classes, it does so by providing a few commonly used templates to ensure that existing functionality is not compromised.

There are some legitimate concerns about how to manage a large team of developers, all of whom can mess around with the core classes. And again, I can see the concern, but think that the practical cost is minimal. Any Rails application that uses plugins is implicitly the work of a larger team, and it all seems to hold together as well or better than you'd expect.

This is another round in the never-ending debate between dynamic-language proponents and static-language fans. I've always felt that, although there is some risk inherent in dynamic features, the amount of time I save as a programmer by using a dynamic language more than makes up for the amount of time I have to spend on increased testing or tracking down the potential flaws. It's not that you can't make mistakes in a dynamic language — it's just that the most dramatic possibilities are both relatively rare, and usually not subtle and easily caught.

Monkey Patching Without Slipping On a Banana Peel

Even a defender of the monkey patch such as I knows that there's a right way and a wrong way to do it. Here are some ways to make sure that your monkey patch doesn't come back and bite you.

I think there are two good reasons to add a utility method to an existing core class with a monkey patch. The first is if a normal object-oriented analysis would cause the method to live in the core class. The Rails ActiveSupport library has several examples of this, such as `Integer#even?` and `Hash#diff`. In both of these cases, the method could easily have been included in the original core class — it's obviously a method that acts on the data of that class. This is your chance to include utility methods that are important to your project, even if they are too obscure to be utility methods for everybody.

I also think that it's reasonable to add a method to a core class purely for readability. Ruby programmers in general are known for putting extra work into their libraries and APIs to make them particularly elegant to read. A good example within Rails is the time functions, such as 3.days.ago and the like. You could argue that days and ago are conceptually methods of the Time class. I suppose that's true, but Time.days_ago(3) doesn't quite have the clarity of 3.days.ago.

You are relatively unlikely to cause a significant problem by adding new methods to an existing class — the biggest risk is that you'll just assume the new method is core, and use it in places where it hasn't been defined, which is an error you'll catch quickly. Things get more dangerous when you start modifying existing methods. The first thing to do is to have an "Is this trip really necessary?" conversation with yourself. Monkey patching to change behavior is desirable only if you are trying to change the behavior of already existing code. If you are just trying to change the behavior in the new code you are going to write, then you should consider creating a subclass of the class you want to use, and overriding the appropriate methods as needed.

There are legitimate reasons not to go the subclass route. You might actually need to affect the behavior of other code, because you are writing a trace utility, or because you want to change default ActiveRecord behavior. Some classes are just awkward to subclass — trying to ensure that you will always use MySpecialString in your application sounds nightmarish.

When you do extend an existing class, it's a good idea to use the alias mechanism similar to the one shown in the next section to ensure that the original behavior is still available for objects that want it. Where possible, use the existing method to provide part of the new functionality — this prevents repetition and allows you to use already tested code.

Finally and always, *test, test, test*. Test your patches to validate correctness. Having 100-percent coverage on your entire program dramatically reduces the possibility of some weird interaction sneaking through and causing havoc.

Alias

A common use of monkey patching is to augment or decorate an existing method. The usual pattern here is to have the new method call the old method while providing an additional piece of functionality. For instance, you might want to write a Rails plugin that specially logs ActiveRecord behavior by tracking the identity of all objects saved to your database. Obviously you still want to preserve the existing save behavior, if for no other reason than that you'll want to call it.

So, you start out doing something like this:

```
module ActiveRecord
  class Base
    def save
      log << "Saving #{class} #{id} at #{Time.now}
      ## Now I want to call the pre-existing save....
    end
  end
end
```

There's kind of a gotcha waiting there — you've redefined save, but then you need to call the original save, and there's no way to access it.

The first step toward resolving this problem involves Ruby's alias keyword. The alias method allows you to specify a new method name as being identical to an existing method name — the new one becomes a literal, also-known-as alias. Now you can try to solve the issue thusly:

```
module ActiveRecord
  class Base
    def new_save
      log << "Saving #{class} #{id} at #{Time.now}"
      save
    end
    alias :save, :new_save
  end
end
```

Sadly, this still won't work. The alias command is called when the module is loaded, but the internal save call doesn't happen until a save is actually triggered. By that time, save has long since been renamed, and you're headed for an infinite loop.

To make this work, you need to have two aliases: one that stores the original version of the method, and another that redirects the original name to the new method. Here's how you define those aliases:

```
module ActiveRecord
  class Base

    def new_save
      log << "Saving #{class} #{id} at #{Time.now}"
      old_save
    end

    alias :old_save :save
    alias :save :new_save
  end
end
```

Because the alias calls still happen at load time, it doesn't matter whether they come before or after the definition of the new method. However, the two lines do have to stay in the same relative order — the alias to the existing method has to come first.

This is a common enough pattern in the Rails source that there's a helper method to simplify it a bit. The Rails idiom for this pattern looks like this:

```
module ActiveRecord
  class Base

    def save_with_logging
      log << "Saving #{class} #{id} at #{Time.now}
      save_without_logging
    end

    alias_method_chain :save, :logging
  end
end
```

The naming convention here is a little different from what the original examples had. The `alias_method_chain` creates two aliases as follows:

```
alias :<method>_without_<descriptor> :<method>
alias :<method> <method>_with_<descriptor>
```

In this example, the method is `:save`, and the descriptor is `:logging`. Therefore, with the usual style of convention-over-configuration, Rails assumes that the new method will be called `save_with_logging`, and the old method can be accessed as `save_without_logging`.

Even though this mechanism saves only one line of code, it imposes a naming convention, and prevents you from making mistakes when dealing with a kind of tangled code structure. It's recommended that you use the method chain whenever you patch an existing method in this pattern.

Plugging In

Over the course of this book, you've seen a couple of Rails plugins work in the `acts_as_something` style. They define a class method declaration or two, which is available to all ActiveRecord subclasses. When that class method is called inside a class definition, it acts as a trigger for several other methods to become available — both at a class and an instance level.

Think about the `acts_as_taggable_on_steroids` plugin. The `acts_as_taggable` declaration is available to any ActiveRecord class. That seems like a straightforward monkey patch — adding a new method to the existing ActiveRecord class object. However, when `acts_as_taggable` is called, then the ActiveRecord subclass in question grows a few new methods: both class methods like `find_with_tags`, and instance methods like `tag_list`. That's monkey patching, of a sort, but it's an even more dynamic version that you've already seen. The plugin is patching a class that is not explicitly defined — in fact, it's likely that the class being patched didn't even exist when `acts_as_taggable` was written. How is that done?

The basic functionality is provided by some hook methods defined in standard Ruby that allow you to get access to some class lifecycle events. That's combined with what has become a sort-of-standard way to use those methods to inject code into new classes.

Two of the Ruby hooks are event triggers, automatically invoked by Ruby in response to code events. The first is `included(other)`, which is a method of the class `Module`. You write this method inside your module, and any time that module is included within another class using `include`, this method is eventually triggered. The argument is the other module object, and you can do whatever you want with that module from here. Obviously, that gives you a lot of power to abuse. For our purposes, you'll be using it just to insert new methods.

The other hook is the analogous one for class inheritance. The method is `inherited(subclass)`, and it's a method of the class `Class`, called whenever a new class is declared with a superclass. Again, you define your behavior within the superclass, and any prospective subclasses have to pass through this method while being defined.

The two methods that actually perform the injection are `include` and `extend`. You've seen `include` all over the place — it's what you always use to add a module to a class. Specifically the methods of the module being included are added to the class as instance methods. The `extend` method works similarly, except that the methods of the module being passed in are added to the original module as class methods, instead of as instance methods.

Acts As Reviewable

In your basic acts_as_*whatever* plugin that affects ActiveRecord, you've got three kinds of methods that you need injected into Rails core behavior. First off, you have class methods that will be accessible to any ActiveRecord subclass. Typically this is the acts_as_*whatever* method itself, along with any other top-level method designed to be used as a declaration. Then you have class methods that are only available to a class after it has invoked acts_as_*whatever*, as well as instance methods that are only available to a class that has invoked acts_as_whatever. Ideally, you'd want the structure of your plugin module to map easily to this structure, so any necessary changes can be made cleanly.

To illustrate the commonly used structure that is used to monkey patch ActiveRecord this way, I'm going to show you a plugin called acts_as_reviewable. This plugin will associate recipes with an arbitrary number of user reviews in much the same way that acts_as_taggable associates a recipe with an arbitrary number of tags. In fact, the design of acts_as_taggable_on_steroids informed this discussion. The actual implementation of the plugin will be covered in the next chapter. Here, the concern is how a plugin might inject its code into an unknown ActiveRecord subclass.

The initial skeleton structure of the main module of the plugin places it in the exiting ActiveRecord module structure as follows (eventually, this file will be vendor/plugins/acts_as_reviewable/lib/ acts_as_reviewable.rb):

```
module ActiveRecord
  module Acts
    module Reviewable
    end
  end
end

ActiveRecord::Base.send(:include, ActiveRecord::Acts::Reviewable)
```

It's the responsibility of the plugin structure to make sure this file is loaded in the first place (which is covered by an init file that's discussed in the next chapter), but this file is responsible for making sure that the right things happen thereafter. To that end, I'll start by setting up the skeleton module structure, and the last line will call the include method of ActiveRecord::Base. In effect, that last line is knocking on the door of ActiveRecord::Base and insisting that the new module be included. This is our first dynamic monkey patch of the plugin: adding a new module's methods to ActiveRecord::Base.

As discussed a couple of paragraphs ago, using include on a module triggers a call to the included method for the module being included. This is still true even when, as in this case, the include call is outside the actual class. Here's what I put in the included method for the Reviewable module:

```
module Reviewable
  def self.included(base)
    base.extend(ClassMethods)
  end
end
```

The single argument, base, is the module to which the plugin is being included — in this case, ActiveRecord::Base. All this method does is extend ActiveRecord::Base with a module called ClassMethods. This is a submodule of Reviewable that contains all the methods defined by the plugin that are expected to be available to all subclasses of ActiveRecord::Base. The full structure looks like this:

```
module Reviewable

  def self.included(base)
    base.extend(ClassMethods)
  end

  module ClassMethods
    def acts_as_reviewable
      #what kinds of goodness need to go here??
    end
  end

end
```

Remember, extend takes all the methods defined in the module and adds them as class methods of the extending class. In this case, the module defines just one method: the actual acts_as_reviewable method.

By the way, given the implementation of included here, it would be possible to bypass the need to implement it and just have the statement at the end of the module read like this:

```
ActiveRecord::Base.extend ActiveRecord::Acts::Reviewable::ClassMethods
```

That's a little more code-efficient because it's a few lines shorter. However, the longer version is more flexible and allows intrepid book authors to show an actual case of how included is used. Feel free to use whichever version you like better.

At this point, the following usage is enabled:

```
class Recipe < ActiveRecord::Base
  acts_as_reviewable

  # and so on
```

That fulfills the first of three requirements. There is now a method that is accessible to all subclasses of ActiveRecord::Base, and any implementation of the second two requirements — class and instance methods for ActiveRecords that decide to act as renewable — will need to take place inside the acts_as_reviewable method inside the ClassMethods module.

I suspect it will not surprise you at this point to discover that the implementation involves two other modules: one for inclusion as instance methods, and one for extension as class methods. Here are the definitions for those modules:

```
module ClassMethods
  def acts_as_reviewable
    # define new relationships and filters here
    extend ActiveRecord::Acts::Reviewable::SingletonMethods
```

```
        include ActiveRecord::Acts::Reviewable::InstanceMethods

      # define aliases and other initializations here
    end
  end

  module SingletonMethods
    def find_reviews_for(options = {})
      # implementation TBD
    end
  end

  module InstanceMethods
    def average_rating
      # implementation TBD
    end

    # and so on...
  end
```

The `acts_as_reviewable` method absolutely needs to do two things. First, it calls `extend` to inject the `SingletonMethods` module into its class. The `extend` method is called without an explicit receiver, meaning that the receiver is `self` in the context when the method is called. Because `acts_as_reviewable` is a class method, when it's called, `self` will be the new class itself — in this example, it would be the `Recipe` class. All methods in the `SingletonMethods` module are therefore added as class methods to the base class. (The module is called `SingletonMethods` because the methods are technically being added to the singleton class of the class instance.) At this point, the plugin has enabled the following usage:

```
Recipe.find_reviews_for
```

The mechanism for injecting the instance methods is similar, but instead of using `extend`, the `include` method is used. Again, the fact that `self` is the class instance enables this to work. This enables the final piece of functionality needed to make the plugin work:

```
r = Recipe.find(1)
r.average_rating
```

At this point, the base functionality of the plugin has been intertwined with `ActiveRecord::Base`. As you'll see in the next chapter, the full implementation of this plugin will need take care of some other logistics in the `acts_as_reviewable` method. For instance, the reviews will almost certainly be stored in a new database table or tables, so the method will need to define the relationships to those tables. If the plugin needs to redefine any ActiveRecord functionality, then any alias definitions also come here.

This should give you a basic idea of how to take advantage of the flexibility of Ruby and the Rails plugin system to add new features to ActiveRecord.

The Case of the Missing Method

In most programming languages, calling a method that doesn't exist is a one-way ticket to Exception-land. As should be clear by now, Ruby isn't like most programming languages, so there are a couple of hook methods defined to allow you to have last-ditch access to any wayward method calls. The first method in question is called method_missing(symbol, *args), where symbol is the name of the nonexistent method and args is the list of all the arguments in the call. (To be fair, the method_missing idea comes from Smalltalk, which uses a similar method called doesNotUnderstand. Python also has a similar feature, although in practice Python programmers tend not to use it quite as often.)

There are all kinds of interesting things you can do with method_missing, if you are so inclined. The default implementation is just to throw an exception. An obvious thing to do in method_missing is to use some kind of different logging of that exception, but still throw the exception anyway.

On a more functional level, method_missing can be used to implement a simple proxy as follows:

```
def method_missing(symbol, *args)
  proxy.send(symbol, *args) if proxy.respond_to?(symbol)
  super
end
```

All this does is redirect the missing method to an object designated as the proxy. The if clause just ensures that the proxy will only get the method if it actually defines the method.

But it's possible to get much more inventive. I really love the example given for method_missing in the official Ruby documentation, which I've modified somewhat here:

```
class RomanNumeral
  def self.method_missing(symbol, *args)
      RomanNumeral.new.roman_to_int(symbol.to_s)
    end
end
```

This, of course, assumes that roman_to_int is defined somewhere in the class itself. This shows that method_missing can be defined as a class method as well. With that in place, you get to do this:

```
RomanNumeral.v
RomanNumeral.vii
RomanNumeral.xvi + RomanNumeral.xx
```

In other words, this definition allows you to treat any Roman numeral as an integer with the simplest possible API.

The Roman-numeral example shows a very common use of method_missing, which is to create a more readable API for other programmers to use. The most famous use of method_missing within Rails has much the same goal. This is, of course, the find_by series of method calls that are trapped by method_missing, parsed, and converted to regular find calls. This is a more aggressive example of parsing the method name to determine the behavior, and it's a good example of how much elaborate behavior can be placed in method_missing.

Ruby also defines an analogous method, `constant_missing`, which is called when you request a constant value from a symbol with a capital letter. This is much less commonly overridden, but it's frequently used to automatically load modules when they are defined — Rails will do this if it can determine that a module is in a known location.

Although `method_missing` is a very cool thing, and it's definitely a tool you should get comfortable with, it's not without its drawbacks. There are two major ones, and which one is a bigger problem depends on your project and general outlook. Using `method_missing` will be slower than using a regularly defined method. This is because Ruby needs to take the method all the way up the class hierarchy to determine that the method is, in fact, missing. In addition, the method name is often parsed in order to determine the appropriate response. The second issue is that it's often difficult to document the behavior defined in `method_missing`. Basically, by definition, method calls that are handled by `method_missing` won't show up in your RDoc, which is normally the lookup of first resort for confused programmers. On a related note, if `method_missing` shows up more than once in the same object hierarchy, you run the risk of name collisions or other difficult-to-predict behavior.

Most of these issues are manageable with some forethought, and you shouldn't let them prevent you from exploring `method_missing`-based solutions where they are applicable. For me, the hardest part is getting into the mindset where you think in a `method_missing` kind of way.

Defining Methods Dynamically

Perhaps the most powerful tool in the metaprogrammer's toolkit is the capability to create brand-new methods at runtime that are indistinguishable from the methods defined when the module is loaded.

Because method declarations are just another kind of command inside a Ruby script, they can actually be placed inside conditionals and invoked based on other program logic. Another programming language might force you to do something like this:

```
def error_messages
  if ENV["RAILS_ENV"] == "development"
    p "A very verbose error message"
  else
    p "A terse message"
  end
end
```

But in Ruby, you can do this:

```
if ENV["RAILS_ENV"] == "development"
  def error_messages
    p "A very verbose error message"
  end
else
  def error_messages
    p "A terse message"
  end
end
```

The second code snippet example (the Ruby one) actually changes which version of the `error_messages` method is defined. The advantage of this is that it performs the conditional test once and only once, whereas the traditional version performs the conditional test every time the method is called. The downside is of the dynamic version is that it looks weird, and will take most programmers some extra time to figure out.

Ruby allows you to create methods with the module-level method `define_method`, which takes a symbol and a block as arguments.

There isn't anything you can do with `define_method` that can't be done another way. In particular, `define_method` is basically syntactic sugar for `class_eval`. As an example, take a look at the following `define_method`:

```
define_method(method_name) do |args|
  print args
end
```

This is basically equivalent to the following `class_eval`:

```
class_eval <<-END
  def #{method_name}(*args)
    print args
  end
end
```

However, because the `class_eval` version takes in its code as a string rather than a block, it's significantly harder to work with (although you do still see that version from time to time). For one thing, doing string processing inside the method body can be a pain. For another, most syntax-coloring editors will treat the whole thing as a string, making it harder to visualize the code. In general, the `define_method` form is more flexible and easier to work with.

You can use `define_method` in a variety of ways. It's commonly placed in a part of a class definition that is always run to define several similar methods that conform to a common template. Using `define_method` in this way reduces the duplication in your code. Here's an example inspired by the Rails source — it's the code that enables the so-called "sexy migrations" such as `t.string :name` and `t.integer user_id`:

```
%w( string text integer float decimal datetime timestamp time date binary ↵
boolean ).each do |column_type|
  define_method(column_type) do |args|
    options = args.extract_options!
    column_names = args
    column_names.each { |name| column(name, '#{column_type}', options) }
  end
end
```

Technically, this code in the Rails source is implemented via the `class_eval` mechanism, rather than `define_method`, but this way is a little nicer. For each of the potential column types, this code block creates a new method named after that column type. When that method is called, the options and column names are extracted from the argument list, and the `column` method is called to create the column, using the same column type that's used to name the method.

Without `define_method`, you'd likely have to do something like this:

```
def column_of_type(column_type, *args)
  options = args.extract_options!
  column_names = args
  column_names.each { |name| column(name, '#{column_type}', options) }
end

def string(*args)
  column_of_type("string", *args)
end

def integer(*args)
  column_of_type("integer", *args)
end

# and so on...
```

That's not horrible, and certainly there's a ton of Java code that looks more or less like this. But it does require the duplication of the structure of each call to `column_of_type`, and extending the method to new types is a little more difficult.

Earlier in this book, `define_method` was used similarly in the `TabularFormBuilder` to reduce the amount of duplication in the different form-helper handlers.

Often, when `define_method` is used within a Rails plugin, the name of the method being defined is also being created dynamically. For instance, the following code shows the method definition for `in_place_edit_for`, from the Rails core plugin for in-place editing. This method is called as a class method in a controller to tell the controller that there's an in-place editor in a view that is going to call this controller:

```
in_place_edit_for :recipe, :description
```

The implementation of this method uses `define_method` to create the `set_recipe_description` method that the in-place editor widget expects to call:

```
def in_place_edit_for(object, attribute, options = {})
  define_method("set_#{object}_#{attribute}") do
    @item = object.to_s.camelize.constantize.find(params[:id])
    @item.update_attribute(attribute, params[:value])
    render :text => @item.send(attribute)
  end
end
```

The snippet also uses some other Ruby and Rails reflective goodness. The first line of the internal method `object.to_s.camelize.constantize` converts the name of the symbol, `:recipe`, into the associated class name, `Recipe`, in a nice use of Rails convention-over-configuration ethos. The `find` method is then called on that class, and `update_attribute` is used to change the arbitrary attribute specified in the method name. Then the `send` method is used to get the new value back from the object and that text is rendered — on the view side, it's recovered by the JavaScript widget that made the edit call in the first place and displayed back in-place in the page.

References

Jay Fields has a nice online discussion of `eval` and bindings at `http://blog.jayfields .com/2006/07/ruby-eval-with-binding.html`. There's an interesting discussion about the benefits and dangers of monkey patching anchored around Chad Fowler's post `www.chadfowler.com/index .cgi/Computing/Programming/Ruby/TheVirtuesOfMonkeyPatching.rdoc,v`.

One of the best general overviews of Ruby metaprogramming and singleton classes is provided by the Ruby programmer known as "why the lucky stiff" at `http://whytheluckystiff.net/articles/ seeingMetaclassesClearly.html`. (My only quibble is with why's naming conventions, which differ from what I used in this book.)

A plugin called Acts As Taggable On Steroids (or AATOS) was the basis for much of the discussion on plugin structure. Its home page is `http://agilewebdevelopment.com/plugins/acts_as_ taggable_on_steroids`.

I want to acknowledge Dave Thomas's excellent talk on Metaprogramming from The Rails Edge in August 2007. It wasn't a direct influence on this chapter (and the slides are, sadly, not online), but it was a great overview of metaprogramming and a strong defense of using that part of Ruby's toolkit. Plus, it contained the quote, "The key to metaprogramming is understanding `self`. Isn't that also the key to life?"

Summary

Rails takes advantage of Ruby's features that enable metaprogramming, or changing the programming context at runtime. Like many languages, Ruby has a statement that enables you to evaluate an arbitrary string. Unlike many languages, Ruby allows you to choose the execution context for that string to be any block or object. The classes `Object`, `Class`, and `Module` all have interesting introspective methods that enable metaprogramming constructs.

Ruby classes are also instances of the class `Class`, which permits class objects to be treated just like any other Ruby object. In addition, every Ruby object has a slot for a singleton class that lets you add methods to any individual instance in the system. When that instance is itself a class, the instance method of the class becomes a class method of instances of that class.

Ruby also allows classes to be reopened for the purpose of adding new methods at any time. This permits some elegant code, but can cause problems if used incorrectly. Ruby's alias feature can mitigate some of the risks, as well as offer an easy way to decorate an existing method. Rails offers an alias chaining feature that simplifies a common-use case. These features used together give the Rails plugin system much of its power.

When a method name is not found in Ruby, a special hook method called `method_missing` is invoked. You can use it to provide flexible behavior based on parsing the method names that are requested. You can also add method definitions at runtime by using `define_method`.

15

Extending Rails with Plugins

Ruby on Rails has become a complex framework, and it has a lot of useful features. But it doesn't have every feature every user wants. The Rails design team has deliberately chosen not to try and put every imaginable feature in core Rails, a decision backed in Rails 2.0 by the removal of several features out of the core (admittedly, there are still a lot of features there). The Rails mechanism for managing feature overload is the plugin system, which does a fantastic job of delivering Rails extensions of all kinds to the user community. The Rails community as a whole has augmented Rails in every imaginable direction, in a vibrant and active ecology. If you're doing something in your website, and it's a feature that applies to other websites, odds are there's a plugin to help you with it. If there's not, bundle one up and distribute it yourself.

This chapter how to extend Rails with plugins. Although several plugins have already been used in the development of Soups OnLine, there are still some features of plugin management that are worth talking about. You'll also see how to create your own plugins and generators.

Using Plugins

Rails plugins cover a wide range of complexity and features. Just within the space of this book, the installed plugins cover everything from the simple addition of a Rake task or two, to text searching, to an entire internationalization system, to graph generators, to in-place editing. And that covers less than half of the plugins that we've explored in Soups OnLine. Still, it's only a drop in the bucket compared to what's actually out there.

Installing Plugins

Every plugin installed thus far in the book uses the entire URL of that plugin's subversion repository, with something like the following:

```
$ script/plugin install http://url/plugin_name
```

Rails attempts to automatically determine the best way to download the plugin. If Subversion is on your system, meaning that the `svn` command is in your path, then Rails will perform a Subversion `export` command to your local system; otherwise, Rails will get the files via HTTP. In either case, a new directory is created in `vendor/rails/plugin_name`, and the files are placed there locally without Subversion metadata and without touching your existing source control repository. Because of this, you'll need to reinstall the plugin to incorporate any later code updates. Ordinarily, Rails will not allow you to install a plugin that is already there; however, the `-f` option will force a load even if the plugin already exists locally.

There are two different command-line options that you can use to incorporate the plugin's Subversion metadata and allow for automatic updates from the remote plugin Subversion server. The `-o` option causes the data to be transferred via a Subversion `checkout`. The `-x` option, which you've seen before in this book, includes the plugin into your repository as a Subversion external. In both cases, the files are copied into your local working copy but are not copied to your project's repository. The `-x` option adds the external property to your repository, meaning that the plugin's repository is automatically included on any `svn` update of your entire project. If the file is acquired via checkout, then an explicit update is required to update the plugin. This can be managed either by using `svn update vendor/plugin/plugin_name` or by issuing the following command:

```
$ script/plugin update
```

If no argument is given, all Subversion-based plugins are installed; otherwise, you can give the command one or more plugin names, which will limit the update to just those plugins.

To use either of the Subversion download methods, you not only need to have Subversion available, but your project must be using Subversion for its own source control — the specific test is whether your project root directory has a `.svn` subdirectory. In addition, the `-x` option requires that the `vendor/plugin` directory be included in the Subversion repository. Try it any other way, and you'll get a helpful message explaining that you can't do that.

The other Subversion-related option for plugin installation is `-r NUMBER`, which takes a specific revision number from the plugin host Subversion server, rather than the most current version. Also, the `-q` option will suppress output from the plugin installation (should that be important to you for some reason).

The flipside of installing a plugin is removing one, which you can do with the following command:

```
$ script/plugin remove plugin_name
```

The argument is the plugin name, which is the same as the name of the plugin's directory in `vendor/plugins`.

Plugin Repositories

Although it seems that the full-URL method is the preferred way of linking to a plugin repository (at least, that's the way about 99 percent of plugins advertise their download links), Rails maintains a list of known plugin repositories and their current plugins. Using that list, you can then install a plugin using just the name, as follows:

```
$script/plugin install <NAME>
```

If you want to see a list of all the plugins that are available via this method enter the following:

```
$script/plugin list
```

You'll get output that's similar to the following (I've included the part of the listing that contains the "official" plugins hosted on the same Subversion server as the Rails core):

```
account_location
http://dev.rubyonrails.com/svn/rails/plugins/account_location/
acts_as_list
http://dev.rubyonrails.com/svn/rails/plugins/acts_as_list/
acts_as_nested_set
http://dev.rubyonrails.com/svn/rails/plugins/acts_as_nested_set/
acts_as_tree
http://dev.rubyonrails.com/svn/rails/plugins/acts_as_tree/
atom_feed_helper
http://dev.rubyonrails.com/svn/rails/plugins/atom_feed_helper/
auto_complete
http://dev.rubyonrails.com/svn/rails/plugins/auto_complete/
continuous_builder
http://dev.rubyonrails.com/svn/rails/plugins/continuous_builder/
deadlock_retry
http://dev.rubyonrails.com/svn/rails/plugins/deadlock_retry/
exception_notification
http://dev.rubyonrails.com/svn/rails/plugins/exception_notification/
in_place_editing
http://dev.rubyonrails.com/svn/rails/plugins/in_place_editing/
javascript_test
http://dev.rubyonrails.com/svn/rails/plugins/javascript_test/
legacy
http://dev.rubyonrails.com/svn/rails/plugins/legacy/
localization
http://dev.rubyonrails.com/svn/rails/plugins/localization/
open_id_authentication
http://dev.rubyonrails.com/svn/rails/plugins/open_id_authentication/
scaffolding
http://dev.rubyonrails.com/svn/rails/plugins/scaffolding/
scriptaculous_slider
http://dev.rubyonrails.com/svn/rails/plugins/scriptaculous_slider/
ssl_requirement
http://dev.rubyonrails.com/svn/rails/plugins/ssl_requirement/
token_generator
http://dev.rubyonrails.com/svn/rails/plugins/token_generator/
tzinfo_timezone
http://dev.rubyonrails.com/svn/rails/plugins/tzinfo_timezone/
tztime
http://dev.rubyonrails.com/svn/rails/plugins/tztime/
upload_progress
http://dev.rubyonrails.com/svn/rails/plugins/upload_progress/
```

And on and on it goes for a few pages. Use this command with the `--local` command switch to see just a list of plugins installed locally.

You can get an updated list of the available plugin repositories with this command:

```
$ script/plugin discover
```

And you can see the available sources that are currently stored with this:

```
$ script/plugin sources
```

You can make manual adjustments to the list of sources with the `source` and `unsource` commands. Each takes one or more repository URLs as arguments. The `source` command adds those URLs to the sources list, and the `unsource` command removes them.

Creating a Plugin

Downloading a plugin is such a simple and quick way to add functionality to your program that it's easy to overlook the value of writing your own plugins. And I don't mean that just in a "there's value in giving back to the Rails community" kind of way — although releasing plugins is a great way get your code out there in the community (disclaimer: as of this writing, I have exactly zero publicly available plugins). Writing your program extensions as plugins is extremely simple, and it's the best way to package snippets of Rails functionality that you might reuse from application to application.

To demonstrate how to write your own plugin, I'll walk you through the process of creating the `acts_as_reviewable` plugin referenced in the previous chapter. The goal of this plugin is to allow a class to automatically reference a separate table of reviews, aggregate the values, and manage the reviews. This plugin includes a migration and integration with ActiveRecord. Many plugins won't need all of the features discussed here. However, this example should be a good guide toward designing your plugins.

As with so many things in Rails, plugin layout is governed by convention. In this case, the convention is enforced by the following generator:

```
$ script/generate plugin acts_as_reviewable --with-generator
create  vendor/plugins/acts_as_reviewable/lib
create  vendor/plugins/acts_as_reviewable/tasks
create  vendor/plugins/acts_as_reviewable/test
create  vendor/plugins/acts_as_reviewable/README
create  vendor/plugins/acts_as_reviewable/MIT-LICENSE
create  vendor/plugins/acts_as_reviewable/Rakefile
create  vendor/plugins/acts_as_reviewable/init.rb
create  vendor/plugins/acts_as_reviewable/install.rb
create  vendor/plugins/acts_as_reviewable/uninstall.rb
create  vendor/plugins/acts_as_reviewable/lib/acts_as_reviewable.rb
create  vendor/plugins/acts_as_reviewable/tasks/acts_as_reviewable_tasks.rake
create  vendor/plugins/acts_as_reviewable/test/acts_as_reviewable_test.rb
create  vendor/plugins/acts_as_reviewable/generators
create  vendor/plugins/acts_as_reviewable/generators/acts_as_reviewable
create  vendor/plugins/acts_as_reviewable/generators/acts_as_reviewable/templates
create  vendor/plugins/acts_as_reviewable/generators/acts_as_reviewable/acts_as_
reviewable_generator.rb
create  vendor/plugins/acts_as_reviewable/generators/acts_as_reviewable/USAGE
```

The generator takes one mandatory argument, which is the name of the plugin, and one optional argument, which is `--with-generator`. It generates the basic skeleton structure of the plugin and places it in a `vendor/plugins` subdirectory with the same name as the plugin itself. Including the `--with-generator` option causes the `generators` directory and subfiles to be included in the new plugin skeleton.

Being in the `vendor/plugins` directory enables several different features. Rails automatically runs through the `vendor/plugins` directory on startup. The following facts are guaranteed for Rails applications that include your plugin:

❑ Your `install.rb` file, if it exists, will be run exactly once, when your plugin is installed into a project via `script/plugin install`. In general, you use this file to ensure that the system setup is as the plugin expects. That might include the existence of other plugins, or a specific Rails version, file structure, or operating system. The file may be deleted from your development repository if it's not needed. Another common usage of this file is to print a message to the console with usage information that the developer can see when the plugin is installed.

❑ The `uninstall.rb` file will be run once when the plugin is removed from a project via `script/plugin remove`. Use this to clean up any structures your plugin created at installation. This file may be deleted from your development repository if it's not needed.

❑ The `lib` directory of your plugin is added to the Rails path. This means that any classes in the directory can be autoloaded by other Rails code, assuming that the filename and class name have the standard Rails relationship. (For example, the class `ActsAsReviewable` is in the file `acts_as_reviewable.rb`.) This is not the only way to load your classes — the `acts_as_taggable` design on which this plugin is based makes only some of its code available via autoloading.

❑ The `Rakefile` generated for the plugin is automatically searched by Rake. Any tasks defined in this file are available from the Rake command-line task for the project that includes the plugin. As initially generated, the rakefile defines two tasks: a documentation task, `rdoc`, which is used by the main project's `rdoc:plugins` task; and a testing task, `test`, which is used by the main project's `test:plugins` task.

❑ Any compliant subdirectories in the `generators` directory are made available to the `script/generate` task. The convention for a generator directory is that the name of the directory is the name of the generator. Inside the directory is a file named `<name of generator>_generator`. The `generator` that is automatically created for you if you use `--with_generate` has the same name as the plugin. So in the example, the directory that is created is named `generators/acts_as_reviewable` and contains a file called `acts_as_reviewable_generator`. The directory also contains another directory named templates.

❑ The `init.rb` script for your plugin is executed when the server starts and initializes Rails. By default, plugins are loaded in an arbitrary order. Normally that's fine because plugins are orthogonal. However, in Rails 2.0, you can specify the load order of plugins by including the following in your `config.rb`:

```
config.plugins = [:plugin_name, :other_plugin]
```

Any plugins not included in the list are loaded after the list is complete, in arbitrary order. If you want the unspecified plugins to be loaded at a different spot — that is, if you want to ensure that a specific plugin is loaded last — then include the special symbol :all in the list, which will cause all unlisted plugins to be loaded at that point.

Figure 15-1 shows the plugin lifecycle.

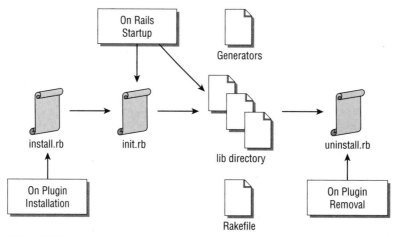

Figure 15-1

In addition to all the code files, you also get some additional text files. The MIT-LICENSE file is the standard license for Rails plugins, with the name of the copyright holder filled in. The license simply allows users to do nearly anything with the code as long as the copyright notice and a disclaimer are included in all distributions. Of course, if you've hung around open source development for any length of time, you know there's nothing simple about a license. You can, of course, change the license if desired. There is a README file that is intended both for text readers and to serve as the front page of your eventual RDoc package. The default file has a skeleton to get you started writing your plugin in RDoc format. Similarly, each generator directory contains a USAGE file. This file is used by Rails to respond to --help requests from script/generate.

Writing a Generator

The Rails generator system is a simple but powerful way to create a family of files from a set of templates based on user commands. The Rails core defines generators for controllers, models, mailers, integration tests, plugins, scaffolds, and a couple of other things. In addition to supporting more complex plugins, generators can stand on their own to automate repetitive tasks. Examples might include custom scaffolding for controllers and models, standard layout templates, or test suites.

Basic Generator Functionality

Generators are called via the script/generate command. The general format is as follows:

```
$ruby script/generate generator_name arg1 arg2 --opt1 --opt2
```

Every generator responds to a set of common option flags, which are described in the following table.

Flag	Meaning
-c --svn	Add new files to subversion, if available.
-h --help	Show the help message.
-f --force	Overwrite existing files without asking.
-p --pretend	Show the list of files that would be created, but don't actually create any files.
-q --quiet	No output.
-s --skip	Skip existing files without asking.
-t --backtrace	Show a stack trace on error.
-v --verbose	Verbose output.

The arguments and options are parsed for you in the parent generator class before your generator is initialized. You have the ability to add new option arguments to your generator.

Generators come in two flavors: basic and named. In a basic generator, the arguments are placed in the instance variable args, and command-line flags are accessible via the accessor options stored in a hash and keyed to the long name of the command, such as options[:svn].

In a named generator, the first argument after the generator name is privileged. A model generator is an example of a named generator, where the first argument is the name of the model to be generated. Named generators do a little extra processing on their first argument. It's inflected multiple ways, and the results are stored in instance variables called name, singular_name, and plural_name. So, for a model named soup_image, the three values are soup_image, soup_image, and soup_images respectively. A side effect of this parsing is that it doesn't matter whether you enter the argument as singular or plural value — Rails will calculate both versions of the name and use the singular version for the class, and the plural version for the database table. Another side effect is that either singular_name or plural_name will match the original name.

Rails also defines the class_name (SoupImage), table_name (soup_images), file_name, and class_path. For the latter two, the full path can be entered either using Unix directory convention (app/model/soup_image) or Ruby module nesting (App::Model::SoupImage).

If you are specifying a set of attributes in name:type format, then the named generator base class will automatically parse them into attributes, which is an array of GeneratedAttribute objects. Here's a big warning, though: If you use attributes, then every argument after the name needs to be in name:type format because Rails will try to parse all the attributes. The following will be an error if you expect attributes:

```
$script/generate model fred barney
```

Rails will try to parse `barney` as an attribute, and will get an error (`fred` is considered to be the name of the model). Worse, the error will be noticed only after some files have already been generated. You can change this behavior in your generator class by overriding the `attributes` method.

The Generator Class

For the `acts_as_reviewable` plugin, the generator is kind of simple. It needs to generate the database migration for the review data table, and that's about it. This is not a named generator — it's always going to create the same basic migration. I see the data structure for a review as having a polymorphic association to reviewable objects, an integer rating, a text description, and a relationship to the user that created the review. To make the generator a little more interesting, I allow an option to change the name of the `user_id` foreign key, and allow the generator to add additional attributes to the database table from the command line.

The first step in the generator is to extract that data from the command line as follows:

```
class ActsAsReviewableGenerator < Rails::Generator::Base

  attr_accessor :user_table, :attributes

  def initialize(runtime_args, runtime_options = {})
    super(runtime_args, runtime_options = {})
    @user_table = init_user_table
    @attributes = @args.collect do |attribute|
      if attribute.include?(":")
        Rails::Generator::GeneratedAttribute.new(*attribute.split(":"))
      end
    end
    @attributes.compact!
  end

  def init_user_table
    return "user" if @args.blank? || @args[0].include?(':')
    @args[0].underscore.singularize
  end
end
```

This is the `ActsAsReviewableGenerator` class, extending `Rails::Generator::Base` (if it was a named generator, it would extend `Rails::Generator::NamedBase`). The class starts by overriding the `initialize` method. The `runtime_args` and `runtime_options` arguments are parsed into `args` and `options` by the parent class, so all this class needs to do is gather the user table name, if entered, and any new attributes. The assumption in the code is that if the first argument does not have a colon, then it's intended to be the user table name; otherwise, it's an attribute. The default user table is `users`: otherwise, it's the suitably inflected version of whatever is entered at the command line. Any command line entry with a colon is converted to an attribute.

The Generator Manifest

The most important part of your generator class is a method called `manifest`. The manifest contains the list of actions that the migration will take. The `acts_as_reviewable` manifest contains only two commands, as shown here:

```
def manifest
  record do |m|
    m.directory "db/migrate"
    m.migration_template "migration.rb", "db/migrate",
      :migration_file_name => "acts_as_reviewable",
      :assigns => {:user_table => @user_table, :attributes => @attributes }
  end
end
```

The first command creates the directory db/migrate in the unlikely event that it doesn't already exist. If it does already exist, then the command does nothing. The second command creates a migration file based on a file in the generator templates directory called migration.rb and will place it in the directory db/migrate. The two key/value pairs in the hash :assigns will be set at local variables when the template is actually generated.

The manifest is what is called by script/generator when your generator is run. The record method gives you a manifest object, and runs the block. The manifest object is where you call your actual generator commands. The following table describes the generator commands that are available in your manifest file's record block.

Generator Command	Description
class_collisions(*class_names)	Raises an exception if any of the class names passed as arguments already exist in Rails. This command does not check the user application space for class names.
directory(path)	Creates a directory at path, relative to the root of the project. Any necessary parent directories are also created. Existing directories are skipped.
file(source, dest, options = {})	Copies the file from source to dest. The paths are relative to the root directory of the Rails project. You can use the :chmod option with this command to specify the access mode for the output file in three-digit Unix format. To override the normal behavior of asking the user what to do on a collision, you can set the :collision option to :ask, :force, or :skip.
	The method takes an optional block. If provided, the block has the input file as an argument, and allows you to manipulate the input file before output, giving a rudimentary template feature. If a block is not provided, then the source file is copied to the destination, and lines beginning with # or ! are ignored. If there is no block, and a :shebang option is provided, it's expected to be the path to the Ruby interpreter in the destination environment, and is inserted at the top of the file.

Table continued on following page

Generator Command	Description
`migration_template(template, dest, options={})`	Identical to `template`, but generates the destination filename based on the next available migration number. You need to explicitly set `dest` to `db/migrations`.
`readme(source)`	Displays the file in the source to the console as a README file.
`route_resources(*resources)`	Adds a RESTful resource set of routes to the `routes.rb` file for each listed resource.
`template(template, dest, options={})`	Converts a template file via ERB and places it in the destination location. All the options that can be passed to file can be passed here. If there is an `:assigns` option with a hash value, then that hash sets the local context that the template is rendered within. Otherwise, the all the key/value pairs in the option hash are available to the template.

Each of these actions has a defined undo equivalent, which is invoked if the generator is called via `script/destroy`.

Testing Generators

Here's the good news: There is a facility in Rails for testing generators, and it's actually quite useful. Here's the bad news: It was clearly intended for use only by the Rails core plugins, so it's buried rather deep in the Rails source and is something of a challenge to get set up correctly. Further complicating matters is the fact that you want to run the migration test outside the Rails environment, so you can control where the generated files go and you don't clobber existing application code to run the test.

Here's how I set up my tests. (I'm not prepared to defend this as the most elegant way to test — there's clearly some room here for augmenting the existing helper.) The test file goes in `vendor/plugins/acts_as_reviewable/test/generator_test.rb`, and the first thing you need to do is require a bunch of stuff as follows:

```
require 'test/unit'
plugin_dir = "#{File.dirname(__FILE__)}/.."
require "#{plugin_dir}/../../rails/railties/lib/rails_generator"
require "#{plugin_dir}/../../rails/railties/test/generators/generator_test_helper"
require "#{plugin_dir}/generators/acts_as_reviewable/acts_as_reviewable_generator"
```

The first `require` line, `test/unit`, should be self-explanatory. The last line is the actual generator class file under test — you'd need to change this line for your own tests. The lines in between are key files from the Rails core that need to be loaded for all the expected classes to be in place. Remember, the Rails environment has not been loaded, so Rails classes are available here only if they are explicitly loaded. The first file, `rails_generator`, contains the actual `Rails::Generator::Base` and `Rails::`

`Generator::NamedBase` classes, and it loads the rest of the generator infrastructure. The `generator_` `test_helper` class contains the actual test helper methods that will be used in this test to make assertions about generator behavior.

Moving on, the next step is to explicitly reset the Rails root directory for purposes of the tests. You do this for two reasons. First, the generator classes depend on the Rails root as the anchor point for the source and destination files, and because this test has not loaded the Rails environment, the value hasn't been set. Second, even if the value had been set, the last thing you want is to use the real Rails root — generating fake migrations into the user's application space tends to be frowned upon. Set the Rails root directory for this test as follows:

```
tmp_dir = "#{File.dirname(__FILE__)}/tmp"
if defined?(RAILS_ROOT)
  RAILS_ROOT.replace(tmp_dir)
else
  RAILS_ROOT=tmp_dir
end
Dir.mkdir(RAILS_ROOT) unless File.exists?(RAILS_ROOT)
```

This sets the Rails root to the `test/tmp` file of the plugin directory, which is more or less arbitrary — it's directory space that this plugin controls, and it's unlikely to be used by anybody else. This snippet, adapted from the existing generator test examples in the Rails core, properly sets the Rails root and ensures that the root directory exists.

Depending on exactly what your migration plans on doing, you may need to stub out some further methods of `ActiveRecord::Base` or `ActiveRecord::ConnectionAdapters::Columns`. In particular, if you are testing a named generator, you may need the following stub inside the `ActiveRecord` module:

```
module ActiveRecord
  class Base
    class << self
      attr_accessor :pluralize_table_names
    end
    self.pluralize_table_names = true
  end
end
```

This allows the name inflection code to work correctly. Again, this is from the existing Rails source generator tests — see those examples if it looks like you need to stub other pieces. A sign that you need to do a stub is if you get a `method_missing` exception on something deep in the guts of ActiveRecord.

You could, I suppose, use Flexmock, Mocha, or a similar mock object tool to manage stubs. I didn't here, largely because examples of generator testing aren't all that thick on the ground, and the examples I have to go on used the direct mechanism.

You also need to ensure that the migration will always get the prefix `001`, or if the migration is run from the regular Rake command line, it will get the next migration prefix based on the current state of the real `db/migrate` directory. There are two options for dealing with this from a test perspective. You can either calclaute the migration prefix you expect to come up and use that in the testing, or you can stub out the appropriate method to always return 001. I think the latter is a bit more stable, so here's how to do it:

```
module Rails
  module Generator
    module Commands
      class Base
        def next_migration_string(padding = 3)
          "001"
        end
      end
    end
  end
end
```

Writing the Generator Test

That takes care of the warm-ups, now you can get to the actual test class. Well, almost — first you need to do the following minor housekeeping inside the test class before you can get to the tests:

```
class ActsAsReviewableGeneratorTest < Test::Unit::TestCase
  include GeneratorTestHelper

  def teardown
    FileUtils.rm_rf "#{RAILS_ROOT}/db/migrate/001_acts_as_reviewable.rb"
  end

  def build_generator(name, params)
    ActsAsReviewableGenerator.spec = Rails::Generator::Spec.new(:plugin,
        "#{File.dirname(__FILE__)}/../generators/acts_as_reviewable", nil)
    ActsAsReviewableGenerator.new(params)
  end
end
```

The `GeneratorTestHelper` is the Rails core module that will provide a lot of the useful test functionality. The `teardown` method removes the migration test that the migration should be creating — notice that it uses the same fake Rails root that you set up earlier.

The `build_generator` method is perhaps a bit of a hack. It's an override of a method provided in `GeneratorTestHelper`. However, the original method checks the standard Rails repository for the generator name, and doesn't seem to want to look in plugin directories. After I tried a series of arguments but still failed to convince it, I decided it was easier to bypass the standard mechanism and just create a new generator object directly. The `Spec` object is used internally by Rails to manage the generator repository.

And now, an actual unit test. Place the following inside the test class:

```
def test_should_create_migration_file
  run_generator('acts_as_reviewable', [])
  assert_file_exists "db/migrate/001_acts_as_reviewable.rb"
  assert_generated_migration :acts_as_reviewable do |body|
    assert_generated_column(body, "reviewable_id", "integer")
```

```
        assert_generated_column(body, "reviewable_class", "string")
        assert_generated_column(body, "rating", "integer")
        assert_generated_column(body, "user_id", "integer")
        assert_generated_column(body, "review", "string")
    end
end
```

The first thing the test does is run the generator, using the handy `run_generator` method provided by `GeneratorTestHelper`. The first argument is the name of the generator, although the `build_generator` override method provided by this test actually ignores it. The second argument is an array of the command line arguments — in this case, the test is for the basic case with no arguments.

After that, the test uses some of the assertions provided by `GenerateTestHelper`. First is `assert_file_exists`, which asserts that a given file exists. Then it uses `assert_generated_migration`, which is one of several assert methods in `GeneratorTestHelper` that validate specific things about the generated file. In this case, the method validates that the generated file contains a subclass of `ActiveRecord::Migration`. The method takes an optional block, which allows you to run arbitrary tests against the body of the generated migration file. In this case, you're asserting that the columns that you expected to create are actually in the migration. This is not, by the way, a full syntactic check of the generated file — it's just a few key regular expression matches.

To run the test, you can use the testing task created by the plugin generator, which you can invoke from the plugin directory with a simple `rake test` command. If you are at the application Rails root, the test directory is automatically seen by the top-level `rake test:plugins` task. Just calling `test:plugins` will get you the test suite for every plugin in the application. You can limit it to just the plugin you want with this:

```
$ rake test:plugins PLUGIN=acts_as_reviewable
```

If you want a Rake task that will specify a set of plugins to run, you're best off writing your own Rake task, which you can place in `lib/tasks` like this:

```
namespace :test do
  Rake::TestTask.new(:acts_as_reviewable => :environment) do |t|
    t.libs << "test"
    t.pattern = 'vendor/plugins/acts_as_reviewable/**/test/**/*_test.rb'
    t.verbose = true
  end

  Rake::TestTask.new(:another_plugin => :environment) do |t|
    t.libs << "test"
    t.pattern = 'vendor/plugins/another_plugin/**/test/**/*_test.rb'
    t.verbose = true
  end

  task :my_plugins => [:acts_as_reviewable, :another_plugin]
end
```

This will allow the Rake `test:my_plugins` command to run both plugin directory tests. If you are developing the plugin alongside your application, you probably also want to add that task to your `rcov` coverage task.

The following two tests cover the case where a user table is specified and where additional columns have been specified:

```
def test_should_create_migration_file_custom_user
  run_generator('acts_as_reviewable', ["critic"])
  assert_file_exists "db/migrate/001_acts_as_reviewable.rb"
  assert_generated_migration :acts_as_reviewable do |body|
    assert_generated_column(body, "reviewable_id", "integer")
    assert_generated_column(body, "reviewable_class", "string")
    assert_generated_column(body, "rating", "integer")
    assert_generated_column(body, "critic_id", "integer")
    assert_generated_column(body, "review", "string")
  end
end

def test_should_create_migration_file_with_attributes
  run_generator('acts_as_reviewable', ["critic", "cuisine:string"])
  assert_file_exists "db/migrate/001_acts_as_reviewable.rb"
  assert_generated_migration :acts_as_reviewable do |body|
    assert_generated_column(body, "reviewable_id", "integer")
    assert_generated_column(body, "reviewable_class", "string")
    assert_generated_column(body, "rating", "integer")
    assert_generated_column(body, "critic_id", "integer")
    assert_generated_column(body, "review", "string")
    assert_generated_column(body, "cuisine", "string")
  end
end
```

GeneratorTestHelper

Within `GeneratorTestHelper`, several assertions are available. All of them take a name as an argument. Where applicable, they also take an optional second argument, which is the parent class. The second argument defaults to whatever the standard Rails parent class for that type would be — for example, the standard controller parent class is `ApplicationController`. The following table describes what the methods check for. All these methods take an optional block for further testing. Unless otherwise specified, all these tests check for the existence of a file, and that the class inside the file is there and has the correct parent class. The name argument is converted to underscore format before the test is applied, so you can pass in the name in CamelCase if that's what you have.

Method	Description
`assert_generated_controller_for`	Asserts the creation of the file `app/controllers/#{name}_controller`.
`assert_generated_fixtures_for`	Asserts that `test/fixtures/#{name}.yml` is a valid YAML file by using the `assert_generated_yaml` method. It also tests to see that the fixtures include timestamp information.
`assert_generated_functional_test_for`	Asserts that `test/functional/#{name}_controller_test` has been created.

Method	Description
assert_generated_helper_for	Asserts that an app/helpers/#{name}_helper file has been created.
assert_generated_migration	Asserts that db/migrate/001_#{name} has been created, and that it has timestamps defined. A separate method, assert_skipped_migration, tests that the migration file does not exist.
assert_generated_model_for	Asserts that a file app/models/#{name} has been created.
assert_generated_unit_test_for	Asserts that a file test/unit/#{name}_test has been created.
assert_generated_views_for	Takes multiple action arguments after the name argument, and validates that app/views/#{name}/#{action} exists for each action specified.

In addition to assert_file_exists, there are a couple of other more generic tests that test for a specific file type. The following table describes the methods used in these tests, and unless otherwise specified, all of these methods also yield to an optional block for further testing.

Method	Description
assert_generated_class	Takes a file path and an optional parent class. Asserts that a file has been created and checks that a class is defined with the name inferred from the filename and the given parent class.
assert_generated_file	Takes a file path as an argument, and asserts that the file exists.
assert_generated_module	Takes a file path, and tests to see if the file has been created with an associated module declaration within it.
assert_generated_stylesheet	Takes a partial path, and asserts that public/stylesheets/#{path}.css exists. It does not do syntax checking on the stylesheet.
assert_generated_yaml	Takes a partial path and asserts that #{path}.yml exists. It also tests that the contents of the file can be loaded via the YAML module. Unlike other methods, this method yields to a block with the result of the YAML load rather than the raw file contents.

There are three assertions that test for specific features within a file, as described in the following table.

Assertion	Description
`assert_added_route_for`	Given the name of a resource, checks that `config/routes.rb` has an associated `map.resources` command.
`assert_genrated_column`	Given a migration file body, a name, and a type, this asserts that the file contains a migration for the column. (See the previous example.)
`assert_has_method`	Given the text of a file and an arbitrary amount of methods, asserts that each method has a `def` statement in the file. For example, `assert_has_method(body, :parse_name, :full_name)`.

I think it's a shame that this test suite hasn't gotten more publicity. A lot of teams would probably benefit from writing more generators to automate common project tasks, and these test helpers go a long way toward simplifying the task.

The Migration that Passes the Tests

At this point, the actual migration template seems almost anticlimactic. The convention for migration templates is to put them in the `templates` subdirectory of the generator directory. The files are ERB files, but the convention is to give them the file extension of the kind of file being generated. The following template will generate a migration file named `migration.rb`:

```ruby
class ActsAsReviewable < ActiveRecord::Migration
  def self.up
    create_table :reviews do |t|
      t.integer :reviewable_id
      t.string :reviewable_class
      t.integer :rating
      t.integer :<%= user_table %>_id
      t.string :review
      <% attributes.each do |attribute| %>
        t.<%= attribute.type %> :<%= attribute.name %>
      <% end %>
      t.timestamps
    end
  end

  def self.down
    drop_table :reviews
  end
end
```

In this file, the `user_table` and `attributes` values come from the `:assigns` option when the migration is invoked from the manifest file.

Writing the Plugin

If your plugin doesn't change `ActiveRecord::Base` or affect Rails data structures in any way, then test-first development for your plugin is quite similar to test-first development of any code.

ActiveRecord Test Setup

If you are trying to modify `ActiveRecord::Base` in your plugin with an `acts_as_whatever` method, then you have some additional setup work to do. Ideally, you'd like to be able to do something like this:

```
require 'test/unit'
require "#{File.dirname(__FILE__)}/../../../../test/test_helper"

class ReviewableThing < ActiveRecord::Base
  acts_as_reviewable
end

class ActsAsReviewableTest < Test::Unit::TestCase

  def setup
    @rt = ReviewableThing
  end

  def test_this_plugin
    assert_responds_to @rt, :reviews
  end
end
```

Unfortunately, if you try that test exactly as written here, it will fail in the depths of ActiveRecord. `ActiveRecord::Base` assumes that it will be able to query a database to get information about its attributes. Because the `ReviewableThing` class doesn't have a database table associated with it, `ActiveRecord` fails to load the class.

This is another manifestation of the larger issue about plugins and testing. The plugin isn't really part of the project that uses it, so it can't depend on that project for test fixtures and setup. Broadly speaking, there are two options for working around this issue. You can either do a lot of setup work to give the plugin its own database setup, which introduces a dependency on a specific database in the developers requirement (any dependency added for testing purposes shouldn't affect a user who just wants to use the plugin). Or you can do a lot of setup work to break the connection between ActiveRecord and the database for the purposes of these tests, which can add a dependency on a mock object package as the mechanism for preventing ActiveRecord from needing the database.

For this plugin, I decided to go with the detached ActiveRecord option, on the grounds that it's much easier to set up. The recipe I'm using to manage this was written by Muness Alrubaie and is available online at http://muness.blogspot.com/2007/06/unit-testing-activerecord-models-now.html.

Chapter 15: Extending Rails with Plugins

Take the code sample in that blog post and insert it into the test file before the declaration of ReviewableThing, or place it in another file to be inserted, like this:

```
class Test::Unit::TestCase
  class ActiveRecordUnitTestHelper
    attr_accessor :klass

    def initialize(klass)
      self.klass = klass
      self
    end

    def where(attributes = {})
      klass.stubs(:columns).returns([id_column])
      instance = klass.new()
      attributes.each do |key, value|
       next if key == :id
       begin
          instance.meta_eval{undef_method(key.to_sym) if respond_to? key}
          instance.meta_eval{undef_method("#{key.to_s}=".to_sym) if respond_to?
"#{key.to_s}="}
          instance.meta_eval{attr_accessor key.to_sym}
          instance.send("#{key}=".to_sym ,value)
        rescue Exception => exception
          instance.stubs(key.to_sym).returns(value)
        end
      end
      instance.id = attributes[:id] if attributes[:id]
      instance
    end

    def where_without_associations(attributes)
      klass.stubs(:columns).returns(columns(attributes))
      instance = klass.new(attributes)
      instance.id = attributes[:id] if attributes[:id]
      instance
    end
    protected

    def columns(attributes)
      attributes.keys.collect do |attribute|
        column attribute.to_s, attributes[attribute]
      end
    end

    def id_column
      column(:id, 0)
    end

    def column(column_name, value)
      ActiveRecord::ConnectionAdapters::Column.new(column_name,
        nil,
```

```
            ActiveRecordUnitTestHelper.active_record_type(value.class),
            false)
      end

    def self.active_record_type(klass)
      return case klass.name
        when "Fixnum"         then "integer"
        when "Float"          then "float"
        when "Time"           then "time"
        when "Date"           then "date"
        when "String"         then "string"
        when "Object"         then "boolean"
      end
    end
  end

  def disconnected(klass)
      ActiveRecordUnitTestHelper.new(klass)
  end
end
```

The code recipe is a fancy piece of metaprogramming that allows you to specify an ActiveRecord object to be detached from a database. ActiveRecord always goes to the database to determine the expected type of the attribute based on the database column type. This code creates an elaborate stub, replacing the database check of the column with an educated guess based on the Ruby class of the attribute value. As such, it has a couple of limitations — perhaps most notably, it doesn't create true `ActiveRecord` association objects. Because it's not actually touching the database, you can't really test `find` or `save` behavior via this recipe, although you could mock those methods separately. Also, the code as written on the website is dependent on the Mocha mock object framework (`gem install mocha`) to stub out the critical piece of `ActiveRecord::Base`.

The recipe used here is not the only way to detach `ActiveRecord` from the database. I chose it because it affects only ActiveRecord objects that are specifically declared to be detached. Another mechanism or two is referenced at the end of this chapter. One of those mechanisms overwrites `ActiveRecord::Base#new`, affecting all ActiveRecords in the test environment — which could be very useful, depending on your overall test structure. Plugins that test the actual database behavior should go through the process of creating a local plugin test database — again, the references at the end of the chapter point you to a good description.

With this recipe in hand, you can set up the tests as follows:

```
require 'test/unit'
require "#{File.dirname(__FILE__)}/../../../../test/test_helper"
require 'mocha'

#### INSERT HELPER RECIPE HERE

class ReviewableThing < ActiveRecord::Base
```

(continued)

(continued)

```
    acts_as_reviewable
  end

class ActsAsReviewableTest < Test::Unit::TestCase

  def setup
    @rev_1 = disconnected(Review).where({:id => 1,
      :rating => 4,
      :created_at => '2007-10-20 11:00:00'})
    @rev_2 = disconnected(Review).where({:id => 2,
      :rating => 3,
      :created_at => '2007-10-18 11:00:00'})
    @rev_3 = disconnected(Review).where({:id => 3,
      :rating => 2,
      :created_at => '2007-10-19 11:00:00'})
    @rt = disconnected(ReviewableThing).where({:id => 1,
        :reviews => [@rev_1, @rev_2, @rev_3]})
  end
end
```

The helper recipe defines a method called `disconnected`, which takes as its argument an
`ActiveRecord::Base` subclass, and returns an instance of that class that is specially metaprogrammed
to not hit the database to get type information. The setup creates four of these objects: three of the
`Review` class that will be built by the plugin, and one of the `ReviewableThing` class that declares that it
`acts_as_reviewable`.

You can see one of the limitations of this test method in the last line, where the `reviews` attribute is
explicitly set to the array of reviews. As mentioned, this is not an ActiveRecord association object, so you
can't mimic a more common way of placing these reviews in the reviewable class, such as `@rt.reviews
<< @rev1`. Also, the foreign key columns of the `Review` class are not automatically set for the `Review`
instances when they are associated. However, that's not really the functionality under test, so I'm not all
that worried about it.

You can now write an initial unit test for basic review functionality, starting with this basic test:

```
def test_reviews
  assert_equal(3, @rt.reviews.size)
end
```

Acts_As_Reviewable Structure

The basic structure of the `acts_as_reviewable` plugin was covered in the previous chapter with
a particular eye towards explaining how the metaprogramming code injection works. This section
expands on that to show how the actual functionality of the plugin is structured.

The plugin point of entry is the `init.rb` file. For many plugins, this file will be only one or two lines. Typical behavior is to require the loading of one or more files in the plugin's `lib` directory, or alternately to extend an existing class with a module stored in the `lib` directory. For `acts_as_renewable`, I chose the following `require` route:

```
require File.dirname(__FILE__) + '/lib/acts_as_reviewable'
```

This places the actual extension of the `ActiveRecord::Base` class within the `lib/acts_as_reviewable` file. There's not a whole lot of practical difference between putting the `extend` in the `init` file or in the `lib` file, but I kind of like the idea of keeping the actual mechanism for injecting the code encapsulated in the `lib` directory. To this end, the following code snippet takes the structure talked about in the previous chapter (the other modules have been left off this snippet for the time being) and adds the highlighted line:

```
module ActiveRecord
  module Acts
    module Reviewable

      def self.included(base)
        base.extend(ClassMethods)
      end

      module ClassMethods
        def acts_as_reviewable
          has_many :reviews, :as => :reviewable

          include ActiveRecord::Acts::Reviewable::InstanceMethods
          extend ActiveRecord::Acts::Reviewable::SingletonMethods
        end
      end

      ### SingletonMethod and InstanceMethod modules here

    end
  end
end

ActiveRecord::Base.send(:include, ActiveRecord::Acts::Reviewable)
```

A class that calls `acts_as_reviewable` gets a `has_many` relationship with the `Review` class. The relationship is polymorphic, allowing multiple reviewable classes in the same project.

The other half of the relationship belongs to the `Review` class, which is defined as part of the plugin, with the following definition in `vendor/plugins/acts_as_reviewable/lib/review.rb`:

```
class Review < ActiveRecord::Base
  belongs_to :reviewable, :polymorphic => true
end
```

At this point, the basic test runs. The ReviewableThing class can call acts_as_reviewable, and it gets the relationship set up correctly (assuming you have the InstanceMethods and SingletonMethods modules set up as outlined in the preceding chapter). Now it's time to augment the test to add a little bit of functionality, like this:

```
def test_reviews
  assert_equal(3, @rt.reviews.size)
  assert_equal(3, @rt.average_review_score)
  assert_equal(1, @rt.best_review.id)
  assert_equal(3, @rt.worst_review.id)
  assert_equal(1, @rt.most_recent_review.id)
end
```

These features are all instance methods of the ReviewableThing class, injected after it calls acts_as_reviewable. In the module structure, that means these methods go in ActiveRecord::Acts::Reviewable::InstanceMethods, as follows.

```
module InstanceMethods
  def best_review
    reviews.max
  end

  def worst_review
    reviews.min
  end

  def most_recent_review
    reviews.max { |a, b| a.created_at <=> b.created_at }
  end

  def average_review_score
    reviews.collect(&:rating).sum / reviews.size
  end
end
```

These implementations are all fairly straightforward. For the best and worst review methods to work as implemented here, the Review class needs to be comparable on the review score. You can set that up as follows:

```
class Review < ActiveRecord::Base
  include Comparable

  belongs_to :reviewable, :polymorphic => true

  def <=>(other)
    rating <=> other.rating
  end
end
```

Alternatively, the reviews can be sorted by explicitly by calling max with a block, the way the most_recent_review function does. In theory, doing this sorting in Rails, rather than in the database, is a potential performance issue. I'm assuming that the reviews will already have been loaded from the database by the time these methods are called, meaning that the Ruby functions would be faster than going back to the database again. To facilitate eager loading of the reviews, the plugin makes the following method available as a class method to all classes that implement the plugin. This method is placed in the `SingletonMethods` module:

```
module SingletonMethods
  def find_with_reviews(*args)
    options = args.last.is_a?(Hash) ? args.pop : {}
    options.merge :include => :reviews
    args << options
    find(*args)
  end
end
```

All this method does is augment an existing `find` call with an additional option to include reviews.

Not all the functionality of the plugin is placed in the reviewable class — some of it needs to go in the actual `Review` class itself. The following code snippet shows an example of a method that converts the rating score into a list of the form `full`, `full`, `empty`, `empty`, `empty`. This is meant to be used to simplify converting the rating into a graphical set of stars or something similar. In addition, the reviewable class should have access to the feature for its average rating. Here's the test, which covers various cases related to fractional scores:

```
def test_star_images
  assert_equal(%w{full full full full empty}, @rev_1.star_images)
  assert_equal(%w{full full full empty empty}, @rt.star_images)
  assert_equal(%w{empty empty empty empty empty}, Review.star_images(0))
  assert_equal(%w{empty empty empty empty empty}, Review.star_images(0.1))
  assert_equal(%w{half empty empty empty empty}, Review.star_images(0.5))
  assert_equal(%w{full empty empty empty empty}, Review.star_images(1))
  assert_equal(%w{full full empty empty empty}, Review.star_images(2))
  assert_equal(%w{full full empty empty empty}, Review.star_images(2.1))
  assert_equal(%w{full full half empty empty}, Review.star_images(2.5))
  assert_equal(%w{full full full empty empty}, Review.star_images(2.9))
  assert_equal(%w{full full full full full}, Review.star_images(5))
end
```

The bulk of the implementation goes into the `Review` class like this:

```
def self.star_images(rating, max = 5)
  partial = rating
  result = []
  max.times do
    if partial > 0.75
      result << "full"
    elsif partial < 0.25
      result << "empty"
    else
      result << "half"
    end
```

(continued)

(continued)

```
      partial -= 1
    end
    result
  end

  def star_images(max=5)
    Review.star_images(rating, max)
  end
```

In this case, `max` is the highest possible rating, and therefore the total number of elements in the array. To allow the reviewable method access to the feature, add the following to the `InstanceMethods` module:

```
  def star_images(max = 5)
    Review.star_images(average_review_score, max)
  end
```

Distributing Plugins

After your plugin is complete, you're encouraged to share it with the Rails community at large. The primary requirement to distribute a plugin is a publicly available Subversion server. If you don't have a public Subversion server that you want to expose to the world, there are a number of hosting services that will provide you with space for your Rails project for the low cost of absolutely free. The most commonly used service is `rubyforge.org`, where you can create a project and get a Subversion server, a project home page, a bug tracker, and a mailing list.

If you place your project on your own Subversion server, you can register the server at `http://wiki.rubyonrails.org/rails/pages/Plugins`. This will cause the server to be added to the sources list generated when somebody does a `script/plugin discover` command.

As I write this, there isn't really an official online plugin repository, although there have been a few attempts to create one. The *de facto* standard location is `http://agilewebdevelopment.com/plugins`, which allows you to register a plugin and assign it to various categories. Plugin users can rate plugins at that site. A newer plugin repository is `www.railsify.com` — it has a nice UI, but as of right now, it doesn't have quite as large a collection of plugins as the Agile Web Development site.

References

Geoffrey Grosenbach has a nice introduction to plugins at `http://nubyonrails.com/articles/2006/05/04/the-complete-guide-to-rails-plugins-part-i`. You also should check out the Rails wiki at `http://wiki.rubyonrails.com/rails/pages/HowTosPlugins`. For more detail, try the O'Reilly Short Cut, *Rails Plugins: Extending Rails Beyond the Core* by James Adam. Another good overview is by Alex Young at `http://alexyoung.org/articles/show/40/a_taxonomy_of_rails_plugins`.

You might also seek out RaPT, which is a replacement for the Rails `script/plugin`. It's available at `http://rapt.rubyforge.org`.

For more information on testing ActiveRecord classes without a database, check out Jay Fields Thoughts at `http://blog.jayfields.com/2007/03/rails-activerecord-unit-testing-part-ii.html`. Muness Alrubaie also discusses this topic at `http://muness.blogspot.com/2006/12/unit-testing-rails-activerecord-classes.html` and `http://muness.blogspot.com/2007/06/unit-testing-activerecord-models-now.html`. For information about the UnitRecord RubyGem, go to `http://unit-test-ar.rubyforge.org`.

Summary

Rails uses the plugin architecture to allow all kinds of functionality to be added to a Rails project without making the core even bigger than it already is. The `script/plugin` script covers the discovery, installation, and removal of plugins.

Creating your own plugin is a great way to package common code for use across multiple projects. The basic skeleton is created by a Rails generator, including hooks for behavior on installation, load, and plugin removal.

Your plugin can create its own generators, which allows your own arbitrary templates to be called from the `script/generator` method. With some judicious environment tweaking, a generator test helper used in the Rails core can be adapted to test your generators. Generator behavior is guided by a manifest file, which accepts several commands that involve the creation of directories and files.

The plugin structure discussed in the previous chapter can be augmented with actual behavior in the modules, and again, tested despite being outside the environment of the Rails application.

After the plugin is developed, it can easily be hosted on one of several freely available servers and distributed to the Rails community at large.

16

Replacing Ruby Tools

Ruby and Rails are linked together tightly, but not so tightly that they can't be pried apart here and there where it makes sense to do so. In this chapter, you'll explore various ways to use Rails and languages or tools other than Ruby itself.

ERB Replacements

The stated design rationale for using ERB as the template language for Rails views is to keep the programming language as consistent as possible — Ruby in the controller, Ruby in the model, and Ruby in the view. There's an admirable consistency to that structure, but nevertheless, Rails has been dogged by complaints about the ERB structure from the very beginning. To some extent, that's because it's a hard problem — I'm not aware of any web tool whose view language is considered completely satisfying. The paradigm of mixing HTML with markup has been around since the first web frameworks, though, and it's certainly a comfortable one for many web developers.

However, there's also a feeling that the mixing of HTML and Ruby code is not always the clearest or most satisfying way of describing a view. For my part, I find the issue of indenting an ERB file properly to be annoying. A table with a header row and then rows within a loop, for instance, winds up with the table rows at two different levels of indentation. (I'm also not happy with the way the ERB delimiters mess up the indentation.) On some level, that's just an aesthetic gripe, but I also feel that it suggests that the structure of the HTML/markup file is wrong, or at least not optimal.

In this section, you'll look at a few replacements that have been developed for ERB views. Design goals of these tools include the desire to create a simpler, more flexible template language, as well as to add a more object-oriented, program-like structure to view output.

Markaby

Markaby is one of the many ingenious Ruby tools from "why the lucky stiff" (http://code
.whytheluckystiff.net/markaby/). Inspired by the core Ruby CGI library, it attempts to make the
output markup look more like Ruby (the name Markaby comes from **Mark**up **a**s **Ruby**). Markaby is
distributed as a Ruby gem (gem install markaby), but for use within a Rails project, you're better off
installing it as a plugin like this:

```
script/plugin install http://code.whytheluckystiff.net/svn/markaby/trunk
```

Markaby Template Files

The basic idea of Markaby is to have the HTML tags in your output represented by Ruby blocks. Here's a
section of Markaby corresponding to a significant chunk of the recipe controller index page:

```
table :width => "75%" do
  tr do
    th "Title"
  end
  @recipes.each do |recipe|
    tr do
      td do
        if recipe.has_image?
          image_tag recipe.soup_image.public_filename(:tag)
        else
          " "
        end
      end
      td do
        link_to h(recipe.title), recipe
      end
    end
  end
end
```

After the Markaby plugin is installed, a Rails controller will search for files with the extension .mab
when looking for an associated view file. To run this, I created a new controller app/controllers
/output_choice_controller, and added the following action called markaby_test:

```
class OutputChoiceController < ApplicationController
  layout "recipes"
  before_filter :load_user

  def markaby_test
    @recipes = Recipe.find_for_index(params[:format])
    respond_to do |format|
      format.html
    end
  end
end
```

The view code was placed in `app/views/output_choice/markaby_test.mab`. You do not need to change the `routes.rb` file for this to work — with the Markaby plugin installed, Rails will include `*.mab` files in its search for valid view files.

So an ordinary HTML tag is represented by a method with an argument representing the text within the tag, like this:

```
th "title" ### <th>title<th>
```

Alternatively, the tag method takes a block, which represents the contents of the tag as follows:

```
tr do
  td do
    span @recipe.title
  end
end ###### <tr><td><span>Title of Recipe</span></td></tr>
```

Tags that don't contain content, such as `br` and `hr`, are treated as simple methods, and block or content attached to them is ignored. As you can see in the preceding code snippet, any variables that would be available to the view (meaning they were specified in the controller action) can be used directly in Markaby. There's no need to surround them in a special syntax to specify that the text should be output — Markaby is smart enough to know that `@recipes.each` should not be directly output to HTML, but that `@recipe.title` should. The general rule is that Markaby knows an instance variable lookup is not a method call and should not be converted to an HTML tag.

Attributes are managed similarly to the way they are in most Rails helpers, as key/value pairs on the method call. For example, the following code:

```
table :width => "75%" do
end
```

gets converted to this:

```
<table width="75"></table>
```

The attributes for CSS class and DOM ID have Markaby shortcuts. To specify a class, treat the class name as though it was a method of the HTML tag, like this:

```
span.subtle "Enter text" #### <span class="subtle">Enter text</span>
```

For a DOM ID, it's the same thing, except the method ends in a bang! For example:

```
span.recipe_name! "Chicken Soup" #### <span id="recipe_name">Chicken Soup</span>
```

Markaby throws an exception if you try to use the same DOM ID multiple times on a page. However, one limitation of this mechanism is that it precludes the use of variable ID or class names, such as `"recipe_#{recipe.id}"`. To do something like that, you need to fall back to the hash mechanism used for other attributes.

You can call any helper method that is available to the view from within your Markaby file. Markaby assumes that the output of the helper method should be placed directly in the stream of text being rendered. For instance, both `image_tag` and `link_to` in the earlier example are helpers that output strings that are part of the final HTML file. Sometimes you may have a helper method whose text you don't want to output at that point — in that case, you can access the method via the special instance method `@helper`. Setting local variables works just fine, too, so you can do something like this:

```
x = @helper.my_helper_method
td x
```

There's a similar issue with named routes. By default, Markaby tends to misnterpret the header in order to put it directly out into the stream, which is not what you want when the route is going to be part of a larger helper that is constructing a form or anchor tag. The workaround for named routes is to explicitly convert to a string, and goes something like this:

```
link_to "Recipes", recipes_path(@instance).to_s
```

You can store the output of a block of code, whether it contains Markaby calls or Rails helpers, using the following `capture` method:

```
header = capture do
  tr do
    th "Column"
    th "Another Column"
  end
end
```

This snippet gives you the following header variable, which you can reuse in multiple tables:

```
table do
  header
end
```

One other issue to be aware of is that in some cases, the tag name will conflict with an existing helper method — the most prominent probably being `select`. You can force Markaby to create a tag using the following `tag!` method:

```
tag! select name => :thingies do
  option "a"
  option "b"
end
```

Markaby Standalone

Using Markaby as an ERB template replacement is pretty nice, but that's not Markaby's only trick. You can also call the `Markaby::Builder` class from any arbitrary location within your Rails project. This makes Markaby a very elegant replacement for `content_tag` and `concat` from within a helper method. To wit, the following helper method is suitable for use in your `ApplicationHelper` class (you must `require 'markaby'` for this to work):

```
def show_a_recipe(recipe)
  builder = Markaby::Builder.new
  builder.html do
```

```
        h1 recipe.title
        p "Servings: #{recipe.servings}"
        p recipe.description
        h2 "Ingredients"
        p recipe.ingredient_string
        p recipe.directions
      end
    builder.to_s
  end
```

That's pretty, if I do say so myself.

There's one unusual feature of the code inside the html do block. You may have noticed that the internal h1, p, and h2 methods (which are technically methods of the Markaby builder) are called without the builder as a recipient. This works because Markaby does a little metaprogramming magic inside its blocks to prevent you from having to type builder. repeatedly. Specifically, the entire block is executed inside an instance_eval call, which effectively points self at the Markaby builder for the duration of the block. The problem is that if you intend to call methods of the class that is calling the Markaby builder, it won't work — you can't access the calling context's self object directly. There are two possible workarounds. The new method takes two optional arguments. The first is a hash of key/value pairs representing variables available within the Markaby builder block, similar to the locals array you'd pass to a partial view, as follows:

```
builder = Markaby.Builder.new(:object => self)
builder.html do
  h1 object.title
end
```

The second argument takes a single object as a helper, and all methods of that object are accessible as though they were methods of the Markaby builder. For example:

```
builder = Markaby.Builder.new({}, recipe)
builder.html do
  h1 title
end
```

Also, the block can be an argument of the new method, rather than of the html method giving a slight shortcut, as follows:

```
builder = Markaby.builder.new do
  html do
    h1 object.title
  end
end
```

If Markaby has a weakness, it's speed. All the metaprogramming and method_missing tricks that make it such a nice API do tend to slow it down some. Still, if you're in a situation where you can take the performance hit (because it's just being cached, for instance), Markaby is a pretty clean way to specify outputs.

Haml

Haml is a very aggressive attempt to rewrite a view template to be as concise as possible — the home page suggests that Haml is "markup haiku." You can get Haml with this:

```
$ script/plugin install http://svn.hamptoncatlin.com/haml/tags/stable
```

It's also available as a Ruby gem (`gem install haml`).

> *As I write this in October 2007, there seems to be a bad interaction between the Haml plugin and the Markaby plugin (they seem to be trying to override the same template method with a different number of arguments). I suspect this is a temporary issue that should be resolved by the time you read this. If you continue to have trouble, though, you may need to remove Markaby to get Haml to work.*

Here's the same recipe page done up Haml-style:

```
%table{:width => "75%"}
  %tr
    %th Title
  - @recipes.each do |recipe|
    %tr
      %td
        - if recipe.has_image?
          %image{:src => recipe.soup_image.public_filename(:tag)}
        - else
           
      %td= link_to h(recipe.title), recipe
```

I invoke this with another controller method, which is identical to the one for Markaby:

```
def haml_test
  @recipes = Recipe.find_for_index(params[:format])
  respond_to do |format|
    format.html
  end
end
```

This means that the view page goes to `app/views/output_choice/haml_test.haml`.

Two things are apparent immediately. The Haml page takes a lot less text than the Markaby or Liquid pages (which you'll look at shortly), and it's also a little opaque on first glance (at least to me). Let's break it down.

Haml uses the percent sign (%) to indicate that a tag is coming. The tag name is optionally followed by one or more special characters, and then by the contents of the tag. Unless the = modifier is used, the text after the tag declaration is assumed to be a string literal — you don't need to enclose it in quotes (in fact, if you enclose it in quotes, the quotes will be part of the output). So, for example, the following code:

```
%th Title
```

gets converted to this:

```
<th>Title</th>
```

Haml does not actually check to see that your tag is part of HTML and will happily convert any string after the % to a tag. That enables Haml to be used to generate XML as well as HTML.

Haml uses indentation to specify the contents of a complex tag. Every line with content that should be contained in the outer tag needs to be indented two spaces relative to the outer tag. The outer tag automatically ends on a line that is set back to the same level of indentation. If you are familiar with Python's use of whitespace to manage blocks, it's the same general idea.

The plus side of Haml's structure is that it encourages readable and consistent layout practice, and makes the code much more compact because blocks don't have to have explicit end markers. The downside is that in long blocks, it can be difficult to keep track of where blocks begin and end (admittedly that can also be a problem in nonindented languages). My experience with Python is that it works largely because the indentation rule subtly encourages refactoring to smaller blocks. In Haml, that would imply refactoring to partials or helpers aggressively to encourage readability.

Here's a longer example. This series of indented blocks in Haml:

```
%table
  %tr
    %td
      %span Hi
    %td
      %span There
```

gets converted to this HTML (indentation cleaned up by me):

```
<table>
  <tr>
    <td><span>Hi</span></td>
    <td><span>There</span></td>
  </tr>
</table>
```

A line that does not begin with a % is considered to be literal text belonging to the containing tag. Haml will expect this text to be indented just as if it was another tag. So the following Haml code:

```
%span
  A line of text
```

becomes this HTML:

```
<span>A line of text</span>
```

Unlike Markaby, which defaults to putting all its HTML characters in a jumble with no new lines or indentation, Haml attempts to make its output more human-readable.

There are about a dozen or so special characters that modify the interpretation of a tag or line of text. Braces after the tag indicate tag attributes. The braces are in standard Ruby hash syntax, just like the HTML options hash that most Rails helpers take. So this:

```
%table{:width => "75%"}
```

becomes this HTML:

```
<table width="75">
```

As in Markaby, `class` and `id` are privileged. The usage is taken from CSS descriptors. The `class` name starts with a period, and the `id` name starts with a pound or hash sign. So this:

```
%span.subtle#try_it_span
```

converts to this HTML:

```
<span class="subtle" id="try_it_span">
```

The `class` and `id` can come in either order.

An object reference placed inside brackets automatically sets the `class` and `id` in a manner similar to the Rails standard `dom_id` method. So this:

```
%span[@recipes[0]]
```

converts to this HTML:

```
<span class="recipe" id="recipe_1"/>
```

The `class` name is the name of the Ruby class of the object, converted to underscore syntax, and the `id` is the class name followed by its ID — for our purposes, this is meant to be an ActiveRecord ID.

If there is just a `class` or `id` specification but no tag name, the tag is implicitly assumed to be a `div`. So the following code:

```
.emphasis#recipe_title
```

is interpreted by Haml to the follwing HTML:

```
<div class="emphasis" id="recipe_title">
```

If you include an equal sign (=) after the tag name, the remainder of the line is evaluated as Ruby code. For example, this:

```
%div= recipe.title
```

becomes this HTML (assuming the exact recipe object, of course):

```
<div>Grandma's Chicken Soup</div>
```

You can also do string interpolation. For example, this:

```
%div= "Title: #{recipe.title}"
```

is converted to this HTML:

```
<div>Title: Grandma's Chicken Soup</div>
```

Starting a line with a hyphen (–)signifies that the line should be evaluated as Ruby code, but not output to the screen. This can be used to define local variables. For example:

```
- days = 3 * 45
```

Or it can be used to specify control behavior with regular Ruby conditional or loop statements. Well, the statements are almost regular Ruby. In keeping with the Haml indentation structure, blocks are started with the normal structure, but are ended using the indentation as a marker. This goes for both language structures like if or for as well as do/end blocks. For example:

```
- if recipe.has_image?
  %image{:src => recipe.soup_image.public_filename(:tag)}
- else
   
```

Notice that the else line is outdented back to the level of the if statement. Or consider this:

```
%table
  - @recipes.each do |recipe|
    %tr
      %td= recipe.title
%h2 End of table
```

Outdenting all the way back for the h2 tag implicitly closes the td, tr, and table tags and the each block. Frankly, seeing Ruby-type blocks with Pythonic indentation is giving me a bit of mental whiplash, although I was always a fan of Python's indentation, and I certainly appreciate the impulse to bring that kind of concise syntax to HTML markup.

Let's look at a few more special characters. A forward slash (/) at the beginning of the line indicates an HTML comment — that is, a comment that is part of the output sent to the browser. Structurally, it behaves like a tag. It can start a line, in which case the contents of the line are placed in the comment tag like this:

```
/ Fred wrote this part
```

which is interpreted as this HTML comment:

```
<!-- Fred wrote this part -->
```

A forward slash at the end of the line indicates that the tag is self-closing. So the following Haml code:

```
%end_of_line/
```

signifies this tag:

```
<end_of_line />
```

Haml already knows about the HTML tags that are self-closing, such as br, so you don't need the forward slash in those cases.

The slash can also be treated as a tag with indented comments. So the following Haml code:

```
/
  On second thought
  %div A bad idea
```

is interpreted as this HTML:

```
<!-- On second thought <div>A bad idea</div>-->
```

The backslash, for its part, fulfills its traditional role as an indicator that a control character should be treated as a literal. For example:

```
%tr
  %td
    + Positives
  %td
    \- Negatives#### <tr><td>+ Positives</td><td>- Negatives</td></tr>
```

A triple-bang (!!!) gets you a standard XHTML document header. The default is XHTML version 1.0 Transitional; however, you can specify alternative versions by placing text after the bangs like this:

```
!!! 1.1 Strict
```

You can include either of the two elements by themselves, and you can add an optional encoding type.

Haml also has a flexible set of filters that act on a set of indented text. The basic structure goes like this:

```
%div
  :plain
    This text is evaluated by the filter
%div This text is not
```

Most of the filters allow you to specify an alternate text-parsing method for the text inside the filter. In the example, the plain filter passes the filtered text through without any further processing. The preserve filter maintains whitespace in the output, similar to the way many blogging text engines do, by converting newlines into HTML new lines. If you are a fan of Textile or Markdown as simple text markup, there are both textile and markdown filters. The textile filter depends on the RedCloth gem being installed, and the markdown filter depends on the BlueCloth gem. There's also a redcloth filter, which uses RedCloth's rendering engine to render either Textile or Markdown. The erb filter evaluates the text using ERB, and the ruby filter evaluates the text as Ruby code, with all text sent to STDOUT (standard output) included in the output. Finally, the sass filter uses the Sass tool to generate CSS.

You can define your own filters. To do so, include a line like the following in your environment.rb file.

```
HAML::Template.options :filters => {:filter_name => FilterClass}
```

You can include as many name/class pairs in the hash as you'd like. The filter class needs to respond to an `initialize(text)` method, where the argument is the text being filtered, and then a `render` method to output the rendered text.

Benchmarks posted by the Haml team suggest that Haml is about 30-percent slower than ERB, but more than 15 times faster than Markaby. The stated goal of the Haml developers is for the 2.0 release to be faster than ERB.

Liquid

Liquid is a Rails templating tool with a very different design goal than Markaby and Haml. Whereas Markaby and Haml are supposed to make markup more elegant for the developer, Liquid is designed to enable a designer separate from the code team to create the output files. Toward that end, Liquid provides a markup language that is much less complex than the ones you've seen previously, and it also allows the coding team to limit what the design template can do with the data objects. One prominent use of Liquid is in the Mephisto blog engine, where Liquid is the language that defines site-specific templates. This is a use case where the template designers are likely to not have any contact with the coding team, and where limiting what a template can do with the data seems like a good idea.

Liquid is available as a Rails plugin:

```
$ ruby script/plugin http://liquid-markup.googlecode.com/svn/trunk/
```

After the Liquid plugin is in place, you can create another test controller method like this:

```
def liquid_test
  @recipes = Recipe.find_for_index(params[:format])
  @recipes.collect {|r| r.to_liquid }
  respond_to do |format|
    format.html
  end
end
```

This controller is slightly different than the controllers for Haml and Markaby in that it converts all the recipes using a `to_liquid` method, which you haven't written yet (more on that in a second).

Here's the recipe index page presented in Liquid, and placed in `app/views/output_choice/liquid_test.liquid`:

```
<table width="75%">
  <tr><th>Title</th></tr>
  {% for recipe in recipes %}
    <tr>
      <td>
        {% if recipe.has_image? %}
          <img src="{{ recipe.image }}" />
        {% else %}
           
```

(continued)

(continued)

```
            {% endif %}
          </td>
          <td><a href="{{recipe.link}}">{{recipe.title | strip_html }}</a></td>
        </tr>
      {% endfor %}
    </table>
```

At first glance, this looks very similar to ERB, but with slightly different marker characters. In fact, Liquid defines only three markers. Double braces (`{{  }}`) denote output — anything inside the braces is evaluated and placed in the output stream. Percent braces (`{% %}`) mark a logic tag. Liquid defines basic tags such as `if`, `for`, `case`, and `cycle`. It's also possible to create your own tag (more on that in a moment). The third marker is the pipe character (`|`), which is used within an output block to indicate a filter. The output block is of the following form:

```
{{ text | filter }}
```

The `filter` is a function that modifies the text — for example, by changing its case. You can have multiple filters in the same output block, in which case they are evaluated left to right. This is the same idea as the Django templates. Again, a standard set of filters is provided, but it's possible to create your own.

If the filter takes an argument other than the string to be modified, the syntax looks like this:

```
{{ recipe.created_at | date: "%Y %m %d" }}
```

The argument is passed following the colon in the filter.

Looking at the example with sharp eyes, you'll notice that the actual code has changed. For one thing, the Rails helpers `image_tag` and `link_to` are not used, and the recipe object appears to have grown a few new methods. Liquid limits the reach of the template. Rails helper methods are not available. In addition, Liquid allows only a special kind of object, called a `Drop`, to be passed to the template. The methods of the `Drop` are the only methods on the object that can be invoked from the template.

This means that the controller method for Liquid is different from the other two output engines because it has to convert `Recipe` to `Drop`, as shown in the following highlighted code line:

```
def liquid_test
  @recipes = Recipe.find_for_index(params[:format])
  @recipes.collect {|r| r.to_liquid }
  respond_to do |format|
    format.html
  end
end
```

The controller bounces control to `Recipe#to_liquid`, which goes like this:

```
def to_liquid(options = {})
  RecipeDrop.new self
end
```

This, of course, requires a `RecipeDrop` class. Here it is (I put the class inside the `app/models/recipe.rb` file, but if you are doing an entire site in Liquid, you probably want to put all your drops in an `app/drops` directory):

```
class RecipeDrop < Liquid::Drop

  def initialize(recipe)
    @recipe = recipe
  end

  def has_image?
    @recipe.has_image?
  end

  def title
    @recipe.title
  end

  def image
    @recipe.soup_image.public_filename(:tag)
  end

  def link
    "/recipes/#{@recipe.id}"
  end
end
```

An instance of the `Drop` class is the object passed to the view, and only methods specifically defined by the `Drop` class can be called by the view. You'll need to create a `Drop` class for any of your objects that you want visible in the view. Base classes (`Array`, `Date`, `DateTime`, `Hash`, `Numeric`, `String`, and `Time`, plus the three constants `true`, `false`, and `nil`) are all predefined by Liquid to act as their own `Drop` class, meaning that objects in these classes behave the same within a Liquid template as they do normally. Admittedly, you could define a similar functionality for your own class like this:

```
def to_liquid
  self
end
```

But doing so would defeat the purpose of using Liquid in the first place.

You can create your own custom filters and tags to augment the standard ones. The standard filters include `capitalize`, `date`, `downcase`, `escape`, `first`, `join`, `last`, `sort`, `strip_html`, `truncate`, and `upcase`. Many of these are simple wrappers around the Rails helper methods of the same name. The `date` filter reformats a date or time and takes a standard format string as an argument. The `escape` filter is also aliased to `h`, and calls `CGI.escapeHTML`. The `first` and `last` filters both work on arrays.

To create filters, place your filter methods in a module. Each method should take at least one argument — the input object to the filter. Additional arguments can be specified, and the argument list will be enforced at runtime when a template is interpreted. To register your template, make the following call somewhere in your code (the last line of the file loading your module is a common spot):

```
Liquid::Template.register_filter(<<Your Filter Module>>)
```

All of the public methods of the module you specify will be available as filters in your Liquid templates.

Tags are a little more complicated to create. By default, Liquid creates the tags described in the following table.

Tag	Description
`assign`	Sets a value for use later in the template, for example: `{% assign var  = value %}`
`capture`	Renders the contents in the block, and assigns them to the variable, for example: `{% capture varname %} some stuff {% endcapture %}` Later on, you can write `{{varname}}` and the output will be inserted. This stores output to be used multiple times in the template.

`case`	Standard `case` statement. The template code in the block where the variable matches the value in the when clause is rendered. If no when block matches, the `else` block is rendered. The syntax is as follows:
	`{% case variable %}{% when 'value' %} stuff {% else %} more stuff`
	`{% endcase %}`

`comment`	Everything inside the block is ignored. The syntax is as follows: `{% comment %} comment text {% endcomment %}`
`cycle`	Similar to the Rails helper; designed to be used inside a loop. This cycles between the values provided, moving from the last back to the first and so on. The syntax is as follows: `{% cycle 'a', 'b', 'c' %}`
`for`	A basic `for` loop with the following syntax: `{% for each in list %} stuff {{each}} {% endfor %}` Takes two possible arguments, `limit` and `offset`, as in `{% for each in list limit: 3 offset: 2 %}`. `limit` sets an upper boundary on the size of the list, and `offset` starts in a location other than the first element in the list. The list can also be a range, using the Ruby range syntax. Within the block, in addition to the loop control variable, there is a series of values of the form for `loop.length` (which returns the length of the list being looped over). Other attributes of the `for` loop include `index` (the number of the iteration, starting at 1), `rindex` (the number of iterations remaining, and `first` and `last`, Boolean markers of the first or last iteration.

`if`	A basic `if` statement with the following syntax:
	`{% if condition %} do something {% else %} do something {% endif %}`
	`%}`
	The condition can be a simple Boolean statement, but Boolean operators aren't available there (complex logic is supposed to be placed in the drop object). There's also no `else if` feature — you should use a case block for that.

Tag	Description
include	Allows the inclusion of another template within the current template, as follows: `{% include another_template %}` This can be called on a collection, as in `{% include other with collection %}`, in which case the template is rendered once for each element in the collection and the element forms the context for the internal template.
unless	The opposite of `if`. It has the following syntax: `{% unless condition %} do something {% endunless %}`

It's possible to create your own tags in Liquid, but at the moment that's not for the faint of heart. Interested parties are invited to check out the source for existing tags in `liquid/lib/tag.rb`, `liquid/lib/block.rb`, and `liquid/lib/tags` — and extrapolate from there.

Liquid is interesting to me because all the messing around with `Drop` classes feels like the kind of redundant task that Rails was designed to prevent. And yet there are certainly use cases, like the blog template example, where I can understand a desire to limit the damage that a user can do from a view. If you think your project has that particular need, Liquid is worth checking out.

JRuby on JRails

Switching gears to cover a different way to incorporate other languages into Rails, we come to JRuby, a 100-percent Java implementation of a Ruby interpreter and compiler. Although there are a number of languages that have Java Virtual Machine (JVM) interpretations, JRuby has one thing that the others don't — official support from Sun, which employs the core JRuby developers and funds JRuby development. The explicit goal of JRuby, at least from Sun's perspective, was to provide a Java-based platform to run Rails web applications.

This naturally begs the question of why you'd want to run a Rails application on top of a JVM. There are at least three potential answers:

- ❑ From JRuby, your Rails application can access Java-based APIs and services. There are still a number of libraries and tools with Java implementations but not Ruby interpretations. With JRuby, you can access those tools from your Ruby code.

- ❑ JRuby allows for deployment using standard Java `.war` files, which you can generate from Rake and deploy in any Java web application environment. This is potentially a much simpler deployment story than exists with standard Ruby and Capistrano, especially because JRuby allows access to large-scale enterprise servers such as Glassfish.

- ❑ JRuby has the only full compiler for the Ruby language. Although the goal hasn't been fully achieved as of this writing, the JRuby team expects that JRuby will soon be faster than the current Ruby interpreter. (It should be mentioned here that there are multiple non-Java–based Ruby interpreter projects that also project speed improvements over the current interpreter.)

Getting Started

JRuby can be downloaded from `http://dist.codehaus.org/jruby`. Because it's based on Java, you'll need a Java Software Development Kit (SDK) on your machine. If you are on a Mac running OS X 10.4.x or higher, you're fine — Java comes preinstalled. For Windows, you should head to `http://java.sun` `.com`, and install Java SDK version 1.5 or later. On Linux, the JDK may come with your distribution, or it may be available via your package installation system. If not, Linux installations are also available at `http://java.sun.com`. You'll need to have the `JAVA_HOME` environment variable set and have the `JAVA_HOME/bin` directory in your PATH — that should be taken care of by the Java installer.

As I write this, the current stable version of JRuby is 1.0.1, and you want `jruby-bin-1.0.1.zip` or `jruby-bin-1.0.1.tar.gz`. The source file and instructions on building from source are available at the JRuby wiki (see the "References" section for more details).

Unpack the file, and place the resulting directory someplace convenient on your file system. I put mine at `/usr/local/lib/jruby-1.0.1` to parallel the location where Ruby installed itself, but it really doesn't matter. What does matter is that you register the `JRUBY_HOME` environment variable. On a Unix or Mac OS X machine, do the following in your `.bash_login` (or other shell equivalent):

```
export JRUBY_HOME="/usr/local/lib/jruby-1.0.1"
```

Again, you'll need to adapt this to your location and command shell. On Windows, set the environment variable in `My Computer` ⇨ `Properties` ⇨ `Advanced` ⇨ `Environment Variables`. It's not strictly necessary, but things will go a lot easier if you add the `JRUBY_HOME/bin` directory to your PATH variable as well.

JRuby is now installed, giving you a completely parallel Ruby environment with its own interpreter command (`jruby`), its own interactive console (`jirb`), and its own version of `gem` and `rake`. You need to be careful with `gem` and `rake` because they share the same name as their regular Ruby siblings — the potential for a name collision is high. If you just type one of these commands at a command line, the PATH variable determines whether the regular Ruby or the JRuby version will be installed — the directory earlier in the list wins. Make sure you know which version you want to be the primary one, and adjust your PATH list so that version comes first. On Unix-derived systems, you can use the `which` command to ask the system to tell you where an executed command is located, like this:

```
$ which gem
/usr/local/bin/gem
```

To access the nonprimary version, you need to explicitly specify its directory at the command line as follows:

```
$ /usr/local/lib/jruby-1.0.1/gem
```

This is a particular issue for `gem` because each Ruby installation maintains its own list of installed gems. You want to make sure the gem gets installed to the Ruby version you expect.

After the setup is complete, `jruby` and `jirb` work exactly as you would expect:

```
$ jirb
irb(main):001:0> 1 + 1
=> 2
irb(main):002:0> x = "a string"
=> "a string"
irb(main):003:0> x.reverse
=> "gnirts a"
```

Now, let's look at what you can do with this stuff.

Crossing the Boundary

If you've used any of the JVM scripting languages (such as Jython, Rhino, or Groovy), you know that one thing that makes them powerful is their capability to interact with existing Java libraries. It's also one of the sources of pain because crossing the language boundary means that the existing code is executed in a new context, and the Ruby code is dealing with new data structures. The possibility for problems is high.

From JRuby, the magic line is this:

```
include Java
```

Once that is placed in your scripts, you have access to any Java class in your `classpath`. There isn't any way to specify a class path in the command-line invocation of JRuby — if you want your application to have a custom class path, you need to set up a batch file that modifies the `classpath`.

You can reference a Java class by using its fully qualified class name, as in this `jirb` session:

```
$ jirb
irb(main):001:0> include Java
=> Object
irb(main):002:0> button = javax.swing.JButton
=> Java::JavaxSwing::JButton
```

Swing programs are good for exploring the use of Java classes from Ruby because the Swing library is so heavily dependent on JavaBeans. Here's a short JRuby program:

```
include Java

include_class javax.swing.JFrame
include_class javax.swing.JButton
include_class javax.swing.JOptionPane
include_class java.awt.event.ActionListener

class ClickAction
  include ActionListener
  def actionPerformed(evt)
```

(continued)

(continued)

```
        JOptionPane.show_message_dialog(nil, "Ouch, that hurts!")
    end
end

frame = JFrame.new("JRuby Test")
button = JButton.new("I'm A Swing Button!")
button.add_action_listener(ClickAction.new)
frame.content_pane.add(button)
frame.default_close_operation = JFrame::EXIT_ON_CLOSE
frame.pack
frame.visible = true
```

This sets up a simple JFrame with one button that triggers an alert message when clicked. Figure 16-1 shows what I see when I run it.

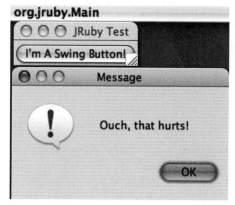

Figure 16-1

From this example, you can see the following facts about calling Java from JRuby:

❑   The shortcut method `include_class` takes a fully qualified Java class name and allows the rest of the script to refer to it by the short name of the class. The fully qualified name is still available should you want to use it.

❑   You can declare your Ruby class to extend a Java interface by calling `include` with the interface class, as in `include ActionListener`. Object inheritance, which isn't shown in this example, is managed exactly the same as it is in Ruby — except with a Java class name, `class MyButton < JButton`.

❑   JRuby does not have a compile-time check to determine that your interface extension class actually implements all the methods needed. If you were to comment out the `actionPerformed` method, the script would fail, but not until the button is actually clicked and the Java runtime attempts to call the method.

❑ Any method you declare in a class will override a parent method of the same name. The Ruby side will not validate the number or type of arguments, but discrepancies will be noticed by the Java side when you attempt to call the Java methods. So, if you try to call add_action_listener with something that is not actually an ActionListener, you get an error on the method call.

❑ New Java objects are created using the Ruby new syntax.

❑ JRuby converts Java CamelCase method names to more Ruby-like name_with_underscore versions. In this example, add_action_listener is an alias for the Java method addActionListener. The Java spellings of these method names are still available.

❑ The Ruby-style method names do not work for the purposes of overriding a parent class or implementing an interface. For this reason, the listener method must be actionListener, not add_action_listener. This may be addressed in a future version of JRuby.

❑ Any JavaBeans property of a Java object (meaning any property with a getter and setter) gets an implicit Ruby attr_accessor. So, for example, you should use frame.visible = true instead of frame.setVisible(true). The original getter and setter methods are still available if you want them. The accessors are also converted to Ruby underscores, as in frame.default_close_operation.

❑ Class methods and constants of Java classes are accessed using the Ruby :: syntax.

❑ You can pass Ruby objects to Java classes where there is an obvious paired class — Ruby strings can be passed as Java strings, numbers can be passed, arrays and hashes become Java lists and maps, and so on.

You can also go the other way and call a Ruby script from a Java class. The basic Java magic is this:

```
Ruby runtime = Ruby.getDefaultInstance();
try {
    runtime.evalScript(script);
} catch (Exception e) {e.printStackTrace();}
```

script is a string with the JRuby code to interpret. You can also instantiate and call methods of Ruby objects from your Java classes, with some limitations. However, because those limitations are somewhat baroque and incidental to our purpose here, I'm going to point you to the "Reference" section later in this chapter for more information on this topic.

Running JRails

Let's get down to the point: running Rails under JRuby. You can install gem Rails from JRuby the same way as from regular Ruby (although if you have memory problems, you may need to change your default Java memory size to at least 512MB). Just enter the following command and watch the results:

```
$ /usr/local/lib/jruby-1.0.1/bin/gem install rails
Bulk updating Gem source index for: http://gems.rubyforge.org
Install required dependency activesupport? [Yn]   Y
Install required dependency activerecord? [Yn]   Y
```

(continued)

(continued)

```
Install required dependency actionpack? [Yn]   Y
Install required dependency actionmailer? [Yn]   Y
Install required dependency actionwebservice? [Yn]   Y
Successfully installed rails-1.2.5
Successfully installed activesupport-1.4.4
Successfully installed activerecord-1.15.5
Successfully installed actionpack-1.13.5
Successfully installed actionmailer-1.3.5
Successfully installed actionwebservice-1.2.5
```

This installs the Rails gems in the JRuby gem directory, and also puts the `rails` application creation script in JRUBY_HOME/bin — in other words, it does exactly what the regular `gem install rails` does.

If you are on a Unix-based system, you may have to change the mode of JRUBY_HOME/BIN/`rails` *to make it executable.*

You can use the JRuby `rails` script to create a new Rails application. You can also run an existing Rails application under JRuby by calling `script/server` with JRuby like this:

```
$jruby script/server
```

There are a couple of issues you'll need to straighten out before you can actually run the Rails application under JRuby. If you've just installed JRuby, the odds are that you'll need to reinstall all the gems that your Rails project depends on. That's easy enough — you just need to run the JRuby `gem` command for each gem. Any gem that is written in pure Ruby should work, but gems that have components written in C won't work. (It's actually possible to specify that your JRuby gem directory be the same as your existing Ruby gem directory, but I recommend keeping them separate.)

Another problem is the database connections. Rails normally uses the ActiveRecord connectors that are specific to each database, but because Java is supposed to have its own database-independent API, those connectors will not work in JRuby. Instead, JRuby Rails applications connect to the database via the Java API called JDBC. The JDBC connections are available as a gem, so naturally, you install them as follows:

```
/usr/local/lib/jruby-1.0.1/bin/gem install activerecord-jdbc --no-rdoc --no-ri
```

For some reason, the JRuby documentation is extremely consistent about recommending the no-documentation options for gem installation. I'm not completely sure why it matters, but I figured I'd pass along the recommendation.

With the gem installed, you need to tell Rails that the JDBC connector is available. The following code shows the recommended syntax, which you need to place in your `environment.rb` file (but check with current documentation — the JRuby team is hoping to automate this step in the future):

```
if RUBY_PLATFORM =~ /java/
  require 'rubygems'
  gem 'ActiveRecord-JDBC'
  require 'jdbc_adapter'
end
```

You also need to go into your `database.yml` file and convert it to JDBC. Here's a sample:

```
production:
  adapter: jdbc
  driver: org.mysql.jdbc.Driver
  url: jdbc:mysql://localhost/soupsonline_production
  username: root
  password:
  encoding: utf8
```

The adapter is now `jdbc` instead of `mysql`. You need to specify the JDBC driver class, just as you would in a Java program. Rather than specifying the database name, the host, and the socket, the database instance is now specified using a JDBC URL. The format for the URL is somewhat dependent on the driver. For MySQL, the basic format is `jdbc:mysql://<hostname>/database_name`. You don't need to include the user name and password in the URL — they will be inserted based on the user name and password entries in the YAML file. You will need to convert all the database references, not just the production version. You might want to do this using a separate working copy from your source control server.

As I write this, ActiveRecord-JDBC supports the following databases: DB2, Derby, Firebird, H2, HSQLDB, MySQL, Oracle, PostgreSQL, and SQL Server. That includes all the most common databases used for ActiveRecord except for SQLite (but Derby makes a good lightweight in-memory alternative for this). Certain kinds of column changing activities are not available for DB2, Derby, Firebird, and SQLServer, but again, check the documentation for current information as development is ongoing.

The actual `.jar` file containing the driver class must also be placed in your class path. To do this, modify the `classpath` either in the batch file that starts your Rails application, or in your shell profile. Alternatively, if you'll be running your Rails application inside Tomcat or some other servlet container, there will usually be some directory to place the `.jar` file in so that it's automatically available to the web application.

At this point, you should be able to run your Rails application locally under JRuby by using `script/server`. That will invoke WEBrick without searching for Mongrel because WEBrick is pure Ruby, and Mongrel is not. If you want something with a little bit more oomph, you'll need to deploy the application to a Java application server.

Deployment via WAR

The generic way to deploy your JRuby Rails application is to convert it to a standard WAR file, suitable for handing off to your Java server. To do this conversion, you need a plugin called GoldSpike. You can get this plugin as follows:

```
script/plugin install http://jruby-extras.rubyforge.org/svn/trunk ↵
/rails-integration/plugins/goldspike
```

With GoldSpike installed, you have access to four new Rake tasks that mange deployment. The two basic ones are `war:standalone:create` and `war:shared:create`. Both of these convert the Rails application to a WAR file. The standalone version includes JRuby itself in the archive, so it can be deployed into an application server with no other dependencies. The shared version assumes that the

JRuby JAR file will be visible to the application at runtime (which it will be if you're in the Tomcat / shared directory, for example), which results in a smaller archive. The shared version is preferred if you want to save space on a server with multiple JRuby applications installed.

You also have the task war:standalone:run, which creates the standalone WAR file and immediately starts up the Jetty web server running the archive (this one assumes you are running JRuby). The task tmp:war:clean cleans up any temporary files left behind by WAR creation.

This WAR file is not a true compile of the Rails application. Instead, it bundles the JRuby interpreter and the Rails files in such a way as to invoke the interpreter to start the Rails application and respond to requests as expected.

As I write this, a compiler deployment solution is in the works, but has not yet been released publicly.

There are two places in your Rails application where you can put external information of interest to the WAR deployment tasks. The lib/java directory should contain all the Java JAR files you need to be deployed in your application. These will be bundled into the WAR file. There is also an optional config/war.rb file that allows you to specify dependencies on RubyGems or Java Maven-based libraries. Refer to external gems with a line in the file for each gem, of the following form:

```
add_gem 'gemname', 'version string'
```

The version string should be something like = 1.5 or > 3.5. Omitting the version string should always get you the most recent version of the gem. Any gem included in this listing will be bundled with the WAR file, which implies that it needs to be already installed locally. Because Rails is a gem, you can use this mechanism to specify a Rails version. For example:

```
add_gem 'rails', '= 1.2.3'
```

Java libraries are added using the following syntax:

```
maven_library 'mysql', 'mysql-connector-java', '5.0.4'
```

The fields are the Maven group ID, the Maven artifact ID, and the Maven version. (See the Maven documentation for details about how to find specific third-party plugins.) You may need to explicitly add a line like this for each JAR file in your lib/java file, although by the time you read this, that step may no longer be necessary. Remember that this is only for bundling the dependent JAR file in your complete WAR file. You can always include third-party JARs in the shared directory of your web application server.

You can specify the JRuby version you want to use with this mechanism:

```
maven_library 'org.jruby', 'jruby-complete', '1.0.1'
```

After you have obtained the WAR file, place it in the application server just like any other file.

GlassFish

Using a WAR file is a pretty straightforward deployment story, but it's possible to make Java deployment even easier. GlassFish is an open-source Java Enterprise server that is available at `http://glassfish.dev.java.net`. (It's also bundled with Sun's Netbeans IDE.) GlassFish supports clustering, and is suitable for production work in a variety of environments. It also supports a brand-new Rails deployment solution.

To get this to work, you need to download the gem. As of this writing, it's still a preview release, and it's not registered with the gem system, so you need to download the gem file from `http://download.java.net/maven/glassfish/com/sun/enterprise/glassfish/glassfish-gem/10.0-SNAPSHOT/glassfish-gem-10.0-SNAPSHOT.gem`. Download it, and then try this:

```
$ cd ~/Desktop/downloads
$ /usr/local/lib/jruby-1.0.1/bin/gem install glassfish-gem-10.0-SNAPSHOT
```

Mac users should note that Safari seems to want to download the file and insert a `.tar` *extension. That can mess up the download a bit. Try using Firefox if possible.*

After the gem is installed, it creates a script called `glassfish_rails` (which you may need to change to executable). You can then run it like this:

```
$ glassfish_rails soupsonline/
```

You'll see something like the following:

```
Oct 26, 2007 9:26:10 PM com.sun.enterprise.v3.services.impl.GrizzlyAdapter
postConstruct
INFO: Listening on port 8080
```

This does bring up GlassFish — unfortunately, Soups OnLine is not completely JRuby ready at this point (for one thing, the Ferret text engine is not pure Ruby). However, with a JRuby-ready application, you get a GlassFish server running Rails without even having to create a WAR file.

As I write this, the GlassFish plugin is at a very early stage, but it's worth keeping an eye on because it could become a very important Rails deployment tool.

References

RDoc documentation for Markaby is available at `http://markaby.rubyforge.org`. Also of interest is the wiki from "why the lucky stiff" at `http://code.whytheluckystiff.net/markaby`. Haml lives at `http://haml.hamptoncatlin.com` — see that page for additional documentation as well as information about Sass, which is an output tool aimed at creating CSS files.

Liquid's home page is `www.liquidmarkup.org`. Bruce Williams and Marcel Molina, Jr. have a great presentation from RailsConf 2007 that discusses all the alternatives listed here and more — slides from this presentation are available at `www.codefluency.com/assets/2007/5/18/VisForVexing.pdf`.

JRuby's home page is `http://jruby.codehaus.org`. There's also a wiki at `http://wiki.jruby.org/wiki/Main_Page`. Charles Nutter maintains a blog at `http://headius.blogspot.com` — watch this blog for announcements and news of new releases. Maven, which is mentioned in the chapter as a tool for managing Java libraries, can be found at `http://maven.apache.org`. There's already a book, *Practical JRuby on Rails Web 2.0 Projects: Bringing Ruby on Rails to Java*, written by Ola Bini and published by Apress (`www.apress.com/book/view/9781590598818`), and I believe another one is forthcoming.

Summary

Although ERB has the advantage of allowing all code in your Rails system to be in Ruby, there are alternative view-output languages that serve some different needs. Markaby is a system that uses Ruby metaprogramming constructs to create a view language that looks as much like Ruby code as possible. It's simple and powerful, but somewhat slow. Haml is an attempt to create very concise views, using a mix of Ruby syntax, Python indentation, and CSS selectors. It's almost as fast as ERB, and quite flexible, but also rather cryptic. Liquid is a templating language designed to completely separate the template from the live model objects. Liquid is particularly well suited to the case where the creators of the templates are widely separated from the coders, or where there's a good reason to do some extra work to limit what can be done from a view.

JRuby is an alternative implementation of the Ruby interpreter that runs inside a JVM. It is not solely intended for running Rails; however, Rails support is a big part of JRuby's reason for existing. JRuby is especially indicated in cases where you want to access a Java library from your Rails program. It also boasts a nice, simple deployment story, converting Rails projects to `.war` files that can be run within any standard Java web application server. JRuby requires some minor changes to the setup of your Rails program, mostly to support database access via JDBC. The JRuby team is also working on a Ruby compiler, and expects to have a JRuby implementation that is faster than the standard Ruby 1.8 implementation quite soon.

Things You Should Download

A Ruby on Rails application is made up of many parts. Although the installation of the gems and plugins used in a Rails application is covered in the main text, the installation of the basic pieces is not covered consistently. This appendix provides a brief guide to what to download and where to get it.

Platform Notes

Ruby on Rails runs on any platform where Ruby itself runs. Most likely, you'll be running a Linux distrubution, Mac OS X, or Microsoft Windows (XP or Vista). Each platform has a slightly different set of steps to follow. Here are some general notes on each platform.

Linux

All the standalone tools here should be available via the package manager for your Linux distribution — in fact, many of them should be preinstalled as part of the general operating system (OS) installation. For updates, the package installer is your first and easiest choice for getting the program onto your system. All the described Linux tools allow for compilation from source — if you want that option, you'll need to have the standard developer tools such as gcc and make installed.

Mac OS X

If you are running the new Mac OS X 10.5 Leopard version, you're in luck because Ruby 1.8.6 and Rails 1.2.3 are both preinstalled. In addition, the Ruby distribution includes RubyGems and several other popular gems. One thing to keep in mind is that the Ruby installation itself has been patched for better integration with the underlying OS and developer tools. This may be an issue when the time comes to update Ruby. You may also want to run a custom Ruby build, in which case, you should go to the URL in the next paragraph.

If you're on OS X 10.4 Tiger, you need to do some work. The Ruby version that shipped with Tiger was a variant of Ruby 1.8.4, and it had some critical bugs that broke MySQL integration. You'll find full instructions for getting everything in order at http://hivelogic.com/narrative/articles/ruby-rails-mongrel-mysql-osx. Dan Benjamin, the maintainer of this page, appears committed to keeping it up-to-date for Leopard as well.

For both system versions, you'll need to have XCode and Developer tools installed if you want to compile from source.

Windows

The Windows installation instructions are pretty straightforward, and should work for both XP and Vista. To compile from source, you need the free Microsoft compiler available at http://msdn2.microsoft.com/en-us/express/aa700735.aspx. You also need nmake, which is available at http://download.microsoft.com/download/vc15/patch/1.52/w95/en-us/nmake15.exe.

Ruby

The current version of Ruby is 1.8.6. That's the version that should be installed on most recent Linux distributions as well as Mac OS X 10.5.

For Windows, a one-click installer for Ruby 1.8.6 is available at http://rubyinstaller.rubyforge.org/wiki/wiki.pl. This installs Ruby, Gems, Rake, and a slew of other commonly used Ruby tools.

Under Linux distributions that support APT, the following command works:

```
% sudo apt-get install ruby irb rdoc
```

A source download is available at www.ruby-lang.org/en/downloads. This distribution contains instructions for building from source. (Dan Benjamin's page noted earlier also has instructions for OS X, and the make/install steps should work for Linux as well.)

The Windows one-click installer includes RubyGems, as does OS X Leopard. For other platforms, head to http://rubyforge.org/frs/?group_id=126 and download the most recent version (0.9.4 as I write this). Unpack the download and run ruby setup.rb from the top level of the downloaded files.

The developer release of Rails 1.9 is brand new as this book heads for production, and Rails is rapidly being patched to accommodate it. While not recommended for production web sites in the immediate future, it's worth keeping an eye on for the future of Ruby development as well as for its promised performance updates.

Rails

Even if you eventually use Edge Rails for your projects, you need to have a version of Gem Rails installed to get the rails command for creating new projects. Here's the command:

```
$ sudo gem install rails --include-dependencies
```

Windows users don't need the `sudo`. This installs all of the various Rails components to your Ruby installation. Upgrading to Edge Rails for your project is covered in Chapter 1.

Subversion

Subversion is covered in depth in Chapter 2. Downloads of Subversion are available at `http:// subversion.tigris.org/project_packages.html`. The source package is official, but binary packages are unofficially maintained for most platforms. Subversion is also available via the APT package manager. Even if you don't plan on using Subversion for your source control, having the client available makes it easier to manage Rails resources that are distributed via their public Subversion servers.

Windows users might be interested in TortoiseSVN, a Subversion client that integrates with Windows Explorer. You can get it at `http://tortoisesvn.tigris.org`. Mac users should try SCPlugin, a similar but less mature tool available at `http://scplugin.tigris.org`. Also keep an eye on the Mac OS X Subversion client called Versions at `www.versionsapp.com` — it hasn't shipped yet, but the screenshots look very pretty.

Databases

Most Rails applications use MySQL, which is available at `http://dev.mysql.com`. The free version is called MySQL Community Edition. Right now, there's a stable 5.0 branch, a beta 5.1 branch, and an alpha 6.0 branch. Choose the binary that corresponds to your operating system.

You should also consider the administrative tools, the MySQL Administrator and the MySQL Query Browser, which are available at `http://dev.mysql.com/downloads/gui-tools/5.0.html`. The interfaces are a little on the clunky side, but they will let you see what's going on in your database. Your platform may have third-party MySQL administrative applications as well.

For smaller projects, consider SQLite, which is available at `www.sqlite.org`. It has binaries for Linux and Windows. An older version of SQLlite was included in Mac OS X 10.4. As of Rails 2.0.2, SQLite is the default database for new Rails applications. The `database.yml` file generated by Rails contains instructions for using SQLite.

Mongrel

The Mongrel web server is available as a RubyGem (`gem install mongrel`). This is not critical for development, but if installed, it will replace WEBrick on your development machine, leading to better performance.

Choosing a Text Editor

You'll need to type your code into something. Here are a few of options to consider.

On the Mac, TextMate (www.macromates.com) has emerged as the clear favorite among Ruby programmers. Unlike the other programs on this page, it's not free, but it is extremely powerful and flexible. It comes with a number of easily extendible shortcuts for Ruby, Rails, and Subversion.

On the Windows side, the E text editor (www.e-texteditor.com) attempts to recreate the TextMate structure, but at the time of this writing, it's not quite mature.

There are a few cross-platform text editors worth a look. Eclipse (www.eclipse.org) includes the Aptana plugin, formerly known as RadRails. At one point, this was pretty much the only game in town for Ruby syntax coloring and such on Windows, but other tools have been catching up fast. If you are already comfortable with Eclipse, this is an easy way to get a Rails tool.

NetBeans (www.netbeans.org) has just added significant Ruby support for version 6.0, with an eye toward supporting JRuby development. It's feature-rich but in a user interface that I've never quite been able to get used to. IntellJ IDEA (www.jetbrains.com/idea) has added Ruby and Rails support for version 7, but I haven't yet gotten a chance to evaluate it. IDEA is also a commercial program.

jEdit (www.jedit.org) is a Java-based text editor that contains a Ruby plugin. It's a little barebones compared to the full IDEs, but it's still quite usable.

If you want to go old-school, both Emacs and Vim have Ruby plugins that provide support for Ruby programming.

One-Stop Shopping

If you want to get everything at once, there are a couple of packages that provide a single installer for most of the components you need for Rails.

Locomotive, at http://locomotive.raaum.org, is the Mac OS X entry into this field. It consists of a bundle with Ruby, Rails, and MySQL. It also has a control panel to monitor all applications created within Locomotive, and a separate bundle with a binary installation of ImageMagick and RMagick.

Instant Rails (http://instantrails.rubyforge.org) is the Windows entry. It installs Ruby, Rails, Apache, Mongrel, and MySQL, as well as any Ruby component included in the OneClick Windows installer.

B

Web Frameworks Inspired by Rails

Rails has had a bit of an influence on the larger world of web frameworks. This appendix introduces you to a series of other frameworks that were inspired by Rails in one way or another. Some are attempts to bring the Rails design philosophy to other languages; others are Ruby-based attempts to create an even more lightweight framework.

CakePHP

CakePHP is a PHP framework to support a Model-View-Controller breakdown in the PHP application. A CakePHP project has a directory framework that is similar to a Rails project, and it allows for database configuration, scaffolding, and models using structures that are inspired by Rails. Naming conventions are also based on the Rails example.

You can download CakePHP from `http://cakephp.org`.

Camping

Camping is a Ruby web framework, written in 60 lines of extremely dense code. Its home page is `http://code.whytheluckystiff.net/camping`. You can download Camping as a gem, either by itself or in a bundle that includes SQLite, ActiveRecord, Mongrel, RedCloth, and the Acts As Versioned plugin.

A Camping application is a Ruby script that calls the framework via a line such as `Camping.goes :MyController`. When the script is run, the Camping framework does some massive metaprograming on itself, changing its names to match the controller created by the `goes` call.

Modules within the script define controllers with actions as well as views. Camping uses Markaby as its view language.

Camping is designed for small web applications that could reasonably fit in a single file. Complex applications that use Camping are expected to be built out of the smaller applications.

Django

Django (www.djangoproject.com) isn't a Ruby clone at all, but a project that became public in a similar time frame using a similar set of design principles. Django is written in Python and includes an ActiveRecord-like mechanism for associating Python classes to database tables. Unlike Rails, where you define the database tables and the models are inferred, in Django, you define the model objects and the database table is inferred. Django also has a flexible URL routing system and a powerful template language. Django does not directly support an Ajax framework, but it allows users to select their own Ajax tool to use within the Django application.

Django is an interesting comparison to Rails because although similar design principles were at work, the two tools came out of very different environments and constraints, which have led to some sharp differences in how the tools are structured. Rails was developed by a small business company to support building a small number of different sites. Django was developed by a media company to allow rapid creation of a number of different content-management kinds of sites. For example, Django maintains a common admin site for all applications, which is important in a newsroom content system, but which was not a necessity for early Rails projects. Conversely, Ajax was much more important to the early development of Rails.

Grails

Grails (http://grails.codehaus.org) uses the Groovy language (a scripting language built on top of the JVM) to implement a web tool that incorporates both the Rails-like convention-over-configuration structure and the model-view-controller (MVC)structure. Like Rails and CakePHP, Grails enforces a standard project layout and database configuration. Grails can also integrate with Java tools like Hibernate and Spring for its data management. Like Django, Grails defines model attributes inside the model object.

Merb

Merb (http://merb.rubyforge.org) is a Ruby web application tool designed to be very lightweight and have a tight integration with Mongrel. A Merb application has a slightly different structure than Rails — it's designed to allow easier partitioning of a project into deployable and non-deployable sections. Merb uses Erubis to define output views and, unlike Rails, allows for multiple render points in a single controller action. Merb allows for RESTful controller definitions.

Merb is specifically designed to hold on to a Mongrel process for less time than a Rails request would, allowing for a much faster web application. For example, Merb allows multiple files to be uploaded to the server at once. Also, Merb allows a controller action to return a block, which can be rendered by Mongrel in a separate thread for output processing.

TurboGears

TurboGears (http://turbogears.org) is a Python framework that was built using some of the best-in-class web tools available around the time Rails was released. Essentially, there were individual Python tools that covered much of the Rails functionality, but which hadn't been combined into a single application stack. TurboGears is made up of separate components for the view template (Kid), the controller logic (CherryPy), the data layer (SQLObject), and a JavaScript library called MochiKit.

Index